Beyond Sovereignty

Issues for a Global Agenda

Third Edition

Maryann Cusimano Love

The Catholic University of America

THOMSON

WADSWORTH

Australia • Brazil • Canada • Mexico • Singapore
Spain • United Kingdom • United States

In memory of
Francis Cusimano, S.J.,

who taught me Africa was only as far away
as your uncle's smile, and that we can imagine and create
a better globalization for our future.

Executive Editor: David Tatom
Editorial Assistant: Eva Dickerson
Senior Marketing Manager: Janise Fry
Marketing Assistant: Teresa Jessen
Project Manager, Editorial Production:
    Marti Paul
Creative Director: Rob Hugel
Art Director: Maria Epes
Print Buyer: Karen Hunt
Permissions Editor: Roberta Broyer
Production Service: Matrix Productions

Text Designer: Paul Lacy
Copy Editor: Janet Tilden
Cover Designer: Bartay Studio
Cover Image: The New York
    Province Jesuits
Cover Printer: Transcontinental Printing/
    Louiseville
Compositor: International Typesetting
    and Composition
Printer: Transcontinental Printing/
    Louiseville

Printed in Canada
2 3 4 5 6 7 10 09 08 07 06

Library of Congress Control Number:
2005938199

ISBN 0-495-09026-3

Thomson Higher Education
10 Davis Drive
Belmont, CA 94002-3098
USA

For more information about our products,
contact us at:
Thomson Learning Academic
Resource Center
1-800-423-0563
For permission to use material from this text
or product, submit a request online at
http://www.thomsonrights.com.
Any additional questions about permissions
can be submitted by e-mail to
thomsonrights@thomson.com.

Contents

Contents

About the Editor

MARYANN CUSIMANO LOVE is an associate professor of politics at the Catholic University of America in Washington, D.C., and a member of the Council on Foreign Relations, the International Policy Committee for the US Conference of Catholic Bishops, the Advisory Board of Jesuit Refugee Services, and the Advisory Board for the Catholic Peacebuilding Network with Notre Dame University's Kroc Institute of Peace. She teaches graduate and undergraduate courses on international relations and US foreign policy at both Catholic University and the Pentagon. She is also an author of children's books, including *You Are My I Love You* and *You Are My Miracle.* She holds a B.A. degree from St. Joseph's University in Philadelphia, an M.A. degree from the University of Texas, and a Ph.D. from Johns Hopkins University.

About the Contributors

CHRISTOPHER A. CORPORA is a senior analyst for the US Department of Defense. He holds a B.A. degree from the University of Illinois at Urbana and an M.A. and Ph.D. from the School of International Service at American University in Washington, DC. He is the author of many professional and scholarly publications and is currently conducting research and writing on illicit political economy and conflict. All statements associated herein with Dr. Corpora are his own and do not reflect the official positions of the U.S. government or Department of Defense.

MARIA GREEN COWLES is an Associate Director of the University Honors Program and Scholar-in-Residence of the School of International Service at American University. She is coeditor of *Developments in the European Union* 2, *Transforming Europe: Europeanization and Domestic Change,* and *The State of the European Union,* Vol. 5. She is the author of numerous articles and book chapters on the European Union's effects on domestic institutions, the role of multinational firms in EU policy making, and the influence of transnational and global business organizations in global regulatory and governance matters. She is a former vice chair of the European Union Studies Association.

MARTHA CRENSHAW is Colin and Nancy Campbell Professor in Global Issues and Democratic Thought and Professor of Government at Wesleyan University, where she has taught international politics and foreign policy, including a course on terrorism, since 1974. Her research has produced many publications, beginning in 1972 with an article titled "The Concept of Revolutionary Terrorism" in the *Journal of Conflict Resolution.* She is the author of *Revolutionary Terrorism: The FLN in Algeria, 1954–1962* as well as *Terrorism and International Cooperation,* and she edited the books *Terrorism, Legitimacy, and Power* and *Terrorism in Context.*

STEPHEN FLYNN is the Jeane J. Kirkpatrick Senior Fellow for National Security Studies at the Council on Foreign Relations, where he conducts research and writes on homeland security issues, most recently, *America the Vulnerable*. From August 2000 to February 2001, Dr. Flynn served as the lead consultant on the border management issue to the U.S. Commission on National Security (Hart-Rudman Commission). He has served in the White House Military Office during the George H.W. Bush administration and as a director for Global Issues on the National Security Council staff during the Clinton administration. A career Coast Guard officer who served twice in command at sea, he retired at the rank of Commander in 2002. He received an M.A.L.D. in 1990 and Ph.D. in 1991 from the Fletcher School of Law and Diplomacy, Tufts University.

TENG FU is a Ph.D. candidate of politics at the Catholic University of America in Washington, DC, where she has been a teaching/research assistant and taught a course on China politics. She has worked for the United Nations Headquarters in New York, Greenpeace USA, and the Campaign Finance Institute in Washington, DC. She is the author of "Unequal Primary Education Opportunities in Rural and Urban China" in *China Perspectives* (July–August 2005). She is active in the Southern, Northeastern and American Political Science Association Annual Conferences. She is currently working on her dissertation on dams and transnational advocacy from the perspective of opportunity structures in the social movement literature. She holds a B.A. from Foreign Affairs College (China Foreign Affairs University) in Beijing, China, and an M.A. from the Catholic University of America.

DORLE HELLMUTH is a Ph.D. candidate at the Catholic University of America in Washington, DC, and a research assistant at National Defense University. She holds M.A. degrees from Marburg University in Germany and the Catholic University of America. She has published in academic and professional journals and is currently working on her dissertation dealing with domestic counterterrorism responses in Europe and the United States.

RICHARD A. LOVE is a Senior Research Fellow and Professor at the Center for the Study of Weapons of Mass Destruction, National Defense University (NDU), Washington, DC. His current projects involve WMD interdiction, foreign consequence management, and combating WMD strategy and operations. He teaches courses on combating WMD and consequence management and incident response at the National War College. Other duties include lecturing on combating WMD for NDU's NATO program, the Joint Forces Senior National Security Course, the CBRN focus study at the Joint Forces Staff College and at the Army Command and General Staff College in Ft. Leavenworth, Kansas. He is an adjunct professor of law and politics at Catholic University and teaches Law of Armed Conflict, National Security Law, Security in the Information Age,

Congress and Foreign Policy and Law and Policy of Homeland Security to Ph.D. and M.A. candidates at the Pentagon and on Capitol Hill. Previously, he served as counsel for the Financial Crimes and Security Project at the Brookings Institution. He holds a B.A. in history and International Relations from the University of Virginia, a Juris Doctor in Law and Economics from George Mason University, and LL.M. in international law from American University.

JOHN T. PICARELLI is a Program Manager at the Transnational Crime and Corruption Center and a Research Lecturer at the School of International Service at American University. His expertise lies in providing training and briefings to policy makers and practitioners in the law enforcement, national and homeland security arenas. He has published widely in academic and policy journals on the topics of transnational organized crime, terrorism and other transnational threats since 1995. He holds a B.A. from the University of Delaware and an M.A. from the Graduate School of Public and International Affairs at the University of Pittsburgh, and expects to complete his Ph.D. from American University in 2006.

DENNIS PIRAGES is Harrison Professor of International Environmental Policy at the University of Maryland, College Park. He received his Ph.D. from Stanford University. He is author or editor of thirteen books on global relations and environmental issues, including *Global Ecopolitics* (1978), *Global Technopolitics* (1989), *Building Sustainable Societies* (1996), *Ecological Security* (2004), and *From Resource Scarcity to Ecological Security* (2005). A lifetime fellow of the American Association for the Advancement of Science, he has been writing about the impact of deepening globalization on the spread of infectious disease for more than a decade.

PAUL RUNCI is a researcher at the Joint Global Change Research Institute in College Park, MD. His research focuses on the politics of global change, energy policy and trends in energy research and development, and institutional responses to global environmental problems. He holds a B.A. from Boston College, an M.A.L.D. from Tufts University's Fletcher School of Law and Diplomacy, and a Ph.D. from the Department of Government and Politics at the University of Maryland, College Park.

LOUISE SHELLEY is a professor in the School of International Service at American University. She is founder and director of the Transnational Crime and Corruption Center (TraCCC), a center devoted to teaching, research and training, and public outreach on these issues. She is the recipient of Guggenheim, NEH, and Kennan Institute grants and received a MacArthur grant to establish the Russian Organized Crime Study Centers. Professor Shelley is the author of *Policing Soviet Society, Lawyers in Soviet Worklife,* and *Crime and Modernization* and numerous articles and book chapters on all aspects of transnational crime and corruption.

Preface to the Third Edition

All people are members of one and the same family. . . . We need to regain an awareness that we share a common destiny.

—Pope Benedict XVI[1]

Oh, the leaky boundaries of man-made states!
How many clouds float past them with impunity;
how much desert sand shifts from one land to another;
how many mountain pebbles tumble onto foreign soil
in provocative hops!
Need I mention every single bird that flies in the face of frontiers
or alights on the roadblock at the border? . . .
Oh, to register in detail, at a glance, the chaos
prevailing on every continent!

—Wislawa Szymborska, Nobel Laureate[2]

What does it mean to live in a world of leaky borders? Globalization is the infrastructure of open economies, open societies, and open technologies. The acceleration of time, compression of space, and decentralization of information and power create a world of leaky borders. Pathogens, pollution, and pirates do not stop at borders, but too often our governing institutions do. Global issues move quickly on global infrastructure, while our sovereign political institutions move slowly. Sovereignty is changing. Institutions are changing. But will our institutions change quickly enough to address pressing global problems before millions more die?

Sovereignty sounds like an arcane and academic term, but it is deadly serious and practical. Some 30,000 Iraqis and 2,300 Americans have been killed in a conflict over sovereignty and global issues. Did and should Iraq have weapons of mass destruction, harbor terrorists, or violate human rights so egregiously that military invasion was the only way to stem the problems spilling over to the world through Iraq's leaky borders?

[1]"World Day of Peace Message," January 1, 2006, www.vatican.va/holy_father/benedict_xvi/messages/peace/documents/hf_ben-xvi_mes_20051213_xxxix-world-day-peace_en.html.

[2]Wislawa Szymborska, "Psalm (1976)," from *View with a Grain of Sand* (New York: Harcourt, 1995), 99.

Millions of refugees live at the seams of fraying borders. They are driven out by hostile sovereignties, yet not welcomed in by other sovereignties. Their lives are witness to the halfway house that is twenty-first century sovereignty—still strong enough to be relevant, yet too weak to solve pressing global issues.

If sovereign states alone cannot solve pressing global issues, who can? Nonstate actors are assuming greater prominence and power in global politics, from NGOs such as Caritas International to MNCs such as Thomson Learning Corporation, publisher of this book. Illicit nonstate actors, such as terrorist or international criminal groups, add to global problems. But some legal nonstate actors, such as NGOs, IGOs, and MNCs, may contribute to global solutions. As states flounder, increasingly the private sector steps in to address global problems. But there are few rules or playbooks for them to follow, creating problems of coordination, communication, capacity, transparency, democracy, accountability, authority, and legitimacy.

This book discusses pressing global problems, attempted and possible global solutions, the various players involved, and the implications for sovereignty, still the creaky default setting for our global political institutions.

As an international relations professor researching and teaching on globalization in Washington, DC, I study these topics as professional concerns. But they are also personal. I teach at the Pentagon as part of Catholic University's graduate programs. On September 11 a faulty car battery kept me out of harm's way while my students were under attack. Friends and colleagues currently fight in Iraq, while other friends and colleagues protest and work to end the war. As a board member of Jesuit Refugee Services, an NGO working to aid refugees and internally displaced persons in fifty countries, I see both the possibilities and limitations of civil society networks working on global issues. As a founding member of the Catholic peacebuilding network, a group that brings together academics and grassroots practitioners to creatively construct peace in conflict-ridden areas around the globe, I see that while sovereignty is often complicit in war, it cannot be ignored in building peace. As an advisor to the U.S. Catholic bishops on international issues of justice and peace, I know the value of nonstate actors pressing for action on global problems, as well as the need for creative partnerships to "bear fruit that will last." This book's table of contents is not a laundry list or academic citation of global problems, but a photo album of friends and colleagues affected by and working on these global issues, where both problem and solution move beyond sovereignty.

Maryann Cusimano Love
Washington, DC
January 10, 2006

Preface to the Second Edition

The first edition of *Beyond Sovereignty* argued that world politics had changed: Nonstate actors operating across international borders were increasingly important; globalization carried unintended consequences (including terrorism) to which even strong states were vulnerable; countries cannot manage pressing global problems alone; and sovereign, military responses are less effective ways to manage global issues. Developments since the first edition reinforce these themes.

The events of September 11 hit home professionally and personally. I teach at the Pentagon every Tuesday through Catholic University's graduate program in international affairs for military officers and government employees. At 9:30 A.M. on September 11, a dead car battery kept me out of harm's way. My students were in the Pentagon offices that were hit. They lost co-workers and offices (including our class materials and books), but they escaped. Except for that day, we continued to meet every week—on the site where 189 people had died, past the emergency vehicles (modified golf carts marked with medical Red Cross symbols) that lined the hallways outside our classroom with stretchers and body bags ready for the next attack, and past the crayon drawings on the walls from grade schools all over the country, "Our hearts are with you. Hope you find your friends. Be strong. You are in our prayers." Like the experiences of colleagues who teach in Ramallah and Beirut, the semester was an interesting experience in teaching about terrorism and global problems at the site of a terrorist attack, during a war against nonstate actors, and with students who were all under attack and charged with carrying out the U.S. military response. As students replaced their copies of *Beyond Sovereignty: Issues for a Global Agenda* burned in the fire (one student recovered a smoke- and water-damaged copy from the FBI evidence team), they encouraged me to quickly produce a second edition. One student, an army chaplain, argued it was our moral responsibility to get information out to the public that could help people to understand what had happened and put events into the context of the challenges of globalization.

I did not need much convincing. For the past three years, colleague and contributor Stephen Flynn had led, and I had participated in, a Council on Foreign Relations project on Homeland Security. We briefed policy makers; government officials in the national security bureaucracy; Congressional representatives; and business, civic, and academic leaders in Washington, D.C., New York, Miami, Houston, Los Angeles, Ottawa (Canada), Port of Spain (Trinidad), and Kingston (Jamaica). We warned of the vulnerabilities of the global trade and transportation infrastructure to exploitation by terrorists and criminals. My "stump speech" line was, "Terrorists and tourists alike use the same global infrastructure." We told leaders the question was not whether an attack would occur, but when.

Our briefings were met with either sympathy or skepticism. The sympathetic said they agreed but were powerless to change the allocation of resources to better respond. The only new security initiative being funded by the United States was missile defense. The Clinton administration had increased anti- and counterterrorism measures, but scandals dissipated any political capital to do more, and the Bush administration favored unilateral rather than multilateral approaches to security. The sympathetic in business argued that they could not convince their shareholders or CEOs to reallocate resources to public security functions. The skeptics argued that if terrorism was such a clear and present danger, then why did only nineteen Americans die in the year 2000 from terrorist attacks? Business leaders in particular argued that the problems, while interesting, were really not their concern. In their view, counterterrorism was the government's job—specifically, the job of the military and law enforcement. We countered that trade and transportation infrastructure are largely privately owned and operated. Government cannot protect critical infrastructure without information, assistance, and cooperation from the private sector.

Since September 11, many of our proposals are being considered (with some adopted) by governments and businesses. However, the status quo is a powerful force, and there is still a disconnect in policy, academic, and public discussions in thinking about global problems. Discussions of global problems, state sovereignty, and globalization too quickly degenerate into either–or, all-or-nothing debates. Advocates of globalization oversell it in their zeal to convert opponents. According to many representatives of international financial institutions, governments, and businesses, globalization promotes progress, life, liberty, and the pursuit of happiness, everything that is good about the enlightenment tradition. Critics respond by overdemonizing globalization. From poverty to injustice to exploitation and environmental degradation, there is no evil in the world that cannot be traced to globalization. Clearly, good and evil existed long before globalization. But in the marketing attempts to persuade converts and win the media public relations battle, careful thought too often loses out. For the past several years, I have been working with various religious groups and nongovernmental organizations on projects that examine the ethical implications of globalization and ways to reform globalization to be more in line with important societal values. But even among ethicists and religious leaders with nuanced and sophisticated understandings of good and evil, the same either–or debates often prevail. The same goes for discussions of the future of sovereignty. Some argue globalization means the sovereign state is dead, while others argue that nothing has changed.

Beyond Sovereignty takes a different approach. We argue that globalization (the interdependent infrastructure of global open economies, societies, and technologies) brings both promise and problems. We cannot get one without the other. Societies pursue policies of economic and political liberalization in order to achieve peace and prosperity only to find they are increasingly vulnerable to a host of global problems that use the same global infrastructure. To create a more just and sustainable globalization, transsovereign problems must be recognized, understood, and carefully managed.

The same logic applies to the future of sovereign states. States do not sign up for globalization policies in order to put themselves out of business. Yet attempts to mitigate global problems produce unintended side effects; sovereignty is changing. Even the most powerful states in the system are increasingly affected by nonstate actors and global problems they cannot solve alone. To maintain legitimacy, domestic and international law, order, peace, and justice, states must become increasingly skilled in coordinating efforts with other states and a host of nonstate actors locally and internationally. Failure to manage global issues further undermines sovereignty. But efforts to solve global problems also must go beyond sovereignty.

Our choices are not between a globalization that puts profits before people or no globalization at all. Similarly, our choices are not between autonomous sovereign states as they existed in 1648 or no sovereign states at all. The world is more complex and adaptive than that. We can imagine globalization without exploitation, and sovereignty with social responsibility acting in concert with nonstate institutions. Imagination is the first step in creation.

The silver lining of the September 11 attacks and the subsequent "war on terrorism" attempts to counter the problems of global terrorism, refugees, nuclear smuggling, crime, and disease may be a greater understanding that no one is immune or invulnerable to global problems and that no one can solve these problems alone. Our hope lies in adapting new systems to coordinate actions across a wide variety of actors and to develop better ways to work together. Because our problems cross state borders and include states and nonstate actors, the public and private sectors, so must our solutions.

Beyond Sovereignty: Issues for a Global Agenda begins with an outline of the debates over globalization; the rise of transsovereign problems and open markets, open societies, and open economies; a historical description of sovereignty; and a review of current theories about whether sovereignty is receding or changing or remaining as powerful as ever. The chapters that follow, written by noted academics and expert practitioners, consider various global issues; their connections with globalization's open economies, societies, and technologies; and potential policy solutions. Chapters describe the changing roles of nonstate actors, including intergovernmental organizations (IGOs), nongovernmental organizations (NGOs), and multinational corporations (MNCs). To manage global issues, institutions must change. Global changes move quickly, while institutions change slowly, creating a variety of institutional gaps. Obstacles and the promise of institutional change are then discussed. The concluding chapter reviews the various policy proposals to combat global issues. Some of the prescriptions focus on the state as savior. Others regard states as ill-equipped to manage global issues and instead suggest that private or nonstate actors intercede. Other proposals suggest that some combination of state and nonstate activities manage global issues. The volume then returns to the theoretical arguments about the future of sovereignty. Do the preceding chapters support or challenge the various theories on the future of the state? If sovereignty has not yet been dethroned by some competing organizational form, does that mean that it remains unchanged and unscathed by current developments?

Beyond Sovereignty is written with students in introductory courses in international relations, U. S. foreign policy, global issues, and globalization in mind. *Beyond Sovereignty* differs from other issue texts. The chapters were written explicitly for this volume. Each chapter addresses the common themes of globalization, the rise of nonstate actors, and the effects on sovereignty, and each proposes potential solutions to pressing global issues. The issues are not presented in an ad hoc, disconnected fashion, as occurs with many issues texts that present descriptive accounts (usually reprinted from journals) without providing the theoretical or historical context that unites current challenges. Instead, readers are offered an understanding of how these issues intersect, why they are on the rise simultaneously, the origins of these issues, and the theoretical and practical problems in policy solutions. Too often, political science books present the problems and criticisms of current policy without presenting alternatives. These books do not meet our moral responsibilities as citizens, students, and scholars not only to describe problems but also to propose possible solutions. In contrast, *Beyond Sovereignty* describes both global problems and possible solutions.

The second edition's chapters are briefer and more on point than those of the first edition, with new chapters on terrorism, the environment, cyberthreats, transnational crime, IGOs, MNCs, and NGOs. Each chapter begins with new and brief minicase examples to launch exploration and discussion of the materials. All chapters were revised in light of new twists in the globalization debates, new data, and the events of September 11. The second edition includes more discussions of developing countries', women's, constructivist, and normative perspectives.

This book benefited from conversations and input from many individuals, although any errors or omissions are purely my own. Discussions with Drs. Richard Love, Stephen Flynn, and Deborah Gerner encouraged me to go forward with the second edition. Meetings with policy makers and bishops from

Latin America, Canada, and the United States on humanizing globalization helped convince me of the need for this book and the importance of its thesis. Discussions with colleagues James Rosenau and James Goldgier of George Washington University, Anne Florini and P. J. Simmons of the Carnegie Endowment for International Peace, Virginia Haufler of the University of Maryland, and Wolfgang Reinicke of the World Bank cross-fertilized ideas and encouraged me to proceed. Many thanks go to the volume contributors who worked with great speed under a tight deadline to produce a quality edition. My undergraduate and graduate students at the Catholic University of America and the Pentagon, especially Nate Frier, David Caldwell, Lance Moore, Greg Brady, Klaus Schmidt, Karen Kwiatkowski, Erin Ennis, Steve Lemons, Paul Sunwabe, Audrey Ammons, James Herrera, Michelle Boomgaard, Jennifer Jaskel, and Emily Levasseur provided lively discussions. The editorial and production staff at Wadsworth, especially Executive Editor David Tatom, Assistant Editor Heather Hogan, and book producer S.M. Summerlight were strongly committed to fast-tracking a September 11 second edition. The manuscript was also helped by the reviewer comments of Lowell Barrington, Marquette University; Deborah J. Gerner, University of Kansas; Darren Hawkins, Brigham Young University; Stacy D. VanDeveer, University of New Hampshire; Joseph Lepgold, Georgetown University; and Thomas Volgy, University of Arizona.

Last, but not least, my husband, family, and friends—especially at St. Aloyius Gonzaga Parish, the Center for International Social Development at Catholic University, Women in International Security, and the Jesuit order—buoyed my spirits and kept me sane throughout. A portion of the proceeds from this book will go to the Francis Cusimano S. J. Scholarship Fund to support the education of children in Nigeria.

Maryann Cusimano Love
The Catholic University of America
Washington, D.C.
July 2002

CHAPTER ONE

Global Problems, Global Solutions

Maryann Cusimano Love

"Let history not say about our age that we were those who were rich in means but poor in will. Let it say that 'we who were strong in love,' as Wordsworth put it, were the ones who really did make poverty history."

—Kofi Annan, July 6, 2005, Speech to Make Poverty History, St. Paul's Cathedral, London

"Don't blow it. Put down the national flags. Look up from the numbers and look to the future."

—Bono, June 9, 2005, statement urging the EU to Make Poverty History

Every hour, 1200 children die from disease and malnourishment—from poverty.[1] More than 8 million people a year die from poverty[2], 30,000 each day. According to Rev. Dr. Ishmael Noko of the Consultation of International Religious Leaders on Global Poverty, "poverty is an issue that has no borders."[3]

In July 2005, hundreds of thousands of protesters, celebrities, religious leaders, and nongovernmental organizations (NGOs) assembled in Gleneagles, Scotland, to urge the G-8 intergovernmental organization (IGO) to increase aid and debt relief to the world's poor. Musicians, celebrities, and entertainers added their voices and pressure to the mix, in a series of highly attended and highly publicized Live 8 concerts held around the world. G-8 leaders were in favor of debt relief in principle, but they debated the means. The International Monetary Fund (IMF) and World Bank wanted commitments that debt forgiveness would be paid for by contributing countries[4] so as not to hurt the IGO's budgets and abilities to give new aid and loans. Should the IMF and the World Bank sell some of their gold reserves to pay for debt relief? Some multinational corporations (MNCs) who deal in gold were alarmed at this prospect and stepped up their lobbying efforts against the proposal, concerned that increased gold supplies on the world market could hurt their businesses. Global media attention to the Live 8 concerts and to the NGO protests raised public awareness of the problems of global poverty and kept the pressure on political leaders.

But the global media attention was diverted from the One Campaign to Make Poverty History as terrorist bombs ripped through London metro "tube" trains and buses on July 7, killing 56 and injuring 700. Individual passengers captured the devastation in photos and recordings on their cell phones, which were then broadcast immediately and globally, even as police were trying to restrict press access to the blast areas as recovery and investigations went forward. Similar to the coordinated Madrid train bombings of March 11, 2004 (which killed 191 and injured 1460), a previously unknown terrorist cell calling themselves "al Qaeda in Europe" claimed responsibility for the bombings in a message posted on the Internet.

The pattern was sadly similar to the attacks of September 11, 2001, when the world witnessed another fiery and fatal demonstration of global issues that move beyond sovereignty. Nonstate actors used nonmilitary means to attack primarily nongovernmental targets. Nineteen terrorists who represented no state inflicted massive casualties and approximately 3,000 deaths against citizens from the most powerful state in the international system as well as from 80 other countries. They used commercial airlines, the tools of transportation and commerce, to attack, and chose as their primary targets the twin towers of the World Trade Center, symbols of global capitalism. Members of the al Qaeda terrorist network, the presumed perpetrators, operate across sovereign borders through cells in an estimated 65 countries. The suicide bombers were Saudis and Egyptians who had been living in the United States, trained in Afghanistan, and organized and financed in Germany, England, and Spain with information and money sent to them from companies, nongovernmental organizations (NGOs), and individuals around the world. The al Qaeda financial network drew from the diamond trade in Sierra Leone and the heroin trade in Afghanistan, effectively linking the terrorist network with global crime and drug trafficking networks. The hijackers exploited the very global transportation, communication, and economic systems they protested—and which they believed carry undue and unwanted U.S. and Western influence around the world. Their high-visibility attacks were planned to maximize global media exposure.

None of these important global actions is captured by the traditional view of International Relations as the activities of states.

This book investigates global issues that move beyond sovereignty in both the nature of problems and solutions. As one UN official observed, "Disease and pollution cross borders without passports."[5] Borders are more permeable, and threats are fast, fungible, fluid, and decentralized. How can global or transsovereign issues be tackled in a system that is based on sovereignty?

How does globalization facilitate both global problems and attempts to manage them? How do the debates over globalization frame our understanding of these issues? We describe the rising importance of nonstate actors and global issues, and the challenges to changing institutions. Finally, we review the various theories on the status and future of sovereignty and assess where sovereignty is heading.

Transsovereign problems represent the downside of globalization. Globalization is the fast, interdependent spread of open society, open economy, and open technology infrastructures. Globalization is not new, but the speed, reach, intensity, cost, and impacts of the current period of globalization are. Earlier periods of globalization moved trade, missionaries, and colonizers far more slowly, with the speed of frigates. Now people and products cross borders in hours. Ideas and capital move around the globe at the touch of a keystroke. Global or transsovereign problems are "problems [that] transcend state boundaries in ways over which states have little control and which cannot be solved by individual state actions alone."[6] Nonstate actors are important players both in creating and managing global issues— from legal groups such as NGOs, intergovernmental organizations (IGOs), and multinational corporations (MNCs) to illicit groups such as international crime cartels and terrorist organizations. The rise of transsovereign problems is made possible by the very changes that have been facilitated and celebrated by many policy makers: the rise of democracies and liberal, capitalist economies, and advances in technology, transportation, and communication. Thus, the rise of global problems is full of irony. It is physically difficult to limit the flow of particular peoples and goods at a time when technological, market, and societal forces make such movement easier than ever before.

Although globalization did not create transsovereign problems, it has facilitated and intensified them. For example, although terrorism existed long before, the modern period of globalization certainly facilitates the work of terrorist groups such as al Qaeda.[7] Open economies, societies, and technologies gave al Qaeda the opportunity to take its complaints to a global stage, to act at a distance cheaply, to perpetrate greater casualties using global technologies, and to elicit greater fear by playing in front of cameras and satellites that broadcast its members' actions instantly and globally.

Globalization gives breakdowns in state authority and capacity and transsovereign problems greater reach, speed, intensity, and impact.

Sovereignty is the form of political organization that has dominated the international system since the Treaty of Westphalia in 1648. Sovereign states have exclusive and final jurisdiction over territory, as well as the resources and populations that lie within such territory. A system based on sovereignty is one that acknowledges only one political authority over a particular territory and looks to that authority as the final arbiter to solve problems that occur within its borders. Sovereign states have four characteristics, three of which are negotiable: territory, population, a government with control over the territory and population, and international recognition. In practice, only international recognition is non-negotiable. If a political entity has territory, population, and a government but lacks international recognition, then it is not considered a sovereign state; the Palestinian Authority is one example. Once a state is internationally recognized, such as Somalia, it does not matter if it lacks a government with the ability to control the territory and population, if territory is contested, or if population varies widely (because of large refugee flows, for example).

Although many policy makers and journalists (and sometimes even scholars) use the term *transnational* in discussing such problems, this volume will instead use the more accurate terms *transsovereign* problems or *global* issues. The term *nation* is not synonymous with the term *sovereign state.* A nation is a group with a common cultural, linguistic, ethnic, racial, or religious identity— such as the Sioux nation of the U.S. plains or the Moluccans in Northern Europe. A sovereign state or country, however, is an internationally recognized unit of political authority over a given territory, such as the United States of America or the Netherlands. National boundaries—where various ethnic or linguistic groups are located—often do not coincide with sovereign state boundaries. For example, the Basques live on either side of the border between Spain and France, and the Kurds live in the region straddling Iraq and Turkey. By some counts, more than 8,000 national groups exist—but only 191 sovereign states.[8] The distinction is not just academic. Each year, tens of thousands of people die trying to make their nations into states. This volume uses the terms *transsovereign* or *global* to keep clear the distinction between sovereign states and national groups.

Twentieth-century international relations were epic battles of behemoth states, a century of "heroic warfare" among strong, competing states—for example, World Wars I and II and the Cold War. In contrast, the twenty-first century is marked by "postheroic warfare."[9] Conflicts now come not from battles among strong states but from the problems posed by nonstate actors and weak or disintegrating states ("Humpty Dumpty wars" in which all the king's forces and men may not be able to put fractured states back together again). Although global issues move beyond sovereignty, the machinery we have to manage these problems is still wired for the sovereign, often state-to-state, military confrontations of a bygone era. Within two months, the U.S. government responded to the September 11 terrorist attacks with a military attack on the Taliban government in Afghanistan not only because it was sheltering Osama bin Laden, but also because this is what the U.S. government knows how to do: fight other states. It is difficult to attack an unknown, moving target, a nonstate actor with no known address.

The post–Cold War era is witness to the collapse of many weak states that had previously been kept afloat by Cold War aid and alliances.[10] These same trends of open societies, open economies, and open technologies can further erode already weak state institutions in many quasi-states, pushing them closer to collapse. Failed states provide a natural breeding ground for transsovereign problems such as terrorism, international criminal activity, flows of refugees, the spread of contagious disease, and trafficking in drugs and nuclear materials. Failed states also attract the relief and development efforts of NGOs and IGOs. In a world primarily organized around state sovereignty, world politics practitioners are challenged by a double bind.

How can transsovereign issues be dealt with effectively in a world of sovereign states? Simultaneously, how can democratization and economic liberalization be promoted in ways that do not undermine already fragile state institutions to the point of collapse, thus increasing the spread and intensity of global problems?

GLOBAL PROBLEMS AND THE GLOBALIZATION DEBATES

Globalization creates a world of paradox. Global transportation, communication, and economic interdependence make possible the vision of a closer human family. Two million people cross an international border every day. Terrorists and dangerous microbes, however, use the same global infrastructure that tourists do. Although capital flows of $2 trillion cross borders each day, most poor people and poor countries see little of it. Building the global infrastructure of open economies, technologies, and societies creates great benefits, but globalization also carries significant costs that are often not equitably dispersed, especially to the world's poor.

Some scholars[11] and advocates argue that globalization is a means to bring peoples and cultures together; rout tyrannical governments; easily and cheaply spread information, ideas, capital, and commerce; and transfer more power than ever before to civil society and networked individuals.[12] For advocates, curtailing globalization would be immoral. Global poverty is a problem—and globalization is the key to solving it. The world's most impoverished countries are those that are least globalized.

Other scholars and critics, however, see globalization as neoimperialism wearing Bill Gates's face and Mickey Mouse's ears, extending the web of global capitalism's exploitation of women, minorities, the poor, and developing regions. It fouls ecosystems, displaces local cultures and traditions, mandates worship at the altar of rampant consumer capitalism, and deepens the divide (digital and otherwise) between the global haves and havenots.[13]

Opposition to globalization comes from many different camps, but critics share a common view that globalization puts profits before people. Globalization benefits a few at the top and in the West at the expense of the rest. Environmental, human rights, and labor advocates charge that globalization brings a race to the bottom in human rights and environmental standards as businesses extend their reach to benefit the corporate bottom line. Local laws and control may be sacrificed to international regimes that are controlled by a few powerful states or corporations. These regimes are not democratic, representative, or transparent. Critics see globalization as a new form of imperialism—whether corporate, cultural, U.S., or Western—that is immoral and unjust. Liberal consumer advocates such as Ralph Nader, conservative protectionists such as the Peronistas in Argentina and Patrick Buchanan in the United States, radicals such as Osama bin Laden and al Qaeda, and anticorporate activists such as anti-McDonald's farmer Jose Bove in France have little in common other than their opposition to globalization. For these opponents, the biggest question is how to stop globalization and the harms that come from it.

Opponents and advocates see globalization differently in part because the costs and benefits of globalization are asymmetrically distributed rather than shared equally. Capitalism is criticized for disparities between rich and poor in terms of income, political power, participation, and opportunities. In parallel, the worldwide spread and intensification of capitalism that globalization represents is criticized for exacerbating capitalism's excesses and exporting the resulting problems to the entire world. For example, before the latest phase of globalization, the disparity between the richest and poorest quintiles of the earth's population was 30 to 1. In 1997, the richest 20 percent were 74 times richer than the world's poorest 20 percent. The wealth of the world's three richest individuals surpasses the combined gross domestic product (GDP) of all the world's underdeveloped countries (with their 600 million inhabitants).[14] Of the 6 billion people now on the planet,

2.5 billion live on less than $2 a day, and 1.3 billion live on less than $1 per day.[15] Sixty countries are poorer than they were in the early 1980s, and 18 countries (460 million people) are poorer than they were in the early 1990s.[16] Critics say globalization widens the gap between rich and poor. Advocates say the lack of globalization causes such poverty.

Does globalization increase income inequality, making the rich richer and the poor poorer? Debates rage over this question, and there is some evidence on each side. On the one hand, China and India have moved their economies toward more industrial and high-tech sectors, and so have been able to benefit from foreign direct investment (FDI), and incomes have improved dramatically.[17] Plenty of poverty remains in these countries, especially among women and people in rural areas, but because of the large populations in China and India, growth in income, life expectancy, and education there allows advocates for globalization to claim that globalization is decreasing global poverty. However, the story is much different in sub-Saharan Africa and economies in transition (such as those in Eastern Europe). The world's poorest countries have experienced declining income rather than economic growth, and advances in life expectancy and education made immediately after decolonization have been reversed in the last decade due to the HIV/AIDS pandemic. African countries find their agricultural products shut out of global markets due to protectionist agriculture policies. Their cheaper labor is excluded from developed country markets due to restrictive immigration policies. These countries do not benefit from FDI, which goes to more developed economies rather than to the poorest economies. Income inequality has increased within countries as well as among countries. If death rates increase among the world's poorest people, does that count as "globalization decreasing poverty"?[18]

Wealth is only one indicator of global asymmetries. Decisions about globalization are made in corporate boardrooms and state capitals generally in economically developed states. Toxic waste from developed countries, however, is shipped to the world's poorest communities as some corporations exploit regions where environmental legislation or enforcement is weak. Most foreign direct investment and corporate shareholder profits go to developed states. "Controlling for the opening of both China and the former Soviet bloc, which attracted almost no investment before 1985, the share of foreign direct investment going to the developing world actually dropped" from 1985 to 1995.[19] All developing countries combined received only 16 percent of FDI in 2000, while the U.S. alone received 26 percent of FDI.[20] Globalization's costs and benefits are unequally distributed, with poor people and poor countries too often not participating in the full benefits that globalization may bring. Maximizing the benefits of globalization while minimizing or managing the challenges is difficult because the institution we generally task with managing global problems—the sovereign state—cannot do the job alone.

Most of the clashes between globalization's proponents and skeptics are peaceful, carried out in op-ed pages, in consumer boycotts, and on the floors of parliaments. But as globalization is embraced by more governments around the world, frustrations are also rising. Tensions rise as opponents are shut out of the boardrooms in businesses, international organizations, and governments where crucial decisions are made about the pace and nature of globalization.

This book takes a third way in this debate: Globalization is neither inherently good nor evil—but both. Terrorists and tourists alike use the same global infrastructure. Transsovereign problems are the unintended side effects of globalization. As globalization advances, so will both opposition to globalization and its unintended adverse effects. To better harness and spread the benefits of globalization, we must take these adverse effects and the ethics of globalization seriously and work to better contain globalization's challenges. As the sides become polarized, this third way is often overlooked. Proponents do not adequately recognize globalization's failures, while opponents do not fully recognize its benefits. Some proponents argue that the way to address global inequities and poverty is more globalization more quickly—and full speed ahead. Some opponents argue that attempts to lessen globalization's downsides are misplaced. Creating a kinder, gentler "globalization with a human face"[21] allows unjust systems to persist longer rather than allowing them to fall from the weight of their problems. Ironically, opponents to globalization use the tools of globalization (global media and the Internet, for example) to organize, mobilize, and publicize their opposition to globalization. And proponents of globalization use the arguments of opponents who are concerned with serious poverty and environmental problems to justify more globalization, arguing that only greater globalization will increase living standards and eventually leave more disposable income to address environmental problems. Too often both sides talk past each other. The same is true in the sovereignty debates. Some argue sovereignty is dead, while others argue it remains unchanged. This book takes the third approach: Sovereignty remains but is changing in important ways.

Understanding pressing global issues means understanding that globalization creates both benefits and challenges that states cannot control or solve alone. Because the problems go beyond sovereignty, so must the solutions. But going beyond sovereignty to manage global problems also carries unintended consequences for the state. The growth of the private sector, often with the aid of deliberate policy choices by states (political, economic, and technological liberalization) now often dwarfs the capacity of the public sector, even in the strongest states. In their attempts to manage pressing global problems, states contract out and form networks and alliances with the private sector (NGOs and MNCs) and with other states and multilateral organizations (IGOs). States enter into these partnerships voluntarily, expecting help in managing global problems. Yet in doing so, states unintentionally lose some autonomy, authority, and legitimacy as they acknowledge their incapacity to solve problems alone and the rising capacity of other actors.

THE DIFFICULTIES IN ADDRESSING TRANSSOVEREIGN PROBLEMS

Transsovereign problems are difficult to solve for many reasons. First, states and the private sector have to figure out how to control or contain them without moving to close off economies, societies, or technologies. Second, because their very nature precludes unilateral solutions, global problems are harder to tackle because they require the cooperation of a greater number of actors. Third, they are complex because they entail both state and nonstate actors, which creates coordination problems. Effective action requires complex coordination among states, NGOs, IGOs, MNCs, and other nonstate actors. These groups have different interests, capabilities, and constituencies. As more groups attempt to coordinate action, more opportunities are created for policy to go awry. As a British minister for the environment explained,

> We face new dilemmas—of problems that cross boundaries, of issues that no single government can control, of shared risk. Nowhere is this collectivity more true than with the environment. Pollution, global warming, ozone depletion, and loss of species do not respect borders. . . . Globalization —in the form of increasing trade, the communications revolution, and increasing cultural exchanges—means that . . . governments have less influence over activities and economic sectors that were formerly under their control. . . . Some people refer to the effect this has on governments as "loss of agency." But the need for intervention in the public interest has not diminished—it is just that the locus has changed. Activities that were formerly national are now international, but the institutional capacity to deal with them has yet to evolve . . . we must manage the changing responsibilities of governments, business and civil society, forming new partnerships, learning from each other, finding new ways of harnessing the expertise and legitimate concerns and aspirations of each.[22]

9

Fourth, global problems are challenging because they often take place in the economic and social spheres, where the arm of liberal capitalist states has the shortest reach. Fifth, addressing global issues is difficult because these problems blur the borders between domestic and foreign policy. As domestic constituencies become mobilized over global issues, policy makers find their tasks complicated because they must address and coordinate the interests of additional groups. Domestic labor, environmental, and industry groups mobilize for international discussions of acid rain, for example. Politics does not stop at the water's edge. Efforts to manage global issues may stumble over contentious and unsettled domestic policy debates. For example, Brazilian government policies toward global warming involve discussions of the rights of indigenous peoples and the private industries that cut, burn, and develop the rain forests.

As a U.S. State Department official described it, transsovereign issues signal a fundamental change in foreign policy:

> Foreign policy as we have known it is dead . . . because it is no longer foreign. The world has invaded us and we have invaded it. . . . The distinctions between domestic and foreign are gone. Look at the issues: The . . . fight against drugs and crime has major international components. Our stolen cars end up in El Salvador or Guatemala or Poland.
>
> Our drugs come from Peru or Pakistan or Burma or elsewhere and transit almost anywhere. Crime cartels spread tentacles from Nigeria or Russia or Colombia. Today it is inconceivable to consider a coordinated attack on crime without working a part of the strategy in the international arena. . . . International terrorism has reached our shores. . . . We cannot deal with the threats to our environment, to assaults on biodiversity with domestic policy. Ozone layer depletion and global warming cannot be addressed by domestic environmental regulations alone. Over and over again we find issues that are domestic in consequence but international in scope. These are the consuming issues of the twenty-first century.[23]

Global problems also can be difficult for states to address because of institutional gaps (these are discussed more fully in Chapter 13). Existing institutions were not created to handle these problems, and they may be slow to change, resist taking on new functions that may divert resources from their traditional missions, and have difficulties coordinating with other institutions. Finally, contracting out or cooperating with the private sector and multilateral organizations to combat or contain global problems may unintentionally further undermine sovereignty.

YESTERDAY: WHERE SOVEREIGNTY CAME FROM

The international system has not always been organized around sovereignty. Prior to the Treaty of Westphalia in 1648, there were overlapping jurisdictions of political authority with no clear hierarchy or pecking order among them. In this feudal system, claims to authority were diffuse, decentralized, and based on personal ties rather than territory. Medieval subjects faced simultaneous and competing claims for allegiance to the pope, the king or emperor, the bishop, and local feudal princes, dukes, counts, lords, and so on.[24] Taxes and military service could be required of a person from several different authorities within the same territory. A person's bonds to an authority figure were based on personal ties and agreements, and "political authority was treated as a private possession."[25] This made secession problematic because contractual obligations might not survive a person's death.

Rather than land, authority claims were based on the divine—on spiritual connections or on the legitimacy of lineage to the Church (and in the days before the Reformation, that meant the Roman Catholic Church). Secular and spiritual authority were intertwined. Kings were anointed with holy insignia (for example, British monarchs took the title "Defender of the Faith"), emperors were crowned as "servants of the apostles," and popes and bishops needed the support of nonclerical leaders to gain and retain power. Both the Church and the Holy Roman Empire sought to fill the vacuum left by the fall of the Roman Empire and made universal claims of authority.

People, not territory, were the primary objects of rule, and "rule was per definition spiritual" rather than spatial.[26] In the struggle between the papacy and the Holy Roman Empire for control, both institutions were weakened in ways that helped new forms of political organization to emerge.

There were many reasons why the feudal system declined and the sovereign state emerged. According to scholar Hendrik Spruyt, the rise of long-distance trade in the late Middle Ages created both a new merchant class of elites and the need for a new political system that could better accommodate the mercantilist economic system. The Church was against the exchange and loan of money and the taking of oaths, but currency and contracts were crucial to long-distance trade. Trade also required more precise and consistent measurements of time, weights, jurisdiction, and private property. As Spruyt notes,

> [t]he result of this economic dynamism was that a social group, the town dwellers, came into existence with new sources of revenue and power, which did not fit the old feudal order. This new social group had various incentives to search for political allies who were willing to change the existing order. The new trading and commercial classes of

11

the towns could not settle into the straitjacket of the feudal order,
and the towns became a chief agent in its final disruption. . . . Business
activity could not be organized according to the . . . system of personal
bonds. . . . Contracts could not depend on the initiating actors.

Sometimes these contracts might have to carry through beyond
the death of the original contractors.[27]

The rise of a new economic system with its own needs, however, was
not enough to bring about the rise of the sovereign state. The currency of
other ideas aided the development of the concept of sovereignty. Martin
Luther and the Protestant Reformation, Henry VIII and his Anglican sepa-
ratists, the rise of scientific knowledge and explorations of the non-European
world, along with the new merchant elites, challenged the authority and
legitimacy of the Church in Rome. Roman ideas of property rights—
which stressed exclusive control over territory—also were on the rise.[28]
Ideas of individual autonomy and freedom from outside interference, later
captured by Immanuel Kant, were important in the development of
sovereignty.[29] Nicholas Onuf cites three conceptual crucial antecedents to
the genesis of sovereignty: *majestas,* or the idea that institutions inspire
respect; *potestas imperiandi,* or the ability to coerce and enforce rules; and the
Protestant idea of stewardship, or rule on behalf of the citizens of the body
politic, not the personal rule of the Middle Ages.[30]

Besides conceptual changes, sovereignty also emerged because of
changes in practical political balances. Sovereign states were more effective
and efficient at waging war and conducting trade than were competing
political organizations.[31] Elites who benefited from the new form of organization sought to delegitimize actors who were not like them (who were not
organized as sovereign states) by excluding them from the international system.

Other forms of political organization competed with the sovereign
state to succeed the feudal system: the city-state, the urban league, and the
empire. Hendrik Spruyt believes that the sovereign state eventually won out
for three main reasons. First, states were better able to extract resources and
rationalize their economies than were other forms of political organization.

Second, states were more efficient and effective than were medieval
forms of organization, especially at being able to "speak with one voice" and
make the external commitments necessary to the new trading system. And
third, social choice and institutional mimicry meant that sovereign states
selected out and delegitimized other actors who were not sovereign states.[32]

Out of these changes in economics, political balances, and conceptual
frameworks came the eventual acceptance of the sovereign state. Authority was

now based on exclusive jurisdiction over territory. Identity became based on geography: You were where you lived—a citizen of French territory, not primarily a member of the Holy Roman Empire or the community of Christians or the Celtic or Norman clans.

In theory, the sovereign state had a monopoly on the legitimate use of force within a territory. Sovereignty was reciprocal. One state recognized the others' exclusive jurisdictions over their territories and the populations and resources that resided on their lands; in return, they recognized that state's exclusive jurisdiction over its territory and everything on its land.[33] From the beginning, sovereignty was based on a social compact. Sovereignty never meant that all states had equal power or resources—some had vast lands, populations, and resources, while the capabilities of other states were meager. But sovereignty meant that only other sovereigns had legal standing in international agreements. States were the main unit of the international system.

From its origins in Europe, the idea and practice of sovereignty spread around the globe as Europeans conquered and carved up the planet into colonial territories. Sovereignty (with its territorial limits) came into conflict with the unlimited, universal Chinese, Japanese, and Ottoman empires, but eventually sovereignty came to dominate worldwide, whether by force or accession. When European colonies became independent after World War II and later when the Soviet bloc disintegrated between 1989 and 1991, the political units that emerged sought sovereign statehood, not recognition of other forms of political organization.

Sovereignty is an equalizing concept. Internally, governments organize themselves in whatever fashion they choose: monarchy, republican constitutional parliamentary system, autocracy, theocracy, and so on. Externally, however, all a state needs is international recognition as a sovereign state.

TODAY: SOVEREIGNTY CHALLENGED

The modern international system is built on the foundation of sovereignty. Today, sovereignty is under siege. There have always been weak states, and distinctions between the theory and the practice of sovereignty, yet both *de jure* and *de facto* sovereignty are now under assault more than ever. The sovereign state will likely continue to be the main unit in the international system for some time, but the operation and legitimacy of sovereignty are being undermined by both external and internal dynamics.

The principle of sovereignty is under siege by those who contend that in grave humanitarian crises the international community (of NGOs, IGOs, and states) has a right to intervene to aid citizens who are not being protected by the state. In Somalia, Bosnia, and Rwanda, the international community intervened in the internal affairs of states to distribute aid directly to individuals in times of grave humanitarian crisis without either the invitation or consent of the sovereignties involved. In the past, only sovereign states, not individuals, had standing in international law; within sovereign borders, a polity could do whatever it pleased with its citizens, even if that meant abusing their human rights or neglecting basic human needs.

Now such thinking is changing among some observers. As Kofi Annan, Secretary-General of the United Nations, said in his speech accepting the Nobel Prize, "In the twenty-first century I believe the mission of the United Nations will be defined by a new, more profound awareness of the sanctity and dignity of every human life. . . . This will require us to look beyond the framework of sovereign states. . . . The sovereignty of States must no longer be used as a shield for gross violations of human rights."[34] These are strong words from the director of an organization founded on the principle of sovereign states and constituted solely of sovereign states as voting members.

The *Wall Street Journal* editorialized in a similar vein, saying that sovereignty is not an absolute right because starvation and wanton killing are "everybody's business," and that in cases such as Somalia or Rwanda, "any absolute principle of nonintervention becomes a cruel abstraction indeed."[35] Editorial writers at the *Economist* agreed, noting that we are

> increasingly concerned not just to see countries well governed but also to ensure that the world is not irreparably damaged—whether by global warming, by the loss of species, by famine or by war. . . .
>
> Increasingly, world opinion, when confronted by television pictures of genocide or starvation, is unimpressed by those who say "We cannot get involved. National sovereignty must be respected.". . . National sovereignty be damned.[36]

Principles of sovereignty took centuries to become established and are not in danger of dissolving any time soon. However, perhaps we ought to take notice anytime the more liberal Kofi Annan and the conservative *Wall Street Journal* and *Economist* agree that the principle of sovereignty is challenged, and that individuals in need might seek international redress if states are unable or unwilling to carry out basic duties to their citizens.

Sovereignty is being challenged not only in theory, but also is under siege in practice. Sovereignty is challenged externally by the globalizing dynamics of open markets, open societies, and open technologies, which make the borders of even strong states permeable by outside forces. Sovereignty is also under siege internally from the rise of internal conflicts and subnational movements, as well as from the reinforcing crises of economic development (resource scarcity, environmental degradation, population growth) that undermine the international and internal legitimacy on which sovereignty stands. Both of these dynamics have led to a growing number of collapsed and collapsing states. But even the strongest states in the system cannot effectively manage global issues alone.

Nearly one third of the people on the planet, more than two billion people, live in failed or failing states. Eight of the top ten failed states are in Africa.[37] In his book *Collapsed States,* I. William Zartman notes that half the states in Africa may be in serious or maximum "danger of collapse, if not already gone."[38] Not coincidentally, Africa has the most wars of any continent on the planet. All major armed conflicts are internal conflicts,[39] showing that sovereign states beyond Africa are feeling the effects of substate challenges.

When sovereign states collapse, the international system feels the shock waves. A state is in a process of collapse when its institutions and leaders lose control of political and economic space. When state authorities can no longer provide security, law and order, an economic infrastructure, or other services for citizens, then government retracts and the countryside is left on its own. Political space broadens as outside actors usurp (as in Lebanon) and intervene (as IGOs and NGOs enter to provide relief services necessitated by state breakdown). Economic space contracts as the informal economy takes over beyond state control, and as localities resort to barter, as occurred in Somalia.[40] In the power vacuum left by state collapse, global problems thrive. For example, as al Qaeda fighters were pushed out of Afghanistan, they moved to Sudan, Somalia, and Yemen—other areas where state control is weak.

When states implode, more than the residents are affected. In an interdependent world, the event can hurt distant international actors. Refugee flows, disease, terrorism, crime, drug smuggling, ethnic conflict, and civil war all thrive as the state recedes and often spread beyond borders. NGOs, IGOs, and criminal organizations are all drawn to collapsed states, whether to help restore law and order or to exploit its absence.

Robert Jackson, in his book *Quasi-States,* notes that the international system used to be based primarily on "positive sovereignty," the actual, empirical ability of a state to control its political and economic space, to "provide political goods for its citizens ... the sociological, economic, technological, psychological, and similar wherewithal to declare, implement, and enforce public policy both domestically and internationally."[41] Weak states existed, but not for long, as it was considered perfectly legitimate for an outside power to conquer and absorb a weak state. The "old sovereignty game" recognized but did not protect weak sovereignties. They were vulnerable links in the international system's food chain. Their digestion by more power-ful states was internationally sanctioned behavior.

This changed with the rise of Woodrow Wilson's idea of self-determination, with the discrediting of the concept of "salt-water colonialism"[42] and the end of colonial empires, and with the rise of democracy. The "new sovereignty game," Jackson contends, is increasingly based on "negative sovereignty," the formal-legal entitlement to freedom from outside interference and the *de jure* norm of nonintervention.[43] Thus, the current norms and practices of the international system create conditions that allow weak, ineffectual quasi-states to exist.

Sovereignty is under siege from internal pressures and conflicts that weaken state institutions. Many states in the developing world are undergo-ing related crises of poverty, disease, environmental degradation, and internal conflict. According to the United Nations, the top twenty worst places to live in the world are all African countries. Life expectancy is dropping pre-cipitously in Africa as HIV/AIDS ravages the continent.[44] High external debt diverts government budgets from critical public health, education, and social welfare investments to making interest payments that further profit Western banks. Corruption flourishes as survival is endangered, a "get mine" mentality permeates public life, and people don't expect to live long enough to face consequences for their actions. Where political institutions are seen as weak and ineffective to meet public needs, cynicism, hostility, and armed conflicts multiply. Most African countries now struggle to respond to this "perfect storm" of poverty, disease, and political instability. The opportunity for conflict among societal groups increases as resources shrink.

Reinforcing economic and political crises are not restricted to Africa. GNP in the former Soviet states fell by as much as 30 percent after the Cold War, while major armed conflicts in the region quadrupled.[45] Pressure on (and disillusionment with) fragile state institutions grows as the state fails to break (or contributes to) the scarcity cycle and as the chasm grows between the lesser developed and the developed states. States that are confronted with reinforcing crises can "harden," resorting to increased repression in an attempt to establish control.[46] Repressive tactics are costly, however. Civil institutions of the state atrophy (and economic and social performance often suffer) as power and resources concentrate in the military and police. State legitimacy and authority is further undermined, and opposition grows with the increase in repressive tactics.

The result is not just a crisis of a particular regime but of the sovereign state itself. Any regime that wins power will face extremely denigrated (to nonexistent) state institutions and societal bases of state power. Thus, the related crises of poverty and internal conflict undermine the foundations of sovereign power. Many areas of Afghanistan respond entirely to tribal and local authorities, not the sovereign state. After decades of warfare, arms are readily available, leaving the state with nothing close to a monopoly on the use of force. As NGOs, IGOs, and states aid Afghanistan's post–Taliban transition, many worry not only about the capacity of any new government, but also whether the area is governable.

Sovereignty also is undermined by external trends that have been heralded since the end of the Cold War: the opening of societies, economies, and technologies. Strong states are not immune to the problems of globalization, as shown by the London bombings, the Madrid bombings, and the September 11 attacks. Developing states are also caught in a bind. Leaders are attracted to the prospect of wealth promised by democracy, capitalism, and technology (which can strengthen the state), yet they fear the loss of control and the decentralization of power that these processes entail (which can weaken the state). Capitalism, democracy, and technology can devolve power away from central state institutions and undermine the state's ability to control its borders.[47] Many developing states desire international capital and jobs, but the process of liberalizing economic and political systems can be quite destabilizing. Citizen demands on government cannot wait until new institutions are built and put into place, so developing states are in the challenging position of trying to modernize and democratize their institutions as these same institutions try to solve critical problems. As Jack Snyder and Edward Mansfield describe the dangers of democratization, it is like changing the steering wheel while driving the car.[48]

The end of the superpower conflict has also increased the pressure on many weak states. More states compete for overseas development assistance. The standard of living has dropped precipitously in many states that had received Cold War assistance, such as Cuba and North Korea (where famine has been a problem in recent years). The underlying ineffectiveness of state political and economic institutions becomes clear without the mask of Cold War aid and alliances. The authority and legitimacy of the state suffer because the state cannot meet citizen expectations, and living standards decline.

It is not just the case, as Max Singer and Aaron Wildavsky argue, that the twenty-first century world is increasingly segregated into two zones—peace and turmoil—with a widening gap between the advanced capitalist democracies and the underdeveloped nondemocratic states. According to Singer and Wildavsky, the stabilizing solution to this dilemma was the advancement of democratization, economic liberalization, and development so that more states would move from the "zone of turmoil" to the "zone of peace."[49]

It is not that simple. Democratization and economic liberalization can undermine already fragile state institutions. During the transition period, attempts to establish open societies and markets can further move a weak state into the zone of turmoil. Even in peaceful and prosperous market democracies, terrorists blow up trains and fly planes into buildings. Singer and Wildavsky might have argued that the zone of peace (even with its problems of drugs and crime) is preferable to the zone of turmoil (with its starvation and war), but surely their argument needs qualification—at least to check the expectations of fledgling democracies. Singer and Wildavsky's zone of peace is not the Promised Land. Democratization and economic liberalization carry their own costs in terms of transsovereign problems. Even strong, wealthy states with healthy internal institutions cannot unilaterally defeat global problems.

Open Economies

Developed countries have long histories of promoting international trade and global capitalist economic systems, sometimes even through force, while also trying to protect some domestic markets from international competition. Squabbles with the Barbary pirates, who were supported by the pasha of Tripoli (present-day Libya—even in the 1790s, the United States had poor relations with Libya because of a form of state-sponsored terrorism), led to the formation of the U.S. Navy and the beginnings of the president's ability to commit troops abroad without a formal declaration of war by Congress, in this case in order to protect commercial shipping engaged in trade. U.S. tensions with China and Japan in the nineteenth and twentieth centuries concerned the opening of Asian markets to U.S. goods.

European imperialism in Asia, Africa, and the Americas also served commercial interests. From the trade in spices, slaves, and rum to the extraction of precious metals, foreign commerce drove earlier periods of globalization. U.S. imperialism in Latin America and the Pacific was also conducted in the name of promoting trade and opening commerce. The American empire— in the form of U.S. protectorates in Puerto Rico, Guam, Samoa, and Hawaii, among others—was acquired largely to assist U.S. commercial interests in their efforts to expand foreign trade. The United States forcibly created the country of Panama (by seizing territory from Colombia) in order to build the Panama Canal to facilitate trade. Military intervention in Guatemala in 1954 was done largely to protect the interests of the United Fruit Company. As one U.S. trade official argued, "For most of America's history, foreign policy has reflected an obsession with open markets for American business. . . . Business expansion abroad was often seen as an extension of the American frontier, part of the nation's manifest destiny."[50]

Given these ties between colonialism and free market economics, it is no wonder that many citizens in developing countries are suspicious of globalization and the spread of international trade and capitalist systems. Many question just how "free" trade is among unequal trading partners and how "open" developed economies are to the goods (especially agricultural products) of lesser-developed countries. Developed countries retain protectionist obstacles to the products in which developing countries enjoy comparative advantage. Some see free trade and monetary policies as neoimperialism, with multinational corporations and international economic organizations such as the IMF and World Trade Organization (WTO) now infringing on the sovereignty of developing states in place of the colonial armies of a previous era. Trade ministers in developed countries counter that open markets, for all their imperfections, perform better than do state-controlled markets.

The Cold War was caused in part by this clash between state and market economies, with the United States opposed to the Soviets closing Eastern European markets to Western goods and trade. During the Cold War, many in the West believed that the superior economic performance of capitalist, free-market systems would eventually bring state-controlled, communist economic systems to their knees. George Kennan presciently predicted that the demise of the Soviet sphere would come about not through the external military confrontation of a globalized and militarized U.S. containment policy, which the United States could not afford, but through the West's building of strong, internal open societies and open markets. Eventually, the Soviet bloc would be "unable to stand the comparison."[51]

> If economic recovery could be brought about and public confidence restored in Western Europe—if Western Europe, in other words, could be made the home of a vigorous, prosperous and forward-looking civilization—the communist regime in Eastern Europe . . . would never be able to stand the comparison, and the spectacle of a happier and more successful life just across the fence . . . would be bound in the end to have a disintegrating and eroding effect on the communist world.[52]

His prediction was confirmed at the Cold War's end. The Marshall Plan and forty-five years of a concerted policy of building open economic and political institutions in Western Europe succeeded in rebuilding a continent destroyed by war. Such rebuilding never took place in much of Eastern Europe. Eventually, even the top leaders of the Soviet Union were forced to admit that their economic system was in need of reform when Gorbachev came to power in the 1980s.

Gorbachev's reforms began as attempts to improve the productivity and efficiency of the state-controlled economy: cutting down on vodka abuse on the job, decreasing bureaucratic red tape, and increasing worker and industry accountability. Quickly, these internal attempts to reform and strengthen the communist system unleashed massive dissatisfaction with the existing system. Gorbachev's reforms tapped into consumer and social unrest over shortages and poor economic performance (for example, exploding television sets in Moscow were a common cause of hospital emergency room visits), including the Chernobyl nuclear disaster. The legitimacy of the communist model was undermined, accelerating the pace of Gorbachev's initially modest reforms into the eventual overthrow of the entire system.[53] Gorbachev soon learned what the Chinese are now grappling with: that it is difficult to uncork just a little economic freedom.

With the demise of communist regimes in Eastern Europe and the former Soviet Union, and with the demise of state-controlled economies and authoritarian regimes in Latin America, many in the West assumed that it had won the Cold War's economic battle. As Paul Krugman put it, "Governments that had spent half a century pursuing statist, protectionist policies suddenly got free market religion. It was . . . the dawn of a new golden age for global capitalism." In addition, there

> was a sea change in the intellectual Zeitgeist: the almost universal acceptance, by governments and markets alike, of a new view about what it takes to develop. This view has come to be widely known as the "Washington Consensus.". . . It is the belief that . . . free markets and sound money [are] the key to economic development. Liberalize trade, privatize state enterprises, balance the budget, peg the exchange rate, and one will have laid the foundations for an economic takeoff.[54]

Of course, while many states "talk the talk" of capitalism, "free-market religion" has not been established universally. Corruption is a huge obstacle to economic development around the world. According to a World Bank study, "40% of customs authorities in Latin America admitted to paying substantial bribes to get their jobs."[55] Property rights remain poorly defined and protected in many parts of the world.[56] Many countries, such as Mexico, are privatizing state-owned industries, but the process is vulnerable to distortion by corruption as the transition to free-market economies is ongoing. This is the case in Eastern Europe, where formerly communist states are constructing the institutions that support free markets, such as laws that allow and protect the private ownership of property, stock exchanges, and laws that govern investment. There are still some states, such as North Korea, with closed economies. Others—such as Vietnam, Cuba, and China—are trying to attract foreign capital and investment and encourage some privatization of the economy, but the central government still owns and plays a key role in many industries. Developed countries retain popular, protectionist, agriculture subsidies and restrictions on certain foreign products. The Asian financial flu in the late 1990s and the collapse of Argentina's economy have led many observers to question the desirability of interconnected economies built on a "one-size-fits-all" Western model.

Yet for all the challenges facing economic liberalization, John Ikenberry contends that the triumph of Western policies of economic openness is so thorough that we often forget that "America is not adrift in uncharted seas. It is at the center of a world of its own making."[57] And the spread of capitalist prosperity, some contend, helps to spread peace and democracy as well. People with economic rights tend to demand political rights. There is some evidence of this today in China, where a growing middle class increasingly demands an end to political corruption, and where there are now contested local elections. Thomas Friedman argues that capitalism and economic interdependence bring peace; no two countries with a McDonald's have ever gone to war with one another.[58]

Yet U.S. and Western dominance of international economic regimes is precisely the point that draws concern from many people around the world. The European Union (EU), WTO, IMF, and World Bank were all created by the United States and its developed allies. Developing countries often have little say in the rules and regimes that govern the global economy. Many poor countries cannot even afford to send delegates to the WTO meetings. For example, until recently, the WTO's rules favored Western pharmaceutical companies that were interested in protecting their patents and profits over developing countries that were interested in producing cheaper generic AIDS drugs to fight a pressing public health crisis. Regardless of the specific conditions in their own countries and economies, developing countries often find that relations with developed countries and access to international loans and aid are contingent on progress in privatization and liberal economic reform.[59]

However, even though open economies often perform better than their state-run counterparts, they also carry costs.[60] Resentment over a widening gulf between rich and poor states and developed countries' dominance of the global economy leads to increasingly violent protests of globalization. The transition to capitalist economic structures also can destabilize states. Argentina's economic difficulties led to five governments in four weeks in early 2002. Amy Chua disputes that "markets and democracy go hand in hand," and instead argues that "Exporting free market democracy breeds ethnic hatred and global instability." When market liberalization helps "foreign minorities" earn disproportionate wealth while the local majority suffers economically, this lights the match to violence. Wealthy ethnic minorities, from Chinese in Southeast Asia to Croatians in the former Yugoslavia, become violently hated, at the same time as emerging democracy "empowers the impoverished majority, unleashing ethnic demagoguery, confiscation, and sometimes genocidal revenge."[61]

Instability provides openings for organized crime to step into the vacuum, as has occurred in Russia. The old order has been pulled down, but new laws and institutions that support free-market economies are still being built, and much turmoil can arise in the interim.

Decreased regulation and increased transborder trade decreases the opportunities for shipments to be searched or monitored. Thus, states lose significant control over their borders, one of the hallmarks of sovereignty.

"Dirty money" follows many of the same paths as "clean money." The same emerging global financial infrastructure useful to legal businesses also increases the opportunity and ease of conducting and covering illicit economic activities, such as the smuggling of narcotics and nuclear materials. Profits from illicit activities can be hidden in legal investments, sprinkled into front companies, bank accounts, and small investments across a range of industries and states. With the Internet and e-cash, the money trail can move quickly and be erased as investments can be changed and moved with a keystroke. Attempts to freeze and seize the monies of terrorist organizations show how difficult it can be to track and stop illicit cash in interdependent economies.

Open economies also decentralize power as more and more actors have autonomous economic power and the central government loses its ability to control economic activities in a global marketplace. Microsoft founder Bill Gates's annual income is more than the annual GNP of many states. The income of prominent drug lords often overwhelms and distorts the legal economy in a state because it is difficult to control or regulate.

Open Societies

Francis Fukuyama argues that the end of the Cold War also signaled the end of history, by which he means that "a remarkable consensus concerning the legitimacy of liberal democracy as a system of government has emerged throughout the world, as it conquered rival ideologies like hereditary monarchy, fascism, and most recently communism."[62] Although liberal democracy has not triumphed and may never prevail in all areas of the globe, Fukuyama contends that the twentieth century was marked by great battles of competing ideologies, and that now no alternative universal ideology of consequence exists to challenge liberal democracy. According to Fukuyama, liberal democracy "gives fullest scope" to satisfying "all three parts of the soul [desire, reason, and spirit] simultaneously."[63]

Fukuyama's thesis may be increasingly challenged by the ideas of some Islamic extremist groups that are intent on challenging Western government forms and promoting fundamentalist Islamic rule. Yet even analysts less optimistic about the liberal democratic form agree that we "are currently witnessing the fourth historical wave of democratization . . . more global in its reach . . . affecting far more countries and more thorough than its predecessors."[64] Democracy is not new and has been around in one form or another since the ancient Greeks. What is new, however, is the number of states that are turning to representative government forms with free multiparty elections and the protection of individual and minority rights including free speech and free press, freedom of association, freedom of movement, and freedom of religion. For the first time in history, a majority of states are either democracies or in transition to democracy.

In the first wave of democratization in the 1800s, universal suffrage was extended in states that were committed to democratic principles so that more than white male property owners could vote. This movement toward democracy ended as monarchies and authoritarian rulers sought to reestablish control in many states after the "springtime of freedom" in Europe in 1848–49. Although the first wave expanded democracy within societies and sought to spread democracy in Western Europe and North America, these same states were involved simultaneously in carving up the non-Western world into colonial empires in profoundly nondemocratic ways.

The second wave of democratization occurred during and after World War I as many states believed that autocracies were more to blame for starting the war than were democratic states. However, many of the democracies established after World War I were weak, such as the Weimar Republic, and many of these states reverted to authoritarianism as fascism swept the globe.

The third wave of democratization occurred with World War II as colonial powers were no longer able or willing to hold onto their overseas possessions, and a tidal wave of decolonization swept the globe. The number of independent states tripled from 1945 to 1979, and many of these former colonies turned to democratic government forms. Once again, however, this wave of democratization was followed by reversals. After historic initial democratic elections, many leaders would not hand over power to others, barring further elections. This pattern was pernicious in Africa. Ironically, the Cold War also caused some democratic backsliding, as the United States and the West supported noncommunist but nondemocratic regimes.

"By some counts, one-third of the globe's democracies had fallen under authoritarian rule by the late 1970s,"[65] as personal rule, military rule, or single-party autocracy replaced democratic political participation and institutions in developing states. Even though there were reverses, with each wave the number of democracies overall increased, as states such as India joined and stayed in the community of democracies.

The fourth wave of democratization differs from previous eras in two important respects. First, it was not the result of a single external event such as World War I or II. Although the end of the Soviet empire led many Eastern European states into the democratic experiment, other states such as Portugal, Spain, and South Africa turned to democracy for reasons other than (and prior to) the end of the Cold War.

Second, the most recent wave of democratization differs from its predecessors in scope and intensity. More states on more continents are becoming more democratic than ever before. This wave is not restricted to Europe or to former colonial empires, and this wave is more intensive, entailing a restructuring of political and economic institutions.

While the fate of these newly emerging democracies is by no means secure, the fourth wave of democratization has advantages that previous movements could not claim. The simultaneous trends of open markets and open technologies support and facilitate political openings. Previous reformers did not have CNN looking in and immediately reporting advances or backsliding to an international audience. Previous reformers also did not have to liberalize political institutions as a prerequisite to receiving international capital investments, whether from international lending institutions such as the World Bank or IMF or from private investors who believe the rule of law as practiced in democratic societies secures a better business environment. The growth of civil society internationally may also help solidify the current wave of democratization.

More than a decade ago, policy makers and scholars thought such extensive opportunities for democratization were unlikely. The opening of societies may lend itself to more open economic systems, as people with some say in their political futures tend to desire openness in their economic futures as well.[66] Of course, movement toward open societies is not complete.

Some states such as China are trying to open their economic systems to achieve prosperity and development without allowing significant political freedoms. Many states, particularly in Africa and the Middle East, retain authoritarian political systems.

Democracy is spreading for several reasons (of course, there are significant disagreements over how best to promote democracy in practice). Global media and cheap and ready access to information technology can help democratization. Democracies are more likely to have free market and free trade capitalist economies (encouraged by international financial institutions) and to have more prosperity and better records of economic development. Democratic protections of property rights and individual liberties provide a rule of law that fosters a more stable investment and business climate and better protects the larger number of citizens now traveling abroad and taking advantage of more advanced transportation and communication links. Perhaps most important, developed democracies tend not to go to war with one another.[67] Democracies are not more peaceful overall. They tend to go to war with nondemocracies, and the transition period of democratization can be fraught with conflict. But the empirical record of democracies not warring with other democracies is strong.

However, democratization carries costs. Transitions to democracy can be destabilizing in the short run, as "[d]emocratization typically creates a syndrome of weak central authority, unstable domestic coalitions, and high-energy mass politics."[68] Democratic elections and liberal protections—of human rights, rule of law, and separation of powers—may not coincide.[69] If privatization and liberalization of the economy are occurring simultaneously with democratization efforts (as is often the case), then corrupt, powerful corporate or criminal organizations may gain assets and influence before the civic institutions of public control and accountability are established (many observers argue that this has occurred in Nigeria, Russia, Ukraine, Tajikistan, Uzbekistan, Kazakhstan, etc.). Any one of these transitions would be highly complex and destabilizing for a society. The simultaneous and often sudden overlapping of these transitions only increases the level of difficulty for polities and increases the pressures for fragmentation that can undermine states.

Open Technologies

Developed countries tend to be enamored with technological advances, and it is easy to understand why. Cellular phones connect areas that are difficult to link by landlines in places such as Hong Kong and Israel. Technology made possible the settlement of the American continent and still undergirds the U.S. military's preeminent position in the world today.

Americans own more computers and televisions than the citizens of any other country,[70] and the United States has the most Internet users by far: 203.3 million (China is second with 103 million; Japan is third with 78 million users; Germany has 47 million; India has 39 million; and Britain has 36 million users).[71] U.S. scientists, industry, and government invented the computer and developed the Internet.

The "information revolution" is profoundly changing the way all states do their business: "Today all of humankind is linked by almost instantaneous communications. There is no corner of the globe that is not accessible to us, or us to them. Marshall McLuhan's global village is upon us with profound consequences . . . a market crash in Hong Kong is felt immediately by pensioners in Dubuque (Iowa)."[72]

Technological advances have been dramatically spurred by advances in computers. The first modern computer, developed in 1946 to calculate firing trajectories for artillery shells, "could execute the then-astonishing number of 5,000 arithmetic operations per second . . . weighed 30 tons, filled an enormous room at the University of Pennsylvania, consumed 150,000 watts of power, and used 18,000 vacuum tubes."[73] (The term "bugs in the system" literally referred to insects in these huge machines that interfered with operations.) Today, a Pentium chip is built on a thumbnail-sized piece of silicon, and laptop computers are smaller than briefcases, weighing less than four pounds.[74]

Many theorists argue that technology drives globalization and that the digital divide between rich and poor countries has kept the world's poor from enjoying the benefits of globalization. Computers, faxes, cell phones, and air travel have shrunk the planet and made sovereign borders less important for economic transactions. Television, radio, video cameras, and computers have made sovereign authorities less able to control the flow of information and ideas and thus made authoritarian control more expensive and difficult to maintain. Anyone with a concealed handheld video camera can record government abuses and instantly transmit these images via the Internet to place international pressure on the offending regime.

Technology, in essence, has undermined sovereign authority, decentralized power, and opened markets and societies.[75] To some extent, this presents a "chicken-or-egg" question. Although technology may in some sense "drive" the process of globalization, technological advances do not occur in an economic or political vacuum. Sustained political and investment decisions drive technological advances. Scientists did not suddenly develop powerful supercomputers, tiny microchips, and fiber optic telecommunications links by accident. These advancements came about through sustained investment, supported by political and social policies that harnessed resources in pursuit of technological progress and innovation as tools to advance economic and political goals. The first mainframe computer and the Internet were developed by the U.S. Department of Defense working in close connection with universities.

Causality flows in all directions, but together the trends of open economies, open societies, and open markets substantially reinforce each other.

When combined, they equal more than the sum of their parts. Technological advances facilitate the opening of markets and of societies, and vice versa.

However, like their counterparts, open technologies also undermine sovereignty and make transsovereign challenges possible. Technology moves legal and illegal information, people, and goods more quickly and efficiently than ever before across borders without the consent or even knowledge of sovereign authorities. Human smugglers use cell phones, e-cash, laptops, the Internet, and encryption software to track and direct their "product" flow.

Noting that globalization has downsides does not mean that sovereignty is dead or that state-controlled economies and authoritarian societies free of advanced technologies would be beneficial. Human history is the unfolding story of numerous and varying social organizing frameworks. The sovereign state has had a good, 350-year run as an organizing unit. Although it is in no imminent danger of disappearing, we cannot expect that the sovereign state will be in the form we know it 350 years from now. For globalization to be both sustainable and just, its costs must be clearly understood and addressed. Sovereignty and globalization carry many benefits, but there is nothing sacrosanct about either.

TOMORROW: DEBATES ABOUT THE FUTURE OF SOVEREIGNTY

There are three main views about the future of sovereignty. According to the first view, we are witnessing the end of the state. The second view argues that the sovereign state continues to be an important actor on the world scene, especially in the military security realm, but that the state is increasingly losing power to markets and nonstate actors. The third view argues that states are still the primary actors in international politics, and other actors (NGOs, IGOs, MNCs) exist and operate only as much as allowed by states.

The first view contends that sovereign states are a "nostalgic fiction" in the global economy. According to Kenichi Ohmae, states "are little more than bit actors." Decisions over investments, production, and exchange rates "are made elsewhere by individuals and institutions over which they have little practical control." National labels are becoming meaningless. Is a Toyota made in Mississippi a Japanese car? This does not mean that international politics will now be marked by the "clash of civilizations" or cultures, as Samuel Huntington contends. "There are now tens of millions of teenagers around the world who, having been raised in a multimedia-rich environment, have a lot more in common with each other than they do with members of older generations in their own cultures." States are losing their capacity to respond to economic bumps in the road, and so regions are becoming more important. Although it may still be politically correct to talk about states as the important actors, "it is a bald-faced economic lie."[76]

The second view sees the state retreating as its functions change.[77] Today, either other actors are increasingly filling these functions or no one fills them. For example, Susan Strange discusses ten important functions or authorities claimed by states that are on the decline. First, the state is responsible for defending national territory against foreign invasion, but in developed countries the threat of foreign invasion is declining or minimal, thereby eroding this source of state authority. Second, the state is responsible for maintaining the value of its currency, but inflation in one country can spread to others, revealing that this responsibility is now a more collective one. Third, the state used to choose the appropriate form of economic development, but open economies now allow market pressures from the IMF, World Bank, and private investors to limit state choice and force convergence on a narrow range of development models (the "Washington Consensus"). Fourth, the state used to be responsible for correcting the booms and busts of market economies through state spending to infuse money into public works or other state enterprises. Franklin Delano Roosevelt fought the Great Depression in the 1930s in the United States by initiating large public works projects, building national parks, the Tennessee Valley Authority dams, and highways and bridges to put people back to work and get the economy moving again. But this option is no longer open to governments, given the market pressures to keep government spending at a minimum. Fifth, states used to provide a social safety net for those who were least able to survive in a market economy by providing assistance to the very old and young, sick, disabled, and unemployed. Today, market pressures are leading states to cut back on their social welfare benefits and protective regulations. Sixth, states used to have the ability to set appropriate tax rates to pay for government public works or social benefits spending. Today, all states are pressured by international market forces to keep tax rates to a minimum, thereby limiting their autonomy and authority to raise funds. Seventh, states used to have great autonomy in control over foreign trade, especially imports. Today, government intervention can only affect the margins because most of the decisions that concern trade flows are the "aggregate result of multiple corporate decisions."[78] Strong international market forces pressure governments to reduce obstacles to cross-border trade.

Eighth, governments used to take responsibility for building the economic infrastructure of the state "from ports and roads to posts and telegraphs. . . . Even where governments, as in the United States, looked to private enterprise to find the necessary capital, they never hesitated in revising the laws on landed property so that landowners could not easily obstruct the infrastructural invest-ment."[79] Today, public utilities are being privatized, and the key infrastructure needed in modern economies are communications technologies, most of which do not depend on government's control over territory. Infrastructure development decisions are being made in corporate boardrooms, not state offices. Eastern European states are being integrated into the modern telecom-munications grid not by governments primarily, but by private corporations that recognize the profit margins that are available to the corporation that gets there first. States may have built the infrastructure of highways, but firms and private actors are building and extending the information superhighways.

Ninth, states used to be able to create or allow public or private monop-olies to dominate the local market, but today international market pressures impose greater costs on state governments that try to maintain monopolies. Finally, states used to entertain one "special kind of monopoly—that of the legitimate use of violence against the citizen or any group of citizens."[80] Now, the globalization of the arms trade and easy access to technology make the means of violence more readily available to nonstate actors. Strong and weak states alike are losing their monopolies on force, as evidenced by the chemical attack on the Japanese subway and the destruction of the World Trade Center in the United States.

In essence, we are witnessing the incredibly shrinking state. States continue to exist, but their powers are not as extensive as they used to be, and other actors take or share power with states over key functions or sectors. The result is "a ramshackle assembly of conflicting sources of authority" in which individuals' loyalties and identities will not necessarily lie with the sovereign state but are spread among professions, civic groups, ethnic ties, firms, etc., just as state power is becoming diffused.[81] As more power shifts away from states and toward markets, accountability and democracy may decrease because corporate leaders are not subject to democratic accountability and market forces cannot be voted upon.

Other theorists agree that we are in a period of transition or turbulence[82] in which the sovereign state is increasingly under challenge but not obsolete yet because alternatives to sovereignty have not established themselves. James Rosenau argues that not just markets but also increasingly skilled individuals are driving the changes. He believes access to the Internet, to personal com-puters, faxes, jet planes, etc., have led to a "skill revolution." People who are plugged in have become better able to assess, compare, and contrast large amounts of data; are more sophisticated in critiquing the information pro-vided to them by states and in seeking alternative information; and are better able to articulate and mobilize around goals. "It is unimaginable that people have not learned and become more complex in order to adapt to an increasingly complicated world."[83] In an evolutionary way, people are adapting to changes in their environment. "People have become increasingly competent in assessing where they fit in international affairs and how their behavior can be aggregated into significant outcomes."[84] Thus, the globalization of democratization is no accident, because the telecommunications revolution that is fueling the skills revolution is global. A people plugged in is a people empowered to bring about change, to end apartheid in South Africa, to tear down the Berlin Wall and the communist empire, and to challenge the dictatorship in Tiananmen Square. Rosenau believes the skills revolution makes governments more responsive to citizens' needs and more democratic, whereas Strange and others believe that increased market and corporate power reduces democracy and accountability.

Because of the digital divide, the rate of change is not uniform. But even though "the information-rich are getting richer at a quicker rate than the information-poor, the trend line is conceived to slope in the same upward direction for both groups."[85] Even citizens in lesser developed countries (where poverty and repressive regimes may limit access to technology) are becoming more skillful. For example, Haitians demonstrating in 1994 to turn back the *USS Harlan County* from intervening and Iranians denouncing U.S. support of the shah of Iran in 1979 carried signs in English and timed their protests to appear on the U.S. evening news broadcasts. Child South African AIDS activist Nkosi Johnson successfully used the media to draw attention to the plight of African AIDS victims and to change policy. As people become more skillful, they also become less deferential. Traditionally, state legitimacy and compliance

> derived from constitutional and legal sources. Under these circumstances individuals were habituated to compliance with the directives issued by higher authorities. They did what they were told to do because . . . that is what one did. As a consequence, authority structures remained in place for decades, even centuries, as people unquestioningly yielded to the dictates of governments.[86]

Today, because of the skills revolution, a pervasive "authority crisis" exists as people are increasingly inclined to question authority and have the means to do so. Legitimacy now derives not from tradition but from performance. States are no longer the only key actors, and they must manage and compete with a variety of organizations. Sovereignty continues to limp along—not because of its strength, but more by default because none of these new organizations has yet delivered a knockout blow.

Another cut at this second view is that sovereignty is losing its identification with territory. Richard Rosecrance argues, "In economies where capital, labor, and information are mobile and have risen to predominance, no land fetish remains. Developed countries would rather plumb the world market than acquire territory. The virtual state—a state that has downsized its territorially based production capability—is the logical consequence of this emancipation from the land."[87] By shedding outmoded functions to nonstate actors and by downsizing territory, states are adapting their logic to market forces. When the Treaty of Westphalia was signed, the economic system was mercantilist and land-based. Wealth and power depended on the control of land, access to raw materials, and control of the means of production. In a world of slow-moving ships and horseback messengers, capital and labor were fixed in place, not mobile. Increasing power meant increasing land, and thus the European colonial empires were born. It is no accident that under this economic system, the political organization that developed—sovereignty—directly correlated authority to territory. But now the economy has changed, and states are changing to reflect the new reality. The new economic system is based on information, technology, and services—none of which depends on the control of land. In a world of open borders and economic flows—and people who have access to computers, faxes, phones, the Internet, e-cash, and other advanced technologies—the means of production, capital, and labor are mobile. States have access to raw materials through trade, not conquest. Thus, for states with modern, information-based economies such as Japan, territory is not the source of their power, so conflict over territory becomes passé. For states with less-developed economies that are still land-based (and primarily dependent on natural resource extraction or agricultural exports), territory will not become passé and may still be a source of conflict. A population explosion might make land important again. But these trends are not sustainable in the long term because land does not produce a better return than knowledge, so states with lots of land (such as Russia) may not be especially powerful in the new economy. Knowledge allows more extraction and more efficient and effective utilization of resources. States recognize the success of "virtual" states such as Japan and will try to emulate them and thus develop modern economies that are less shackled to land.

The virtual state no longer commands resources as states did in the mercantilist yesteryear. It negotiates, deriving its power from direct foreign investment, an educated workforce, and market savvy, not from military superiority or control over territory. This brings a crisis for democratic politics as states lose some of their autonomy over electing and enforcing policy to unelected, nonstate actors. Citizens can, however, vote with their feet if they are unimpressed by their state's performance.[88]

The final view argues that nothing fundamental has changed. Stephen Krasner argues that weak states have always existed, and that sovereignty has always been "organized hypocrisy," challenged in theory and practice.[89] But even examples of problematic sovereignty only show how embedded the concept of sovereignty is.[90] It continues to be our default assumption. Changes in the environment do not readily or easily translate into institutional changes. Sovereign states persist over time, even when their functions are not in sync with a changed international environment because of vertical and horizontal linkages:

> Vertical depth refers to the extent to which the institutional structure defines the individual actors. Breadth refers to the number of links that a particular activity has with other activities, to the number of changes that would have to be made if a particular form of activity were altered. . . . With regard to both breadth and depth, sovereign states have become increasingly formidable institutions. They influence the self-image of those individuals within their territory through the concept of citizenship, as well as by exercising control, to one degree or another, over powerful instruments of socialization. With regard to breadth, states are the most densely linked institutions in the contemporary world. Change the nature of states and virtually everything else in human society would also have to be changed. Hence, even though environmental incentives have dramatically changed since the establishment of the state system in the seventeenth century, there is little reason to believe that it will be easy to replace sovereign states with some alternative structure for organizing human political life.[91]

Despite interdependence, weak states, and compromised or problematic sovereignty, the sovereign state is not retreating. The costs of changing to an alternative system would be prohibitive, and people cannot conceive of a plausible alternative to sovereignty.

Others in this school of thought argue that no such fundamental change away from sovereignty is imminent because existing states have little incentive to alter the system. States are the gatekeepers to the international system, so it is difficult for actors other than states to be accorded equal participation in that system. The growth of the European Union is providing an alternative model to traditional sovereignty, but there are few other serious challengers to sovereign arrangements. Hendrik Spruyt argues that, for sovereignty to be replaced, there must be competition among alternative models of organization—as there was at sovereignty's initiation after competition with the urban league and city-state. If anything, sovereignty is becoming more entrenched because ethnic, religious, and nationalist challenges to sovereignty reinforce the state as a prize worth fighting for. Although sovereignty is not the optimal institutional arrangement, new institutional challengers have not yet arisen. Sovereignty took centuries to emerge, Spruyt argues. It is too early to declare its demise.

Another perspective argues there is no such thing as globalization, only Americanization. Kenneth Waltz contends that we are witnessing the advance of one incredibly powerful state—the United States—rather than the retreat of the state.[92] This third viewpoint paraphrases Mark Twain's famous observation by noting that the territorial state is being "buried too soon." William O'Neill believes that challenges to the existing sovereign state do not mean its death but that "pride of place [will go] to whatever authorities are able to organize and maintain superior armed force. This implies that their requiem for the Westphalian state is premature. So far, no promising alternative to the territorial organization of armed force has even begun to emerge."[93] To this assertion, the other schools of thought argue "Yes, but so what?" If state military power is less able to prevail against non-state threats in an interdependent world, then the state may retain coercive powers that are less and less useful. The state still exists but is more compromised in its ability to act in the economic and social spheres that increasingly affect citizens' everyday lives.

Mapping out these debates in the scholarly literature helps establish questions to consider in reading the chapters of this book. Do global problems challenge not only the interests of states (as the traditional realist International Relations theory stipulates) but also the very architecture of states? How can transsovereign problems be dealt with in a system of sovereign states? Do the responses to transsovereign problems (greater reliance on NGOs or IGOs, for example) undermine sovereignty? Are alternatives to sovereignty evolving as people struggle to respond to global problems? Or is the state becoming more entrenched as people rely on old responses to combat new threats?

THE NEW SECURITY DILEMMA

Security has been the dominant realm of sovereign states, but even this is changing. Weakened sovereignty and transsovereign challenges create a new security dilemma. In previous eras, threats came from strong states. The "old security dilemma" was how one state could contain another strong state without provoking counteractions on the other side that would make the state stronger. This spiral of insecurity was often cited in arms races, the outbreak of World War I, and the Cold War. The temptation was to overrespond and appear offensive, thus triggering a heightened response from opponents that further decreased one's own security. In a self-help international system of strong sovereign states, how could a state provide for its own military security against another state without setting off a self-defeating spiral of counteractions by other states?

But if the old security dilemma was how states could protect against strong states without making them stronger, then the new security dilemma is how to protect against global challenges and the implosion of weak states without taking actions that make weak states weaker and transsovereign problems more severe. Globalization plus weak states and transsovereign problems equals the new security dilemma. Globalization gives breakdowns in state authority and capacity and transsovereign problems greater reach, speed, intensity, and impact. Borders are more permeable, and threats are decentralized, fast, fungible, and fluid. The twenty-first century security dilemma is how to respond to the problems of weak states and nonstate threats without making these problems worse. Responding with the predominant tool of the old security dilemma—military force—may not be effective. For example, using force may make terrorist organizations stronger because they can appeal to messianic visions and have heightened international importance. Failure to respond to nonmilitary threats, however, allows these problems to grow until they present a threat of violence and instability that cannot easily be met by force. As HIV and AIDS spread throughout sub-Saharan Africa, millions of orphans (especially boys) live in gangs on the streets, supported by begging and crime and without socialization into families or community values. Although these growing numbers of hardened throwaway children pose real threats to security, military forces can do little to prevent the spread of HIV and AIDS or care for orphans.

The new security dilemma requires both creation of more powerful nonmilitary tools (including more effective involvement of the private sector), and the retooling of military forces to meet nonstate threats. This presents a challenge even for the world's most powerful military. But even if doctrine, organization, training, and equipment priorities are changed to better prepare for the type of conflict that now predominates, military force is just not sufficient to combat global problems, which often stem from economic or other causes. Threats are decentralized, as are the resources needed for the fight, which are not primarily military. We must go beyond the military tools of sovereignty to contain security dilemmas that go beyond sovereignty.

Realizing this, militaries are increasingly reaching out to the private sector to help manage pressing security problems. The British government debates hiring mercenaries. The U.S. government enlists the private sector in the war on terrorism, and in curtailing the proliferation of weapons of mass destruction. When the strongest military in the strongest state needs the private sector to help manage security problems (traditionally, the state's strong suit), then sovereignty is changing.

ENDNOTES

1. World Bank, *World Development Report 2006,* 1, <http://hdr.undp.org/reports/global/2005/pdf/HDR05_overview.pdf>.
2. Jeffrey Sachs, *The End of Poverty: Economic Possibilities for Our Time* (New York: Penguin Press, 2005); Jeffrey D. Sachs, *Investing In Development: A Practical Plan to Achieve the Millennium Development Goals* (UN Millennium Project), (Earthscan Publications, 2005).
3. "Religious Leaders Say Global Poverty Has No Borders," *The Christian Post,* (Sept. 13, 2005), <http://www.christianpost.com/article/church/2293/section/religious.leaders.say.global.poverty.has.no.borders/1.htm>.
4. This is the agreement reached, as described by Jeannine Aversa, "Plan to cancel poor nations' debts OK'd," *The Washington Times* (Sept. 25, 2005), <http://washingtontimes.com/world/20050924-111439-8691r.htm>.
5. Gillian Sorensen, *The United Nations and Civil Societies: Redefining the Partnership for the 21st Century.* Keynote address to Women in International Security summer symposium, Washington, DC, June 15, 1998.
6. Donald Snow and Eugene Brown, *Beyond the Water's Edge* (New York: St. Martin's Press, 1997).
7. Maryann Cusimano Love, "Globalization, Ethics, and the War on Terrorism," *Notre Dame Journal of Ethics, Law, and Public Policy* (special "Violence in America" edition, 2002), 65–80; Maryann Cusimano Love, "Morality Matters: Ethics and Power Politics in the War on Terrorism," *Georgetown Journal of International Affairs* (Summer–Fall 2002): 7–16.
8. Ernest Gellner, "Nations and Nationalism," in Richard Betts (Ed.), *Conflict after the Cold War: Arguments on the Causes of War and Peace* (New York: Macmillan, 1994), 286.
9. Edward Luttwak, "Toward Post-Heroic Warfare," *Foreign Affairs* 74 (May–June 1995): 109–122; Francis Fukuyama, *The End of History and the Last Man* (New York: Free Press, 1992).
10. I. William Zartman, *Collapsed States* (Boulder, CO: Lynne Rienner, 1995); Robert Jackson, *Quasi-States: Sovereignty, International Relations, and the Third World* (New York: Cambridge University Press, 1990); Foreign Policy and the Fund for Peace, "The Failed State Index," *Foreign Policy* (July/August 2005), <http://www.foreignpolicy.com/story/cms.php?story_id=3098>; Gerald B. Helman and Steven R. Ratner, "Saving Failed States," *Foreign Policy* (Winter 1992–1993): 3–20; Alex Rondos, "The Collapsing State and International Security," in Janne E. Nolan (Ed.), *Global Engagement* (Washington, DC: Brookings Institution, 1994), 481–503; Ted Robert Gurr, "The State Failure Project," <www.bsos.umd.edu/cidcm/inscr/stfail/>; James C. Clad, "Old World Disorders," in Brad Roberts (Ed.), *U.S. Security in an Uncertain Era* (Cambridge: MIT Press, 1993); Chester Crocker, "The Global Law and Order Deficit: Is the West Ready to Police the World's Bad Neighborhoods?" *Washington Post* (Dec. 20, 1992), C1; Michael Brown, "Introduction," *The International Dimensions of Internal Conflict*

(Cambridge: MIT Press, 1996); Pauline H. Baker and John A. Ausink, "State Collapse and Ethnic Violence: Toward a Predictive Model," *Parameters* (Spring 1996): 19–31.

11. The following remarks are taken from Maryann Cusimano Love, "Globalization: A Virtue or a Vice," Chapter 5 in Siamack Shojai (Ed.), *Globalization: A Virtue or a Vice?* (New York: Praeger, 2002).

12. Jagdish N. Bhagwati, *In Defense of Globalization,* (New York: Oxford University Press, 2004); Martin Wolf, *Why Globalization Works* (New Haven, CT: Yale University Press, 2004); John Micklethwait and Adrian Wooldridge, *A Future Perfect: The Challenge and Hidden Promise of Globalization* (New York: Random House, 2000); Thomas Friedman, *The Lexus and the Olive Tree* (New York: Farrar, Straus, & Giroux, 1999).

13. Robin Broad (Ed.), *Global Backlash* (Lanham, MD: Rowman & Littlefield, 2002); Joseph E. Stiglitz, *Globalization and Its Discontents* (New York: Norton, 2003); Lester R. Brown, *Outgrowing the Earth: The Food Security Challenge in an Age of Falling Water Tables and Rising Temperatures* (New York: Norton, 2005); William Easterly, *The Elusive Quest for Growth: Economists' Adventures and Misadventures in the Tropics* (Cambridge, MA: MIT Press, 2002); John Cavanagh, *Alternatives to Economic Globalization: A Better World Is Possible,* 2nd ed. (San Francisco: Berrett-Koehler Publishers, 2004); Noreena Hertz, *The Silent Takeover: Global Capitalism and the Death of Democracy* (New York: Simon & Schuster, 2002); James H. Mittelman, *The Globalization Syndrome: Transformation and Resistance* (Princeton, NJ: Princeton University Press, 2000); Dani Rodrik, *Has Globalization Gone Too Far?* (Washington, DC: Institute for International Economics, 1997); Benjamin R. Barber, *Jihad vs. McWorld: How Globalism and Tribalism Are Reshaping the World* (New York: Ballantine Books, 1995); Hans-Henrik Holm and Georg Sorensen, *Whose World Order?* (Boulder, CO: Westview Press, 1995).

14. United Nations Development Program, *Globalization with a Human Face* (New York: United Nations, 1999).

15. United Nations, Human Development Report 2005, 4, <http://hdr.undp.org/reports/global/2005/pdf/HDR05_overview.pdf>.

16. Ibid., 3.

17. Clyde Prestowitz, *Three Billion New Capitalists: The Great Shift of Wealth and Power to the East* (New York: Basic Books, 2005).

18. World Bank, *World Development Report 2006,* Chapter 3, <http://wdsbeta.worldbank.org/external/default/WDSContentServer/IW3P/IB/2005/09/20/000112742_20050920110826/additional/841401968_200508263001617.pdf>.

19. Wolfgang Reinicke, "Global Public Policy," *Foreign Affairs* (Nov.–Dec. 1997): 128.

20. *World Bank Global Development Finance Report,* 2000.

21. United Nations Development Program, *Globalization with a Human Face* (New York: United Nations, 1999).

22. Michael Meacher (UK minister for the environment), speech at the Royal Society of Arts, April 1998.

23. L. Craig Johnstone, *Strategic Planning and International Affairs in the 21st Century.* Address to the Conference Series on International Affairs in the 21st Century, U.S. Department of State, Washington, DC, Nov. 18, 1997.

24. F. H. Hinsley, *Sovereignty* (London: C. A. Watts, 1966). The Treaty of Westphalia is a commonly used if somewhat controversial marker for a historical process that took centuries. Scholars such as Bruce Bueno de Mesquita claim that the move toward sovereignty actually came much earlier, while others such as Stephen Krasner point out that even after Westphalia there were struggles between religious and secular leaders and contested and overlapping authority claims.

25. Hendrik Spruyt, *The Sovereign State and Its Competitors* (Princeton, NJ: Princeton University Press, 1996), 40.

26. Ibid., 47.

27. Ibid., 62, 75.

28. Friedrich Kratochwil, "Sovereignty as Dominium: Is There a Right of Humanitarian Intervention?" in Gene M. Lyons and Michael Mastanduno (Eds.), *Beyond Westphalia: State Sovereignty and International Intervention* (Baltimore: Johns Hopkins University Press, 1995), 21–42.

29. Nicholas Onuf, "Intervention for the Common Good," in *Beyond Westphalia,* 43–58.

30. Ibid.; Nicholas Onuf, "Sovereignty: Outline of a Conceptual History," *Alternatives* 16 (1991): 425–446.

31. Charles Tilly, *The Formation of National States in Western Europe* (Princeton, NJ: Princeton University Press, 1975).

32. Spruyt, *The Sovereign State and Its Competitors.*

33. Michael Ross Fowler and Julie Marie Bunck, *Law, Power, and the Sovereign State: The Evolution and Application of the Concept of Sovereignty* (University Park: Pennsylvania State University Press, 1995), 5–6.

34. UN Secretary-General Kofi Annan, Nobel Prize for Peace acceptance speech, Dec. 10, 2001; International Commission on Intervention and State Sovereignty, *The Responsibility to Protect* (Ottawa, Canada: International Development Research Centre, 2001), <http://www.iciss-ciise.gc.ca/pdfs/Commission-Report.pdf>.

35. "Everybody's Business," *Wall Street Journal* (Aug. 24, 1992): A8.

36. "New Ways to Run the World," *Economist* (Nov. 5, 1991): 11.

37. Foreign Policy and the Fund for Peace, "The Failed State Index," *Foreign Policy* (July/August 2005), <http://www.foreignpolicy.com/story/cms.php?story_id=3098>.

38. Zartman, *Collapsed States,* 3.

39. Stockholm International Peace Research Institute (SIPRI), "Major Armed Conflict," *SIPRI Yearbook 2005,* <http://yearbook2005.sipri.org/ch2/ch2>. The report notes, however, that the wars in Iraq, Rwanda, and the war on terrorism had significant international components.

40. Zartman, *Collapsed States,* 1–11. State collapse is more than a succession struggle over which group will control the levers of state—it is the failure of function of those very state institutions. Although groups may be involved in leadership contests, state collapse continues no matter who wins the helm, because state authority, legitimacy, and competence have badly disintegrated. States that have protracted or persistent leadership battles are vulnerable to collapse as state institutions atrophy during continued warfare and as the legitimacy and authority enjoyed by these institutions is undermined by the conflict. *Civil war* and *state collapse* are not synonymous terms. Internal war can occur in states that are not in the process or in danger of collapse—as in Britain and Israel. More rarely, states can collapse without violence—as in the breakup of Czechoslovakia. Not surprisingly, however, state collapse is highly correlated with internal violence, which can weaken state institutions and precede and contribute to state collapse. Alternatively, state collapse can provide the opportunity for groups to use violence as they try to assert authority in the power vacuum left by state failure. See also Foreign Policy and the Fund for Peace, "The Failed State Index," *Foreign Policy* (July/August 2005), <http://www.foreignpolicy.com/story/cms.php?story_id=3098>; Gerald B. Helman and Steven R. Ratner, "Saving Failed States," *Foreign Policy* (Winter 1992–1993): 3–20; Alex Rondos, "The Collapsing State and International Security," in *Global Engagement,* 481–503; Gurr, "The State Failure Project"; James C. Clad, "Old World Disorders," in *U.S. Security in an Uncertain*

Era, 181–188; Robert D. Kaplan, *The Coming Anarchy,* Vintage, 2001; and Jackson, *Quasi-States.*

41. Jackson, *Quasi-States,* 29.

42. Morton Halperin, *Self-Determination in the New World Order* (Washington, DC: Carnegie Endowment for International Peace, 1992).

43. Jackson, *Quasi-States,* 27.

44. United Nations, UN Human Development Report 2005, <http://hdr.undp.org/reports/global/2005/pdf/HDR05_overview.pdf>.

45. SIPRI, *SIPRI Yearbook 1995* (New York: Oxford University Press, 1995), 23–24.

46. Zartman, *Collapsed States,* 7–10.

47. Terry Lynn Karl and Philippe C. Schmitter, "Democratization Around the Globe: Opportunities and Risks," in Michael Klare (Ed.), *World Security: Challenges for a New Century* (New York: Palgrave McMillan, 1998).

48. Edward D. Mansfield and Jack Snyder, "Democratization and War," *Foreign Affairs* (May–June 1995): 79–97.

49. Max Singer and Aaron Wildavsky, *The Real World Order: Zones of Peace and Zones of Turmoil* (Chatham, NJ: Chatham House, 1993).

50. Jeffrey E. Garten, "Business and Foreign Policy," *Foreign Affairs* (May–June 1997): 68.

51. George Kennan, "Moscow Embassy Telegram #511: 'The Long Telegram,' February 22, 1946," *Foreign Relations of the United States: 1946,* Vol. I, 696–709.

52. George Kennan, 1948, as quoted in John Lewis Gaddis, *Strategies of Containment* (New York: Oxford, 1982), 45.

53. Jessica Tuchman Matthews, "Lessons of Chernobyl," *Washington Post* (April 1996); "Sunshine and Shadow: The CIA and the Soviet Economy," John F. Kennedy School of Government case program.

54. Paul Krugman, "Dutch Tulips and Emerging Markets," *Foreign Affairs* (July–Aug. 1995): 28–43.

55. Stephen E. Flynn, *Globalization and Eroding Border Control: Developing a New US–Caribbean Regime to Meet the Challenge.* Paper prepared for the Council on Foreign Relations Homeland Security Group, Dante B. Fascall North-South Center, University of Miami, Florida, Nov. 17, 1999.

56. World Bank, World Development Report 2006, Equity and Development, 162, <http://wdsbeta.worldbank.org>.

57. John Ikenberry, "The Myth of Post–Cold War Chaos," *Foreign Affairs* (May–June 1997): 91.

58. Thomas Friedman, *The World Is Flat: A Brief History of the Twenty-first Century* (New York: Farrar, Straus and Giroux, 2005); Thomas Friedman, *The Lexus and the Olive Tree* (New York: Anchor, 2000).

59. Jeffrey Sachs, *The End of Poverty: Economic Possibilities for Our Time* (New York: Penguin Press, 2005); Michael Barnett and Martha Finnemore, *Rules for the World: International Organizations in Global Politics.* (Ithaca, NY: Cornell University Press, 2004).

60. John Lewis Gaddis, "Toward the Post Cold War World," in Steven L. Speigel and David J. Pervin (Eds.), *At Issue: Politics in the World Arena* (New York: St. Martin's Press, 1994), 27–42. Clearly, many more costs have been attributed to global economies than those discussed here. These include exploitation of labor (John Sweeney, Address to the Bishops of Latin America, Canada and the United States on Humanizing the Global Economy, Washington, DC, Catholic University of America, Jan. 31, 2002; Vatican Special Advisor to the International Labor Organization Fr. Dominique Peccoud, S.J., Address to the Bishops of Latin America, Canada and the United States on Humanizing the Global Economy, Washington, DC, Catholic University of America, Jan. 31, 2002); the exploitation (even the apartheid) of the developing South by the developed North (Richard Falk, "Democratizing,

Internationalizing, and Globalizing," in Yoshikazu Sakamoto (Ed.), *Global Transformation: Challenges to the State System* [Tokyo: United Nations University Press, 1994], 475–502); and environmental degradation and endangerment of indigenous peoples and their civilizations (Falk, "Democratizing, Internationalizing, and Globalizing," 475–502).

61. Amy Chua, *World On Fire: How Exporting Free Market Democracy Breeds Ethnic Hatred and Global Instability* (New York: Anchor, 2004).

62. Francis Fukuyama, *The End of History and the Last Man* (New York: Free Press, 1992), xi.

63. Ibid., 337; see also Michael Mandelbaum, *The Ideas That Conquered the World: Peace, Democracy, and Free Markets in the Twenty-First Century* (New York: Public Affairs, 2003).

64. Terry Lynn Karl and Philippe C. Schmitter, "Democratization around the Globe: Opportunities and Risks," in *World Security: Challenges for a New Century*, 43–44. This description of the four waves of democratization is based on Karl and Schmitter's work. It should be noted that some theorists, such as Samuel Huntington, merge waves one and two into an overly long and undifferentiated category and thus count only three waves of democratization.

65. Ibid., 60.

66. This has been a problematic point for states such as Singapore, which have tried to open up free market, capitalist economic systems while restricting political participation and democratic political reforms.

67. Michael Doyle, "Liberalism and World Politics," in *Conflict after the Cold War*, 263–279.

68. Mansfield and Snyder, "Democratization and War," 88.

69. Fareed Zakaria, *The Future of Freedom: Illiberal Democracy at Home and Abroad* (New York: Norton, 2004), <www.freedomhouse.org>.

70. Daniel F. Burton, Jr., "The Brave New Wired World," *Foreign Policy* (Spring 1997): 32.

71. Internet World Usage Stats, October 2005, <http://www.internetworldstats.com/stats>.

72. Johnstone, *Strategic Planning and International Affairs in the 21st Century*.

73. Burton, "The Brave New Wired World," 26.

74. Ibid.

75. Gaddis, "Toward the Post Cold War World," 27–42.

76. Kenichi Ohmae, *The End of the Nation State: The Rise of Regional Economies* (New York: Free Press, 1995).

77. Susan Strange, *The Retreat of the State: The Diffusion of Power in the World Economy* (Cambridge, UK: Cambridge University Press, 1996), 189.

78. Ibid., 78.

79. Ibid., 79.

80. Ibid., 81.

81. Ibid., 77, 199.

82. James N. Rosenau, "Sovereignty in a Turbulent World," in Gene M. Lyons and Michael Mastanduno (Eds.), *Beyond Westphalia? State Sovereignty and International Intervention* (Baltimore: Johns Hopkins University Press, 1995), 193; James N. Rosenau, *Turbulence in World Politics* (Princeton, NJ: Princeton University Press, 1990).

83. James N. Rosenau and W. Michael Fagen, "A New Dynamism in World Politics: Increasingly Skillful Individuals?" *International Studies Quarterly* 41 (Dec. 1997): 660. Although he does not draw this comparison, Rosenau's arguments dovetail those of Neil Postman in *Amusing Ourselves to Death*, in which he maintains that the media technologies available to a generation affect not just the mode of their public discourse but also its content, as well as the way they think about and interact with the world. Postman sees the move to a visual era as negative, reducing public discourse to sound bites, whereas Rosenau points up the positive effects that a skills revolution can have on political outcomes and dismembering repressive regimes.

84. Rosenau, "Sovereignty in a Turbulent World," 204.
85. Ibid., 206–207; Rosenau, *Turbulence in World Politics,* 90–113.
86. Rosenau, "Sovereignty in a Turbulent World," 206–207; Rosenau, *Turbulence in World Politics,* 90–113.
87. Richard Rosecrance, *The Rise of the Virtual State: Wealth and Power in the Coming Century* (New York: Basic Books, 2000); and "The Rise of the Virtual State," *Foreign Affairs* (July–Aug. 1996): 59–60.
88. Ibid., 59–61.
89. Stephen D. Krasner, *Sovereignty: Organized Hypocrisy* (Princeton, NJ: Princeton University Press, 1999).
90. Stephen D. Krasner, *Problematic Sovereignty: Contested Rules and Political Possibilities* (New York: Columbia University Press, 2001).
91. Stephen D. Krasner, "Sovereignty: An Institutional Perspective," *Comparative Political Studies* 21 (April 1988): 74.
92. Kenneth Waltz, "Globalization and Governance," *PS: Political Science & Politics* (Dec. 1999): 693–700.
93. William H. McNeill, "Territorial States Buried Too Soon," *Mershon International Studies Review* 41 (1997): 269.

CHAPTER TWO

Intergovernmental Organizations

Global Governance and Transsovereign Problems*

Maria Green Cowles

"Anyone who attacks the U.N. for failing to serve the global interest should, as part of that exercise, critically examine the decisions of each nation within the body.... [They] should also remember that the U.N., like the U.S. and other great democracies, is a work in progress—always struggling to lessen the gap between reality and the ideals which gave it birth. That such a gap exists is all the more reason why those who value freedom and peace should work to build the U.N. up, not tear it down."

—Kofi A. Annan, Secretary General of the United Nations[1]

Intergovernmental organizations (IGOs) are increasingly in the spotlight but difficult to define. Some scholars recognize intergovernmental organizations such as the United Nations as vestiges of the nation-state system.[2] Others view the same IGOs as actors who increasingly operate independent of their member states.[3] Some policy makers identify intergovernmental organizations such as the World Bank, International Monetary Fund (IMF), and World Trade Organization (WTO) as important forces in promoting economic development throughout the world. Many nongovernmental organizations (NGOs), however, regard these organizations as a means for the wealthy North to continue to dominate the economies, despoil the environment, and denigrate the cultures of the Global South. More recently, certain U.S. policymakers have expressed concern that IGOs have become hostile entities designed to constrain American power and delimit U.S.

*Special thanks go to Stephanie Curtis for her research support on an earlier version of this chapter. I also thank Tammi Gutner and Maryann Cusimano Love for their comments and suggestions.

sovereignty.[4] Others argue that the principles that emerge from these supranational bodies reflect compromises among member states, and not campaigns to thwart U.S. hegemony.

There is much on which to disagree when defining and analyzing IGOs. They have been called the "ugly ducklings" of international relations studies, in part because they are misconstrued and do not fit easily into our understanding of how the international system of states functions.[5] But supporters and detractors of IGOs may agree on one point: It is increasingly difficult to discuss transsovereign problems today without any mention of IGOs. It is inconceivable, for example, to address the refugee situation in collapsed states such as Sudan and Rwanda without reference to the UN High Commissioner for Refugees. It is rather difficult to understand the effects of international financial flows on East Asian countries without citing the policies of the IMF. Moreover, it is unimaginable to contemplate the rebuilding of tsunami-ravaged countries such as Indonesia or war-torn countries such as Bosnia without citing the UN. Ugly ducklings or not, IGOs serve and will continue to serve an important function in a world where problems can no longer be addressed by individual member states. They have also become a focal point for competing views on how these transsovereign problems should be addressed.

This chapter explores the changing nature of IGOs and their governance in the international system. The first two sections define IGOs, examine their rise in the twentieth century, and then highlight some of the key challenges they face in this increasingly interdependent world. The chapter then examines the global governance of—as well as the reform efforts aimed at—four key IGOs: the United Nations, the International Monetary Fund, the World Trade Organization, and the European Union. The chapter concludes with prescriptions for and reflections on the future of IGOs.

INTERGOVERNMENTAL ORGANIZATIONS: AN INTRODUCTION

Intergovernmental organizations are organizations whose members are state governments. In many respects, IGOs are creatures of the twentieth century. Their roots, however, can be traced back to basic ideas and practices that promote international cooperation and stem from diplomacy, rules of warfare, and international law in preceding centuries.

Today, there are more than 300 formal IGOs—that is, organizations that are permanent and have a secretariat to carry out functions, a voluntary membership, and a specific structure.[6] Many of the "classic" institutions are formal intergovernmental institutions: the United Nations, the International

Monetary Fund (IMF), the Organization for Economic Cooperation and Development (OECD), the World Trade Organization (WTO), and the World Health Organization (WHO). Another 200 to 700 informal IGOs lack permanent bureaucracy and structure but function nonetheless to promote cooperation among governments.[7] An example of an informal IGO would be the Group of Eight (G-8). Its members—the large industrialized states of Canada, France, Germany, Italy, Japan, Russia, the United Kingdom, and the United States—regularly meet in an attempt to coordinate economic policies.

Intergovernmental organizations also differ significantly in terms of their scope and purpose. IGOs can be global, regional, and even bilateral in scope. At the same time, the organizations may hold broad, overarching purposes or more specific technical ones. The United Nations is an example of a global organization with a broad mandate. By contrast, the Universal Postal Union (UPU)—the world's second oldest international organization (established in 1874)—is a global organization (190 member countries) with a technical focus. The UPU sets the rules for international mail exchange and makes recommendations for improving the quality of mail services around the world.

The European Union (EU), comprising 25 European countries, is arguably the most important regional intergovernmental organization. The EU covers a broad range of activities, including agricultural policy, commercial policy, competition policy, currency, customs union, and an embryonic foreign and defense policy. Some scholars argue that the EU, with its strong supranational bureaucracy and multilevel system of governance, should no longer be classified as a traditional international organization. Other regional organizations include the Association of South East Asian Nations (ASEAN), Mercosur, and the African Union.

There are differing views of the relationship between states and IGOs in the international system. Some scholars believe that IGOs are created to serve the interests of states and to encourage cooperation among states by reducing transaction costs—the costs of making and enforcing agreements.[8] As such, IGOs are designed to reflect the wishes of the most powerful nation-states. If an IGO does not effectively champion the interests of these countries, then the countries can pick and choose other intergovernmental organizations to suit their purposes. Thus, IGOs themselves have minimal influence on—and do not challenge the sovereignty of—the member states that formed them.[9]

Other scholars disagree. They point out that the purpose of IGOs is not merely to represent states' interests or reduce transaction costs. IGOs "may be created not for what they do but for what they are for, what they represent symbolically and the values they embody."[10] Although states may still be the dominant actors within IGOs, they do not dictate the behavior of the organization. Many IGOs can and do exercise power autonomously, notably in the areas of human rights and refugees. They are purposive actors that can develop their own agendas, rules, and norms. Thus, states may choose one IGO over another not because one organization serves its interests better than another, but because some organizations are more adept at creating, developing, and implementing policies than intergovernmental bargaining alone.[11]

Globalization processes, it is argued, bring greater autonomy to IGOs because they offer IGOs more tools at their disposal.[12] IGOs may be better positioned than states to respond to the challenges of open societies, open economies, and open technologies and the resulting call for greater international cooperation. Understanding the effects of globalization on the rise and development of IGOs is the point to which we turn next.

THE RISE OF IGOs: THE RESPONSE TO GLOBALIZATION

Intergovernmental organizations increasingly became visible and important global actors in the twentieth century, particularly after World War II. Since 1945, the number of IGOs has increased fivefold. The creation of several institutions in the 1943–45 period—the IMF, World Bank, and United Nations—promised to usher in a new era of international cooperation and dialogue in the aftermath of the Second World War. However, the advent of the Cold War and the growing geopolitical concerns of the United States and the Soviet Union dampened any expectations that these organizations would rival powerful states for global leadership. IGOs often found themselves part of the Cold War battlefield with the United States and Soviet Union opposing each others' positions in the World Health Organization, the Universal Telecommunications Union (UTU), and the International Atomic Energy Agency.[13] Even UNICEF, the UN International Children's Education Fund, was tainted by superpower conflicts during this era.

At the same time, decolonization in the 1960s and 1970s produced new tensions within IGOs as the number of newly independent states increased. Many of these new countries did not cast their votes along the lines of their Western counterparts. Soon, certain organizations became forums for highlighting North-South conflicts—the differences between the wealthier countries of the North and the poorer countries of the South. The Group of Seventy-Seven (G-77), for example, was established in 1964 at the end of the first session of the UN Conference on Trade and Development (or UNCTAD, as it is more commonly known). As part of its mandate, the G–77 sought to improve the terms of trade between industrialized northern and poorer southern countries. Because of these Cold War and North–South tensions, countries such as the United States grew increasingly distrustful of key IGOs that were purportedly designed to promote international cooperation.[14]

IGOs created during this period, however, were still relevant. The North Atlantic Treaty Organization (NATO) and its Eastern bloc counterpart, the Warsaw Pact, proved to be powerful organizations. The creation of the Organization of Petroleum Exporting Countries (OPEC) in 1960 also demonstrated how an IGO could influence international economic and political relations. If anything, the oil crisis and growing environmental awareness in the 1970s brought home all too clearly to some countries the need to cooperate in international forums.[15]

The fall of the Berlin Wall in 1989 signaled the end of paralysis within many IGOs. When President George H. W. Bush called for a "new world order" that emphasized multilateral cooperation in solving global issues, institutions such as the United Nations stood poised to gain further prominence in international affairs. The initial euphoria over this new world order was short-lived, however, with failed UN peacekeeping missions in Bosnia, Rwanda, and Somalia.[16] Although the new world order held promise for some IGOs, it threatened the existence of others. NATO, for example, found itself lacking a central mandate and having to reinvent itself. The Warsaw Pact, on the other hand, lost its overarching purpose and collapsed with the fall of the Berlin Wall.

The end of the Cold War and the emergence of what Thomas Friedman has called the "turbo-charged" era of globalization[17] have infused many IGOs with new life, new roles, and newfound influence. The opening of societies, for example, has led to greater roles for IGOs. The breakup of the Soviet Union and the democratic developments in Central and Eastern European states have provided new members and new agendas for organizations such as the Council of Europe and the Organization for Security and Cooperation in Europe. The new wave of democratization has also meant a growing role for IGOs in election monitoring around the world.

The opening of economies has also empowered IGOs as people and governments call for greater regulation of the world economy and rules for international investment and finance. The IMF's "seal of approval," for example, became vital for governments that wished to attract greater foreign investment.[18] The IMF was thus able to set down rules and conditions that governments were required to meet to receive the organization's blessing and funding. Although no sovereign government was forced to accede to these conditions, many accepted IMF recommendations that called for restructured government agencies, reprioritized government programs, and restricted government practices.

Globalization and the opening of technologies have also increased the number and types of parties who are interested in international policy making. This, in turn, has empowered international organizations. For example, people can now follow international political activities on a real-time basis over the Internet and buy and sell foreign countries' bonds in online trading. They are thus given greater incentive to follow and affect international policy making by working alone or within NGOs to make their interests known and heard. Moreover, states must now consider these domestic political actors in their foreign policy calculus.[19] In this respect, globalization empowers more actors who, in turn, limit the policy choices of individual states and encourage them to cooperate in international policy making.

Many IGOs have sought to take advantage of these globalization trends to attain greater autonomy and influence in global affairs. They have reached out to domestic organizations while building their own transnational coalitions with NGOs to promote agendas that, at times, contradict those of key member states. The United Nations, for example, allied itself with the International Campaign to Ban Landmines despite the U.S. government's position against the ban.

It would be a mistake, however, to assume that the opening of societies, economies, and technologies solely supports IGOs that are dedicated to promoting these new globalization trends. Paradoxically, globalization also strengthens certain international organizations as bulwarks *against* globalization. On the one hand, the European Union advocates the opening of economies through its single market program, which was designed to remove barriers to trade among its member states. At the same time, however, the EU espouses policies that effectively seek to limit or counter globalization forces. The creation of the European currency, the euro, was not merely designed to integrate European economies more effectively. It was also promoted as a means to challenge the U.S. dollar in global finance. The rise of Mercosur, the "Common Market of the South," is another example of a regional IGO that both welcomes the opening of economies and seeks to contain them. Mercosur countries have opened their economies through the signing of a free trade agreement with the European Union, resulting in a significant increase in trade between the two regions. At the same time, several Mercosur countries have considered creating their own currency that could impede the U.S. dollar's global reach.

Globalization, therefore, has led to the rise of IGOs that both promote and resist the opening of societies, economies, and technologies.

Globalization has also prompted many new challenges to the roles, effectiveness, and legitimacy of IGOs in the world today.

CHALLENGES TO INTERGOVERNMENTAL ORGANIZATIONS: PROBLEMS, PERFORMANCE, AND PERCEPTIONS

The challenges faced by IGOs can be placed in three broad yet interrelated categories: the number and nature of today's problems, the emphasis on IGO performance, and the perceptions of IGO legitimacy, transparency, and fairness.

The Number and Nature of Problems

The past three decades have seen an explosion both in the number of transsovereign issues and in the demands for international policy coordination. According to some observers, the opening of societies, economies, and technologies has created a more informed population that calls on states to undertake greater international problem solving and global public policy making.[20] With President George H. W. Bush's appeal for a new world order, for example, there was the expectation that transsovereign issues would increasingly be addressed in the multilateral forums of IGOs.

Flying in the face of these expectations, however, is the problem of "mandate congestion" and what Oran Young calls the growing "gap between the demand for governance and the supply of governance at the international level."[21] For example, many countries now demand that the United Nations assume more peacekeeping operations—without any significant increase in funding or meaningful revisions of the rules of engagement. Simply put, IGOs are asked to put more and more on their agendas without necessarily having the proper means to address these expanding issues.

It is not only the demand that has changed, but also the nature of the problems themselves. While the United Nations' founders assumed that it would address interstate disputes, most wars today are the result of intrastate conflict. Recent wars in Rwanda, Bosnia, Kosovo, and Sudan, for example, have intrastate conflict roots, although there were outside influences in each case. Today, the United Nations finds itself addressing not only refugee, human rights, health, and environmental matters in the aftermath of intrastate conflict but also the prospects of "state building."[22] Often, the United Nations is charged with rebuilding the administrative, political, judicial, and economic structure of these collapsed states.[23] Such failed states form the core of today's security dilemma and now dominate the agendas of many IGOs.

Performance

Of course, it is difficult for IGOs to perform and address these new and varied problems without the necessary financial and leadership support. This point was made to the United States more than once after it fell more than $1.5 billion behind in dues to the United Nations. Critics of U.S. foreign policy have charged that by withholding funds and refusing to support specific programs, the United States has set up IGOs for failure.

Others, notably certain members of the U.S. Congress, have maintained that many traditional IGOs have not adequately responded internally to the changed international agenda, or have been hostile to U.S. efforts to address this agenda. They reason that just as the private sector needs to restructure itself in light of economic trends, so too must IGO bureaucracies reform and transform themselves to better address today's political and economic environment. The United Nations in particular has come under criticism for its bloated bureaucracy.

Some countries have decided to sidestep these "ineffective" organizations and create their own "shadow institutions" or informal sessions where problems and issues can be addressed. Critics argue, for example, that the G-7 meetings were designed for the wealthiest countries to create a united front on issues that will later be discussed in other organizations. They also charge that these same countries move important issues, such as the Code of Conduct for Multinationals and the Multilateral Agreement on Investment (MAI), to rich countries' "clubs," such as the Organization for Economic Cooperation and Development, instead of addressing them solely in the United Nations.[24] The result, according to some critics, is a "crisis of multilateralism."[25]

Nonetheless, certain IGOs have succeeded in "reinventing" themselves and their purposes in the post–Cold War, globalizing world. For example, although still not "lean and mean" as bureaucracies go, NATO has been successful in redefining its mission. Similarly, the IMF has shifted dramatically from being a short-term balance-of-payments provider to a major supplier of liquidity in times of global financial crisis. The International Telecommunications Union (ITU)—the oldest IGO (created in 1865)—has developed into a significantly streamlined organization by ridding itself of obsolete departments.

Other IGOs have sought to reinvent themselves and/or strengthen their performance by developing NGO partnerships and building transnational coalitions around key agenda items. These "born-again institutions" are often infused with new life and influence as a result.[26] Yet the coalitions themselves can hinder an IGO's performance if it is "captured" by an NGO, which is a common phenomenon in domestic policy making of member states. Determining the proper role for NGOs in organizations that comprise nation-states is problematic. The participation of NGOs can lead to perception problems for the organization.

Perception

Perceptions—whether based on truth or fiction—can have considerable consequences for IGOs. As noted above, critics—as well as many NGOs and developing countries—view the OECD as a tool of rich countries and big businesses setting their international agendas. The OECD's failed behind-the-scenes meetings to develop an MAI with representatives of multinational corporations are cited as a classic case of this collusion. Other critics, however, charge that certain organizations, including programs within the United Nations, are being run by zealous NGOs that have developed their own global public policy fiefdoms. Government officials at the 1992 UN Conference on the Environment and Development in Rio de Janeiro, for example, found themselves surrounded by 1,500 NGOs accredited to the conference. In the conference's final days, officials opted to work behind closed doors to escape the NGOs and complete the work at hand.[27]

Even well-respected IGOs can suffer perception problems. For example, the World Health Organization has been hailed in recent years for its progressive approach to eradicating disease. According to former WHO Secretary General Gro Bruntland, the WHO's forging of partnerships with both NGOs and multinational corporations (MNCs) to carry out these global public policies has been key to its success. Nonetheless, certain NGOs have argued that the WHO's reputation and prestige will forever be tainted because of its working relationships with the multinational firms.[28]

Arguably the most important challenge to IGOs today involves the perception of legitimacy. For too many IGOs, the lack of transparency and meaningful participation in IGO policymaking form the core of this perception problem. As IGOs address more and more transsovereign issues, they are taking actions that have far-reaching implications for millions of people. The role of the IMF in the Asian financial crisis in the late 1990s prompted Asian governments to make important policy changes in employment, taxation, environmental and even health policies. These changes in turn led to massive protests in the streets of South Korea and the downfall of the political leadership in Indonesia. The IMF was criticized for both the policies undertaken and how these issues were decided in the first place. Managing the IMF is a technocratic elite that meets and consults with high government officials from its membership. Members of civil society are rarely involved in these discussions. Little, if any, democratic accountability or control is exercised over the IMF. This democratic deficit is compounded by the lack of transparency. More often than not, key IMF negotiations are made behind closed doors. How decisions are made, who makes them, and for what reasons are rarely disclosed—much to the dissatisfaction of many citizens, NGOs, and even MNCs.

Thus, whether IGOs like the IMF have or should have this influence in other states' public policymaking is controversial. Whether these IGOs are the legitimate decision makers in sovereign states is contested. It matters not whether the alleged crisis of legitimacy is valid—the perception is real.

THE IGOs: GLOBAL GOVERNANCE AND CALLS FOR REFORM

Four key IGOs will now be examined in greater detail: the United Nations, the International Monetary Fund, the World Trade Organization, and the European Union.

The United Nations

Established by 51 countries in 1945, the United Nations boasts a membership of 191 countries some sixty years later. The organization has six main bodies: the General Assembly, the Security Council, the Economic and Social Council, the Trusteeship Council, the Secretariat, and the International Court of Justice. The UN Charter identifies four main purposes for the organization: "to maintain international peace and security, to develop friendly relations among nations, to cooperate in solving international problems and in promoting respect for human rights, and to be a centre for harmonizing the actions of nations." These objectives result in a rather broad mandate that has been expanded upon over the years. In September 2000, UN members approved the Millennium Declaration, identifying a global agenda for the new century that addresses seven key areas: peace, security and disarmament; development and poverty eradication; protecting our common environment, human rights, democracy and good governance; protecting the vulnerable; meeting the special needs of Africa; and strengthening the United Nations.[29]

The United Nations also has several independent organizations, special programs, and funds that make up what is known as the UN family or UN system. For example, the Office of the UN High Commissioner for Refugees (UNHCR) and UNICEF are UN programs with separate government bodies, budgets, and secretariats that also are linked to the UN system.[30] The

International Monetary Fund, the World Bank Group, and specialized agencies such as the World Health Organization and Universal Postal Union are all linked to the United Nations through cooperative technical agreements but are autonomous organizations in practice.

The United Nations is recognized as a provider of "international public goods," including international air traffic control, telecommunications and posts, humanitarian relief for refugees and victims of natural disasters, and protection of the environmental commons.[31] In recent years, it has been heralded as a promoter of "human security"—protecting states and individuals from danger and promoting individuals' political, social, and economic human rights.[32] Since they were first deployed in 1948, UN peacekeepers have taken part in sixty operations (including fifteen underway in 2006) and were awarded the 1988 Nobel Prize for Peace.[33] Moreover, the United Nations has established international tribunals to prosecute individuals accused of war crimes and genocide in Rwanda and the former Yugoslavia. The United Nations protects more than 20 million refugees each year, buys vaccines for half of the world's children, and champions human rights around the globe.[34]

Despite these UN successes, critics charge that the United Nations is in need of serious reform. While the demand for UN reform is not novel—various groups have called for significant changes to the organization since its inception—the intensity of this call is new.[35] In recent years, UN reform has become a regular feature on news stories and a source of constant discussion within think tanks. Reform efforts have also captured news headlines. In June 2005, the U.S. House of Representatives introduced the "Henry J. Hyde United Nations Reform Act" that threatened to cut U.S. monetary contributions to the UN in half if major reforms were not undertaken.

UN critics charge that the IGO is a bloated, unruly bureaucracy prone to fraud and abuse. The "Oil for Food" scandal highlighted the "serious mismanagement and outright corruption" of this major UN program.[36] The "Oil for Food" program—initially designed to safeguard Iraqi citizens from starvation in light of economic sanctions—allowed then-Iraqi president Saddam Hussein's government to garner over $1.7 billion in illicit oil revenues. Moreover, million-dollar kickbacks to certain UN officials and contracting companies were discovered.[37] To prevent another Oil-for-Food scandal in the future, U.S. critics advocate for "results-oriented" changes to the organization. Their solution is a fundamental overhaul that would include cutting unneeded or unnecessary programs and trimming the ranks of bureaucrats. Critics point out, for example, that although the United Nations devotes most of its time to development issues, it provides only 5 percent of the development aid to poorer regions of the world. The rest of this aid comes from private corporations, states, and NGOs.[38] Critics maintain that instead of being an organization that tries to cover everything under its broad mandate, the United Nations should focus on "global problems that nobody else can tackle" such as refugees and peacekeeping.[39]

While acknowledging the need for reform, UN supporters charge that a "results-oriented" reform campaign based on cost cutting alone is misguided. They point out that the UN's inability to carry out certain missions effectively may in fact be due to member states' weak UN support and lackluster funding. Peacekeeping efforts are a prime example. Creating a small standing army to bring peacekeepers to trouble spots immediately instead of wrangling with member states over troop numbers, contributions, and commands would render the UN more effective in this core function. Yet it is unlikely that certain countries would give the United Nations the funding to do so. Nor would countries like the United States support giving the UN something as symbolic of sovereignty as an army—or allow any of their own troops to operate under a UN commander. Thus, few foreign observers trust the intentions of U.S. congressional leaders in UN reform efforts. They view American actions as an excuse for not paying U.S. dues in the past and "doubt that America really wants to see a more efficient [United Nations]—just a smaller one."[40]

Another area for UN reform focuses on the expansion of the UN Security Council to better reflect the current configuration of power in the world by including countries such as Japan and Germany. Both countries are key contributors to the regular UN budget and the largest contributors to UN special programs.[41] Many UN member countries also believe that the Security Council should be more representative of other regions and populations of the world by permanently including countries such as Brazil, India, Egypt, and Nigeria. The current permanent members, however, are reluctant to revamp the body out of concern that such revisions would reduce their own powers.

Not surprisingly, countries' concern over their power in the UN features prominently in reform debates. While everyone agrees the UN needs reform, there is little consensus over the shape and purpose of the reform. U.S. efforts to bring "results-driven" reform are eyed warily by countries in the global South that do not want to see development programs cut and are reluctant to support any efficiency reforms that might undercut their own voices in the UN system.

Similarly, the U.S. looks warily at Secretary General Kofi Annan's own reform efforts. While U.S. congressional leaders call on the Secretary General to reduce bureaucratic bloat and run the IGO more like a private company, they and other government leaders are unwilling to grant him the administrative powers to hire and fire at will. As the *Economist* noted,

> [t]he job of secretary-general at the United Nations is not unlike that of a medieval pope. In one sense, you are the leader of Christendom. Yet, at the same time, your power is limited: you have no battalions of your own (all those peacekeeping troops are only on loan); your own organisation is a hotchpotch of feuding bishoprics, most of whom feel more loyalty to temporal rules than to you; and you are normally broke.[42]

Nonetheless, the UN Secretary General proposed a major reform program, the Millennium+5 reforms, in March 2005. Designed, according to some observers, to placate the U.S., the reforms focused on accountability measures but failed to address the UN's more fundamental financial woes or the final structure in the UN Security Council. Perhaps as a consequence, the UN summit on institutional reform in September 2005 produced "watered-down results."[43]

How the UN develops and its reform efforts unfold over the next decade remains to be seen. Some critics suggest the UN will simply "fade into irrelevance."[44] Others charge that the UN will continue to play an important role in global governance. Annan points out that while the U.S. led initial relief efforts to tsunami-ravaged countries in 2005, it agreed a week later with other countries that the UN and its Office for the Coordination of Humanitarian Affairs should take over as the lead relief coordinating agency for two reasons. First, the UN office has a "light structure" with a track record for such coordination efforts. The second and most important reason, however, is others' perception of the UN:

> ... everyone was willing to work with the U.N.: the governments and people of the affected countries, the donors, and the nonprofit organizations whose role is so essential in all emergencies, great and small. All of them recognize that the U.N. is the right body to lead, because it is in no one's pocket. It belongs to the world.[45]

The International Monetary Fund

Since its conception in 1944, the IMF has lent hundreds of billions of dollars to countries in need of economic assistance. The IMF charter, and that of its sister IGO, the World Bank, was formulated during a three-week conference held in Bretton Woods, New Hampshire. Both organizations and their respective organs are commonly referred to as the Bretton Woods system. The World

Bank was tasked with postwar reconstruction. The IMF's mandate was to promote international monetary cooperation through exchange rate stability and to facilitate the expansion of international trade by addressing balance of payment problems among the initial twenty-nine member countries.

In recent decades, IMF members have significantly expanded the IGO's mandate. As national economies have grown increasingly integrated, the global economy has become considerably more complex. The introduction of new technologies, coupled with a staggering increase in private capital flows and international transactions, has required organizations such as the IMF to broaden their functions.

The collapse of the gold standard in 1971, and the subsequent switch to floating exchange rates, for example, forced the organization to seek out a new *raison d'être*. Beginning with the debt crisis in Mexico and other Latin American countries in the 1980s, IMF members discovered a new and important role for the IGO in the international system. In addition to offering financial support and credit, the IMF began providing fiscal and monetary advice to governments and local economists. The organization increased its monitoring activities and vastly expanded the scope of conditions attached to the aid packages. For instance, the fund demanded that politicians make specific macroeconomic policy changes to improve the economic health of their countries in exchange for IMF loans.

Later economic crises in the former Soviet bloc countries and in Southeast Asia triggered an even greater expansion in the functions and monetary support of the IMF. For example, in 1997 the fund was called upon to aid the struggling economies of South Korea, Thailand, and Indonesia. The South Korean package alone amounted to $57 billion. The IMF "bailouts"—as some have termed the action—"provided enough credit to prevent formal government defaults and maintain future access to capital markets."[46] Had the IMF not intervened, the future of the Asian economies could have been even more precarious. In addition to constructing aid packages intended to avoid liquidity crunches, the IMF has begun providing loans to developing countries to assist with poverty alleviation and good governance programs. Consequently, the IMF has grown increasingly involved in the political affairs of certain countries.

Despite continual requests for its assistance, the IMF has received its share of criticisms.[47] Critics, for example, have found fault with the clandestine workings of the organization. Most of the fund's activities "are shrouded in secrecy, and even when it releases statements or documents to the public, it tends to hide behind a smoke screen of technical jargon."[48] The secrecy surrounding the organization translates into a lack of transparency and accountability. IMF country documents and annual economic surveys remain private. As a consequence, its warnings and speculations about weak economies fail to reach the same international bankers and investors that the organization later bails out. Various reform agendas have sought to redress the problem of transparency through requests for increased public input and scrutiny, an independent evaluation board, and an overall demystifying of the fund.[49]

A second set of IMF criticisms is directed at the fund's country pre-scriptions for economic recovery. According to Joseph Stiglitz, a former chief economist and vice-president of the World Bank, during the Asian crisis the IMF delivered the "same medication for each ailing nation that showed up on its doorstep . . . even as evidence of the policy's failure mounted."[50] Moreover, the IMF attempted to temper the Asian financial crisis with a set of austerity measures similar to those prescribed to the Latin American governments in the 1980s—even though the reasons behind the Asian crisis were far different from those in Latin America. Critics argue that behind these poor prescriptions lay a group of inadequate economists who "are more likely to have firsthand knowledge of [a country's] five-star hotels" than of its social, political, and cultural makeup.[51]

Finally, more liberal critics claim that the IMF's policies "are a not-so-thinly disguised wedge for capital interests."[52] The fund has been criticized for being divided between the strong, Western economies and the poorer, developing member countries. Because the major economic powers are rarely forced to borrow from the IMF, they fail to foresee problems with continual expansion of the IMF's power and role.

To address the organization's many criticisms, critics have offered three broadly defined sets of reform proposals: abolishing the fund, significantly restructuring it, and scaling back its role to the original Bretton Woods mandate. Of course, selecting any one of these reforms would placate some groups and anger others. As Devesh Kapur joked, "If the IMF had a dollar for every criticism of its purpose and role by the Right, the Left, and the Center, it would perhaps never again have to approach its shareholders for more money to sustain its operations."[53]

The World Trade Organization

The primary purpose of the WTO is to facilitate free trade through trade agreements and negotiations, trade dispute settlements, assistance to developing countries on trade matters, and cooperation with other IGOs on international trade matters. Almost 150 countries, accounting for more than 97 percent of world trade, represent the WTO membership.[54]

The WTO is the youngest of the major IGOs. It also is an example of an informal institution or regime that developed into a formal intergovernmental organization. WTO agreements are based on those of its predecessor, the General Agreement on Tariffs and Trade (GATT) (1947–1994), a one-time "temporary" agreement that became increasingly institutionalized over the years. Whereas the GATT focused solely on the trading of goods, the WTO agreements also include agreements on the trading of certain services (General Agreement on Trade in Services, or GATS) and the protection of intellectual property rights (Trade Related Intellectual Property Rights, or TRIPS). When creating the WTO, these future members also established the Dispute Settle Understanding (DSU), a specific process that encourages countries to settle trade disputes through consultation or, if that fails, to bring the disputes before a specially appointed panel of experts for a ruling. Through the DSU, the WTO "has profoundly changed the nature of trade disputes" by ending a country's ability to retaliate unilaterally against another country with sanctions and various protectionist policies.[55] Under the disputed settlement rules, a country that is found to have violated its WTO commitments must either change its domestic law, regulation, or practice, or accept retaliatory trade sanctions to compensate for the aggrieved parties' losses.

A look at the WTO's membership and the list of applicant countries clearly shows the importance that governments attach to WTO membership. China's accession to the WTO is a case in point. A sign of the WTO's success is that China's communist leaders participated in fifteen years of multilateral and bilateral negotiations with WTO members, and adopted significant market-oriented laws and trade practices to meet WTO requirements.

Yet the WTO is also one of the most controversial IGOs. Forty thousand activists and union members protested the organization and its free trade agenda at the December 1999 WTO ministerial meeting in Seattle, Washington. The result was the infamous "Battle in Seattle" during which protesters succeeded in shutting down the meeting and much of the city.

Perhaps one reason why the WTO is so controversial is that people from every part of the political spectrum can find fault with it. Problems of perception challenge the WTO's governance in global trade matters today. In the United States, some conservatives are wary of the organization because they believe it takes away U.S. sovereignty through the voting procedures and the DSU. Unlike with the IMF and its weighted vote system, the United States is a coequal in the organization: Its vote counts the same as that of Jamaica. Moreover, under the DSU, the United States can no longer respond unilaterally to trade problems and instead must bring its grievances to the Dispute Settlement Body (DSB). Of course, the United

States has been the target of other countries' grievances in the WTO process and has "lost" some of these cases.

On the other hand, protesters on the left of the political spectrum deride the IGO because the WTO focuses exclusively on trade issues and not on environmental and labor concerns. Accordingly, this results in a "race to the bottom"—the idea that countries and companies in the name of trade competition will push for lower and lower environmental and labor regulations. They often cite the classic tuna–dolphin ruling that occurred under the old GATT dispute settlement process. In that case, Mexico brought a grievance against the United States for banning the importation of tuna caught with purse seine nets that were deemed unsafe for dolphins.[56] When Mexico won the case, environmentalists in the United States and elsewhere viewed this ruling as a dangerous case of free trade trumping environmental concerns.

Still another category of protesters comes from the developing countries. They argue that the WTO is biased toward wealthy countries and their multinational corporations. They point out that the United States and Europe pushed the developing world to accept new trade rules on services and intellectual property rights—areas where the Global North has the comparative advantage. Yet the United States and European Union were unwilling to quickly lift restrictions on textile imports or, in the case of the EU, end agricultural subsidy programs—two sectors where the Global South is more competitive. At the same time, the developing countries question the intentions of U.S. labor and environmental activists. Requiring all WTO members to adhere to stricter labor and environmental standards would raise the costs of production in the Global South—and thus keep more jobs in the United States. The developing countries' other complaint concerns the rules and informal procedures that preclude developing countries from actively and effectively participating in negotiations. For example, unlike the United States and EU, the developing countries do not have the staff or resources to participate in complex multiple negotiations simultaneously. Thus, they are either railroaded through the process or forced to delay the process through vetoes or other tactics.[57]

The most telling criticism of the WTO, however, is its perceived lack of democratic accountability and transparency. The *Economist* magazine explained the perception in the following way:

> According to skeptics, the WTO takes powers away from elected governments and grants them to faceless bureaucrats . . .The WTO is a kind of embryonic world government, but with none of the checks

57

and balances that true democratic government requires. In short, it is an embryonic world tyranny. That is why, in the view of many skeptics, it is the most dangerous of all the institutions of globalisation.[58]

Not everyone blames the WTO secretariat with its 600-plus-person staff in Geneva for this perception. It is the member states themselves who conduct the trade negotiations, insist that they take place behind closed doors, and maintain that the DSB deliberations remain secret.[59]

In the aftermath of the 1999 Seattle ministerial meeting, the WTO began to address more seriously the criticisms and perceptions surrounding it. The need to take account of developing countries' concerns took on even greater urgency following the 2001 terrorist attacks in the United States. At the Doha, Qatar, ministerial in Fall 2001, members agreed to launch another round of trade liberalization designed to address a broader range of issues of concern to developing countries. The so-called Doha Development Round (DDR) was launched to reform trade rules and, in particular, to reduce or eliminate agricultural food and cotton subsidies in the Global North, notably in the United States and European Union. The elimination of these subsidies would improve developing countries' competitiveness, allow them greater market access to wealthier countries, and promote their economic development. Whether WTO members will meet the DDR commitments, however, is debatable given farm lobby efforts and national politicians' reluctance to reform agricultural programs in the United States and the European Union.

The Doha Round raised expectations for the WTO to be "reformed to serve as a vehicle for a more benign kind of globalization."[60] The question for some observers is not whether the Doha effort will be successful, but whether or not the IGO can afford *not* to reform itself.

The European Union

The European Union is a classic example of a regional (as opposed to global) intergovernmental organization.[61] Since its creation as the European Coal and Steel Community in the early 1950s, the EU has emerged as an important actor on the regional and global stage. Today, the EU represents twenty-five countries and nearly 457 million people, and it boasts a $9.7 trillion gross domestic product.[62]

The EU distinguishes itself from other IGOs in an important way. Member states "pool" their sovereignty within the EU. In effect, they share or grant part of their sovereignty to the EU itself in particular policy areas. For example, in January 2002, the twelve participating members of "Euroland" replaced their national currencies with a European currency, the euro. Instead of twelve central banks making decisions, a single European Central Bank now oversees monetary policy in much of Europe.[63]

Membership in the European Union also requires significant conformity to the *acquis communautaire*—the policies, rules, and regulations that form the legal and political basis for the European Union. EU law must be transposed into national law. The ten new member states, for example, were required to rewrite—and continue to rewrite—their environmental, consumer protection, competition policy, and other laws and policies to conform to the *acquis*.

The EU is also different from other IGOs in terms of the powers granted to its supranational bodies: the European Commission, the European Parliament, and the European Court of Justice. Located in Brussels, the European Commission is the policy-making body that initiates legislation primarily in economic matters and oversees the implementation of various EU-wide policies and programs, among other duties. It is the European Commission, for example, that represents the European Union in trade negotiations with the United States and in the WTO.

The European Parliament (EP) has evolved from a relatively weak assembly to a body whose voting power is equal to that of the member states in several policy areas. Scholars who study the EP argue that it is more powerful than most national parliaments in Europe.[64] The European Court of Justice (ECJ), however, is arguably the most powerful supranational body in the European Union. Today, ECJ rulings have precedence over national law in matters pertaining to EU treaties and secondary legislation. Moreover, national courts in EU member states may refer questions on particular cases to the ECJ to determine how the European law should be applied at the national level.

In many regards, the EU is at a crossroads in its development. While EU member states have not relinquished sovereign authority in all policy areas—taxation is a prime example—the global fight against terrorism has prompted member states to increasingly work through the EU on matters such as border control, visas, immigration, and money laundering. And while retaining their right of policy initiation and individual veto, member states often seek European positions in Common Foreign and Security Policy (CFSP) and have appointed a "High Representative" or "Mr. CFSP" to officially present EU policy on foreign and security policy matters to the outside world.

The 2004 enlargement in which the EU admitted ten new members from Central and Eastern Europe remains the biggest challenge to the EU. The unprecedented enlargement poses considerable collective action problems for the European Union. Governing an EU of twenty-five members—especially when it includes countries who only recently transitioned to Western democratic ideals and capitalist markets—is considerably more challenging than governing an EU of fifteen. Some naysayers suggest that the EU will no longer be able to embrace a wide-ranging agenda and will need to focus its efforts on the maintenance of the Single Market program and the euro. For these observers, the question focuses on the extent to which the EU will dilute its powers and become more like a mini-United Nations "with much less political and legal authority, or none at all."[65] Others, however, are more confident that EU institutions and member states will embrace the challenge of enlargement and will make the reforms necessary to ensure that the EU can continue to evolve and govern effectively.

Nonetheless, there remains considerable debate over the autonomy of the EU institutions vis-à-vis that of its member states.[66] The EU's distinctive traits have led some scholars to refer to it as a "multilevel system of governance" in which certain activities or forms of governance are carried out at the supranational level, others at the national level, and still others at the subnational or regional levels. Indeed, several scholars have argued that the EU should no longer be treated as an IGO but as a "polity."[67] Thus, instead of using international relations theory to explain member state cooperation, these scholars maintain that comparative politics theory can better explain how the EU functions. As noted above, for example, the European Parliament's powers can be judged by comparing the EP to other national assemblies. Similarly, the European Central Bank's role and functions can be ascertained by comparing it to other central banking systems.

Like other IGOs, however, the European Union faces many interrelated challenges. Perhaps the most fundamental is the perceived "democratic deficit" or what some term the "legitimacy deficit" of the European Union. Over a fifty-year period, the European Union developed from a small coal and steel community to today's complex organization. During this time, political elites generally encouraged EU expansion and allowed the EU institutions to define their scope, methods, and functions—all while the mass public remained largely unaware of these developments.[68] The 1992 Danish referendum on the Maastricht Treaty, in which the Danish people voted against the expansion of EU powers, signaled the end to this permissive consensus. Public opinion polls revealed that Danes and other Europeans were increasingly wary of decisions made by unknown "Eurocrats" in Brussels (the EU capital) on such matters ranging from the size of apples to the elimination of national currencies. Government leaders who in the past found it easy to blame Brussels for forcing change on national policies now struggled to explain the functioning and relevance of the EU to their citizens. In recent years, member states and EU institutions alike have sought to better clarify their policy decisions. For example, a major sustained publicity campaign accompanied the introduction of the euro as a currency in 1999 and as legal tender in 2002.

The transparency of the EU institutions is a related problem. Critics have long complained, for example, that the Brussels machinery is too complex and obtuse to allow observers and lobbyists alike to track EU legislation. To successfully influence legislation in the early draft stages, for example, one had to develop an extensive intelligence network to monitor European Commission activities.[69] The body has endeavored to make its machinery more transparent by providing organization charts, listing contact numbers of key personnel, and issuing status reports on various pieces of legislation on its official Web site. More recently, the European Commission issued a governance paper that suggested reforms in policy making and decision making that would render the EU legislative process more efficient, open, and timely.

Compared to the European Commission, efforts by the Council of Ministers—the member states—to address the perceived democratic deficit have been less impressive. The key decision making body of the European Union has been reluctant to publish the voting records of its members. Major newspapers have sued the Council of Ministers to make its meeting and voting records more public. These actions, along with the prodding by Sweden and Finland, have prompted the Council to begin opening up their decision-making processes. Whether or not the member states will take larger steps to address the democratic deficit remains to be seen.

Reform of EU institutions is linked to legitimacy and transparency concerns. In 1999, the European Commission resigned *en masse* in response to perceived mismanagement problems. Individual commissioners were alleged to have improperly hired friends and relatives and misappropriated funds. For years, the European Commission doled out management positions according to an unofficial quota to ensure the representation of all member states. As a result of the 1999 debacle, the European Commission has undergone and continues to pursue significant institutional reforms, including the establishment of a promotion process based on meritocracy instead of national quotas. The European Parliament, however, whose scrutiny of the European Commission led to the 1999 resignation, has yet to embrace such reform. EP members, for example, enjoy a questionable system of salaries and expenses that has not helped their reputation in the polls.[70] The fact that the 626-member European Parliament continues to meet in three different places—Brussels, Strasbourg, and Luxembourg—only reinforces the perception of an institution out of touch with its public.

EU leaders sought to address the challenges of legitimacy, transparency, and reform by creating a European constitution. A special Convention on the Future of Europe, led by former French Prime Minister Valerie Giscard d'Estaing, met to identify the EU's core principles and to condense the provisions of numerous EU treaties into a single document. The result was a long, detailed constitution—many would argue that it is too long and detailed—adopted by the governments on June 17 and 18, 2004. While government leaders sought to engage the European public in a dialogue over the constitution, European citizens, who historically had been excluded from EU treaty matters, remained largely disengaged from the process. As EU leaders soon discovered, the lengthy constitutional text failed to capture the European public's attention. Their decision, however, to expand the EU's boundaries to include the ten new Eastern and Central European countries did weigh heavily on people's minds as they considered the enlargement's potential impact on employment, immigration, and competitiveness policies. Thus, when French and Dutch citizens went to the polls to cast their votes on the constitution, their negative vote was as much, if not more, a protest against EU enlargement—and the failure of politicians to adequately address citizen concerns regarding the expansion—as it was against the constitution itself. In an ironic twist, EU member states' failure to engage with the public in a transparent manner over EU enlargement prompted the veto of a constitution designed to further the principles of transparency and legitimacy.

While EU observers generally consider the formal EU constitution to be a moribund issue (all twenty-five member states must ratify the constitution before it can enter into force), they do not see its ratification as necessary for the EU to function. Legal scholars have long argued that the EU is already constitutionally grounded in the various EU treaties.[71] Others point out that many provisions in the treaty simply codified existing EU policies and practices and that many of the "new" provisions such as greater foreign policy coordination will likely take place with or without a ratified constitution. The real challenge will be for EU political leaders to allow for greater transparency and to consult with the European public on major changes facing the European Union, including future enlargement. As politicians learned, constitutions alone cannot address the EU democratic deficit.

PRESCRIPTIONS

Globalization has infused new life and purpose into IGOs. Far from being the ugly ducklings of the past, IGOs now occupy center stage in addressing the most important transsovereign issues of the day. Yet globalization has also prompted increasing criticism of IGOs. Individuals and NGOs increasingly question not only IGO policies but also the raison d'être of the IGOs themselves, as evidenced by the WTO Battle in Seattle, the debates over the United Nations on the U.S. House floor, and the IMF and World Bank protests around the world. To remain relevant, IGOs and their members must address three core issues: reform, transparency, and legitimacy.

Reforming IGOs is not a question but a necessity. As companies and countries adjust to globalization pressures, so too must IGOs. Many IGOs are not organized effectively to deal with today's transsovereign issues. Parts of the United Nations are prime candidates for reform because of bloated bureaucracies and poor management. However, reformers must take care to embrace efficiency without compromising the overarching values of the organization. For some countries, assessing the United Nations' performance solely in terms of an Anglo-Saxon measure of effectiveness is not appropriate. Different countries have different expectations regarding the United Nations. For some, the organization's primary role has been and still should be as a venue where dialogue can take place and where countries are treated as independent and equal—at least in the General Assembly meetings. To reform the United Nations or any other IGO, reformers need to find a balance.[72]

Transparency is the second core issue. The WTO, for example, touts the benefits of free and open markets. The IMF demands that states develop free and open financial systems. The EU requires open borders and the free movement of goods, services, people, and capital. Yet all three organizations fail to practice what they preach, conducting their primary decision-making sessions in secrecy, behind closed doors. Who is making the decisions, why, and under what circumstances? Protesters argue that they have a right to know. Transparency allows for greater scrutiny of IGOs and "provides the basis for a highly democratic, albeit nonelectoral, system of transnational governance based on the growing strength of global civil society."[73]

Legitimacy is arguably the most important concern facing IGOs—in a sense, the umbrella issue under which all other concerns can be found. For example, whether an IGO is reforming or transparent will affect the public's determination of its legitimacy. Relations with NGOs, fairness, and adequate resources are three key factors that play an important role in enhancing the public and political support for IGOs. Today, IGOs seek to enhance their legitimacy by building coalitions and networks with NGOs and MNCs. Positive examples of such cooperation abound—from the WHO's compact with MNCs to eradicate disease, to the United Nations' alliance with the International Campaign to Ban Landmines. Relations between IGOs, NGOs, and MNCs, however, must be developed carefully to ensure that IGOs are not beholden to or co-opted by particular groups or interests.[74]

Failure to do so would result in the demise of the very legitimacy IGOs sought to achieve in the first place.

IGOs—including their members—must also seek to enhance fairness as a means to promote their policies. Who does the IGO represent? Western protesters in Seattle maintained that the WTO favored MNCs at the expense of the environment and laborers. At the same time, poor countries argued that the IMF, WTO, and other economic organizations were biased toward the richer North. Of course, schisms between rich and poor countries, environmentalists and economists are not new. Today, however, IGO policies that fail to consider these tensions are ripe for failure.

Providing adequate resources—funding, staff, and political support—is also critical to ensuring the future health and legitimacy of IGOs. Today, IGOs serve as primary, if not *the* primary, entities responsible for addressing the economic, political, and cultural fallout of failed states. They are the guardians of refugees, the lenders of last resort, and, in some cases, the bulwarks against the excesses of globalization. Yet they are often not given the resources to carry out these important policies in the most effective manner. Although critics and member states may complain about ill-advised programs, they often need not look beyond their own pocketbooks to explain why an IGO's performance is less than optimal.

Of course, critics of IGOS are not going away anytime soon—nor should they. Member states recognize that they are ill equipped to address today's transsovereign problems and thus, IGOs are likely to persist. Addressing the core issues of reform, transparency, and legitimacy would ensure that they are here to stay and better poised to carry out the demands of global governance.

ENDNOTES

1. Kofi A. Annan, "Our Mission Remains Vital," *Wall Street Journal* (Feb. 22, 2005): A14.
2. A. LeRoy Bennett and James K. Oliver, *International Organizations: Principles and Issues,* 7th ed. (Upper Saddle River, NJ: Prentice Hall, 2002), 3.
3. Michael N. Barnett and Martha Finnemore, "The Politics, Power, and Pathologies of International Organizations," *International Organization,* 53(4): 699–732; Bob Reinalda and Bertjan Verbeek, *Autonomous Policy Making by International Organizations* (New York: Routledge, 1998).
4. Jeffrey Laurenti, *The World Today,* 61 (8/9, Aug./Sept. 2005): 4.
5. Clive Archer, *International Organizations* (London: Allen & Unwin, 1983).
6. Bennett and Oliver, *International Organizations,* 2.
7. The actual number of international organizations varies widely, depending on various scholars' definitions of organizations and institutions. Keohane, for example, suggests there are currently more than 1,000 international institutions [Robert O. Keohane, "International Institutions: Can Interdependence Work?" *Foreign Policy* (Spring 1998): 82–94]. The term *regime* is yet another word used to describe these informal institutions.

See Stephen D. Krasner, "Structural Causes and Regime Consequences: Regimes as Intervening Variables," *International Organization* 36(2): 185.

8. Keohane, "International Institutions," 86.

9. John J. Mearsheimer, "The False Promise of International Institutions," *International Security* 19(3): 5–49.

10. Barnett and Finnemore, "Politics, Power, and Pathologies," 703. See also Reinalda and Verbeek, *Autonomous Policy Making.*

11. Reinalda and Verbeek, *Autonomous Policy Making,* 5.

12. Bertjan Verbeek, "International Organizations: The Ugly Duckling of International Relations Theory?" in Reinalda and Verbeek, *Autonomous Policy Making,* 25.

13. Ibid., 17.

14. According to Daniel Moynihan, a former U.S. representative there, the United Nations itself had become "a dangerous place." See Keohane, "International Institutions," 84.

15. Ibid.

16. Oran R. Young, "Governance without Government," in *Governance in World Affairs* (Ithaca, NY: Cornell University Press, 1999), 1.

17. Thomas Friedman, *The Lexus and the Olive Tree* (New York: Farrar, Straus & Giroux, 2000).

18. Jessica T. Mathews, "Power Shift," *Foreign Affairs* (Jan.–Feb. 1997): 58.

19. Reinalda and Verbeek, *Autonomous Policy Making,* 6–7.

20. Wolfgang Reinicke, "The Other World Wide Web: Global Public Policy," *Foreign Policy* (Winter 1999–2000): 44–57.

21. Oran R. Young, "Governance without Government," in *Governance in World Affairs* (Ithaca, NY: Cornell University Press, 1999), 2.

22. Donald C. F. Daniel and Bradd C. Hayes (Eds.), *Beyond Traditional Peacekeeping* (New York: St. Martin's, 1995); Lori Fisler Damrosch, ed., *Enforcing Restraint: Collective Intervention in Internal Conflicts* (New York: Council on Foreign Relations, 1993).

23. Bruce Russett, "Ten Balances for Weighing UN Reform Proposals," *Political Science Quarterly* 111(2): 262.

24. Steve Kobrin, "The MAI and the Clash of Globalizations," *Foreign Policy* (Fall 1998): 97–109. As Kobrin notes, NGOs were largely responsible for stopping the MAI negotiations in the OECD. Today, the issue is headed for the WTO.

25. Martina Metzger and Birgit Reichenstein, eds., *Challenges for International Organizations in the 21st Century: Essays in Honor of Klaus Hufner* (New York: St. Martin's Press, 2000), viii.

26. Mathews, "Power Shift," 50–66.

27. P. J. Simmons, "Learning to Live with NGOs," *Foreign Policy* (Fall 1998): 5–6; available at <www.ceip.org/files/Publications/simmfp.asp?from=pubtopic>.

28. Corp Watch, "UN and Corporations Fact Sheet, March 2001"; available at <www.corpwatch.org/press/PPF.jsp?articleid=928>.

29. "The UN in Brief"; available at <www.un.org/overview/brief.html>.

30. Ibid.

31. David Held, Anthony McGrew, David Goldblatt, and Jonathan Perraton, *Global Transformations: Politics, Economics, and Culture* (Stanford: Stanford University Press, 1999).

32. Russett, "Ten Balances," 260.

33. UN Secretaries-General Dag Hammarskjöld and Kofi Annan were also given the Nobel award in 1961 and 2001, respectively. Annan's prize was shared with the United Nations. The UNHCR and UNICEF have also been recipients of the Nobel Prize for Peace.

34. "Reforming the United Nations: Pope Kofi's Unruly Flock," *Economist* (Aug. 8, 1998): 19.

35. See, for example, Ronald I. Meltzer, "Restructuring the United Nations System: Institutional Reform Efforts in the Context of North-South Relations," *International Organization* 32(4): 993–1018.

36. Yochi J. Dreazen, "U.N. Fires Midlevel Staffer for Oil-for-Food Role," *Wall Street Journal* (June 2, 2005): A11.

37. "U.S. Responses to Alleged Abuse of Oil-for-Food Program," *The American Journal of International Law* 99 (Jan. 2005): 254–255.

38. "Reforming the United Nations," 20.

39. Ibid.

40. Ibid., 22.

41. Ibid., 20.

42. "Reforming the United Nations," 19.

43. Howard LaFranchi, "Enough Reform to Satisfy Congress?" *Christian Science Monitor* (Sept. 30, 2005), available at <www.csmonitor.com/2005/0930/p02501-usfp.htm>.

44. Charles Hill, "How to Save the U.N. (If We Really Have To)," *Wall Street Journal* (Dec. 7, 2004): A14.

45. Annan, A14.

46. David D. Hale, "The IMF, Now More than Ever," *Foreign Affairs* 77(6): 107–113.

47. One of the most common policy criticisms of the IMF is the "moral hazard" argument in which critics fear that countries will take excessive risks knowing that the IMF will later come to their rescue. See Hale, "The IMF, Now More than Ever," 10.

48. Paul Bluestein, "At the IMF, a Struggle Shrouded in Secrecy," *Washington Post* (March 30, 1998), A1.

49. Carol Welch, "In Focus: The IMF and Good Governance," *Foreign Policy in Focus* 3(33); available at <www.foreignpolicy-infocus.org/briefs/vol3/v3n33imf_body.html>.

50. Joseph Stiglitz, "The Insider," *New Republic* (April 17 and 24, 2000): 56; available at <www.tnr.com/041700/stiglitz041700.html>.

51. Ibid., 57.

52. Devesh Kapur, "The IMF: A Cure or a Curse?" *Foreign Policy*, Summer 1998, pp. 115.

53. Ibid.

54. Another thirty countries are negotiating membership. See "The WTO in Brief" on the WTO Web site at <www.wto.org/english/thewto_e/whatis_e/inbrief_e/inbr02_e.htm>.

55. Marcus Noland, "Learning to Love the WTO," *Foreign Affairs* (Sept.–Oct. 1999): 81.

56. See "Beyond the Agreements: The Tuna–Dolphin Dispute" on the WTO Web site at <www.wto.org/english/thewto_e/whatis_e/tif_e/bey5_e.htm>.

57. John Audley and Ann M. Florini, *Overhauling the WTO: Opportunity at Doha and Beyond,* Policy Brief: Carnegie Endowment for International Peace, Oct. 2001, p. 4.

58. "Who Elected the WTO? The Case for Globalisation Survey," *Economist* (Sept. 29–Oct. 5, 2001): 26.

59. As the *Economist* argued, "The WTO is no would-be tyrant. It is democratic to a fault, and has few powers of its own." Ibid.

60. Focus on the Global South, "The End of an Illusion: WTO Reform, Global Civil Society and the Road to Hong Kong," March 31, 2005, <www.focusweb.org/Article602.html>.

61. There are still technical distinctions when referring to the European Union and the European Community, the previous name for this organization. For simplicity's sake, only the term *European Union* is used in this text.

62. Data for 2000. See "Facts and Figures" at <www.eurunion.org/profile/facts.htm>.

63. Denmark, Sweden, and the United Kingdom opted not to adopt the Euro. The ten member states that joined the EU in 2004 will have the opportunity to join the Euro area once they meet the economic convergence criteria.

64. Roger Scully, "Democracy, Legitimacy, and the European Parliament," in Maria Green Cowles and Michael Smith (Eds.), *The State of the European Union: Risks, Reform, Resistance, and Revival,* vol. 5 (Oxford, UK: Oxford University Press), 228–245.

65. "A Survey of the EU's Eastern Borders," *The Economist,* June 25th, 2005, 3.

66. See, for example, Mark Pollack, "Delegation, Agency, and Agenda-Setting in the European Community," *International Organization* 51(1): 99–134.

67. Simon Hix, "The Study of the European Community: The Challenge to Comparative Politics," *West European Politics* 1(1): 1–30.

68. Helen Wallace, "Politics and Policy in the EU: The Challenge of Governance," in Helen Wallace and William Wallace (Eds.), *Policy-Making in the European Union,* 3rd ed. (Oxford, UK: Oxford University Press, 1996), 3–36. See also Thomas Banchoff and Mitchell Smith (Eds.), *Legitimacy and the European Union: The Contested Polity* (New York: Routledge, 1999).

69. Maria Green Cowles, "The EU Committee of AmCham: The Powerful Voice of American Firms in Brussels," *Journal of European Public Policy* 3(3): 339–358.

70. Ian Black, "Euro Group Calls on MEPs to Reform," *Guardian* (March 15, 2001); available at <www.guardian.co.uk/europarl/Story/0,2763,452061,00.html>.

71. For example, see J. H. H. Weiler, *The Constitution of Europe: "Do the New Clothes Have an Emperor" and Other Essays on European Integration* (Cambridge: Cambridge University Press, 1999).

72. Russett, "Ten Balances," 259–269.

73. Ann M. Florini, "The End of Secrecy," *Foreign Policy* (Summer 1998); available at <www.ceip.org/files/Publications/annfp.asp?from=pubtopic>.

74. "The Non-Governmental Order," *Economist* (Dec. 9, 1999): 3; available at <www.economist.com/PrinterFriendly.cfm?Story_ID=266250>. See also P. J. Simmons, "Learning to Live with NGOs," *Foreign Policy* (Fall 1998): 82–96; available at <www.ceip.org/files/Publications/simmfp.asp?from=pubtopic>.

CHAPTER THREE

Nongovernmental Organizations

Politics Beyond Sovereignty

Maryann Cusimano Love

"We're not asking you to put your hand in your pockets, but we are asking people to put their fist in the air. This is your moment. Make history by making poverty history."

—Bono, lead singer of U2

Three billion people, nearly half the world's population, watched the Live 8 concerts to Make Poverty History on July 2, 2005. More than a million music fans packed ten concerts on four continents, another two billion watched on television, and the remainder tuned in online. The concerts were designed to pressure world leaders assembling for the G-8 meetings in Gleneagles, Scotland, to aid the world's poor, especially in Africa, by increasing development assistance, funding for HIV/AIDS prevention and treatment, and debt relief. Free concerts were held in Berlin, Johannesburg, London, Moscow, Paris, Philadelphia, Rome, Tokyo, and Toronto; celebrities from Nelson Mandela, Brad Pitt and Tom Hanks to Paul McCartney, U2, Bob Geldof, Green Day, Elton John, Coldplay, REM, The Who, Destiny's Child, Stevie Wonder, P. Diddy, Jay-Z, Robbie Williams, and Madonna contributed their time and talent to the concerts and media campaigns.[1] The concerts were part of the One Campaign to "Make Poverty History" organized to raise global awareness, mobilize citizens, and pressure governments to address global poverty. In addition to the concerts, millions signed petitions and protested in the streets. The efforts largely succeeded. The G-8 leaders committed to double aid to Africa (an increase to $25 billion immediately and $50 billion by 2010), cancel the debt of some of the world's poorest countries, provide greater access to HIV/AIDS treatment drugs, and work to reform trade practices that hurt the world's poor. The movement continues to pressure world leaders to keep and expand upon these promises.[2]

The One Campaign is a successor to the Jubilee movement, and both are curious coalitions. The pope, Bono (lead singer of the Irish rock band U2), Harvard economist Jeffrey Sachs, and a coalition of religious organizations and nongovernmental organizations (NGOs) united in an effort to get the debts of heavily indebted poor countries (HIPCs) forgiven in the millennium year. In a perverse form of foreign aid, HIPCs pay private banks and international financial institutions more in debt repayments each year than they invest in education and health care or receive in aid or foreign direct investment. Each year, $13.5 billion—$200 million per week—is drained away from Africa alone, while $7 billion to $10 billion would treat HIV and AIDS, tuberculosis, and malaria combined in Africa in one year.[3] Many of the original loans went to corrupt governments and dictators who were useful to the West during its Cold War fight against communism. For example, at least 30 percent of World Bank funds to Indonesia were pocketed by the Suharto family or its associates, according to some estimates.[4]

The idea behind these campaigns is that poor people have paid enough. Most have paid the original lending amounts three or four times over—and they will never be able to pay the escalating interest owed on loans that have profited the banks of some developed countries as well as corrupt rulers, but have deprived citizens in indebted countries of resources and basic services. Initially, the Jubilee effort was declared politically dead by officials in the U.S. Department of the Treasury, which is a strong proponent of debt repayment (U.S. banks hold some of these debts). But through dogged persistence and savvy lobbying, the Jubilee effort prevailed on several fronts in a short time. The debate moved from whether debt should be forgiven, to the questions of whose debt should be forgiven, how quickly, and using what instruments. Through a pincer movement of pressure commonly used by NGOs, these movements press democratic governments internally and externally. Through rock concerts and media campaigns, the movements appeal directly to the public, making the abstract problem of Third World poverty and debt concrete to mobilize public opinion. Leveraging celebrity activism, Bono and others worked the halls of Congress, Parliaments, the UN, and EU, winning over conservatives by quoting scripture and discussing religious obligations to help the poor.

In a similar story of NGOs affecting foreign policy, Canadian housewife Jody Williams had had enough. NGOs had warned governments about the dangers of landmines for years, but governments were not taking sufficient action. Long after wars were over, antipersonnel landmines remained in more than ninety countries, killing and maiming an estimated 26,000 people each year—or creating one new landmine victim every twenty minutes.[5] Landmines violate the rules of war because they cannot distinguish between combatants and civilians. Many victims of landmines are children, who, out of curiosity, pick up these shiny but dangerous objects. Many governments found landmines to be cheap weapons of war. They did not want to stop using them, and they did not want to pay for difficult and often deadly mine-removal programs.

So Jody Williams used the personal computer in her kitchen to organize the many NGOs that had a stake in this fight. Using e-mail and faxes, she inexpensively, quickly, and efficiently brought diverse groups on board and founded the International Campaign to Ban Landmines (ICBL). With the help of the Canadian government, the ICBL brought pressure to bear on governments to quickly ban, remove, stop producing and stockpiling antipersonnel landmines, and to increase landmine education and reduce the pain and suffering of landmine victims. The ICBL enlisted celebrity spokespeople such as Princess Diana in a direct media campaign that bypassed obstructionist governments and made emotional appeals directly to the public. Internally, governments were pressured by their own populations. Externally, they were pressed by the coalition of NGOs and states such as Canada, which led the movement to ban landmines. In record time, the ICBL succeeded in getting states to adopt an international treaty banning antipersonnel landmines in December 1997. One hundred forty-nine states have already ratified the treaty, despite opposition from the United States. In each year since the treaty's signing, landmine use, production, and stockpiling has decreased while landmine decommissioning, education, and services to landmine victims has increased. The ICBL continues to be active, using a network of NGOs to monitor compliance with the treaty and pressuring states that have not joined the treaty. Jody Williams won the Nobel Peace Prize for her efforts.

These examples illustrate four main themes that will be explored in this chapter. First, not only are the power and number of NGOs increasing, but also they are more frequently joining forces in transnational advocacy networks, or mobilizations of principled actors who are committed to social change.[6] Second, NGOs are active in more sectors, taking on increased functions that were once the sole preserve of states (such as international finance) and serving as the legal monitors of arms control treaty compliance. Third, NGOs use tactics that are aimed directly at the public, multinational corporations (MNCs), or intergovernmental organizations (IGOs). They are not focused only on governments—and this is one of their greatest strengths. NGOs come with weaknesses, however, including democracy deficits, North–South divisions, and coordination complexity. Fourth and finally, these changing ideas and practices of transnational politics affect sovereignty.

NGOs: PEOPLE POWER

Although NGOs predate the current period of modern globalization, their numbers, sizes, budgets, ranges of activities, power, transnational networks, and levels of international recognition have drastically increased in recent years—to the point where commentators have suggested that "we are in the midst of a global 'associational revolution.'"[7] NGOs are an odd category, defined negatively by what they are not rather than by positive definitions of what they are. NGOs are not governments, but they may receive resources from or offer resources to governments, or they may only involve themselves in certain areas or issues with the permission of governments. NGOs are a broad and eclectic group, however, and some never accept government aid. A strong tradition of autonomy prevented the Red Cross, for example, from accepting U.S. military airlift capabilities to transport food into Somalia during the famine in 1992.[8] After the Bush administration had publicly announced the airlift, it learned that the Red Cross could not allow its food to fly into Somalia in military-marked planes.[9] Other NGOS, such as CARE and World Vision, derive significant portions of their budgets and resources from governments as states contract out developmental assistance to NGOs.

NGOs range from small, grassroots groups run on shoestring budgets to huge international organizations with deep pockets, from single-issue outfits to umbrella organizations. NGOs are private-sector organizations but are often assumed to be public interest groups, which leads to contention. Who elects NGOs and who do they speak for? Many in the United States refer to NGOs as PVOs, or private volunteer organizations. But the term *volunteer* can be misleading, because most international NGOs have permanent, full-time, paid professional staffs. NGOs are nonprofit groups. Although community development banks or Habitat for Humanity often turn a profit, the resources generated are reinvested in the community. Profit is not the organization's primary goal but a means to achieving the NGO's goals such as stabilizing communities by developing homes and businesses in poor areas where banks will not lend money.

Table 1

Worldwide NGO Growth

	1909	1951	1960	1968
Traditional NGOs	176	832	1,268	2,577
Special NGOs	–	–	–	741
Total	176	832	1,268	3,318

	1976	1978	1983	1985
Traditional NGOs	5,155	8,347	11,523	13,768
Special NGOs	1,067	1,174	5,507	6,866
Total	6,222	9,521	17,030	20,634

	1987	1989	1991	1993
Traditional NGOs	14,943	14,333	16,113	12,759
Special NGOs	8,305	5,730	7,522	16,142
Total	23,248	20,063	23,635	28,901

	1995	1997	2001/2002	2005
Traditional NGOs	14,274	15,965	18,323	20,928
Special NGOs	21,780	24,341	28,775	30,581
Total	36,054	40,306	47,098	51,509

Data from Union of International Associations (Ed.), *Yearbook of International Organizations,* Vol. 1 (Brussels: K. G. Saur Verlag, 2005), Appendix 3.

Counts of NGOs vary, although scholars agree that their numbers are increasing. They are often referred to as part of civil society or as the third sector (government and for-profit businesses being the other two sectors).

The Union of International Associations tracks NGOs and IGOs (see Table 1) and listed 20,929 traditional international NGOs in 2005, such as universal membership organizations and internationally oriented national organizations. Another 30,581 special NGOs (such as religious orders) brings a total of 51,509 international NGOs.[10]

Despite their rising numbers, NGOs raise some puzzles. NGOs have no armies. They command no states. They collect no taxes and can compel no one to follow them or to contribute to their treasuries. So what is the source of their power? NGOs trade in the currency of ideas, especially ideas of good and evil, right and wrong. The ideas compel, even when the organizations cannot. NGOs attract support more than they can enforce compliance.

Many NGOs are transnational moral entrepreneurs, agents who act as reformers or crusaders to change rules out of an ethical concern to curtail a great evil.[11] Their very names are often cast as moral imperatives, proclaiming both what they value and what they do—as in Human Rights Watch and Save the Children.

Governments have legal authority, but advocacy NGOs rely on moral authority. Generally, where states have military power and MNCs have economic power, the strength of NGOs lies in their idea power. They seek to occupy the only high ground available to them, the moral high ground. If an NGO can succeed in redefining a problem as a moral issue, then it will have a greater chance of prevailing, because states and MNCs may not be able to speak credibly as bastions or brokers of morality. Religious organizations in particular often have well-developed ethics and rich institutions, resources that are useful to transnational advocacy networks and greatly needed today given the ethical and institutional gaps of globalization (discussed in Chapter 13). For example, consider the importance of church networks and leaders in abolishing slavery, as well as the importance of Archbishop Desmond Tutu in the South African anti-apartheid movement. Morally, religious organizations have legitimacy speaking on moral issues and a treasure chest of well-developed ideas available for use by transnational advocacy networks. Tactically, religious organizations can pool their power with other religious and civil society groups and use their direct pulpit access to citizens (who may be business or government decision makers) as well as their ability to attract media. Although secular NGOs may not command institutional networks (such as schools and hospitals) that are as extensive as those of religious organizations, they also develop and trade in moral ideas, such as when environmental transnational advocacy networks construct and promote environmental ethics.[12]

NGOs have information power. Especially when networked transnationally, NGOs may have access to grassroots information about how particular policies affect particular people, information that governments or IGOs overlook or do not have. People with greater and cheaper access to information technologies can force greater transparency. Transparency and sunshine politics are important tools for NGOs. By expanding the information base of a public's or elite's discussion of previously closed matters, NGOs often impose a "Dracula" test: Will a particular policy or practice be able to survive in the daylight? Transparency alone can do much to shrink both government and corporate abuses. And discussions about opening the decision-making process to greater transparency help to reframe issues as moral issues, again moving the issue to where NGOs have some home court advantage.

Some NGOs can use the power of their reputations as a "force multiplier" to enhance their values, ideas, and information power. Reputational power may derive from important, well-known, or respected figures who are members of the group, or it may come from the NGO's own track record of strong advocacy. Or, like an MNC, an NGO may build a "brand name" around the quality and reliability of the organization's information products. Some NGOs emphasize building such reputational power through quality information products—for example, Transparency International's work on corruption worldwide.

NGOs use media and communications power as a force multiplier for their values, ideas, and information power. Although NGOs vary in their skills and access to global media, they do have certain media advantages. Global media simplify issues to attract wider audiences and compete against ever-shorter sound bites to sell their products. If NGOs often emphasize how policies or practices affect particular individuals or groups, or how global issues present clear moral choices, then they may be able to attract media attention. NGOs can use media as a megaphone for their message if they understand the care and feeding of the media and can deliver compelling stories and good pictures with clear good guys and bad guys in arenas where government, IGO, or corporate responses may be slow or lack credibility. Because MNCs may have huge marketing investments in their brand names and do not want these brands sullied or their reputations trashed, even the threat of negative media coverage can bring greater attention to an NGO's ideas. It is more difficult to wield this media power against naked, anonymous commodities and unknown, unbranded companies, however. Media and communications power are important to groups that trade in ideas. NGOs, like others who can persuade but cannot compel, must be good salespeople as well as good preachers to effectively mobilize their ideas.[13]

NGOs also have female power. Women are underrepresented in the governments of states and in leadership positions in MNCs and IGOs. But women are better represented as both leaders and members of NGOs. Women make up the majority of people on the planet, but many governments, MNCs, and IGOs throw away or underutilize the talents of more than half their populations. This can be a moral and strategic advantage for NGOs. They can provide a means for women to participate in and affect international structures that may otherwise exclude them. If women perceive NGOs as more likely to represent their interests, then this may add to popular support and reputational advantages for NGOs. Like human society in general, NGOs are certainly not free from gender conflicts; relative to other institutions, however, NGOs are more likely to be run by and for women, taking up issues—such as women's rights, human smuggling, and female genital mutilation—that other institutions ignore.[14]

NGOs also have the power of individuals. They do not accept the traditional view that states are the fundamental unit in international politics and that individuals can have little effect. Believing individuals can make a difference, they create ways for them to do so. Without getting bogged down in the question of which came first, the idea or the activist, activists are central to NGOs.[15] Individuals may start NGOs, splinter NGOs, and use NGOs as vehicles for both personal and community expression and activism. Even when NGOs network internationally in large campaigns, testimonials of how global problems affect real people are an enormous strength for NGOs, helping to put a face on global politics.

Although NGOs are generally legal groups that do not advocate violence, they share similarities with other nonstate actors that form transnational networks in pursuit of particular ideas: terrorists. For both groups, "victims" are strategically useful if a wider society empathizes with them either as innocent civilians, or because people can envision themselves in their shoes. A "poster child factor" also helps NGOs gain sympathy and concrete identification with their cause from either elites or masses. For terrorists, sympathy with the victims helps generate fear that is out of proportion to the acts they commit. The similarities end there, however, because terrorists target their victims with the intention of harming them, whereas NGOs target their groups with the intention of aiding them. The success of their very divergent strategies, however, depends on the esteem with which society regards them, their cause, and their targeted groups.

Another source of power for NGOs can be consumer power. If an NGO can credibly argue a connection between a corporate policy and some objectionable wider practice, then it can marshal the market power of customers, consumers, or shareholders through boycotts or pressure on advertisers and shareholders, among other forms of market pressures. This can put an economic price on objectionable practices that may make corporations or states notice and respond to NGO concerns. This is how "dolphin- safe tuna" came to a grocery store near you.

NGOs have network power. They are typically organized as flatter, more flexible organizations than governments, IGOs, or MNCs. This may give NGOs greater speed to respond to pressing global issues or to get their views to the media faster than some government bureaucracies. More important, networks allow NGOs to forum shop—that is, to press their issues in more favorable state or international arenas. For example, with the help of human rights NGOs, the families of four U.S. churchwomen who had been abducted, raped, and murdered while serving the poor in El Salvador in 1980 are trying to have their day in court in the United States.

Feeling that justice was blocked in the political system of El Salvador, NGOs helped to move the issue to the United States, where there are stronger legal protections on human rights and greater access to the international media.[16] What can possibly be accomplished by this? The women are dead and the civil war has ended. But NGOs trade in ideas. The trials may help shed light on the poor human rights practices of governments, as well as open a new forum for hearing other cases blocked by local governments. Margaret Keck and Kathryn Sikkink refer to this as the "boomerang pattern":

> Governments are the primary "guarantors" of rights, but also their primary violators. When a government violates or refuses to recognize rights, individuals and domestic groups often have no recourse within domestic political or judicial arenas. They may seek international connections finally to express their concerns and even to protect their lives. When channels between the state and its domestic actors are blocked, the boomerang pattern of influence characteristic of transnational networks may occur: domestic NGOs bypass their state and directly search out international allies to try to bring pressure on their states from outside.[17]

Keck and Sikkink are correct that transnational networks often emerge as a back way around blocked local politics, but NGOs go global for other reasons as well. Even when an NGO enjoys a good relationship with the local government, as Jody Williams and the ICBL enjoyed with the Canadian government, the goal may require activating a global advocacy network. Or NGOs may perceive a better target internationally, even when local politics are not blocked.

Outlining these potential sources of power for NGOs does not mean that all organizations have all of these resources at all times. Some NGOs have denser networks that allow them to pool or access greater resources than others with fewer or sparser networks. Some issues are easier to put a face on than others. Environmentalists who are concerned with global climate change have thus far lacked a poster child, which makes it difficult for them to translate the abstractions of global warming into more concrete concern over those who are affected. If ideas are a crucial source of power for NGOs, then clearly some ideas are better than others, and some play better to particular audiences than do others. Some NGOs can craft an easily recognizable and universally sympathetic message better than others. NGOs that promulgate values and ideas with greater resonance will have advantages over NGOs with narrower and less appealing idea bases. For example, it may be easier to mobilize against child labor than to save the dwarf wedge mussel. As in all things political, context matters in assessing NGO power. It is easier to sell the idea that child labor is wrong in rich countries than in poor countries.

Different NGOs have different resources, expertise, networks, issues, and contexts. However, NGOs use their variegated supplies of people power in several common ways. NGOs raise consciousness regarding issues with elites, masses, or both. NGOS often practice resurrection politics, taking issues previously thought dead on arrival (such as landmines and debt relief), and raising them up onto the public and political agenda. NGOs also practice ideas, information, and symbolic politics, expanding the idea base surrounding issues by introducing new or discrediting accepted information, or introducing alternative norms by which to evaluate information. NGOs frame or reframe issues. NGOs change language, beliefs, and symbols surrounding issues (which may later translate into behavioral changes). NGOs move issues to a forum more amenable to a favorable response. NGOs practice leverage politics by enlisting celebrities to bring attention and leverage to their cause.[18]

NGOs change government, IGO, or MNC policy, or individual behavior. They adapt or create institutional structures or advocacy networks to further particular issues. NGOs practice Dracula politics, transparency politics, and sunshine politics, shining a light on problems and shaming and naming perpetrators. Like Dracula, many abusive international practices can only persist in the dark, and die off when exposed to the light of day. NGOs monitor compliance with norms or regimes once created, making actors live up to the promises they make.

Yet NGOs come with their downsides as well. Coordinating action among a wide variety of eclectic organizations with different agendas, cultures, and operating procedures is difficult. As Andrew S. Natsios, head of the U.S. Agency for International Development (USAID) and former director of the NGO World Vision, observes, "Many of the institutional players really don't like or trust one another."[19] The abilities of NGOs to work well with states, IGOs, and MNCs in combating transsovereign problems is often inhibited by poor communication and coordination among the various groups. IGOs, MNCs, and government foreign policy organizations too often deal with NGOs in an ad hoc, nonsystematic manner. Increased numbers of NGOs in complex combinations make coordination, communication, transparency, and accountability difficult, as is determining which groups should be included in government and IGO decision processes. NGOs may compete against one another for the supremacy of their ideas, funding, and recognition. As private-sector organizations, who do NGOs speak for or answer to beyond their own governing boards or contributors? NGOs have asymmetrical resources and influence, and even within NGO advocacy networks, conflicts arise between Northern and Southern NGOs. Who guides the network? Southern NGOs are critical of donor-driven development. However, media power and reputational power can also be tools to check and balance rising NGO power. For example, public pressure against the Red Cross decision to use funds donated to the victims of September 11 for other purposes indicates these tools can yield results. Many NGOs adopt voluntary codes of conduct and publish their budgets to encourage transparency and accountability. The same questions that plague corporate codes of conduct, however, may be raised regarding NGOs: How seriously are these codes implemented, and what are the sanctions if voluntary codes are not implemented? Because NGO power frequently derives from moral and reputational capital, NGOs may have greater incentives to address democracy deficits than other organizations.

NGOs AND GLOBALIZATION: OPEN SOCIETIES

Open societies, open technologies, and open economies make it easier to establish, organize, and run NGOs. We are witnessing an explosion of NGOs worldwide precisely when liberalizing trends are spreading. The spread of democracy lowers the barriers to forming NGOs. Some of the hallmarks of democracy are freedom of expression and freedom of association.

Certainly, the democratization process encourages the creation and spread of NGOs as part of the effort to build civil society. One Hungarian activist, Andras Biro, describes his efforts: "For the first time in forty years we are reclaiming responsibility for our lives."[20] Nondemocratic governments may make NGOs illegal, fearing they may form a base of opposition to the government. Organizing people in states with closed political systems —North Korea, for example—can be a dangerous proposition to the activist, who risks imprisonment, torture, and death.

The fears of authoritarian governments are justified because NGOs have worked to bring about the fall of nondemocratic regimes. Lester Salamon notes that "under Pope John Paul II Catholic churches in Warsaw, Gdansk, Krakow, and elsewhere in Eastern Europe provided a crucial neutral meeting ground and source of moral support for those agitating for change in the latter 1980s. The Lutheran Church played a comparable role in East Germany."[21]

NGOs also have been instrumental in pressing for open societies and advocating for human rights and democratization. During and after World

War II, NGOs kept the issue of human rights on the international agenda when state representatives meeting to construct the postwar international organization (which became the UN) tried to exclude or water down such concerns. States were skeptical about including human rights in the UN Charter. They feared a loss of sovereignty over internal treatment of their citizens if the topic were broached in the UN Charter. But NGOs such as the American Jewish Committee, the American Bar Association, the National Association for the Advancement of Colored People, and the League of Women Voters reminded states that the failure to protect individual and minority rights after World War I had contributed to the conflict and genocide of World War II. Sustained lobbying by NGOs ensured that respect for human rights became one of the four purposes of the United Nations set forth in its Charter, and that the Charter called for the creation of a UN Commission on Human Rights. NGOs provided expert advice and research and helped to draft language and lobby for the adoption of the 1948 Universal Declaration of Human Rights and other subsequent human rights treaties.[22]

NGOs often are created as the locus of resistance to nondemocratic regimes. One dramatic example was the emergence of NGOs in opposition to the military dictatorships in Argentina and Chile in the 1970s and 1980s. Citizens who criticized or were seen as threats to these regimes, as well as many who happened to be in the wrong place at the wrong time, became the *desaparecidos,* or the "disappeared." They were kidnapped, imprisoned, tortured, and killed. In a final insult, the children of many of the disappeared were sold to childless military couples. "One torturer estimated that about sixty babies passed through [his clandestine detention center], and that all but two—whose heads were smashed against the wall in efforts to get their mothers to talk—were sold."[23]

> Children were tortured in front of their parents, and parents in front of their children. Some prisoners were kept in rooms no longer or wider than a single bed. And the torture continued for days, weeks, months, even years, until the victim was released or, more often, killed. The sadistic brutality did not always even end with the death of the victim. "One woman was sent the hands of her daughter in a shoe box." The body of another woman "was dumped in her parents' yard, naked but showing no outward signs of torture. Later the director of the funeral home called to inform her parents that the girl's vagina had been sewn up. Inside he had found a rat."[24]

In a heroic response to such brutality, a small group of middle-aged mothers of disappeared children organized in 1977. Calling themselves the

"Mothers of the Plaza de Mayo," at first they numbered only fourteen. Frustrated in their attempts to locate their children, they began a silent vigil every Thursday afternoon in the main square of Buenos Aires in front of the president's residence and seat of government. Although the women were subject to harassment and attack (some of them even disappeared themselves), they continued their efforts to draw attention to the atrocities of the military government. They were followed by the "Grandmothers of the Plaza de Mayo," who attempted to trace and recover the trafficked children and babies. Quickly, the numbers of these groups swelled across Latin America, and they soon became the NGO known as Federación Latinoamericana de Asociaciones de Familiares de Detenidos-Desaparecidos (FEDEFAM, Federation of Families of Political Prisoners and Disappeared Persons). Working with a wide transnational network of NGOs, they fought the military dictatorships and their brutality, always at great personal risk to themselves. When the dictatorships eventually fell, these groups helped to build democracies, strengthen the legal protections for human rights, and reunite political prisoners with their families.[25]

NGOs promote open societies in many ways. They expose the abuses of regimes by tracking facts and disseminating information, as well as by mobilizing public opinion to try to end the abuses and improve conditions. They communicate with decision makers locally and globally, dispensing information and advocating for legal changes. They are direct service providers, offering education, advocacy, and legal aid services. They teach citizens what their rights are and "how to act upon them."[26]

NGOs AND GLOBAL TECHNOLOGIES

Open technologies also greatly assist the formation and maintenance of NGOs, as seen in the landmines case. Any group with a personal computer can maintain a database and mailing list, circulate a newsletter, or e-mail information to its members. Cheap and easily available information technologies allow citizens to more easily gather and disseminate information and ideas, identify members, solicit funds, network with others, and coordinate activities. Decentralization of phone and communication companies has made it more difficult for governments to control access to or censor use of the Internet. Many governments still try to censor the Internet, although as former President Clinton put it, the attempt may be as futile as "nailing Jello to a wall."[27] NGOs also rely on independent news media to directly communicate with the public, publicize their causes, and pressure governments. For example, Greenpeace relies on satellite communications technology to launch direct media campaigns on environmental causes. When Shell Oil wanted to dump retired oil rigs at sea, Greenpeace seized one of the rigs, the Brent Spar in the North Sea, and broadcast directly from there. Media wishing to cover the controversy had to rely on Greenpeace's satellite uplinks, putting Shell and the British government at a disadvantage in getting out their side of the story. Eventually Greenpeace was successful in mobilizing public opinion to pressure the oil companies (via boycotts) and governments to stop decommissioning oil rigs at sea, in large part because of Greenpeace's effective media strategies and use of communications technologies.[28] Media attention also raises public attention and funding to NGOs.[29] Compelling media coverage of the 280,000 killed in the tsunami in Southeast Asia brought record contributions. The International Red Cross discontinued fund raising on January 26, 2005, because so much money (over 1.2 billion in contributions) had been pledged in the first 30 days.[30]

NGOs also actively work to expand the reach of open technologies. Typically, international NGOs work with local counterparts, thereby spreading technology. For example, when the NGO known as Women Waging Peace began, one of the first projects it funded was equipping women's peace organizations with laptop computers and providing training in the use of the Internet and media strategies. In similar ways, environmental NGOs press for the adoption of cleaner, greener technologies, such as water- and air-filtration systems that make it possible for factories to emit fewer toxic pollutants into the environment. Public health NGOs disseminate health technologies such as filtration systems for drinking water and X-ray and diagnostic equipment as parts of their disease eradication programs.

Development NGOs disseminate technologies for agriculture, irrigation, water systems, and electrification.

NGOs AND OPEN ECONOMIES

The rise in NGOs is also facilitated by open economies. The information economy brings advantages for NGOs that trade in ideas and information. Economic liberalization also allows money to flow freely across borders, allowing NGOs to solicit and contribute money across sovereign jurisdictions. In addition, capitalism encourages the growth of the private sector, of which NGOs are a part. Free-market economies tend to emphasize grassroots, private-sector responses to societal problems rather than top-down, state-sponsored solutions. NGOs thus fit with the entrepreneurial and pluralistic norms of capitalist societies. Privatization of the economy is even encouraging the growth of NGOs in China:

The Chinese government and party have announced a new slogan. They refer to it as "small government, big society." They want to shrink government, and they want to grow society, that is, they want to shift functions from the government sphere to the private sphere....The vehicle for doing this, in part, is to create a private nonprofit sector that can shoulder some of the social tasks that have traditionally, in recent Chinese history, been state functions.[31]

Although there are limits to the independence of Chinese NGOs, the small government, big society approach shows the spread of ideas concerning the value of the private sector.

NGOs vary in their receptiveness to open markets, however. While some trade and professional associations lobby to expand free-market arrangements such as the WTO and the North American Free Trade Agreement, social advocacy NGOs in the labor, development, environment, and human rights arenas are often skeptical of economic globalization—as seen in the Battle in Seattle.

NGOs AND STATES

NGOs may work with donor states to aid people in weak or failing states, as relief and development organizations such as Catholic Relief Services are doing with the Afghan and Pakistani governments in ministering to the needs of Afghan refugees. Donor governments increasingly prefer to funnel aid through NGOs rather than give it directly to recipient foreign governments that may be neither efficient nor accountable in their use of the funds. In states undergoing transitions, new institutions may be weak and lack proven track records.

Governments believe that aid funneled through NGOs is more politically acceptable than direct government-to-government assistance. They believe that NGOs can better reach the grassroots level and are more efficient because they involve less bureaucratic red tape and overhead. They also believe that working with NGOs helps to develop the private sector.

Many see contracting out to NGOs as a win–win situation. The government "has found an efficient, less costly means of carrying out its legislative mandate, while the [NGO]s have discovered a relatively dependable source of money, available in large sums."[32]

There are downsides, however. NGOs risk losing the perception of their autonomy and independence from governments if they rely too heavily on state sources for funding, which can compromise an NGO's reputational power. One NGO executive director described the question of accepting funding from the USAID as the dilemma of not wanting "to look like the tool or the fool of the United States government."[33]

NGOs are also concerned about the potential for conflict of interest between their goals and the goals of government donors. NGOs are concerned about becoming dependent on states for resources and potentially neglecting their traditional bases of support. They do not want to change their focus to fit more closely with government priorities in order to attract state funding. The "strings" that may come attached to accepting government funds (such as the "Buy American" requirement that goes along with U.S. aid dollars) may detract from their program principles (such as, whenever possible, to buy locally to help the local economy). And NGOs fear that the reporting and accounting procedures required of government contractors may make them more bureaucratic, entangle them in red tape, and drive up costs (the results donors wanted to avoid by funneling aid through NGOs in the first place).

When recipient governments are cut out of the aid loop because of corruption or weakness, animosity may develop between state institutions and NGOs. For example, in Haiti, short term concerns for quick and accountable projects may come at the cost of developing long term state capacity in crucial sectors such as education and public health.[34]

As citizens turn to NGOs as service providers, the state is further undermined, which can perpetuate a feedback loop. NGOs may become involved to attend to problems that states are not addressing. In so doing, NGOs may further undermine the capacity and legitimacy of states, which can exacerbate transsovereign problems rather than fight them.

As an increasing number of states collapse, this is becoming a larger issue. Many NGOs do not wait for a state invitation before entering a country to provide services. This is especially true in countries such as Somalia, Rwanda, and states of the former Yugoslavia where there were no working state governments. If NGOs fulfill the functions of states where there are no functioning sovereignties, then how are sovereign states rebuilt? Some NGOs are not concerned with the question. Individuals in need, not states, are their priorities. They regard sovereignty not only as a right to nonintervention (negative or *de jure* sovereignty), but also as a responsibility to provide some benefit to citizens (positive or *de facto* sovereignty). If states are unable or unwilling to fulfill their responsibilities toward individuals in need, then NGOs must step in.

The NGO known as Doctors Without Borders (Médicins Sans Frontières) developed specifically out of the creed that physicians would provide medical assistance where needed, regardless of whether government actors existed or welcomed them.[35] Save the Children developed out of the

efforts of a British woman, Eglantyne Jebb, to provide aid to the children vic-
timized by World War I, regardless of whether they were the citizens of a winning or losing state in the conflict.[36] Similarly, Amnesty International began in
1961 with the efforts of a London lawyer, Peter Benenson, to win the release
of some Portuguese political prisoners. His campaign soon developed into a
worldwide watchdog and advocacy organization for human rights. Amnesty
International is fundamentally concerned with protecting the human rights
of individuals and groups. It is less concerned with the effect its activities may
have on state capacities. Faith-based NGOs likewise are concerned with
higher principles. The major world religions existed before the advent of the
modern nation-state, and they likely will be around long after its demise.
Although not necessarily antagonistic to states, faith-based NGOs feel they
answer to a higher authority than the state.

Understandably, then, NGO–state relations are often adversarial
because NGOs are often created to curb the abuses of states or to attend to
issues that states ignore. In Central America in the 1970s and 1980s, NGOs
were targeted by the state, particularly four types of NGOs—human rights,
training, humanitarian, and organizations that represented those citizens
uprooted by the violence and civil wars:

> Physical attacks on NGOs started in the 1970s. . . . Governments
> responded violently to the growth of peasant groups in El Salvador, and
> to the expanding Guatemalan cooperative movement. Self-help farmers'
> organizations were also systematically destroyed. In the 1980s uprooted
> populations were methodically subjected to harassment, army abuses,
> disappearances, and assassinations. . . . Governments have tried to destroy
> human rights NGOs since their creation. They have endured because of
> personal courage, the mix of financial, technical, and political support
> received from international NGOs, and survival strategies crafted to
> suit local conditions. For example, the Catholic Justice and Peace
> Commission and El Salvador's Tutela Legal operated under the umbrella
> of church protection. . . . Most survived because of strong international
> links and small, low budget, decentralized administrative operations;
> some . . . perished. NGOs documenting and researching issues related to
> uprooted populations were also intimidated because of their infringe-
> ment into policy areas considered the armed forces' preserve.[37]

One sign of the adversarial relationship between states and NGOs is the
establishment of "front" NGOs by governments "to infiltrate and gather
information on the NGO community. These 'government NGOs' are of
particular concern in the field of human rights."[38]

NGOs AND STATE FUNCTIONS

Not only do some NGOs commandeer more resources than do many states, but also the activities of these organizations increasingly impinge on functions that previously were jealously guarded by states. NGOs carry out health, education, welfare, and development functions, especially in weak states. In abdicating educational functions to NGOs, states lose opportunities to proselytize and socialize their youth in the viewpoints of the state, as many poor Muslim states are realizing. They had welcomed Saudi charities that set up madrasas, or schools that educate students in the Wahabi form of Islam, an extreme fundamentalist version of that religion. Even in strong states, NGOs are increasingly active in issues such as economic and environmental policy making, land use, and even arms control.

Although only states make laws and sign treaties, NGOs increasingly help to write laws and treaties, lobby for their acceptance, and monitor compliance with them:

> Nongovernmental organizations play an increasingly prominent role in international environmental institutions, participating in many activities—negotiation, monitoring, and implementation—traditionally reserved to states. . . . For better or worse NGOs are now a regular part of the cooperative process. Within limits, they address delegations as a state would. They participate actively in the corridor diplomacy which is so central to negotiations, receive documents, present proposals, and are consulted by and lobby delegations. These changes are all relatively new. . . .[39]

Because environmental problems are indifferent to state borders, and the information and technical expertise needed to make environmental policy often exceeds the capacity of states, NGOs provide valuable services on environmental issues. They can track environmental problems and effects on resources across borders, presenting the wider perspective needed to write treaties and create and monitor regimes. For example, in negotiations on global warming, "NGOs set the original goal of negotiating an agreement to control greenhouse gases long before governments were ready to do so, proposed most of its structure and content, and lobbied and mobilized public pressure to force through a pact that virtually no one else thought possible when the talks began."[40] NGOs also provide policy research and development, serve on government delegations, participate in small working-group meetings at international negotiations, monitor state commitments, report on negotiations, lobby participants, and facilitate negotiations. NGOs even have legal standing in most of the major environmental treaties negotiated in the last decade.[41]

NGOs also develop and implement "soft law," or the voluntary codes that often serve as stepping stones to the eventual passage of "hard law." Finally, NGOs may change attitudes and behavior directly, changing the ideas held by individuals and institutions. In this way, NGOs may work to manage pressing global problems with or without the cooperation or capacity of states.

NGOs WORKING BEYOND SOVEREIGNTY

NGOs go beyond sovereignty not only in their organization, membership, and activities across borders, but also in their ideas and the targets of their activities. If the public sector is shrinking or not growing as fast as the private sector, then the nonprofit part of the private sector may be needed as a counterweight to the for-profit private sector. Citizens who believe globalization is out of balance or tilted in favor of corporations look to NGOs to serve as a check or counterbalance. Networks of international environmental NGOs, for example, directly pressure MNCs and the public to change environmental behavior. They do not restrict themselves to lobbying governments and IGOs for strengthened legislation or treaties. By taking their arguments directly to corporations, consumers, and public opinion worldwide, NGOs operate beyond sovereignty. McDonald's stopped using styrofoam burger packaging largely in response to NGO-fueled direct-public and consumer-pressure campaigns.[42] NGOs often prefer direct action campaigns to legislative campaigns because state actions to pass and enforce laws on particular environmental problems can be slow and are only effective within a country's territory with enforcement measures. Direct corporate and consumer campaigns, on the other hand, can achieve results across borders without government legislation or enforcement. Convincing individuals not to purchase products made from rain-forest wood can be more effective in preserving rain forests than pursuing government legislation.

Religious organizations also work beyond sovereignty, often targeting their activities directly toward individuals and communities. Religious organizations reach globally with rich, interconnected institutions in health care, education, relief and development, and refugee and resettlement services. These institutional infrastructures are so extensive, well developed, and multifaceted that some consider it misleading to consider a religious organization "just another NGO" because NGOs may be more singular in focus and rarely run global networks of schools and hospitals, for example.

Too often, when religious organizations are considered at all in international relations, they are presented as parties to ethnic and nationalist conflict and opposed to globalization, change, and modernity (or what some have termed "Jihad versus McWorld"). Samuel Huntington, among others, predicts an inevitable clash of civilizations with religious groups at war—that is, of the West versus the rest. There are alternative views, however.[43] Corporations and states are neither the only engines of globalization nor its only beneficiaries. Religious organizations have long been globalizing forces, spreading ideas, institutions, flows of people, and capital across international borders. Today, religious organizations (like other civil society groups) continue to play active roles in globalization as both global actors and mediating institutions, responding to the challenges of globalization and offering alternative ethical visions of it (beyond market or consumer dynamics).[44]

NGO ideas go beyond sovereignty. Corporations see the world as a market. In this material world, people are all customers, shareholders, or investors. States see globalization as a world to be governed. People are either governed or ungovernable, citizens or those beyond government and posing problems (for example, illegal immigrants, refugees, terrorists, and criminals). Social advocacy NGOs, however, present alternative ethical visions, seeing a world in which we are all people with fundamental human dignity. Rather than mere opposition to globalization as the clash of civilizations "Jihad versus McWorld" formulations suggest, NGOs present more varied and constructive reactions to globalization. Their formation of transnational networks that work to acknowledge and bridge North–South conflicts may represent one of the best ways for globalization to proceed "with a human face,"[45] thereby unleashing greater human potential than can mere materialism—and for more of the planet than currently participates in the benefits of globalization.

As NGOs (sometimes in partnership with IGOs or MNCs) fill functions instead of states and challenge the ideas of states, what effect does this have on sovereignty? Keck and Sikkink note, "If sovereignty is a shared set of understandings and expectations about state authority that is reinforced by practices, then changes in these practices and understandings should in turn transform sovereignty."[46]

The state is not going away. Rather, it is increasingly contracting out. As states downsize and decentralize in response to the pressures of globalization, and as states innovate in response to global problems, nonstate actors such as NGOs perform functions previously assumed by states and promote ideas that have unintended consequences for sovereignty.

ENDNOTES

1. Michael Warner, "2 billion unite to help the starving," *The Herald Sun* (July 4, 2005).
2. The One Campaign, "ONE Reaction to G-8 Communique," July 8, 2005, <www.one. org/g8countdown.html>.
3. Jubilee USA, "Debt and AIDS," February 2002, <www.jubileeusa.org/jubilee.cgi? path=/learn_more/&page=debt_AIDS.html>.
4. Rick Rowden, "A World of Debt," *American Prospect* 12(12). <www.prospect.org/ print/V12/12/rowden-r.html>.
5. International Campaign to Ban Landmines, "A Brief History of the ICB," <www.icbl.org>; Richard Price, "Reversing the Gun Sights: Transnational Civil Society Targets Land Mines," *International Organization* 52(3): 613–644; Anne Peters, "The International Campaign to Ban Landmines," case study for the Global Public Policy Network, <www.f 2.efresh.de/public/peters%20gpp%202000.pdf>.
6. Margaret E. Keck and Kathryn Sikkink, *Activists Beyond Borders* (Ithaca, NY: Cornell University Press, 1998), 1.
7. Lester M. Salamon, "Interview on Global Civil Society," *Johns Hopkins Gazette,* Jan. 3, 2000, <www.jhu.edu/~gazette/2000/jan0300/03lestxt.html>; Lester M. Salamon, *Global Civil Society: Dimensions of the Nonprofit Sector* (Baltimore: Johns Hopkins University, Institute for Policy Studies, Center for Civil Society Studies, 1999).
8. Technically speaking, the International Committee of the Red Cross (ICRC) is not an NGO. It is an international organization with a mandate assigned to it by international law in the 1864 Geneva Convention and in subsequent protocols. However, unlike most other IGOs, it is not composed of states as members, and it is not part of the UN system. Instead, it is made up of national Red Cross and Red Crescent societies, which are NGOs. Thus, the ICRC resembles a hybrid NGO–IGO. See Andrew Natsios, "NGOs and the UN System in Complex Humanitarian Emergencies," in Thomas G. Weiss, Leon Gordenker, and Thomas Watson (Eds.), *NGOS, the UN and Global Governance* (Boulder, CO: Lynne Rienner, 1996), 73–74.
9. Maryann K. Cusimano, "Operation Restore Hope: The Bush Administration's Decision to Intervene in Somalia," in *Pew Case Studies in International Affairs* (Washington, DC: Georgetown University, Institute for the Study of Diplomacy, 1995).
10. Union of International Associations (Ed.), *Yearbook of International Organizations 2005* (Brussels: K.G. Saur Verlag, 2005).
11. Howard S. Becker, *Outsiders: Studies in the Sociology of Deviance* (New York: Free Press, 1963), 148; Ethan A. Nadelmann, "Global Prohibition Regimes: The Evolution of Norms in International Society," *International Organization* 44(4): 482.
12. Paul Wapner, "Politics Beyond the State: Environmental Activism and World Civic Politics," in John S. Dryzek and David Schlosberg (Eds.), *Debating the Earth: The Environmental Politics Reader* (New York: Oxford University Press, 1999), 518–519; Paul Wapner, *Environmental Activism and World Civil Politics* (Albany: SUNY Press, 1996).
13. Richard E. Neustadt, *Presidential Power and the Modern Presidents: The Politics of Leadership from Roosevelt to Reagan* (New York: Free Press, 1990).
14. Valerie Sperling, Myra Marx Ferree, and Barbara Risman, "Constructing Global Feminism: Transactional Advocacy Networks and Russian Women's Activities," *Signs: Journal of Women in Culture and Society* 26(41): 1156.
15. Martha Finnemore notes that actors and interests are constituted in interaction. Martha Finnemore, *National Interests in International Society* (Ithaca, NY: Cornell University Press, 1996).

16. Specifically, the families filed a civil lawsuit under the Torture Victim Protection Act passed by the U.S. Congress in 1991. "This federal statute permits civil lawsuits against those accused of committing torture or murder under actual or apparent authority, or color of law, of any foreign nation. As the language intended, victims or their representatives may confront not only the perpetrators of such crimes but also their superiors who bear responsibility." Information available at <www.pbs.org/wnet/ justice/elsalvador.html>.

17. Margaret E. Keck and Kathryn Sikkink, *Activists Beyond Borders* (Ithaca, NY: Cornell University Press, 1998), 12.

18. Margaret Keck and Kathryn Sikkink, *Activists Beyond Borders: Advocacy Networks in International Politics* (Ithaca, NY: Cornell University Press, 1998).

19. Andrew S. Natsios, "The International Humanitarian Response System," *Parameters* (Spring 1995): 68–81.

20. Andras Biro as quoted in Lester M. Salamon, "The Rise of the Nonprofit Sector," *Foreign Affairs* (July–Aug. 1994): 112.

21. Salamon, "The Rise of the Nonprofit Sector," 113.

22. Felice D. Gaer, "Human Rights, Nongovernmental Organizations, and the UN," in Weiss et al., *NGOS, the UN and Global Governance,* 52–53.

23. Jack Donnelly, *International Human Rights,* 2nd ed. (Boulder, CO: Westview Press, 1998), 43; John Simpson and Jana Bennett, *The Disappeared: Voices from a Secret War* (London: Robson Books, 1985), 110.

24. Donnelly, *International Human Rights,* 39; Simpson and Bennett, *The Disappeared,* 225.

25. Donnelly, *International Human Rights,* 44–45.

26. Gaer, "Human Rights," 52–53.

27. "Nailing Jello in China," *Washington Post* (Aug. 26, 2000): A16.

28. Samuel Passow, *Sunk Costs: The Plan to Dump the Brent Spar, and Epilogue* (Cambridge, MA: Harvard University, 1997) (John F. Kennedy School of Government Case 1369), <www.ksgcase.harvard.edu/case.htm?PID=1369>.

29. Richard Morin, "Aid from the Gray Lady?", *The Washington Post* (March 13, 2005): B05.

30. "International Red Cross Needs for Tsunami Relief Met," January 26, 2005, <http://www.redcross.org/pressrelease/0,1077,0_314_4043,00.html>.

31. Salamon, "Interview on Global Civil Society."

32. Charles Downs, "Negotiating Development Assistance: USAID and the Choice between Public and Private Implementation in Haiti," in *Pew Case Studies in International Affairs* (Washington, DC: Georgetown University, Institute for the Study of Diplomacy, 1994), 7.

33. Ibid., 8.

34. Ibid., 4–5.

35. Médicins Sans Frontières, *Life, Death, and Aid: The Médicins Sans Frontières Report on World Crisis Intervention* (New York: Routledge, 1993).

36. Angela Penrose and John Seaman, "The Save the Children Fund and Nutrition for Refugees," in Peter Willetts (Ed.), *The Conscience of the World: The Influence of Nongovernmental Organisations in the UN System* (Washington, DC: Brookings Institution, 1996), 241–248.

37. Peter Sollis, "The State, Nongovernmental Organizations, and the UN," in Willetts (Ed.), *The Conscience of the World,* 194–195.

38. Willetts, *The Conscience of the World,* 6.

39. Kal Raustiala, "States, NGOs, and International Environmental Institutions," *International Studies Quarterly* 41 (Dec. 1997): 719–724.

40. Jessica Tuchman Mathews, "Power Shift: The Age of Nonstate Actors," *Foreign Affairs* 76 (Jan.–Feb. 1997): 55.

41. Raustiala, "States, NGOs, and International Environmental Institutions," 726–731.

42. Wapner, "Politics Beyond the State," 518–519.

43. Max L. Stackhouse (Ed.), *God and Globalization,* Vols. 1 and 2 (Harrisburg, PA: Trinity Press International, 2001); Benjamin Barber, *Jihad vs. McWorld*; Samuel Huntington, *The Clash of Civilizations.*

44. Maryann Cusimano Love, "Globalization, Faith Based NGOs, and Peacebuilding" Presentation to the Leadership Institute Conference on Religion and U.S. Foreign Policy, Washington, DC, October 12, 2005; "Bridging the Gap: Globalization and Religion," *Journal of Social Thought,* 2003; R. Scott Appleby, "Catholic Peacebuilding," America Magazine 189(6) (Sept. 8, 2003), <www.americamagazine.org/gettext.cfm?articleTypeID=1&textID=3145&issueID=449>.

45. United Nations Development Program Report, *Globalization with a Human Face* (New York: United Nations, 1999).

46. Margaret E. Keck and Kathryn Sikkink, *Activists Beyond Borders* (Ithaca, NY: Cornell University Press, 1998), 37.

CHAPTER FOUR

Multinational Corporations

Power and Responsibility

Richard A. Love and Maryann Cusimano Love

Globalization makes a business such as Nike possible. The founders of Nike began by selling Tiger athletic shoes, a Japanese brand, in the U.S. market in 1964.[1] Phil Knight (later Nike's co-founder and CEO) soon realized that rather than peddle another company's brand, he could use the global supply chain to produce shoes inexpensively in Asia and sell them in developed economies for a handsome profit. Over time, Nike has shifted production from Japan and South Korea to Indonesia, Taiwan, the Philippines, Vietnam, and China in search of lower costs. The labor costs are approximately $1.44 per pair of shoes. Nike buys a pair of shoes from its suppliers for approximately $20, adds transportation and marketing costs plus a profit, and sells the pair to a retailer for $40. The retailer then adds its costs and profits and sells the product to consumers for $80 and up.[2]

But why buy Nike shoes rather than another brand? The sportswear market is competitive and crowded. More than sportswear, Nike sells ideas. In Greek mythology, Nike is the winged goddess of victory, which gave rise to the company's signature winged "swoosh" symbol and the practice of making

its products into wearable advertisements. Through aggressive global marketing and promotions, Nike sells an image, a lifestyle, and a creed more than a
product. Close your eyes and you would be hard-pressed to tell the difference
between Nike shoes and other brands. Nike is selling the dream of being a
world-class athlete, the desire to belong to the club of premier athletes, and the
inspiration to become the best you can be. You may never be able to play golf
like Tiger Woods or basketball like Lebron James or Michael Jordan, but you
can wear the same brand of shoes. As one Nike official puts it, "We don't know
the first thing about manufacturing. We are marketers and designers."[3] Nike
pioneered the process of creating a market through product design, promotion, and innovative global advertising, and of associating the Nike brand
swoosh with world-class athletes, male and female, of every race, from the inner
cities to the more privileged classes. Nike went from $2 million in sales in
1972[4] to more than $14 billion in revenues in 2005[5]—or more than the GDP
of Iceland and 100 other states.[6] And Nike is willing to pay for the marquee
endorsement, offering a reported multiyear $90 million endorsement contract
to LeBron James in 2003 when he was an 18-year-old awaiting the NBA draft.

The same global media that made Nike a household name and a billion
dollar company, however, also made it vulnerable to charges of labor and
environmental abuses. NGOs and activists concerned with labor, environment, and human rights brought public attention to the sweatshop practices
of Nike factories abroad and the disconnect with Nike advertising themes
of empowerment, diversity, and women's equality. Reports of sexual harassment of women workers in Nike production facilities in Asia and of seven-
year-old children stitching soccer balls in Pakistan gained media and
consumer attention. A young woman in China making Nike shoes would
have had to work nine hours a day, six days a week, for fifteen centuries to
earn the yearly salary of Nike CEO Phil Knight.[7]

At first, Nike's response to the critics was denial. The factories are subcontractors to Nike, the company argued; therefore the employees who
made Nike products were not company employees, and Nike was powerless
to change subcontractors' behavior. When abuses at Nike's Indonesian factories came to light in the early 1990s, the Nike general manager in
Indonesia responded, "It's not within our scope to investigate. I don't know
that I need to know."[8] The workers were lucky to have jobs at all, Nike representatives maintained, and it was not the company's fault if governments
in developing countries had poor labor or environmental laws or enforcement. By some estimates, more than 80 percent of the workers are young
women. The company says these workers are good at sewing. Critics say
they are more docile and easily intimidated than older workers or men.

"I don't think the girls in our factories are treated badly. It's better than no job at all, than harvesting coconut meat in the tropical sun," said a company official.[9] But as the controversy grew, so did negative media coverage (undermining Nike's $280 million annual advertising budget at the time).[10] Reports continued of women being beaten by supervisors and forced to work 65 hours a week for $10 in pay without bathroom or meal breaks. Nike began to admit there were "isolated problems" that it was determined to correct, yet an internal audit done by the company and leaked to *The New York Times* revealed that workers in one factory were exposed to 177 times the legal limit of carcinogens, with 77 percent of the workers suffering from respiratory problems. Rather than being unaware, the company knew of the problem.[11]

In 1998, consumer boycotts and shareholder unrest grew while company profits fell. CEO Phil Knight announced a new course for the company. Nike would (1) increase the minimum age of its workers to 16 in apparel factories and 18 in shoe factories; (2) follow U.S. Occupational Safety and Health Administration standards for air quality at factories abroad, especially seeking substitutes for the adhesives that were causing respiratory problems in workers; and (3) allow local NGOs and independent auditors to monitor and release information about the company's subcontracting factories. Nike joined corporate responsibility groups such as the Apparel Industry Partnership, the Fair Labor Association, the Global Alliance for Workers and Communities, and the United Nations' Global Compact, and increased community development loans for small business and education projects in the areas of its overseas production facilities.[12]

Nike believes it is now a leader in corporate responsibility, and some observers credit Nike with raising standards and awareness of the issues across the apparel industry. Critics charge the pronouncements are more public relations efforts than real accomplishments and that Nike's corporate codes of conduct are voluntary and unenforceable. Nike still does not pay workers adequate wages or allow international NGOs that might be more critical to participate in monitoring. College students have organized into groups such as the Workers Rights Consortium, the Clean Clothes Campaign, and United Students Against Sweatshops to pressure suppliers of college sportswear not to use sweatshop labor. Nike has withdrawn advertising sponsorships of athletic programs at many colleges and universities such as Brown University, the University of Michigan, and even for a time Phil Knight's alma mater, the University of Oregon, due to student protests of Nike and activism in these groups. While collegiate licensing is only a small part of Nike's overall business, image is everything for a company like

Nike, especially image among young athletes, the company's key market. As CEO Phil Knight acknowledged, "The brand is sacred. I messed that up."[13]

The Nike example illustrates pressing debates that will be discussed in this chapter about the rising power and global reach of multinational corporations (MNCs). Do MNCs raise labor and environmental standards internationally or are they leading a global race to the bottom? Are states effectively able to regulate MNCs, or do MNCs have increasing power over states? Are MNCs exercising their power responsibly, and how do they interact with other actors (NGOs, IGOs, and states) in setting standards for responsible corporate behavior? Are corporate codes of conduct a way to go beyond sovereignty to manage pressing global problems and to make private actors better stewards of the public good? Are they nontariff trade barriers or protectionist measures that hurt development in the Global South? Or are they merely a way for corporations to deflect state regulation and public criticism? What are the effects on sovereignty?

THE GLOBAL REACH OF MNCs

Multinational corporations are enterprises that control and manage commercial ventures and operations outside their countries of origin.[14] Fueled by open economies and distributed technology, enhanced financial mechanisms and the ease of transborder trade, their power and influence is growing dramatically. In 2005, of the world's 150 largest economic entities, 95 (63 percent) are multinational corporations, not countries.[15]

MNCs are not new. Foreign investment, banking, resource extraction, trade, and production were part of imperial expansion and colonial trade by the Romans, Venetians, Genoese, English (British East India Company), and Dutch (Hudson Bay Company). What is new is the global reach and influence of modern multinational firms. In 1969, there were 7,000 MNCs.[16] By 2005, there were 70,000 multinational parent corporations with 690,000 foreign affiliates worldwide.[17] The sheer scope of these entities represents a rise in private, nonstate power across the globe.[18]

MNCs are a diverse and eclectic group. MNCs are organized internationally to achieve several corporate objectives: open new markets and gain access to new consumers, acquire natural resources at lower costs, and produce efficiencies through the reduction of production and labor costs or by taking advantage of lower environmental regulations and taxes. Some allow "host" subsidiaries greater autonomy; others insist on a high degree of "parent" company control. They range from corporations such as Royal Dutch Shell Oil and British Petroleum, which extract raw materials and natural resources; to manufacturers such as Siemens, Coca Cola, Samsung, Walt Disney Corporation, and Nokia, which produce consumer goods; to companies such as Lloyd's of London, Barclays, and Credit Suisse, which offer banking, investment, insurance, and consulting services. Many MNCs are hybrids of these functions—such as IBM, which sells computer and business products and provides consulting services.

MNCs are not simply companies that engage in foreign trade or market their products abroad. MNCs engage in foreign direct investment (FDI) and carry out production in foreign countries. They engage in FDI because local firms have a "home court advantage." They are more knowledgeable about local business practices and consumer tastes, and it is generally less costly for local firms to do business in their home markets. Foreign firms that seek entry into a locality have an incentive to "hook up" with local firms. FDI may take many forms: buyouts of a foreign subsidiary, joint ventures, licensing agreements, or strategic alliances. The top recipients of FDI are the United States, the United Kingdom, and China, while all of Africa combined receives only 3 percent of global FDI.[19]

MNCs AND THE GLOBALIZATION DEBATES

The global reach of MNCs can be a positive force for profits as well as development. MNCs can assist in transferring capital and know-how to the developing world and often bring in capital goods and technology. They may create jobs and assist in developing training and education programs. MNCs also provide avenues for access to other international markets and exposure to the region that may result in additional investment. MNCs often have the incentive to develop a host state's infrastructure to maximize commerce. UN Secretary-General Kofi Annan notes that business is the best hope of alleviating global poverty, and that "economics, properly applied, and profits, wisely invested, can bring social benefits within reach not only for the few but for the many, and eventually for all."[20] For example, Nakornthon Bank works with poor villages in rural Thailand, offering training and small, low-interest loans for microdevelopment. As a result, "[i]ncome levels skyrocketed. . . . People returned to work in the village. The payoff rate for loans was 100%, and our bank now has a loyal base of customers. The project has been so successful that development agencies and the government have kept asking how it was done."[21]

But there is also a downside. MNCs can overwhelm a locality and drive traditional firms out of business. MNCs normally insist on maintaining control over technology, management, and intellectual property, which means that technology and expertise are never transferred to the host state. CEOs, boards of directors, and shareholders may all be located in developed countries so that MNC decision making and profits flow disproportionately back to developed economies. MNCs often become advocates at the local level for changing local systems in favor of gaining preferential treatment. These take the form of tax breaks, favorable laws, dispute resolution mechanisms, and ownership and property rights. In seeking lower-cost alternatives globally, MNCs exploit resources, labor, and the environment, leading critics to charge that MNCs lead a race to the bottom in worker, regulatory, safety, and environmental standards.

For example, one IGO, the International Labor Organization, reports that 250 million children under age 14 are working half- or part-time.[22] Some of these children work for MNCs or their subcontractors, such as in high-profile cases (e.g., Nike) and as forced child slave labor in Africa picking the cocoa beans for major chocolate companies like Nestles, Mars, and Hershey. Yet MNCs counter these arguments by noting that working conditions are generally no worse and are often better than those of the local employers, and prominent MNCs are likely to comply with standards that are higher than those maintained locally.[23] They also argue that age and wage standards cannot be universal but must be considered in the context of local economies.

MNCs AND OPEN ECONOMIES

It is no surprise that many MNCs are in the forefront of lobbying to increase free market economic systems and reduce barriers to FDI and trade.[24] Whether through regional trading blocs such as NAFTA, CAFTA or the EU, or multilateral free trade agreements such as GATT and the WTO, MNCs generally seek to decrease tariff and nontariff barriers to trade and investment, as well as decrease state control of state subsidies to key industries.[25] MNCs lobby states and multinational organizations to open up economies to market forces. In the democratizing states of the former communist bloc, Latin America, and South Africa, MNCs are pressing for protections of private property and the free movement of goods and capital in their newly liberalized economies. Once established, MNCs or their local affiliates often try to get the local host states to protect their advantages by enacting exclusionary laws and giving the established MNCs monopoly advantages. Host countries can be subject to intense pressure to acquiesce to MNC investment already in place and to appease international pressure to open their economies and markets. Each year, at least $365 billion is spent in protections and subsidies by developed states, which keep many of the goods from developing countries out of developed countries. This is why developing countries question how "free" the free market and free trade really are—free for whom?

Many MNCs have pushed hard for harmonizing international law, although some prefer to exploit differences in legal codes in local venues that profit foreign companies. For example, on the night of December 2–3, 1984, Union Carbide Chemical Corporation was responsible for the worst industrial accident in history. Its plant in Bhopal, India released forty-one tons of poisonous gas, killing 14,000 people and inflicting permanent disabilities on 150,000 more:[26]

> As people ran with their families, they saw their children falling beside them, and often had to choose which ones they would carry on their shoulders and save. This image comes up again and again in the dreams of the survivors: in the stampede, the sight of a hundred people walking over the body of their child. Iftekhar Begum went out on the morning after the gas to help bury the Muslim dead. There were so many that she could not see the ground—she had to stand on the corpses to wash them.[27]

After the accident, Union Carbide worked to see that a more lenient judge in India would hear the case so that the company could avoid having to face a stricter U.S. judicial system that might have imposed hefty fines. After years of legal battles, the MNC agreed to pay survivors generally $2,857 for each death (a few received as much as $4,286). Ninety-five percent of the victims who were compensated received only $500. These are the gross figures; subtract the legal fees, administration costs, and sometimes bribes survivors had to pay to stake their claim, and most survivors actually netted much less. These settlements are low even by Indian standards. The standard compensation offered by Indian Railways is $5,714 for accidental death and $3,429 for disability, which is disbursed quickly and with minimal additional fees.[28]

While some companies prefer to take their chances with local legal codes, most MNCs have a powerful interest in harmonizing global laws to decrease transaction costs. It is costly for them to do business internationally when each country has separate standards and rules for trade, investment, intellectual property rights, and so on. MNCs push for greater harmonization to decrease their costs and risks and create a better business climate, and they stress that developing states benefit as well from such measures. They argue that international trade, global supply chains, and FDI helps developing economies and that developing states are better served by a system of established rules with transparent and regular procedures for making rules than by trying to negotiate ad hoc agreements with more powerful actors on a deal-by-deal basis. In general, developing countries have agreed and voluntarily signed up for these international agreements out of a desperate desire to attract MNCs and FDI that may bring jobs and alleviate poverty in their countries. Often, developing states fear that not to acquiesce will mean that FDI and jobs will go elsewhere and that they will be left behind. Not surprisingly, there is unequal bargaining power among the parties. Developing states riddled with poverty cannot compete with the deep pockets of MNCs that lobby state governments and the international bodies that create the rules of the road for international trade. Developing countries often lack the resources to send delegations to the international meetings that decide the rules.

MNCs AND OPEN TECHNOLOGIES

Cheap, easily available global information and transportation technologies make the growth of MNCs possible. New technology also creates new industries and presents the hope of "leapfrog" development for some developing countries. For example, Bangalore, India, is now a thriving center of the computer services industry. India is aided by an educated workforce that speaks English and a time zone differential that allows Indian computer programmers to service the information systems of companies in many developed countries while the companies' main workforces sleep. Although this model is not replicable in many developing countries, many developing countries aspire to the Bangalore model as they seek to profit from the global economy and technologies. It is not only large corporations that benefit from global technologies, but also medium, small, and even microbusinesses that can go global thanks to the Internet and shipping companies such as United Parcel Service. Australian sheepskin slippers, Turkish towels, and Mexican crafts can be marketed and sold to consumers globally without large overhead investments.

MNCs may disperse technologies in the countries where they operate as a part of their business presence, but some MNCs restrict technology transfers out of concern for retaining proprietary and competitive advantages. MNC and state interests regarding technology transfers are not always correlated either. The U.S. government wanted limits on the sale of powerful computer encryption technologies so that law enforcement officers would have the keys to crack the codes of illicit actors using encrypted communications. Businesses did not want a lucrative new market in encryption programs regulated—and business won. States often want to restrict the sale of sensitive technologies that can have military applications, whereas MNCs may favor trade in dual use technologies. The German, British, and U.S. governments fought the Persian Gulf War against an Iraqi army that German, British, and U.S. firms had supplied with weapons and the ingredients to make chemical weapons. In 1987, while the United States, Japan, and Norway were officially allied to fight the Cold War against the Soviet Union, both a Japanese and a Norwegian MNC—Toshiba and Kongsberg—violated export restrictions and sold technologies to the USSR to help it build quieter and less detectable nuclear submarines.

MNCs AND OPEN SOCIETIES

The relationship between MNCs and open societies is hotly contested. In states such as China, Indonesia, and Nigeria, MNCs have pursued a capitalist economic agenda without pushing hard for democratic political reforms. In corporatist societies (such as Chile and Argentina in the 1970s), authoritarian regimes ally with and co-opt business elites, protecting business interests while repressing democratic rights and principles. Order is central for the stable, efficient, and profitable conduct of commerce. Political upheavals, even those associated with democratization, create costs and uncertainties for the investment, production, and trade of MNCs. Do MNCs favor repressive regimes as a way of ensuring a stable, orderly, and favorable business environment? In Nigeria, Shell Oil was accused of helping to arm and finance a repressive military government, as long as the government helped to keep Shell's oil flowing. According to Mr. Austin Onuoha of the Nigerian Center for Social and Corporate Responsibility, the oil companies claim to invest millions in "community development," but the money they spend to hire security forces is counted as part of their Corporate Social Responsibility (CSR) projects. Royalty and licensing agreements between the government and oil companies on how oil money will be split are not made public, and Nigerians see little benefit from the oil industry. The World Bank estimates that Nigeria has received over $350 billion from the oil industry since 1960, but corrupt business-government practices mean that the money has not benefited the Nigerian people, 70 percent of whom live on less than $1 a day.[29] Exxon–Mobil, Chevron-Texaco, and Petronas, with the aid of World Bank loans, have been building and operating an oil pipeline since July 2003 in Chad and Cameroon, extremely poor countries with two of the most corrupt governments in the world according to ratings of government corruption by Transparency International.[30] These governments are not democratic, and human rights and environmental abuses have been reported in the project. The government of Chad has illegally diverted World Bank loans for military purchases. According to Fr. Antoine Berilengar, SJ, a representative on the Petroleum Revenue Oversight and Control Committee in Chad, the oil companies do not hire local workers to build the pipeline, but instead bring in Mexican, Egyptian, and Filipino workers, who do not pay local taxes and are less concerned about environmental and human rights abuses in Chad.[31]

Others disagree. One study analyzed MNC cash flows to developing states from 1975 to 1986 to determine whether MNCs are more or less likely to invest in repressive states with abusive human rights records. The study concluded that "MNCs in general [avoid] locating larger amounts of [foreign investment] in those [developing states] that consistently implement fewer human rights reforms. . . . [It] does not appear that MNCs view a lack of human rights reforms and the high use of repression in [developing states] as acceptable."[32] MNCs may not favor repressive regimes for several reasons. Arbitrary exercise of police powers and military brutality affect MNC executives, workers, and citizens alike. Repressive regimes may rule by force rather than law, but respect for law (and particularly for property rights) is crucial for successful business transactions. Without the rule of law, business transactions become uncertain and potentially more costly.

The effects of MNCs on human rights can cut both ways. Sometimes just the presence of a multinational corporation can place the international media spotlight on local worker conditions, creating a "race to the top."[33] Concerned with protecting their image, companies will pressure local governments to improve workers' conditions or take the initiative to do so themselves. A multinational's instinct to protect its reputation, and thereby its bottom line, can have the beneficial side effect of exporting a concern for human rights. This may be MNC specific, however, as image-conscious branded products have a greater concern for reputation than do unbranded or extractive industries. Thus, even though MNCs generally promote open economies and open technologies, their record of promoting open societies (including respect for human rights) is contested and mixed.

RISE OF PRIVATE POWER: DO CORPORATIONS RULE THE WORLD?

We are witnessing the rise of private power. Even in developed states, private standard-setting bodies, contract law, and private arbitration mechanisms now fulfill regulatory functions once performed by states.[34] In emerging information technology sectors, this trend of private governance is particularly pronounced. For example, Internet commerce is often untaxed and self-regulated by companies, not by governments. A private body assigns Internet domain names and adjudicates disputes.

The critique that corporations rule the world[35] runs even stronger given the unequal bargaining power of developing states against MNCs. In developing states, grinding poverty leads states to court corporate investments because the private sector has more money than the public sector, and state-to-state aid and investment is drying up. Developing states often do not have the capacity to check corporate power, as law and order and institutions may be fragile at best in countries without resources to adequately pay, staff, equip, and train government officials. As corporations enter developing states, they often do so free of taxes (in export processing or free trade zones). The most powerful companies are also able to avoid taxes even in developed states. For example, the majority of U.S. corporations do not pay their full income tax rates. "U.S. taxpayers subsidize U.S. businesses to the tune of almost $125 billion, the equivalent of all the income tax paid by 60 million individuals and families.[36] Export processing and free trade zones are often free of other government regulations (environmental and worker safety law enforcement).

MNCs encourage the multilateral organizations to pressure developing states to privatize their remaining state-controlled industries, such as telephone systems. Although it is done in the name of rationalizing economies and making them more efficient, privatization may also bankrupt governments because poor countries do not have the tax bases to finance basic government services—education, public health systems, clean water, roads, public safety, customs, courts, and law and order. When telephone revenues, for example, are the primary government income and the business is privatized, after the initial windfall in money from the sale of state-owned industries, states may lack financing for basic government activities.

Many states have no tradition of payment of personal income taxes, and governments are too weak to be able to get citizens to pay taxes (this is a problem in Russia, Italy, and many Caribbean states). Because so many goods and incomes go untaxed, states charge exorbitant tax rates on those few goods or people that they are most able to tax—for example, automobile imports, or imports of washers and dryers. This creates greater incentives to smuggle, commit fraud, and evade taxes because taxes on the few pay for the services provided to the many. Inability to finance basic good governance makes all government ripe for corruption because government workers are not paid a living wage and need to supplement their income with "overtime" (the euphemism for bribery in the Caribbean). Thus, governments in developing states often do not have the capacity to challenge or contain the power of corporations, and the actions of corporations (to lower their tax rates, privatize industries, and pay government bribes) may actually contribute to the weakness of state structures and governance.

Developing states sign agreements that allow corporations to operate in their territories; such arrangements are examples of bargaining among unequal parties. A developing state is signing a contract with a gun to its head—the gun being grinding poverty, unemployment, and death—and it is trying to lure corporations with its low wages and lack of unionization. A state has less ability to wrest many guarantees of good behavior, local management power, and so on from a corporation when poverty is a state's comparative advantage. The corporation has many poor states from which to choose, and it is often not building plants and capital investments from scratch but is contracting out to local subsidiary agents. The corporation can easily find another poor country that will accept its business. Literally, beggars can't be choosers.

Even strong states cannot contain corporate power alone because MNCs operate across international borders, and jurisdiction often stops at the border. Attempts to harmonize legal codes to help law enforcement work multilaterally across borders or to rein in corporate power are weak, new, and without teeth. They often are exports of Western contract law and procedures that are advantageous to corporations. They show how corporations can get laws that work for them rather than how states can effectively counterbalance the weight of corporations.

The rise of private contract law epitomizes the rise of private power in the global age. A relatively few MNCs exercise power to create law in their own interest and for their own benefit. Developed states not only condone this practice, but also support the trend because they hope to rationalize commercial disputes and benefit from increased tax revenue from their MNCs. The result is that local governments, especially in the developing world, experience a loss of control and influence over trade practices within their borders.

MNCs worldwide are seeking ways to fashion enforceable rights. One way they do this is by expanding private contract rights in order to avoid foreign laws. This is generally not a difficult challenge. The three most common ways of doing so are through choice of law, stabilization, and arbitration clauses. These clauses ensure the protection of property rights, right of entry into new markets, and the availability of natural resources. The effect of these clauses is not only to avoid the law of a host state, but also to develop a legal system outside traditional sovereign courts. It sets up external and private law to resolve disputes, based on the concept of the sanctity of the contract and party autonomy. Courts allow these contractual decisions, often with little or no respect for the public policy concerns of host states. Courts will often refuse to hear a controversy where clauses using alternative dispute resolution (ADR) or arbitration exist in a contract. For example, when Mexico denied Metalclad, a New Jersey metal company with toxic waste by-products, permission to build a facility because of concerns about the site's environmental impact, the NAFTA court required Mexico to pay $16.7 million to Metalclad in breach of contract compensation for earnings Metalclad could have received if it had been allowed to proceed. The case had a chilling effect, sending the message that private contract rights take precedence over sovereign concerns.

Choice of law clauses are perhaps the most common among the three and allow a party to avoid local law and remove issues from local courts by predetermining where controversies will be resolved and under whose law the controversy will proceed. Arbitration clauses determine who has the authority to decide controversies and usually include a reference to the specific rules that will guide arbitration. Arbitration courts have established procedures and remedies that can be adopted or amended by the terms of a contract, and the arbiters have powers similar to those of sovereign courts.[37] A stabilization clause freezes the law at the time the contract is entered into and prevents law made after a contract enters into force from having any effect on a controversy's ultimate disposition.

These clauses allow a contract to avoid the laws of sovereign states and propel controversies to a "supranational" legal arbitration body or to a court outside a local jurisdiction. Thus, they insulate foreign corporations from uncertain and unfamiliar locales. Yet this new worldwide body of private law runs counter to the sovereign concept of regulating affairs within one's state borders. These contract provisions are increasingly offensive to local legal and political institutions and affront the concept of equal dignity of sovereigns. The contract terms effectively let the parties opt out of local jurisdictions. Private contract also gives MNCs a procedural advantage since many parties in the developing world lack the expertise needed to enter into agreements with a full appreciation of the costs and consequences. Firms located outside such traditional centers of commerce as New York, London, and Geneva may also lack the resources to fully protect their rights under contract. The travel costs alone may make pursuing a dispute prohibitively expensive.

While MNCs work to enlarge the private sector and earn profits, they also can facilitate the illicit economy. Money laundering, for example, is facilitated by the international banking and financial services industries. Between $640 billion and $1.6 trillion are laundered through banks every year.[38] Money laundering involves complex financial and product transactions that mask and perpetuate the underlying criminal activity that generates the illegal gains. Money laundering finances the most egregious crimes in the global age from terrorism and drug trafficking to human trafficking, illegal arms transactions, and nuclear smuggling. It propagates corruption and corrupt regimes by providing an avenue for using illegal proceeds. Money laundering also provides a way to avoid taxes.

The underlying purpose of money laundering is to conceal the true source of the funds for free use in the open market. The mechanisms for laundering money are complex and diverse and often involve multiple transactions among several (and sometimes unsuspecting) parties, fraudulent alterations of prices for goods, and outright bribes and kickbacks. Money laundering is illegal, but some MNCs prefer the benefit of the infusion of capital. The most common form of money laundering is transfer pricing, where prices are falsified on import and export transactions in order to generate artificial values. The difference between the fair value and the artificial value is pocketed. Real estate transactions and securities trades, often between related parties and improperly priced and paid for in order to shift money across borders, offer creative avenues for generating illegal capital flight. Money laundering activities must first hide the source of the illegally received proceeds and then provide a legitimate explanation for the proceeds. Through complex, layered transactions, money laundering blends criminal proceeds into the licit economy.

Most laundered money winds up in the United States and Europe through Western banks. As the beneficiaries of such an enormous inflow of capital, the banking and financial establishment traditionally favors informal money laundering controls and reporting requirements. Government efforts to curtail money laundering have failed in the past because of the lack of "buy-in" from the private banking and business sector. The attacks of September 11 changed how many political and commercial leaders view money laundering, and they increased state and IGO pressure to regulate these industries. However, state anti–money laundering policies rely on industry self-reporting of suspicious financial activities. Even in strong, developed states, governments do not have the capacity to curtail money laundering without cooperation from the private sector, which demonstrates the extent of private power.

PRIVATE POWER AND PUBLIC RESPONSIBILITY

Does the rise in private power mean MNCs can act with impunity and with no responsibilities to the common good? No. States still regulate corporations, although, as the previous section showed, MNCs may have the ability to forum shop—to have a dispute heard in a forum more amenable to their interests—and may have deeper pockets and better lawyers to evade states' regulatory capacities. However, other bodies are stepping in to fill these governance gaps. IGOs increasingly regulate global commerce, and MNCs are increasingly self-regulating, in part because of greater attention to corporate social responsibility (CSR).

There has been an explosion of CSR mechanisms for MNC voluntary self-regulation, especially in the past decade. They fall into several categories. First are internal codes of conduct and statements of company core values. Most MNCs have or are writing such in-house codes of conduct. They are frequently broad, general guidelines, such as those of Levi Strauss, which state in part that the company will "embrace diversity; be responsible, but not afraid."[39] Optimists say these codes of conduct are important barometers of changing corporate culture. They are attempts to educate and socialize large workforces into common values, such as the belief that good corporate citizenship is as important as bottom-line profit margins. Even broad guidelines can be helpful as a first step to more specific standards and concrete benchmarks. They are also useful because they provide a public commitment by companies to particular values. If company behavior falls short later, then the codes of conduct and value statements give reformers a basis to discuss criticisms. Skeptics argue that the codes are little more than window dressing designed to diffuse criticism and deter regulation, that they are frequently so vague and general that they cannot be implemented or measured, and that they are unenforceable because they are voluntary.

The second genre of CSR measures are sector-wide agreements among companies within an industry to adopt certain standards or shared best practices. Sector-wide agreements can vary from narrow technical codes on specific industrial processes to broader statements of larger CSR commitments such as the Apparel Industry Partnership to improve working conditions in the garment industry. Some sectors may develop regimes or private professional bodies to monitor and report on implementation and compliance with the standards. Many rely on the companies themselves to choose methods of monitoring and transparency to show implementation and compliance with adopted codes.

The third approach is to develop general CSR codes that are not specific to particular organizations or industries. For example, the UN Global Compact challenges businesses to comply with nine principles drawn from UN treaties concerning human rights, labor, and the environment. The Global Compact is quite broad, as are other codes such as the Coalition for Environmentally Responsible Economies (CERES) principles on environmental responsibility, and the Caux Round Table Principles for Business. These set overarching corporate goals and rely on companies to decide their own monitoring and transparency measures. The International

Standards Organization (ISO) has its own set of standards, such as ISO 9000 and ISO 14000. The Council on Economic Priorities has SA 8000. These standards come with more specific operational guidelines and measurable benchmarks to monitor progress and implementation. As industries "buy into" ISO labeling and accreditation, they agree to undergo regular inspections and audits by accredited auditors.

There are vigorous debates over which codes, standards, and reporting techniques are more effective in raising corporate behavior and improving labor, human rights, and environmental practices. Many are too new to be fully assessed; MNCs are still in the adoption and implementation phases. Some critics argue that internal audits are more rigorous because only people familiar with the processes and layouts of particular factories will know where to look for problems or abuses. Others argue that internal audits lack credibility because companies have few incentives to blow the whistle on themselves. This leads to arguments in favor of external auditing procedures, but again this raises questions of competence and independence. Although using professional auditors trained in particular standards sounds like an attractive way to ensure more reliability and comparability of results over time and across companies, critics argue that auditors hired and paid by industry have few incentives to issue negative reports and "bite the hand that feeds them." NGOs argue they can offer independent assessments and should be a part of the process, but this again raises the questions of which NGOs should be involved and how qualified they are to make assessments. Some corporations do not see NGOs as unbiased and believe NGOs will never acknowledge improvements in corporate practices or issue favorable assessments. Some corporations such as Nike choose to involve local NGOs as a form of outreach to the local community where facilities are located. International NGOs question whether local NGOs are more easily manipulated to issue favorable reports because they may fear losing local jobs or may not have the resources or access to complete information to make fully informed and more critical judgments. Finally, reporting varies widely. Some reports are little more than press releases, while others are substantive and concrete assessments. The Global Reporting Initiative is a UN-sponsored effort to increase the comparability, credibility, and consistency of CSR reporting and to highlight best practices.

The UN is taking action to increase CSR. The Secretary-General has established a special representative on human rights and transnational corporations, in response to the 2005 UN High Commissioner on Human Rights' report, which noted that "there are gaps in understanding the human rights responsibilities of business."[40] Over the past decade, the UN has been reaching out to businesses, forming more partnerships with civil society, both MNCs and NGOs. Partnerships vary widely on topic and breadth. "Who Cares Wins" brought together twenty financial institutions with combined assets of over $6 trillion to develop guidelines on socially responsible asset management. "Health in Your Hands" is a public health campaign to promote hand washing with soap. Development projects help provide market access for indigenous micro businesses, such as the Shea Butter Production Inititative in Burkina Faso or the UNIDO Automotive Industry Partnerships.[41]

This explosion of CSR codes and implementation techniques shows a rising acknowledgment of the power of private governance and the power of corporations to implement social and economic change. It testifies to increased attention among corporations to the "triple bottom line," a rising awareness that the environmental and social as well as economic concerns can affect business.

But why is there such growth in CSR standards and attention? Margaret Keck and Kathryn Sikkink argue that blocked politics cause activists to take their grievances to other forums,[42] including pressuring MNCs to focus on issues ignored by states. Because groups cannot lobby for environmental or human rights change in China or Vietnam, NGOs and moral entrepreneurs search for a forum where democratic politics, independent media, voters, and consumers can exert some pressure for change rather than be excluded. MNCs based in developed democracies are open to civil society pressures, whereas authoritarian states may be less susceptible to these pressures. Blocked politics explains some of the increased attention to CSR, but not all of it.

Corporations often argue that they are not the correct targets for labor, environment, and human rights demands and that governments should be pressured to change. Yet even in democratic countries such as the Philippines, MNCs are targeted for CSR campaigns rather than governments, even though politics are not blocked and procedures exist for citizen advocacy. Moving away from state activism and toward CSR campaigns focused on MNCs is a way for NGOs to focus their resources and to get more bang for the buck. NGO resources are constrained, so dividing them among 191 countries may mean there will be too few resources for any one NGO to be effective, reach critical mass, and overcome threshold effects of inertia and the status quo. Just as opponents of the U.S. civil rights movement in the 1960s tried to splinter the movement by arguing that local state governments should decide the civil rights of African Americans, NGOs find that if they successfully lobby MNCs to raise standards, the effects will be felt broadly across borders, rather than in one country only.

There are other reasons for the increased number and attention to CSR codes as well. Virginia Haufler studied private standard setting across a variety of sectors and industries and concluded that risk assessments, concern for reputation, and corporate learning were critical factors in adoption and implementation of CSR standards.[43] Previous crises certainly can alert decision makers to the risks of ignoring CSR. In this way, the CERES principles were created in response to the *Exxon Valdez* oil spill.[44]

Only publicly traded companies are vulnerable to shareholder activism, and unbranded products are less vulnerable to consumer boycotts and negative publicity. But ideas matter in pressuring corporations to address global issues. Even unbranded food products are vulnerable to claims about health and safety. And not all brands are equally vulnerable to CSR pressures. It matters what values and ideas the brand proclaims. Nike was vulnerable not just because it was an identifiable brand, but also because it advertised values of diversity, emancipating young people, and women's equality. This made it more vulnerable to brand devaluation by charges that women were being abused and children were forced to work in diverse countries. Similarly, Mattel Toys has been a leader in the Business Anti-Smuggling Coalition because, as its chief security officer puts it, "The last thing we can afford is Barbie on drugs." A shipment of Barbie toys compromised by drug traffickers would be extremely harmful to the toy's wholesome role model identity in a way that would be less damaging to a shipment of Lysol toilet bowl cleaner. It is not just the brand, but the ideas behind the brand that give traction to CSR efforts.

Several factors are important in determining whether an MNC will adopt CSR standards. The internal leadership of the company is important. Anita Roddick, founder of The Body Shop, has been a force for CSR within her global franchise and throughout the wider business community.[45]

Company culture, the competitive environment, and consumer demand are important. In recent years, Chiquita Brands International, the banana importer and exporter, has changed its company practices and adopted some of the industry's most enlightened age and wage policies. But if grocery stores and consumers do not factor CSR into buying decisions, then CSR policies may not be sustainable,[46] either because leadership will backslide if companies believe CSR policies are a drag to their costs that competitors avoid and consumers do not reward, or because the company goes under.

Shareholder activism also can spur attention to CSR as investments are withdrawn from companies with poor practices or ratings. For example, the Interfaith Center on Corporate Responsibility, a coalition of 275 religious investors from the Catholic, Jewish and Protestant communities with a combined investment total of over $110 billion, promotes socially responsible investing. TIAA–CREF, the largest private pension fund in the United States, negotiates directly with companies regarding their CSR records. The U.S. Jesuit Conference has been negotiating with Occidental Petroleum, accused of questionable human rights practices in Colombia. As a result of this shareholder activism, Occidental has agreed to write and implement a corporate code of conduct.[47] Shareholder activism does not produce quick results. Daniel Rosan of the Interfaith Center compares it to the effect of water on stone, a slow reshaping that can produce great effects over time.[48] Media attention to corporate shortcomings spurs MNC attention. Companies engage not only in immediate damage control within a targeted company but also in longer-range policy change across companies as MNC leaders learn lessons from the crises of others. NGOs threaten to use the sticks of negative media publicity, protests, consumer boycotts, and shareholder activism, but they can also offer the carrots of positive attention to favorable examples of CSR. Too often, however, NGOs rely more on the sticks than the carrots. Finally, IGOs and states can offer incentives for positive CSR behavior and threaten regulation or adversarial treatment to companies with negative CSR records. A combination of these factors leads companies to decide whether and which CSR policies may enhance their reputation, change their market share, or reduce their risks of adverse consumer, media, IGO, government, or shareholder reactions.

Through the CSR movement, MNCs are finding that open societies, open technologies, and open economies cut both ways. These infrastructures facilitate the operations and profits of MNCs. Yet global technologies that broadcast MNC advertising also serve as an instant and global megaphone for news of corporate abuses. Open societies allow critics to organize and apply political pressure to MNCs, and open economies allows consumer and shareholder market pressures to be brought to bear on MNCs.

MNCs, STATE FUNCTIONS, AND SOVEREIGNTY

Beyond social, environmental, and economic regulatory and arbitration functions, MNCs are also performing security functions that traditionally have been reserved for states, such as arms control negotiations, homeland security, disarmament, de-mining operations, and military activities. Functions traditionally reserved for the state are increasingly contracted out. For example, in 1978, when the negotiation process for the chemical weapons convention (CWC) began, few government officials had more than superficial knowledge of the chemical industry. U.S. arms control negotiators requested assistance in the negotiation process from the chemical industry.

Recognizing the importance and effect of the chemical weapons ban for their industry, the chemical manufacturers assisted the U.S. government. An industry group, the Chemical Manufacturers Association (CMA), helped develop procedures for on-site inspections and participated in special sessions of the Conference on Disarmament. What resulted was an unprecedented industry–government partnership in forging an effective treaty. For industry, opposition to the treaty not only would have resulted in negative publicity, but also would have risked the creation of a treaty that was technically unsound and detrimental to industry interests.

The private sector has a critical role to play in protecting critical infrastructure from illicit activities, from terrorism to cybercrime. Ninety percent of critical infrastructure in the United States is privately owned.[49] Critical infrastructures are systems whose incapacity or destruction would have a debilitating effect on a state's defense or economic security. They include telecommunications, electrical power systems, gas and oil industries, banking and finance, transportation, water supply systems, government services, and emergency services. The events of September 11, 2001, highlighted security concerns over physical and electronic threats to critical infrastructures. Such threats are global, blur public–private distinctions, and render states, commercial interests, and individuals mutually vulnerable and interdependent.

There are limits to what governments can effectively do to provide adequate security in the absence of private cooperation. Private infrastructure owners are in the best position to understand the technology and vulnerabilities and must recognize their stake in infrastructure protection. Many challenges to effective public–private cooperation exist. Trust needs to be established between stakeholders. Public–private lines of communication and response activities need to be clarified. Technical training and expertise needs to be furthered in both sectors. Government and industry leaders must recognize the need for cooperation. Process buy-in is essential to success.

Governments of the strongest states are ceding security functions to private companies. For example, with troops stretched thin in peacekeeping operations abroad, the British government debates whether to hire and regulate private mercenary forces that would work alongside British troops. And with the U.S. government's blessing, mercenaries trained the Bosnian army. The U.S. government itself uses private security companies to disassemble former Soviet nuclear weapons through the Cooperative Threat Reduction program, as well as to conduct de-mining operations in support of U.S. troop deployments.

Private organizations are increasingly seen not just as contributors to global problems but as crucial players in designing and implementing effective global solutions. We are witnessing a creative period as new private organizations arise and increased partnerships are formed with business to manage pressing global problems. As MNCs become the target of citizen demands for social, environmental, and economic goods, ideas of authority change. As governments cede or contract functions to the private sector (even security functions), state power, capacity, legitimacy, and authority change relative to other actors—and thus sovereignty is changing.

ENDNOTES

1. Phil Knight and Bill Bowerman, the head coach of the University of Oregon's track and field teams, each contributed $500 to start Blue Ribbon Sports Company, Nike's predecessor. As conflicts grew with Tiger concerning control over the company and exclusive rights to U.S. distribution, Knight ordered 6,000 pairs of shoes with the now-familiar "swoosh" logo in 1971. The company subsequently broke with Tiger and became Nike.
2. Peter Schwartz and Blair Gibb, *When Good Companies Do Bad Things: Responsibility and Risk in an Age of Globalization* (New York: Wiley & Sons, 1999), 52.
3. Miguel Korzeniewicz, "Commodity Chains and Marketing Strategies: Nike and the Global Athletic Footwear Industry," in Frank J. Lechner and John Boli (Eds.), *The Globalization Reader* (Malden, MA: Blackwell, 2000), 158–159.
4. Ibid., 157.
5. Nike, Inc. Annual Report 2005; available at <http://www.nike.com/nikebiz/nikebiz.jhtml?page=0>.
6. World Bank, 2001 World Development Indicators database, July 16, 2001, <www.worldbank.org/data/>.
7. Schwartz and Gibb, *When Good Companies Do Bad Things,* 51, 53.
8. Michael Clancy, "Sweating the Swoosh: Nike, the Globalization of Sneakers, and the Question of Sweatshop Labor," in *Pew Case Studies in International Affairs* (Washington, DC: Georgetown University, Institute for the Study of Diplomacy, 2000), 5.
9. Ibid.
10. Schwartz and Gibb, *When Good Companies Do Bad Things,* 51, 53.
11. Clancy, "Sweating the Swoosh," 9.
12. Nike Web site, corporate responsibility page, <www.nikebiz.com/labor/index.shtml>.
13. Clancy, "Sweating the Swoosh," 13.
14. "Firms are considered to be more multinational if (1) they have foreign affiliates or subsidiaries in foreign countries; (2) they operate in a wide variety of countries around the globe; (3) the proportion of assets, revenues, or profits accounted for by overseas operations relative to total assets, revenues, or profits is high; (4) their employees, stockholders, owners, and managers are from many different countries; (5) their overseas operations are much more ambitious than just sales offices, including a full range of manufacturing and research and development activities. . . . MNCs are firms that have sent abroad a package of capital, technology, managerial talent, and marketing skills to carry out production in foreign countries." Joan E. Spiro and Jeffrey A. Hart, *The Politics of International Economic Relations* (New York: St. Martin's Press, 1997), 96, 98.
15. "Corporations among largest global economic entities, rank above many countries; Corporations make up 63% of 150 largest global economic enterprises," Report summary of Fortune Magazine available at mongabay.com, July 18, 2005. Available at <http://news.mongabay.com/2005/0718-worlds_largest.html>.
16. *Economist* (July 30, 1994): 57, reprinted in James Lee Ray, *Global Problems* (New York: Houghton Mifflin, 1998), 465.

17. United Nations Conference on Trade and Development (UNCTAD), *World Investment Report 2005,* 10, <http://www.unctad.org/en/docs/wir2005overview_en.pdf>.

18. Ibid.

19. United Nations Conference on Trade and Development, World Investment Report 2005, overview, <http://www.unctad.org/en/docs/wir2005overview_en.pdf>.

20. Kofi Annan, address to the World Economic Forum, New York, Feb. 4, 2002.

21. Schwartz and Gibb, *When Good Companies Do Bad Things,* 85.

22. Sixty-one percent of these are in Asia, 32 percent in Africa, and 7 percent in Latin America. Human Rights Watch, Child Labor, <http://www.hrw.org/children/labor.htm>.

23. For example, MNCs are under growing pressure to conform to higher environmental standards from home country regulations and consumers. See UNCTAD, *World Investment Report: Foreign Direct Investment and the Challenge of Development, Overview* (New York: United Nations, 1999), 46; UNCTAD, *World Investment Report, 1999* (New York: United Nations, 1999).

24. A. Claire Cutler, Virginia Haufler, and Tony Porter, *Private Authority and International Affairs* (Albany: SUNY Press, 1999), 16.

25. In practice, this varies by MNC and country. Companies that receive subsidies favor continuing them, and industries that are hurt by foreign competition pressure governments for protection.

26. Ward Morehouse and M. Arun Subramaniam, *The Bhopal Tragedy: A Report for the Citizens Commission on Bhopal* (New York: Council on International and Public Affairs, 1986); William Board, *The Bhopal Tragedy: Language, Logic, and Politics in the Production of a Hazard* (Boulder, CO: Westview, 1989); Paul Shrivastava, *Bhopal: Anatomy of a Crisis* (Cambridge, MA: Ballinger, 1987); Rama Lakshmi, "India Seeks to Reduce Charge Facing Ex-Union Carbide Boss," *Washington Post* (July 8, 2002): A12.

27. Suketu Mehta, "Bhopal Lives," *Village Voice* (Dec. 3, 1996): 51.

28. Ibid., 55; Lakshmi, "India Seeks to Reduce Charge Facing Ex-Union Carbide Boss." Warren Anderson, CEO of Union Carbide at the time of the accident, was charged with culpable homicide in India and faced a civil suit in the United States over the accident. In June 2003, the Indian government requested Anderson's extradition to stand trial. A year later, on July 13, 2004, the U.S. government rejected Anderson's extradition request on technical grounds. He currently resides in Long Island, New York.

29. Mr. Austin Onuoha, "African Oil and Poverty," speech at Catholic University of America, Washington, DC, October 17, 2005.

30. The Global Corruption Report 2005, Transparency International, <http://www.globalcorruptionreport.org/gcr2005/download/english/country_reports_a_j.pdf>.

31. Fr. Antoine Berilengar, SJ, "African Oil and Poverty," speech at Catholic University of America, Washington, DC, October 17, 2005.

32. Bret L. Billet, "Safeguarding or International Morality? The Behavior of Multinational Corporations in Less Developed Countries, 1975–86," *International Interactions* 17 (1991): 171, 184; quoted in Ray, *Global Problems,* 476.

33. Deborah L. Spar, "The Spotlight and the Bottom Line: How Multinationals Export Human Rights," *Foreign Affairs* 77 (March–April 1998): 7–12.

34. Cutler, Haufler, and Porter, *Private Authority and International Affairs.*

35. David C. Korten, *When Corporations Rule the World* (West Hartford, CT: Kumarian Press, 1995).

36. Public Citizen, "Corporate Welfare," <http://www.citizen.org/congress/welfare/index.cfm>; Sarah Anderson and John Cavanagh, *Top 200: The Rise of Corporate Global Power,* Institute for Policy Studies, 2001.

37. These include the power to compel discovery, dispose of property and property rights, order monetary damages, and, depending on the nature of the contract and the rules of arbitration chosen, even order specific performance.

38. Raymond W. Baker, *Capitalism's Achilles Heel* (Hoboken, NJ: Wiley & Sons, 2005), 163.

39. Schwartz and Gibb, *When Good Companies Do Bad Things,* 92.

40. United Nations, "Report of the United Nations High Commissioner on Human Rights on the responsibilities of transnational corporations and related business enterprises with regard to human rights," February 2005, <http://www.ohchr.org/english/bodies/chr/docs/61chr/E.CN.4.2005.91.doc>.

41. Jan Martin Witte and Wolfgang Reinicke, UN Global Compact Office, "Business UN usual," 2005, <http://globalpublicpolicy.net/businessUNusual/>; Witte and Reinicke, "Partnerships: Opportunities and Challenges of Partnering with the UN," Global Compact, July 10, 2005, <www.globalpublicpolicy.net>; Sarah Murray, "UN Partnerships: Mistrust of Corporate World Wearing Off," *Financial Times* (Sept. 13, 2005).

42. Margaret E. Keck and Kathryn Sikkink, *Activists Beyond Borders* (Ithaca, NY: Cornell University Press, 1998).

43. Virginia Haufler, *A Public Role for the Private Sector: Industry Self-Regulation in a Global Economy* (Washington, DC: Carnegie Endowment for International Peace, 2001), 106.

44. "The Coalition for Environmentally Responsible Economies (CERES) was formed in 1989 as a groundbreaking partnership between leading environmental groups and institutional investors. Ceres emerged just as the Exxon Valdez oil spill in Alaska motivated the environmental and investor communities to push for higher standards of corporate environmental performance and disclosure. That work resulted in the creation of the Ceres Principles, a pioneering 10-point code of corporate environmental conduct that has led to the widespread adoption of environmental principles by companies worldwide." <http://www.ceres.org/ceres/>

45. Jack Quarter, *Beyond the Bottom Line* (Westport, CT: Quorum Books, 2000), 119–133.

46. Presentation to the Humanizing the Global Economy Conference of the Latin American, Canadian, and US Catholic Bishops, Washington, DC, Catholic University, January 29, 2002.

47. Schwartz and Gibb, *When Good Companies Do Bad Things,* 77; John Kleiderer, US Jesuit Conference, "African Oil and Poverty," speech at Catholic University of America, Washington, DC, October 17, 2005.

48. Richard Galant, "Faith-Based Investors Demand Policy Shifts in Major Pharmas; Reforms Aim to Save Lives and the Drug Industry's Future," *Newsday* (May 16, 2005).

49. "Economic Security and Critical Infrastructure Protection," address by Kenneth I. Juster, Undersecretary of Commerce Bureau of Industry and Security, The Information Technology Association of America/Prudential Securities Conference on e-Security and Homeland Defense, New York, May 22, 2002, <http://www.bxa.doc.gov/news/2002/KIJNYSpeech5_22_02.htm>.

CHAPTER FIVE

Networked Terror

Martha Crenshaw and Maryann Cusimano Love

Terrorism is not new. What is new is the way terrorists today can take advantage of globalization. Terrorists use cheap and instant global infrastructure to recruit members; raise money; train individuals and cells; gather intelligence; move people, money and material; conduct operations; and spread their messages. Terrorists do not respect sovereign borders. But governments do respect sovereign borders in their efforts to stop, arrest, and eliminate terrorists.

Consider these examples. Al Qaeda training is now available cheaply and globally on the Internet 24/7, despite the efforts of U.S. and coalition forces who raided and shut down al Qaeda training camps in Afghanistan in 2001 and 2002. According to Osama bin Laden biographer Hamid Mir, as al Qaeda scattered from Afghanistan into exile, Mir watched "every second al Qaeda member carrying a laptop computer along with a Kalashnikov." Internet training videos and manuals include "how to's" for building and wearing a suicide bomber belt; creating biological weapons and spreading the plague; poisoning techniques; extracting and recycling explosives from missiles and land mines; bomb recipes, instructions, and country-by-country explosives shopping lists and availability information; hostage taking; assassination; shooting a rocket-propelled grenade; firing an SA-7 surface-to-air missile; blowing up cars; and using the internet to organize a cell and plan an operation. In 1998 there were 12 terrorist-related Web sites; today there are over 4500. As government authorities shut down a terrorist Web site, hundreds of successors crop up with mirror postings. Concerned that fixed Web sites are too vulnerable, al Qaeda uses more mobile and difficult to track postings on bulletin boards, in Internet storage sites, and chat rooms.[1]

Seized laptop computers offer a window into al Qaeda. After a failed assassination attempt on Pakistani President Musharraf, Pakistani officials cracked down on al Qaeda operatives in Pakistan and made a series of high-profile arrests in July 2004. Among those arrested was Muhammad Naeem Noor Khan, a British computer engineer of Pakistani descent. He was caught with laptops containing scouting reports, detailed surveillance information, and hundreds of photographs of financial institutions in the United States, including the World Bank headquarters in Washington, DC. Khan cooperated with law enforcement officials and sent e-mails in a "sting" operation to gather evidence on other al Qaeda operatives. Khan's Pakistan arrest led British authorities to arrest his cousin Babar Ahmad, another British citizen of Pakistani descent. The U.S. government is trying to extradite Ahmad to the United States on charges that he ran an influential network of English-language jihadist web sites that raised money and spread propaganda for Islamic extremists. He is charged with raising money for Chechen rebels in Russia and the Taliban in Afghanistan and Pakistan, as well as arranging for the training and transportation of Islamic fighters and al Qaeda affiliates.[2]

In another example of global networks, Australian authorities arrested a Caribbean-born French citizen whom they believe was sent by a little-known Pakistani group to scout possible targets for attacks. The group, Lashkar e Taiba, was previously thought to be focused only on the India-Pakistan border struggle in Kashmir, but now is thought to be working with al Qaeda, substituting training camps in Kashmir for the ones U.S. and coalition forces destroyed in Afghanistan.

Or consider the case of the millennium bomber. On the evening of December 14, 1999, U.S. Customs agent Deana Dean decided to search the last rental car leaving the ferry from Vancouver, British Columbia, into Washington state. The driver had a Canadian driver's license that identified him as Benni Antoine Noris of Montreal, but his answers to her routine questions seemed hesitant and nervous. Customs agents removed the cover over the spare tire in his trunk and found garbage bags of white powder, as well as aspirin containers and olive jars filled with liquid resembling honey. The suspect bolted, ran across lanes of traffic, bounced off a moving vehicle, and tried to commandeer a car. Customs agents apprehended and handcuffed him and continued to search his vehicle. Thinking they had found drugs, the border guards lifted, examined, and shook the containers, while the suspect ducked behind a car. Later they learned they had by chance apprehended a 32-year-old Algerian man named Ahmed Ressam, who was wanted in France and Canada for suspected terrorist activities. Rather than narcotics, Ressam was carrying 100 pounds of volatile, high-powered explosives that could have detonated if accidentally dropped by the customs agents. His intended target had been the Los Angeles International airport. The press quickly dubbed him the "Millennium Bomber."[3]

Ressam worked with his father in a coffee shop in Algeria until intrastate hostilities intensified in Algeria in 1992. An Islamic fundamentalist party was on the verge of winning national elections, but the government prevented it from taking power and a civil war broke out. Ressam became associated with Islamic militants and then moved to France for the next two years. During that time, Algerian terrorists calling themselves the Group Islamique Armé (GIA), or Armed Islamic Group, conducted a series of bombings of the Paris Metro subway system, killing 22 people and injuring more than 200 others. In an eerie preview of the September 11 attacks, in 1994 they hijacked an Air France plane, which they intended to crash, fully loaded with fuel and passengers, into a Paris landmark, preferably the Eiffel Tower. French commandos successfully stormed the plane, freed the passengers, and shot the hijackers, thus spoiling the plan.[4]

Ressam left France, using a fake French passport, and applied for political asylum in Canada. He moved in with a group of Islamic extremists in Quebec, where he supported himself on Canadian welfare assistance and petty theft and fraud, usually by robbing tourists and using or selling their traveler's checks, cash and credit cards, passports, driver's licenses, and other identification papers. When French police upset a GIA plot to bomb a G-7 economic meeting in France, they seized an electronic organizer filled with phone numbers and addresses of others in the terrorist network. Ahmed Ressam in Montreal was included in the electronic records. Bureaucratic obstacles and delays between the French and Canadian governments and within the Canadian government kept law enforcement from apprehending Ressam. In the meantime, he forged a false Canadian birth record and obtained a Canadian driver's license and passport as Beni Noris. Posing as Noris, he traveled to Pakistan, where he met with al Qaeda members and was taken to Osama bin Laden's terrorist training camps in Afghanistan. He received training in explosives manufacturing, destruction of a country's infrastructure, use of chemical weapons, and other terrorist activities. He left with new skills, $12,000 in "seed money" from the al Qaeda network to pursue terrorist activities, and a request from one of bin Laden's chief lieutenants to steal and send them original Canadian passports so they could help establish operatives in the United States. As investigating French Judge Jean-Louis Brugiere noted, "You can't move around if you don't have false papers and passports. For these groups, passports are as important as weapons."[5] Ressam returned to Canada via South Korea, with a layover in Los Angeles International Airport. While there, he surveyed the site, calculating how long he could leave explosives-laden luggage before it would be discovered and moved, and the length of time he would have to escape the premises (apparently, he did not plan a suicide bombing).[6]

Ressam was arrested days before the millennium, and his cooperation with law enforcement helped secure the arrests of some of his associates in Canada and Brooklyn, New York. International law enforcement efforts foiled other millennium plots in Jordan, Yemen, the Phillipines and elsewhere.[7] After the September 11 attacks, Ressam was again interrogated in a high-security prison in Seattle. He said he did not know any of the September 11 hijackers, but he gave authorities additional information about terrorist sleeper cells and about al Qaeda's interest in chemical and biological weapons. In return, he is seeking reduced prison time from his potential maximum sentence of 130 years.[8]

These examples illustrate many trends in modern terrorism: global operations, use of cheap and easily available modern technologies, networked organizational structures, and a desire to increase casualties. The case also demonstrates how difficult it is for states to cooperate effectively to combat terrorism in a timely fashion. The purpose of this chapter is to put the transsovereign problem of modern terrorism in context:[9] in the context of the debates over defining terrorism compared to other forms of political violence, in the context of globalization,[10] in the context of what the private sector and states can do to prevent and respond to terrorism, and in the context of how terrorism ends.

DEFINING TERRORISM

Terrorism has been around for centuries. The word *terrorism* was first used in describing the Reign of Terror phase of the French Revolution in 1793–94 as a newly installed regime systematically attempted to consolidate power. In nineteenth-century Russia, the People's Will proudly admitted using terrorism in its fight against the autocracy, seeing its members as "noble, terrible . . . the martyr and the hero." A successor group later proclaimed, "The terrorists are the incarnation of the honor and the conscience of the Russian revolution."[11]

Using the term *terrorism* has always been controversial. The British army in Palestine in 1947 banned use of the word *terrorist* to describe members of Menachem Begin's Irgun group, the principal Jewish rebel force, because it implied that British forces had reason to be terrified by the resistance fighters.[12]

Defining terrorism today is no less controversial, in part because the concept is "overlaid with questions of value, usually centered on the legitimacy of the use of violence. Attitudes toward terrorism are frequently based on deep moral commitments . . . the morality of political systems and governments; one has to ask what values are to be defended."[13] Because of the word's pejorative connotation, many people seek to label any use of violence they perceive as illegitimate or with which they disagree as *terrorism*. Israel tends to refer to any Palestinian violence as terrorism, whereas Palestinians call Israel a terrorist state. Pakistan regards Muslims fighting for the autonomy of Kashmir as freedom fighters, yet India regards them as terrorists. Al Qaeda contends that the United States engaged in terrorism because sanctions on Iraq kill millions of innocent women and children, and because the United States used weapons of mass destruction against civilian populations—as when it dropped atomic bombs on Hiroshima and Nagasaki in 1945.

Distinct from the word's use as an insult, however, is some core of agreement about the definition of terrorism. Why is terrorism considered to be an illegitimate use of force? One reason is that terrorism typically refers to force directed against noncombatants, which violates centuries of natural law and international law regarding the rules of war.[14]

Unlike other "isms"—communism, fascism, socialism—terrorism is a strategy or tactic, not an ideology. It is used by widely divergent groups, from Maoists in the mountains of Peru to conservative Islamic extremists in the Arabian desert. Although George W. Bush's administration has not portrayed it this way, its "war on terrorism" is similar to other efforts to delegitimize particular tactics internationally, such as the effort to ban the use of antipersonnel landmines. Similar to the campaign to ban landmines as an illegitimate tool of force against noncombatants, international coalitions, treaties, and conventions against terrorism also seek to globally undermine the use of terrorism as a tool. The war against terrorism is not a fight against a particular state, territory, group, person, or ideology. It is a battle to curtail the use of a specific method of violence.[15]

Terrorism can be defined as organized and purposive political violence that is perceived as unacceptable by society because of its cruelty and unexpectedness:

> Terrorism usually occurs in situations of peace rather than war, and comes as a surprise to its victims . . . who are noncombatants, not prepared to defend themselves against attack and only in the most tenuous way responsible for the actions of the governments that terrorists oppose. . . . Terrorists intend, if not to terrorize (that is, to create the emotion of terror, a form of panic), at least to produce outrage and shock. Terrorism is a strategy of surprise. It is meant to . . . produce psychological and political effects far out of proportion to the magnitude of physical destruction. . . . [T]he physical victims of terrorism are not the targets. That they are terrorized is important only in so far as their terror is communicated to a watching audience, whose emotions the terrorists seek to manipulate.[16]

Terrorism depends on surprise to gain attention and generate fear, so terrorists must constantly be innovative in their means of attack or they lose the power to shock. If terrorist violence becomes routine, then their actions will not pressure change and their goals will no longer receive attention. Surprise is one way of compensating for what they lack in numbers. "Terrorists rarely attack well defended targets. The two factors of weakness and the desire to excite passions encourage terrorists to attack ordinary civilians."[17]

Terrorism is an inherently political act designed to achieve particular goals, generally to bring public pressure to bear on government decisions. For example, al Qaeda's terrorist campaign against the United States is an attempt to pressure the United States to withdraw its support from the Saudi and Egyptian regimes, which al Qaeda regards as illegitimate. The calculus assumes that raising the costs to the United States will undermine support and encourage change of U.S. policies in the Middle East. Thus, even though some people regard such terrorists as "mad," as a group terrorists are engaged in conscious, goal-directed, and premeditated rather than random behavior.

As opposed to mass uprisings or spontaneous violence, "Terrorism is clandestine violence organized by small groups. . . . [T]errorism is highly intentional or purposeful violence. It is not spontaneous or unplanned."[18] For example, the four simultaneous hijackings of September 11 revealed a vast, complex, and highly organized conspiracy.[19]

Because terrorism aims to arouse or intimidate civilian audiences more than reduce an opponent's military effectiveness, "Victims are representative and symbolic. Their usefulness to the terrorist lies in the regard society has for them."[20]

There are other official definitions of terrorism. The International Convention for the Suppression of the Financing of Terrorism sponsored by the United Nations defines terrorism as "an act intended to cause death or serious bodily injury to any person not actively involved in armed conflict in order to intimidate a population, or to compel a government or an international organization to do or abstain from doing any act."[21] Other UN documents stress that terrorists are nonstate actors motivated by political goals.[22]

The U.S. Department of State defines terrorism as

> premeditated, politically motivated violence perpetrated against non-combatant targets by subnational groups or clandestine agents, usually intended to influence an audience. The term "international terrorism" means terrorism involving citizens or the territory of more than one country. The term "terrorist group" means any group practicing, or that has significant subgroups that practice, international terrorism.[23]

The definitions generally share the idea that terrorism is the use of violence against noncombatants, generally by nonstate actors to generate fear in furtherance of other political goals. The "nonstate" component of the definition is important, if not universally accepted. If terrorism is conducted only by nonstate actors, then by definition U.S. and Israeli actions against noncombatants are not terrorism, whereas similar actions by Palestinians may be so termed. If states deliberately and intentionally target and terrorize noncombatants, it is a violation of the laws of armed conflict, not terrorism. International conventions, because they are signed by states, are likely to support definitions of terrorism that are more favorable to states.

It is important to note that all uses of violence by groups labeled as terrorist may not be terrorism, and not all violence by nonstate actors is terrorism. Terrorism is distinct from other low-level forms of political violence by nonstate actors such as guerrilla warfare, ethnic or nationalist separatist violence, and violent efforts to overthrow governments, among others. Depending on the context, nonstate groups may use a medley of tactics that includes both terrorism and other forms of political violence.[24] Sometimes terrorist groups may engage in traditional insurgent activities of using force against military and government targets in order to gain territory or strategic advantage, not to strike at noncombatants in order to cause fear. Terrorism means not only conducting illegal actions (such as killing noncombatants), but also having certain intentions behind those actions (causing fear and psychological reactions to achieve political or other goals rather than destroy something of material value).

Traditional guerrilla or insurgent actions to diminish a government's abilities to project power into a disputed region may not be terrorism. These distinctions between terrorism and other forms of low-level violence can confuse policy makers and the public, because generally once a group is labeled as terrorist, all its actions are labeled as terrorism, even though groups may employ a variety of tactics, only some of which are terrorism.

Developing common definitions of terrorism is important as antiterrorism laws are increasingly enacted domestically and internationally. In the case of the millennium bomber, what difference does it make whether we call his actions terrorism? He committed fraud, theft, illegal immigration, and perjury, and he created and carried illegal explosives across state lines in a conspiracy to commit multiple homicides. Unlike many acts of cybercrime, which are not illegal in some states, terrorism is not primarily a problem of a lack of law. Most everything terrorist organizations do is already illegal: fraud, theft, murder, hijackings, bombings, conspiracy. What value is added by enacting additional domestic and international legislation that labels these activities as terrorism? The purpose of additional antiterrorism legislation is primarily political: to help free additional resources to combat terrorism, to build international political consensus and harmonize international law regarding these acts, and to further undermine the tactic's legitimacy.

GOING GLOBAL

Additional international legal conventions are also sought against terrorism because, although terrorist networks are increasingly global, intelligence, military, and law enforcement efforts are still stymied by state borders and jurisdictions. For example, the U.S. government complains that European governments are more lax in prosecution of suspected terrorists. Many of those apprehended in Germany in connection with the September 11 plot were either released or served minimal jail sentences. In contrast, the Saudi government beheaded suspects apprehended in connection with the USS Cole bombing. This was also a blow to officials in the U.S. government, who were not afforded an opportunity to question the suspects. Because the suspects were Saudi citizens in Saudi territory, the Saudi government was well within its sovereign rights. Terrorists may go global, but state actions to pursue terrorists are constrained by sovereignty.

Although terrorism has existed for centuries, the modern period of globalization changes it. If terrorism is a form of "advertising discontent,"[25] then globalization offers terrorists the opportunity to easily and cheaply take their complaints to a global stage.[26] For example, al Qaeda's attacks on

U.S. targets can be seen as a strategic reaction to American power in the context of a globalized civil war. The United States is susceptible to international terrorism because of its global engagement and its choice of allies, most of whom face significant opposition at home.

> For many of the militants now engaged in al Qaeda, opposition to authority at home, whether peaceful or violent, was ineffective. Local regimes countered dissent with severe repression. As a result, radical frustrations apparently were transferred to the United States as a symbol of both oppression and arrogance. As a free and affluent society, America is a target-rich environment, and one where sensational attacks elicit gratifying media attention. Portraying the United States as an immoral enemy justifies terrorism to the audiences of the dispossessed, especially young men without life prospects whose only education is religious. These various strands have been knitted together in the transnational conspiracy that is al Qaeda. One cannot understand al Qaeda without understanding the domestic politics of Egypt and Saudi Arabia, or now much of the Muslim world.[27]

Globalization takes local fault lines farther afield. Terrorists can go global by using global media as shrewdly as other political actors. Journalist Peter Bergen recalls being contacted by Osama bin Laden's media advisors, who were considering appropriate venues for bin Laden's first television interview. The advisors had a large stack of media requests, but they had narrowed it down to the BBC, CBS News's *60 Minutes* program, or CNN. Bergen, employed by CNN, recalled, "I pointed out that CNN's programs were shown in over a hundred countries, while CBS was broadcast only in the United States."[28] A month later, CNN was called on to do the interview. Bergen and his crew were blindfolded and escorted to an undisclosed location in Afghanistan and allowed to use only al Qaeda's video equipment in case their cameras were bugged or rigged with explosives.[29] After the interview, the media advisor reviewed the tape and cut out any unflattering footage of bin Laden.[30]

Besides global media, terrorists use other cheap and easily available off-the-shelf technologies. A laptop computer left behind by one of the terrorists responsible for the 1993 bombing of the World Trade Center revealed an evidence trail to other co-conspirators, as well as an al Qaeda "how-to" terrorist manual. The September 11 hijackers used the Internet to download specific airport maps, directions, flying instructions, and information about the targeted buildings. They even purchased many of their tickets online. To hide their trail, they often used general access computers in public libraries. Terrorist groups routinely set up Web sites and broadcast their political aims and encourage recruits. They create and copy homemade videotapes for use in international recruitment. From fax machines to Palm Pilots and cell phones, terrorist networks use the same technologies that global business networks use.

Globalization increases terrorists' casualties, due to greater access to lethal technologies and reduced taboos on killing. Experts have noted rising casualties and increased lethality in terrorist violence in recent years. Although the Japanese group Aum Shinrikyo's release of poisonous sarin gas into the crowded Tokyo subway system in 1995 "only" killed twelve people, more than 5,500 were injured. Many more would have died if the group had been more expert in its use of chemical agents. Local terrorist groups in the past faced diminishing returns on increased bloodshed. If their activities caused too many casualties, it could decrease critical social support, recruitments, financial support, and legitimacy. The Irish Republican Army (IRA) often faced this dilemma. But today, terrorism experts fear greater casualties in coming years as terrorist groups train in and explore the use of chemical, biological, and nuclear devices. Because terrorist groups are increasingly networked globally, with training, recruitment, financing, and operations carried out in several countries, increased deaths of one country's citizens may not reduce sympathy, support, and recruitment for the group in other countries. Increased casualties may actually build support as the group gains media exposure and international recognition that it is a force to be reckoned with. Terrorists may also capitalize politically on governments' increased use of violence to combat terrorism. For example, increased violence by British troops and Protestant paramilitary units in Northern Ireland—including the British Army's firing into a crowd of unarmed Irish Catholic demonstrators in Londonderry on "Bloody Sunday" (January 30, 1972)[31]—led to the establishment of the Provisional Irish Republican Army and increased sympathy for the IRA's cause for a time, as many people asked, "Who are the real terrorists here?"[32] Similarly the Iraq War has proved to be a huge rallying point and recruitment tool for jihadist terrorists.

Globalization also facilitates the financing of terrorist groups, because dirty money moves in the same cross-border financial flows as clean money. Terrorists can finance their operations through private charitable foundations. These NGOs may conduct social service works (such as education, health care, and care of widows, orphans, war victims, and refugees), but some of the funds raised may be diverted to illicit activities. Terrorists also engage in strategic cooperative ventures with transnational criminal groups. Terrorist groups in Latin America, for example, often derive significant financial benefit from the drug trade, just as al Qaeda profited from the Afghan heroin trade.

Terrorist organizations may also conduct legal businesses. The Aum Skinrikyo sect used its software development companies as a major source of revenue. (Computer sales at Aum-related retail shops in the cities of Tokyo, Osaka, and Nagoya alone earn the group approximately $65 million a year.) The Japanese defense ministry even used Aum-developed communications programs at twenty ground bases across Japan to gain more rapid access to the Internet. Aum programs were also used for airline-route management and mainframe computer operations. The software companies earned the business through indirect subcontracting relationships and by underbidding competitors by 30 to 40 percent because their employees, all Aum members, worked for virtually no pay. In an incredible irony, the Japanese government purchased software from the very group that perpetrated the sarin gas attacks in the hope of causing chaos that would lead to the overthrow of the Japanese government.[33]

Terrorist organizations may also network with other terrorist organizations. For example, the Provisional IRA historically has prized "its links with foreign terrorist movements such as the Popular Front for the Liberation of Palestine, the Red Brigades, the Red Army Faction, and the ETA [Euskadi Ta Askatasuna, a Basque separatist group that inhabits the Spanish–French border region]. . . . Italian terrorists shared a huge consignment of Palestinian weapons between the ETA and the IRA."[34] More recently, IRA members have been arrested in Colombia, helping to train the Revolutionary Armed Forces of Colombia (Fuerzas Armadas Revolucionarias de Colombia, or FARC).

THE MISSING LINK: THE PRIVATE SECTOR AND CURTAILING TERRORISM[35]

Global infrastructures were built for speed and profit, not security. People and packages now move faster, farther, more easily, and for a lower price than ever before—but at the cost of preventive, multilateral security measures. Although attention has been placed on increasing government activities against terrorism after September 11, the private sector remains key in safeguarding infrastructure from terrorist attack.

For example, although government has increased its attention to airline security, security as a whole has not been adequately addressed in the rest of the global transportation and trade infrastructure, particularly commercial shipping. Airline passengers have their tweezers and nail clippers seized at the gates, but commercial shipping cargo is loaded on these same aircraft with few security precautions. Whether by land, sea, or air, more than 21 million cargo containers enter the United States every year. Less than 2 percent of those containers are inspected in "needle in the haystack" random checks by border, customs, or Coast Guard agents. This is how most illegal drugs enter the United States, and cargo containers are increasingly used in human smuggling. It would not be difficult for terrorists to ship and explode a chemical, biological, or nuclear device via container cargo. The current system favors shippers and businesses who can cheaply speed inventories for just-in-time delivery and avoid warehousing and storage costs. The shippers say they have few incentives to change the system and engage in greater public–private cooperation with government on security issues. They are rarely required to do so by law. Their clients, customers, and shareholders are concerned more with the bottom line than with security measures. They do not trust government competence or motives. Would information volunteered to government land in the hands of their competitors or result in higher tax bills?

Without action by shippers and businesses, however, terrorists can easily exploit the vulnerabilities of the global trade and transportation infrastructure, as they did on September 11.

Unfortunately, such a scenario is not science fiction. Businesses do little to police themselves, and pressure to facilitate trade means that established shippers receive little scrutiny from government authorities, even though they are easily compromised. In early January 2002, Federal Express unknowingly shipped a highly radioactive, 300-pound package that was emitting radiation at an estimated rate of 10 rem (radiation equivalent man) per hour. In one-half hour, a person exposed to that much radiation would exceed the annual limit for exposure and suffer the symptoms of radiation poisoning within just a few hours. Despite this case, FedEx officials do not believe the incident shows any need for greater security precautions on their part. A terrorist organization would not have been able to ship dangerous materials, the company hypothesized, "because extra precautions would have been taken in the case of an unknown shipper or recipient."[36] Would terrorists really use their own return address?

Because terrorists seek easy targets, private-sector responses are crucial. The private sector is increasingly partnering with states. For example, the financial sector is working to curtail money laundering, and pharmaceutical companies are rapidly producing smallpox vaccine to prepare for potential bioterrorist attacks. Yet more private-sector cooperation is needed in the war on terrorism.

Increasing the number of border control agents and the amount of equipment and increasing searches and seizures at borders are efforts that are still bound to fail because even the most up-to-date and efficient government agents cannot keep up with the volume of global trade flows. Speed and volume are crucial to maintaining the economic health of global trade and transportation systems. Just-in-time shipping and narrow profit margins that are dependent on speed and volume mean that closing down borders for old-fashioned search and seizures is an unsustainable approach and equivalent to imposing an economic embargo on ourselves.[37] Luckily we have other choices.

Stephen Flynn, a senior fellow at the Council on Foreign Relations and a retired Coast Guard Commander, offers suggestions for increasing public–private sector cooperation to safeguard against terrorist attacks. Rather than focusing efforts on border control, security checks should be done at the point of origin in trade and transportation flows. Trying to manage security at borders is like "trying to catch minnows at the base of Niagara Falls."[38] Border checks should be the last defense, not the first or main check for security. Thorough security background checks should be required of all private-sector employees in the shipping and transportation sectors. We must move more quickly away from paper passports and paper-based manifest and information systems globally. Modern off-the-shelf technologies such as bar coding, GPS transceivers, sensors, smart cards, and advance electronic manifests should be adopted by government and private-sector agents; these would allow real-time transparency and accountability about the contents of the shipping or transportation stream at any given time. This is how United Parcel Service and FedEx track packages in transit to customers. Shippers that comply with standards and do thorough and strict self-policing will be accorded fast-track processing at borders that would be the equivalent of an "EZ pass" lane. Border checks would continue but be based on intelligence and risk management baselines rather than purely on hunches. Flynn concludes:

> Governments around the world that share an interest in sustaining the free flow of people, goods, capital, and ideas must be encouraged to develop and enact common prevention and protective measures to facilitate legitimate crossborder movements while stopping illegitimate and dangerous ones. Washington has the leverage necessary to gain support for such a process, since all roads lead to and from U.S. markets. It must now put that leverage to good use. Most of the owners, operators, and users of the global transportation networks are from the private sector, however, and they must also be enlisted into

any efforts to enhance security and controls. The result will be an imperfect system, but one that will do a much better job at controlling the risks and consequences of catastrophic terrorist attacks than do the arrangements prevailing now.[39]

STATE RESPONSES: HOW TERRORISM ENDS[40]

So far the discussion has focused on how to manage or curtail terrorism. More international cooperation, greater information sharing and cooperation across and within government bureaucracies, and more sustained and systematic cooperation between government and the private sector are all needed. But how does terrorism end? Context matters. As we try to formulate governmental policies aimed at ending terrorism, we must ask how such policies are likely to affect the evolution of terrorism.

The first set of questions involves the terrorist groups themselves. First, internal factors must be assessed. How does the organization make decisions? How does the organization perceive its environment? What are its internal psychological dynamics? Is the organization divided internally? The answers to all of these questions are important to know but often difficult to ascertain.

Next, external factors must be considered. How does the relative strength of the terrorist organization compare with that of the government it opposes? Are the terrorists ideologically or ethnically motivated? What kinds of ties do they have to outside groups that may support them? Is the conflict best characterized as a secessionist struggle or does it involve a battle over civil society and representation?

The options that a government uses to respond to terrorism, many of which can be pursued simultaneously, must be adapted to the type of group and situation. There is no one-size-fits-all policy.

First, governments can try deterrence. They can use their coercive capacity to make terrorism too costly for those who seek to use it. They can do this by military strikes against terrorist bases, assassinations of key leaders, and collective punishment. There are several drawbacks to this approach, however. It can lead to unacceptable human rights violations, and groups may not come to government attention until their movements are so well developed that containing them through deterrent methods is insufficient.

An alternative is to use the criminal justice system to end terrorist activities and groups. Governments can treat terrorism primarily as a crime and therefore pursue the extradition, prosecution, and incarceration of suspects. One drawback to this approach is that the prosecution of terrorists in a court of law can compromise government efforts to gather intelligence on terrorist organizations. For example, al Qaeda members drastically reduced their usage of cell phones after court testimony revealed that governments could easily intercept cell phone conversations. In addition, criminal justice efforts (like deterrent efforts) are deployed mostly after terrorists have struck, meaning that significant damage and loss of life may have already occurred.

Governments can enhance prevention and defense. They can make targets harder to attack, and they can use intelligence capabilities to gain advance knowledge of when attacks may take place. As targets are hardened, however, some terrorist groups may shift their sights to softer targets. An example is the targeting of the U.S. embassies in Kenya and Tanzania in August 1998 by truck bombs. Although the attacks were coordinated by al Qaeda, targets in Africa were chosen because of their relatively lax security compared with targets in the Middle East.

States also may try negotiations. Governments can elect to negotiate with terrorist groups and make concessions in exchange for the groups' renunciation of violence. The Good Friday Peace Accords and the associated peace process in Northern Ireland, and the Colombian government's outreach to insurgency and terrorist groups are attempts to reach negotiated settlements and end violence. Governments are often reluctant to do so when terror campaigns begin, but negotiations may be the only way to resolve long-standing disputes, especially ethnonationalist claims that have significant popular support.

The end of terrorism may result from one or more of the following situations. Success may end it. The terrorists may accomplish their objectives, such as the overthrow of a government, the end of an occupation, or a policy change. Terrorism per se cannot achieve long-term goals such as revolution or independence, but it can sometimes do so in conjunction with less violent political action. The terrorists may also achieve partial or preliminary success. A corollary to achieving objectives is having at least achieved public recognition for an organization and the cause it espouses. It can put the issue on the public agenda. In this case, continued terrorist actions may alienate supporters, sponsors, or key third-country actors for whom continued violence is unacceptable.

Terrorists may experience organizational breakdown, as has been the case for the Tupac Amaru group in Peru. After some of its members died when a four-month siege of the Japanese embassy in Peru was put down by Peruvian forces in 1997, the group has not mounted a significant terrorist action and appears to be in organizational disarray, with dwindling numbers focused mainly on freeing their imprisoned compatriots.[41] Terrorist organizations, like any organizations, must constantly work to maintain themselves. If recruiting dries up, or if funding becomes unavailable, then the organization may be unable to sustain itself. On the other hand, the necessity of self-preservation may force organizations to continue terrorist activities even if the leadership otherwise wishes to give them up. It may be that the only way for the organization to continue to attract new recruits and financial support is to continue to gain publicity for its terrorist actions.

Terrorist groups also may face dwindling support. Organizations may lose the support of their various constituencies—the populations they seek to represent or the governments or other organizations that support them. They can do so for reasons of ideological or strategic differences, personality clashes, or simple fatigue. Terrorist actions can also provoke moral outrage and undermine support.

New alternatives to achieve political or other goals may emerge. At times, other options for political change emerge. They can include more traditional forms of warfare or revolution, mass protests, or political negotiations.

As suggested above, many of the factors and consequences already outlined may occur simultaneously. Both governments and terrorist organizations can pursue many tracks at once, and organizations may confront a wide series of challenges simultaneously.

Governmental decisions about how to confront terrorism are made more difficult by the frequently high degree of uncertainty governments have about the nature of terrorist organizations, their motivations, and the effects of government actions on those organizations. The need for understanding terrorist organizations is highlighted by the fact that such groups' calculations are based on their perceptions of costs and rewards, not those of the authorities who confront them or of objective observers.

So called get-tough measures against terrorist groups can have unintended consequences. Trying to decapitate a movement may radicalize the whole movement or some splinter faction. Assassinations and military force can provoke a desire for revenge, and raids and arrests can reinforce martial images, create mythologies of martyrdom, and feed paranoia and secretiveness (which makes the movements even harder to penetrate for reasons of either understanding motivations or foiling actions). Success in combating terrorism in one place may merely push it to another region. After the assassination of Egyptian President Anwar Sadat, Egyptian authorities cracked down on the Egyptian Islamic Jihad group. Many of its members fled Egypt and joined forces with Osama bin Laden's al Qaeda organization, becoming bin Laden's chief lieutenants. Some observers are concerned that success in toppling the Taliban and routing al Qaeda fighters from Afghanistan may simply have pushed the organization into Yemen, Sudan, Somalia, or Pakistan.

In the event that organizations are primarily motivated by a desire for recognition, how should policy makers respond? Should the government recognize the organizations and eliminate their motivation for terrorism? Because terrorist actions most often are considered newsworthy events by media organizations, governments cannot control whether the actions garner attention. Governments can play an effective role, however, in influencing how terrorist events are portrayed to the public and thus influence (but not control) how the public interprets those events.

Public opinion is important because it can determine the amount of financial and operational support the terrorists enjoy. In some cases, support comes from abroad and is difficult for governments to control. In other cases, governments have control over populations that are sympathetic to the terrorists. In this event, they must walk a difficult line. On the one hand, repressive measures can encourage antigovernment hostility and support for the terrorists. On the other hand, fear of punishment for the terrorists' excesses can undermine a population's willingness to support terrorist activities. In this balance, the terrorists have two weapons on their side. The first is their ability to mete out punishment against those who do not support their actions, and the second is their ability to build on group solidarity to overcome reservations about their methods.

One effective tactic against many terrorist organizations may be to promote their disintegration from the inside. Governments can demonstrate to such groups that their support among the populations they supposedly represent is waning. Even where such allegations are true, however, groups may resolutely believe they enjoy support even after it has dissipated.

Governments can also try to split off members from a group either by offering large rewards for information that undermines group solidarity or by making promises of leniency for imprisoned group members. Finally, governments can unilaterally enact reforms that reduce public support for the terrorists without rewarding the terrorists directly, or they may choose to negotiate with terrorist leaders.

Another tactic may be to put pressure on states that are sympathetic to a terrorist group's goals, even if the states are not outright sponsors of the group. Expulsion from a haven often causes financial pressures or logistical difficulties and can sometimes end a group's viability. In many cases, however, affected countries lack the necessary ties to effect such pressure, or laws that govern free expression make it difficult to crack down on an organization's activities.

If the efforts to eliminate a terrorist group through compulsion fail, however, governments are left trying to reach a peaceful settlement with that group. In civil conflicts, such a settlement usually entails negotiations for amnesty of both individuals and the group. In trying negotiations, governments must confront opposition on two fronts: from the group's rank-and-file members, who may be more disposed toward violence than the leadership; and from the inside—that is, from their own populations, who may oppose the government sitting down with killers and "rewarding violence." Groups that are opposed to a peaceful reconciliation will act to undermine the peace, often by undertaking terrorist actions of their own, as has been the case in the peace process in Northern Ireland. In this event, governments that have only a precarious grip on power will find it difficult to move decisively toward peace.

In addition, governments must time their peace overtures carefully: first, by making such gestures when their ability to reward good behavior and punish bad is strong; and second, by making them when the terrorist organization is going through some period of internal questioning. In such situations, effective intelligence can be crucial in identifying auspicious times for a peaceful gesture and in defining the context of that gesture. Yet lack of timely intelligence is often cited as the crux of the problem.

CONCLUSIONS: CONSIDER THE CONTEXT[42]

Deciding when to employ what strategy is one of the hardest problems facing government officials who deal with terrorism. There is no single solution. Governments must carefully consider the nature of their terrorism problem in context. Negotiations with those who are perpetrating violence are not the solution to every problem. By the same token, many terrorist campaigns cannot be stopped by military or law-enforcement actions alone. Many people suggest that a decisive factor that determines the effectiveness of law-enforcement activities is the support that the terrorist groups enjoy among their base. Narrowly based terrorist groups can be rooted out, but groups that rely on a broad base of support (some of them from beyond a nation's borders) have a durability that may defy such efforts. For that reason, ethnically based groups may be harder than class-based groups to eliminate through force because ethnicity has proven a stronger tie than class in most cases.

If negotiations are pursued, then two conditions should be present. First, the government should enjoy a strong popular mandate. Political opponents often portray negotiating with terrorists as "giving in" to terrorism. Such an attack can topple a weak government or, short of that, block whatever agreement has been reached through negotiations. Second, the terrorist organization should be undergoing a period of self-evaluation. In such a circumstance, the government may be able to successfully split off pragmatists

131

from hardline terrorists, bring the population along with the pragmatists, and dry up popular support for those who continue to pursue violence.

Intelligence is important throughout. In confronting terrorism, the nature of the grievance does matter, as does the nature of the organization that puts forth the grievance. Intelligence is important not only to prevent terrorist attacks but also to understand how the organization works and how its decision-making processes can be affected. Because terrorism is global, intelligence becomes an almost intractable problem. How can intelligence collection, analysis, and dissemination be conducted or shared globally? This is resisted by sovereign states.

Terrorism is an international problem and therefore requires policies that go beyond unilateral state actions. Money and weapons flow across borders, and supporters of terrorism (if not the terrorists themselves) often have established bases in other countries. Increasingly, law enforcement efforts aimed at stemming terrorism have an international component, and such a strategy will only require more international cooperation in the future. The nature of the terrorists' grievances matters. Although political violence by itself can rarely achieve its aims, it can sometimes do so in conjunction with less violent political action. By the same token, deterring terrorism and prosecuting terrorists may be insufficient to end terrorism, especially when a large population supports the terrorists' cause. In this regard, the war on terrorism may be as unsuccessful as the war on drugs if efforts to curtail terrorism focus exclusively on military, defensive, and law enforcement approaches. Without addressing underlying factors of what terrorists are fighting for, where they draw their strength from, and how to address their grievances or separate organizations from their base, it will be difficult to manage or end terrorism. The means and targets of terrorism may be global, but grievances are often still local, ensuring that governments will need to use a range of responses to manage networked terror.

Which measures are chosen will depend on the nature of the terrorist threat as well as the domestic political context. The diffusion of power in democratic governments poses a challenge for formulating and coordinating policy.[43] In addition, democracies generally promote the idea of protection of the rights of the individual, bringing pressure on governments to respond to terrorist attacks on innocent civilians. "Democracies can survive the assassinations of leaders . . . but they cannot tolerate public insecurity."[44] However, choosing a response must be tempered by the fact that no democratic regime has ever been conquered by terrorism. Terrorists often miscalculate. Their attacks may rally support for their opponent and strengthen rather than undermine the power of the state. The magnitude of terrorist destruction must also be considered in context. Terrorist destruction "is small compared not only to other forms of political violence such as civil wars or communal rioting but also to other sources of casualties in modern societies."[45] This is particularly true after September 11. The public perception of risk from terrorism generally far exceeds the reality. Citizens in developed countries are more likely to die from firearms or car accidents than from terrorism. In 2004, 42,646 Americans died in traffic accidents.[46] Citizens in developing countries are more likely to die from tuberculosis, malaria, or AIDS than from terrorism. The spread of democracy and global media make open societies more vulnerable to terrorist attacks and place great pressure on governments to respond. Yet in choosing a response, democracies must be careful not to overreact. In fighting the war on terrorism, we must not become more like our opponents than we would like and less able to address the underlying vulnerabilities and grievances of globalization that can fuel terrorism.[47]

ENDNOTES

1. Steve Coll and Susan B. Glasser, "Terrorists Turn to the Web as Base of Operations," *The Washington Post* (Aug. 7, 2005): A01.
2. Craig Whitlock, "Briton Used the Internet as His Bully Pulpit," *The Washington Post* (Aug. 8, 2005): A01.
3. Terrence McKenna, "Trail of a Terrorist" (transcript of *Frontline* documentary, Public Broadcasting Service [PBS], Oct. 25, 2001, <www.pbs.org/wgbh/pages/frontline/shows/trail/etc/script.html>); Ahmed Ressam, testimony in July 2001 as a witness for the prosecution at the New York trial of co-conspirator Mokhtar Haouari, federal district court of the Southern District of New York, <www.pbs.org/wgbh/pages/frontline/shows/trail/inside/testimony.html>.
4. McKenna, "Trail of a Terrorist"; Ahmed Ressam testimony, July 2001.
5. McKenna, "Trail of a Terrorist." 4. Ibid.; Ahmed Ressam testimony, July 2001.
6. Ibid.
7. Vernon Loeb, "Terrorists Plotted Jan. 2000," *Washington Post* (Dec. 24, 2000): A01; *Frontline,* "Other Millennium Plots," PBS, Oct. 25, 2001, <www.pbs.org/wgbh/pages/frontline/shows/trail/inside/attacks.html>.
8. McKenna, "Trail of a Terrorist."
9. Martha Crenshaw, "Terrorism in Context," in Martha Crenshaw (Ed.), *Terrorism in Context* (University Park: Pennsylvania State University Press, 1995).
10. Maryann Cusimano Love, "Globalization, Ethics, and the War on Terrorism," *Notre Dame Journal of Law, Ethics, & Public Policy* (Violence in America issue, 2002): 65–80; Maryann Cusimano Love, "Morality Matters: Ethics, Power, Politics, and the War on Terrorism," *Georgetown Journal of International Affairs* (Summer–Fall 2002): 7–16.
11. Martha Crenshaw, "Organized Disorder: Terrorism, Politics, and Society," in Ray C. Rist (Ed.), *The Democratic Imagination* (New Brunswick, NJ: Transaction Publishers, 1994), 140.
12. Ibid., 141.
13. Ibid., 143.
14. Saint Augustine, *City of God* (trans. Thomas Merton) (New York: Modern Library Paperback Classics, 2000).

15. Cusimano Love, "Globalization, Ethics, and the War on Terrorism," 65–80; Cusimano Love, "Morality Matters."

16. Martha Crenshaw, *Terrorism and International Cooperation,* New York: Institute for East-West Security Studies (Boulder, CO: Westview, 1989), 6–7.

17. Crenshaw, "Organized Disorder," 150.

18. Ibid., 143–144.

19. Martha Crenshaw, "Why America? The Globalization of Civil War," *Current History* (Dec. 2001): 425.

20. Crenshaw, "Organized Disorder," 143.

21. United Nations, "International Convention for the Suppression of the Financing of Terrorism," December 9, 1999, <http://untreaty.un.org/English/tersumen.htm#4>.

22. Jonathan R. White, *Terrorism,* 3rd ed. (Belmont, CA: Wadsworth, 2002), 12.

23. U.S. Department of State, *Patterns of Global Terrorism 2000* (Washington, DC: U.S. Government Printing Office, April 30, 2001); <www.state.gov/s/ct/rls/pgtrpt/2000/2419.htm>.

24. Crenshaw, *Terrorism and International Cooperation,* 8.

25. Irving Louis Horowitz, "Political Terrorism and State Power," *Journal of Political and Military Sociology* (Spring 1973): 145–157.

26. Cusimano Love, "Globalization, Ethics, and the War on Terrorism," 65–80.

27. Crenshaw, "Why America?" 425.

28. Peter L. Bergen, *Holy War, Inc.: Inside the Secret World of Bin Laden* (New York: Free Press, 2001), 6.

29. It is ironic that Afghan rebel leader Ahmad Shah Massoud, an ardent opponent of the Taliban government and the al Qaeda camps in his country, was later assassinated by opponents disguised as a camera crew.

30. Bergen, *Holy War, Inc.,* 23.

31. Prime Minister Tony Blair, "Prime Minister's Statement, Bloody Sunday Inquiry," House of Commons Official Report (Jan. 29, 1998), Parliamentary Debates (Hansard) (London); <www.bloody-Sunday-inquiry.org.uk/index2.asp?p=7>.

32. Paul Wilkinson, "The Orange and the Green," in Martha Crenshaw (Ed.), *Terrorism, Legitimacy and Power* (Middletown, CT: Wesleyan University Press, 1983), 117.

33. Maryann Cusimano Love, *Public Private Partnerships and Global Problems: Y2K and Cybercrime.* Paper delivered at International Studies Association, Hong Kong meeting, July 2001; Calvin Sims, "Japan Software Suppliers Linked to Sect," *The New York Times* (March 2, 2000): A6.

34. Wilkinson, "The Orange and the Green," 120.

35. This section derived from Cusimano Love, "Globalization, Ethics, and the War on Terrorism," 65–80.

36. Matthew L. Wald, "Fed Ex Shipped a High Radiation Package without Knowledge," *The New York Times* (Jan. 10, 2002).

37. Stephen Flynn, "America the Vulnerable," *Foreign Affairs* (Jan.–Feb. 2002): 60–75; Stephen E. Flynn, *America the Vulnerable: How Our Government Is Failing to Protect Us from Terrorism* (New York: Harper Collins/Perennial, 2005); Stephen E. Flynn, *The Age of Disaster: Terror, Catastrophe, and the Unmaking of a Great Nation* (New York: Random House, 2006).

38. Ibid.

39. Ibid.

40. This section is drawn from Martha Crenshaw, *How Terrorism Ends* (Washington, DC: U.S. Institute of Peace, May 25, 1999), <www.usip.org/oc/sr/sr990525/sr990525.html>.

41. U.S. Department of State, *Patterns of Global Terrorism 2000.*

42. This section is drawn from Crenshaw, *How Terrorism Ends.*

43. Martha Crenshaw, "Counterterrorism Policy and the Political Process," *Studies in Conflict & Terrorism* (Oct. 2001): 329–337.

44. Crenshaw, "Organized Disorder," 149; Irving Louis Horowitz, "The Routinization of Terrorism and Its Unanticipated Consequences," in Martha Crenshaw (Ed.), *Terrorism, Legitimacy, and Power* (Middletown, CT: Wesleyan University Press, 1983).

45. Crenshaw, "Organized Disorder," 145.

46. U.S. Department of Transportation, National Highway Traffic Safety Administration, "2004 Traffic Safety Annual Assessment," August 2005www-nrd.nhtsa.dot.gov/pdf/nrd-30/NCSA/RNotes/2005/809897.pdf.

47. Cusimano Love, "Globalization, Ethics, and the War on Terrorism," 65–80; Cusimano Love, "Morality Matters," 7–16.

CHAPTER SIX

Global Crime Inc.

Louise Shelley, John Picarelli, and Chris Corpora

On a chilly Monday evening in early March 2005, Steve MacQueen, the Chief of the World Bank's Microfinance Investment and Support Facility for Afghanistan, stepped out of a bar called the Elbow Room and into his Ministry of Rural Rehabilitation four-wheel-drive vehicle. This was meant to be his last week in Kabul, but it turned out to be his last few moments of life.[1] MacQueen oversaw the World Bank project aimed at converting poppy farms into other, legal activities. The Ministry of Rural Rehabilitation was universally understood to be the financial arm of the opium eradication efforts in Afghanistan, and MacQueen embodied an activity many resisted. It is nearly impossible to know who drove the two black Toyota Landcruisers that approached MacQueen in expert fashion and boldly killed the 41-year-old directly in front of Dutch Embassy. The complexity of determining the actual killers, or those who had arranged for the murder, stems from the transnational complexity surrounding the opium trade in Afghanistan. Varying reports suggest a range of 60 to 80 percent of the Afghan GDP is associated with poppy cultivation into opiates and production of heroin.[2] The poppy trade has long been a crucial commodity for raising much-needed funds for forming necessary strategic alliances across the divided country. These activities clearly crossed the borders of the shattered country in the early 1990s, when Afghanistan jumped past Myanmar as the world's largest opium exporter.[3] This tainted success could only come with the corrupt support of government officials, within and surrounding Afghanistan, and with a growing international smuggling interest that was finding new access in the Post-Soviet North. The threat MacQueen and his activities posed to the multi-billion dollar transnational trade in heroin went deeper than the fledgling Afghan Anti-Narcotics Teams, which were already limited by corruption, or the solemn rhetoric of many international leaders. MacQueen represented a true and direct threat that could cause international traffickers' business costs to rise, which would in turn shrink the funds available for bribes and equipment. The message sent through MacQueen's assassination could have come from any number of entities threatened by the program he oversaw: narcotics-funded Taliban or Pakistani-trained terrorists, Central Asian smugglers, or corrupt government officials whose wealth and power would be compromised by the program's success. Each of these potential instigators exemplify the complex nature and challenge of transnational organized crime and corruption to legitimate, transparent governance and security; the rule of law and a vibrant civil society; and regional development. It also explains why this purposefully public and violent crime remains unsolved.[4]

TRANSNATIONAL ORGANIZED CRIME: DIFFERENT VIEWS

The "global mafia," the "next war," a "pax mafiosi," the "dark side of globalization," the "illicit global economy," the "retreat of the state"—all are recent terms and expressions in the literature of world politics that describe the appearance of transnational organized crime. However, such crime has a lineage that scholars have traced back to the times of pirates on the high seas and the African slave trade. So is this a new phenomenon or something that scholars of world politics have just begun to notice and explore? Furthermore, what makes the phenomenon "transnational"? Finally, what is the significance of using a term such as *transnational* or, in the context of this volume, *transsovereign?*

These are valid and often asked questions about the study of transnational organized crime. In the span of some two decades, practitioners and scholars alike have begun to explore and analyze the different activities and processes that compose the phenomenon, developing and revising definitions as they go along. Furthermore, especially in the scholarly realm, we have attempted to explain transnational criminal groups, focusing both within the traditional analytical unit of world politics—the state—as well as the state system. Finally, we have sought to identify objects and methods for responding to these criminal enterprises. This chapter will address these important issues while engaging the debates throughout the literature. It concludes by fashioning a framework for composing strategy that will respond to transnational organized crime.

TRANSNATIONAL ORGANIZED CRIME

Over the past two decades, scholarship that addresses the phenomenon of transnational organized crime has blossomed. In the 1990s, the scholarly literature began a more serious focus on transnational organized crime as a phenomenon unto itself, whereas earlier literature had focused on domestic organized crime or organized criminal activities that span borders, such as the trafficking of narcotics. The scholars and practitioners who have contributed to this growing corpus of knowledge have sought to answer fundamental questions: What is transnational organized crime? Why the label *transnational* versus others such as *international?* What kinds of activities compose this area of inquiry? In what ways does transnational organized crime interact with the state? What kinds of approaches are most appropriate for examining transnational organized crime? Each question leads us to important answers that affect the ways we view and approach world politics.

Definitional Issues

One of the first major issues that researchers and practitioners tackled was defining transnational organized crime. The United Nations established the term *transnational crime* more than twenty-five years ago, but it was a catchall term that incorporated some eighteen categories of activity, including terrorism and hijacking, alongside organized crime activities.[5] The distinction between domestic forms of organized crime and transnational organized crime developed from the increased study of narcotics trafficking and the growth in organized crime operating across international borders during the 1980s. The generation of a definition had to overcome traditional and novel hurdles ranging from the minimum number of individuals in a group to the basis for considering a group a transnational criminal entity—decisions that greatly affect the inclusiveness of the definition.

The definition of organized crime has evolved, reflecting the increasing complexity and international nature of the phenomenon. One of the first definitions of organized crime came from U.S. law enforcement, primarily the Federal Bureau of Investigation, which states that organized crime is "continuing and self-perpetuating criminal conspiracy, having an organized structure, fed by fear and corruption, and motivated by greed."[6] With time, the FBI began to use this definition to describe what it referred to as *international* organized crime—that is, organized crime groups operating in more than one country. Note, however, that this definition retains the notion of organized crime operating internationally, and it does not seek to identify the criminal activity as a transnational phenomenon.

Thinking of crime as transnational better illustrates the ways in which these criminal organizations seek to operate outside of the state system— in essence, transcending the sovereignty that organizes the modern state system and leveraging it for their own gain. One of the first to make this distinction was Phil Williams, who in 1996 demonstrated that organized crime was recasting itself by leveraging the changes in global political economy and society being rendered by globalization and the technology revolution.[7] What resulted were criminal organizations that came to "resemble transnational corporations" that operated across the globe from a home base using networked structures to perpetuate their activities, all the while seeing borders as hindering law enforcement more than their own activities.[8]

More recently, the United Nations Convention on Transnational Organized Crime sought to provide a unified definition that is likely to serve as the benchmark for identifying transnational criminal organizations:

> "Organized criminal group" shall mean a structured group of three or more persons, existing for a period of time and acting in concert with the aim of committing one or more serious crimes or offences established in accordance with this Convention, in order to obtain, directly or indirectly, a financial or other material benefit. "Serious crime" shall mean conduct constituting an offence punishable by a maximum deprivation of liberty of at least four years or a more serious penalty. "Structured group" shall mean a group that is not randomly formed for the immediate commission of an offence and that does not need to have formally defined roles for its members, continuity of its membership or a developed structure. . . . [A]n offence is transnational in nature if: (a) It is committed in more than one state; (b) It is committed in one state but a substantial part of its preparation, planning, direction or control takes place in another state; (c) It is committed in one state but involves an organized criminal group that engages in criminal activities in more than one state; or (d) It is committed in one state but has substantial effects in another state.[9]

The United Nations' definition is one of the most comprehensive, addressing the issue of size, duration, and the transnational nature of criminal groups. Furthermore, it provides the flexibility to examine transnational organized crime outside of such traditional ethnic groups as the Russian Mafiya, Chinese Triads, Japanese Yakuza, and Italian Mafia families.

Transnational Criminal Activities

Transnational criminal activity involves a broad range of activities in both the legitimate and illegitimate sectors of the economy. Some groups function primarily in the illegitimate sector, such as drug trafficking groups, whereas others span both sectors of the economy searching for high profits. The massive privatizations of the 1990s have given many transnational organized crime groups a large and important foothold in the economies of their home countries and in many others. Money laundering and corruption, two associated activities, are vital to the conduct of transnational organized crime.

TYPES OF CRIMINAL ACTIVITIES

Experts and practitioners have identified more than a dozen criminal activities engaged in by transnational criminal organizations. The major component of most of these activities is smuggling of diverse commodities and the provision of illicit goods and services. Narcotics trafficking, as Stephen Flynn details in Chapter 7, is the most common and profitable activity. Many organizations and countries cite narcotics trafficking as the most significant transnational organized crime in terms of annual profits.

Furthermore, scholars such as Pino Arlacchi have demonstrated that narcotics trafficking has often served as the gateway for domestic organized crime groups to enter the transnational realm.[10] Hence, it comes as no surprise that the drug trade is often cited as the most commonly known transnational organized criminal activity.

The next most significant transnational organized crimes are trafficking in persons and in arms. An important distinction characterizes these forms of organized crime. Arms deliveries involve the transfer of inanimate goods that are used to commit other crimes or to arm regional conflicts. In contrast, trafficking in persons involves the movement of live human beings who are exploited continuously after their delivery. Likewise, human trafficking provides ongoing revenues for transnational organized crime, whereas the arms trade, if it is to be sustained, requires the perpetuation of conflict.

Trafficking in persons and migrant smuggling, a similar activity that does not incorporate the pernicious aspects of slavery, both involve the recruitment, movement, and delivery of migrants from a host to a destination state. The profits from such activities are significant and believed to be rising—a recent

Federal Bureau of Investigation estimate placed the annual profits of trafficking in persons at $9.5 billion.[11] Crafting even inexact estimates of the number of people trafficked annually is difficult at best, and thus few solid estimates exist. Yet most every expert on trafficking in persons, practitioner and scholar alike, agrees that the problem is significant and increasing as both demand and supply are rising. The rise in demand for cheap services and labor in developed countries and the growth of population in developing countries without adequate employment will result in a rise in this phenomenon in coming decades.

Trafficking and smuggling in persons is pernicious because of both the large profits and the physical and emotional toll it takes on the victims. Numerous trafficking studies note the physical violence and mental strain that victims suffer at the hands of their captors. For example, it is not uncommon for these victims to become addicted to alcohol or narcotics, contract HIV and AIDS or other diseases, or die from strain or violence. Those that do survive often face difficult and time-consuming recoveries.

The fact that transnational criminal organizations are increasingly gravitating toward the trafficking in persons as a source of profits is even more pernicious as it is these groups that have a profound interest in perpetuating the trade in persons. A range of transnational criminal organizations are trafficking in persons, particularly Chinese and Taiwanese, Thai, Indian, Pakistani, Japanese, Russian-speaking, and Balkan organized crime groups.[12] Indeed, Shelley has identified at least five business models for trafficking syndicates globally, and another study highlights the integration of trafficking and smuggling enterprises in organized crime's portfolio.[13]

None of this activity can function without the complicity of some law enforcement and the corruption of officials in source, transit, and destination countries. This telling quote from Kevin Bales also applies outside the Thai context: "To be sure, a brothel owner may have some ties to organized crime, but in Thailand organized crime includes the police and much of the government. Indeed, the work of the modern slaveholder is best seen not as aberrant criminality but as a perfect example of disinterested capitalism."[14]

Arms trafficking is another significant form of transnational organized crime. The rise of regional conflicts in the postwar era has provided transnational organized crime groups with a huge market for small arms. In some cases, transnational organized crime groups help foment regional conflict to increase demand for weapons.[15] This has been particularly true in Africa but also applies in the Balkans, Latin America, and Asia. Many of the weapons come from former Soviet states and Eastern Europe. The trafficking in arms has also led to an insidious partnership between military forces and mafia groups, especially in the post–Soviet transition states of Eastern Europe and the former Soviet Union. Graham Turbiville, Jr., for example, outlines the ways in which organized crime and the Russian military coalesced after the end of the Soviet Union, going so far as to refer to the Russian armed forces as "mafia in uniform."[16]

Transnational criminal organizations have found a niche supplying arms to areas suffering from continued conflict with small arms and even major arms systems. Organized crime has also positioned itself as the arms supplier of last resort, oftentimes delivering arms to regions under arms embargo. For example, in April 2001, Italian authorities arrested members of a Russian and Ukrainian criminal network that, for more than seven years, had supplied more than 13,500 tons of arms, including thousands of assault rifles and hundreds of missiles and antitank shells, to groups fighting in the Balkans, including the Croatian army.[17] Italian authorities then dismantled a similar Russian organized crime controlled network soon afterward that was supplying arms to Charles Taylor's forces in Sierra Leone.[18] The problem is very apparent in the Caucasus where the smuggling of arms and other commodities has prolonged the conflict in Abkhazia and Ossetia regions. In both areas, border controls are weak and individuals guarding the borders are profiting significantly from the trafficking of contraband. This contraband, comprised of both arms and different commodities, makes it difficult to solve these conflicts.[19]

The largest profits for organized crime have been in the small weapons area, but the threat of organized crime trafficking in nuclear materials and biological and chemical weapons remains a major concern. Richard Love has identified organized crime as a potential facilitator for the theft and smuggling of strategic weapons and materials.[20] In the end, transnational organized crime involvement in arms smuggling is a major concern for states and international organizations concerned with maintaining international security and peace.

Smuggling and trade-related transnational criminal activities are a major profit source for transnational organized crime. For example, trade in cigarettes, once a national trade, has been internationalized by transnational criminal groups, who often work with legitimate cigarette manufacturers to obtain their commodities. These links between crime groups and legitimate corporations are now the subject of major criminal investigations within the European community.[21] Such illicit trade also thrives across the U.S.– Canadian border.[22] Furthermore, organized crime groups are important actors internationally in the illicit trade in environmental products, ranging from banned chlorofluorocarbon-based refrigerants to toxic waste and even endangered fauna and flora.[23] Likewise, scholars have identified transnational organized crime as a player in the theft and smuggling of art and antiquities and have linked the latter to international money laundering.[24] The thefts from the Iraqi Museum, many of which were unregistered antiquities, provided money for the skilled thieves who were able to smuggle the antiquities out of the country.[25] These antiquities could then be translated into cash once they had been sold to collectors outside the country. Finally, there is the smuggling of stolen automobiles, an activity that is especially prevalent in central Europe and the southwestern United States.[26] Roughly $1 billion worth of stolen vehicles is removed from the United States annually and sent to other countries.[27] The theft of vehicles exists in Asia as well. Stolen Japanese vehicles are transported to Russia for sale in the Far East and parts of Siberia.[28]

The return of a trade-related organized criminal activity that many had thought was relegated to the past—the piracy of ships in international waters—also involves the activities of transnational criminal organizations. Pirating now benefits from cheaply available global technologies. "One pirate ship captured recently in Indonesia was outfitted with bogus immigration stamps, tools to forge ship documents, and sophisticated radar, communications, and satellite-tracking equipment."[29] According to the International Chamber of Commerce, a piracy incident reporting clearinghouse, ship seizures increased 57 percent in 2000 over the previous year's numbers and were significantly more than 400 percent higher than 1991 numbers.[30] Organized crime is closely linked to these incidents, either conducting the piracy itself or supporting piracy. The benefits for the organized crime groups are significant as they can move cargo and illegal immigrants and engage in insurance fraud. The problem is most pronounced in Asia but also is common in Latin America and Africa. The crime groups are increasingly focusing on the theft of high-technology cargo.[31] Hijacking of cargo is not confined to the sea. Analysts have identified transnational organized crime involvement in the theft of land-based cargo, such as hijackings of truck and rail cargo.[32]

Increasingly, analysts have documented links between transnational organized crime and terrorism. Although it is clear that international terrorist organizations have routinely used organized crime tactics to raise money and move equipment and personnel, it was historically rare to find an alliance between groups separately motivated by economics and politics.[33] However, some recent studies on Abu Sayyef, Islamic Jihad, and HIG suggest these activities overlap increasingly beyond convenient opportunities. Furthermore, the growing evidence of far-reaching international corruption challenges formal interpretations of legitimacy and formal behavior.

Many significant transnational criminal activities are now linked to the licit economy. Fraud scams originating in western Africa, primarily Nigeria, use official-looking fax and electronic mail correspondence to obtain banking information from victims that is then used to steal funds from their accounts.[34]

Transnational criminal organizations have also engaged in massive credit card and identity theft rings using stolen account numbers and identities to amass millions in fraudulent charges. Recent arrests in Spain of members of a terrorist cell revealed that they supported themselves by producing fraudulent documents and airplane tickets.[35] Al Qaeda profited from heroin trafficking. The MacQueen assassination was only one act of violence aimed at challenging the slow-starting international anti-narcotics effort in Afghanistan. Slowly, international institutions are beginning to understand the depth and breadth of the Afghan poppy problem—ranging far beyond an Afghan-centric drug cultivation issue into international terrorism and regional politics. Therefore, organized crime for profit not only is the domain of criminals who seek profits but also is being used by politically motivated groups.

Crime groups cash counterfeit checks, trade in bearer bonds, and manipulate the stock market in the United States, Canada, and Italy. Asian organized crime groups operating in Las Vegas were earning close to $500,000 monthly from the cashing of counterfeit checks in casinos.[36] Finally, some organized crime groups in the United States have recently infiltrated the U.S. stock markets, purchasing or creating their own brokerage houses to engage in "pump and dump" and other types of stock manipulations for illicit gains. For example, a scandal occurred in Canadian markets with the manipulation of stocks by Russian organized crime in the metals trade. Italian organized crime, according to Italian investigators, is now also active in market manipulation.[37]

Violence and corruption, the traditional methods of organized crime once applied on the local level, are now being applied internationally. Protection rackets, the backbone of domestic organized crime groups, have been retained as an important activity for transnational criminal organizations, who also frequently engage in contract killings for profit or power projection. For example, the use of violence for protection rackets and other purposes is referred to as the "defining characteristic" of Asian organized crime groups operating in the United States.[38] Furthermore, Russian-speaking organized crime groups have used threats of violence to extort Russian hockey players in the National Hockey League.[39] Contract killers have been sent from Russia to carry out their hits and returned home after carrying out their missions.

A significant area of growth for transnational criminal activity is within the realm of information and high technology. Just as pirates are now focusing on high-technology cargo, criminals are realizing high profits from pursuing the hardware of technology, and their Internet schemes reveal their capacity to engage in cybercrime.[40] For example, John Picarelli and Phil Williams have identified several ways criminals can use information technology as a criminal milieu, as a tool, and even as a weapon to further their activities.[41] Likewise, a conference that examined the ways in which organized crime, terrorist, and other groups use information technology noted that such technology can assist in the conduct of traditional criminal activities as well as serve as the gateway to new criminal endeavors. For example, panelists noted that Nigerian criminal gangs were abandoning fax machines and using e-mail in their elaborate fraud schemes, and that criminal groups were becoming increasingly involved in the piracy of intellectual property such as compact discs and computer software.[42] Finally, Richard Love notes in Chapter 9 how criminal organizations are operating online rather than in the bricks and mortar world.

ACTIVITIES THAT SUPPORT TRANSNATIONAL CRIME

Transnational criminal activity cannot survive solely in the illicit realm. Its profits must be moved into the legitimate economy to be invested. Furthermore, it requires corruption to function—to fend off arrests, obtain lucrative contracts, and obtain legitimacy in the community.

Money Laundering

Money laundering is a universal and crucial activity for transnational criminal organizations. The previous section described the numerous methods by which transnational organized crime generates profits. These profits remain useless, however, unless the criminal groups can somehow place them into the licit global financial infrastructure without the knowledge of law enforcement or regulators. Hence, almost all transnational criminal organizations engage in some form of money laundering to dispose of their profits.

Money laundering has increased in both scope and sophistication. Although the estimates of global money laundering have continued to prove difficult to quantify, estimates of $500 billion to $1 trillion annually is a commonly held figure.[43] More anecdotal estimates provide a basis to demonstrate the significant size of money laundering. For example, in 1995 Australian officials estimated that close to $3 billion of laundered funds passed through their country.[44] Canada recently estimated that laundered funds from the narcotics industry alone accounted for roughly $5 billion to $14 billion annually from Canada.[45]

The methods that money launderers use range from placement in the licit financial sector through phony corporations, bank accounts, and the use of offshore banking centers to less traditional means such as using Internet-based banking and informal banking systems, including the *hawala*.[46] This informal remittance system is used to move funds into and from South Asia and the Middle East, and it has recently gained attention because of its uses by terrorist organizations such as al Qaeda.[47] One study

145

showed that because increases in crime have recently been coupled with a decrease in the demand for currency, money launderers apparently are "moving away from the banking system and cash and toward parallel financial markets, sophisticated nonmonetary instruments (such as derivatives), and possibly barter (such as an exchange of boats and guns for drugs)."[48]

In the end, money laundering is the bridge that connects the illicit and licit global economies. Money laundering uses licit financial markets as a method of transfer and placement for illicit funds. Such activities, more importantly, skew economic indicators and policy in significant ways. Tanzi, for example, demonstrates that large capital inflows and outflows from money laundering affect interest rates, that the demand for dollars from money launderers supports an implicit seigniorage for U.S. currency markets, and that money laundering generates distrust in markets, which then amplifies reactions to rumors or false statements.[49]

In recent years, international investigations have gone after the proceeds of organized crime. In the United States and Switzerland, more than $1 billion has been seized from drug traffickers and other criminal groups. In Georgia, a case was discovered involving one billion U.S. dollars of laundered money in which the money moved through the bank was entirely illicit. The laundered money was the proceeds of organized crime activity from crime groups from the former Soviet Union who were active in crime all over the world.[50]

Extensive money laundering was detected at Riggs Bank, which received the largest fine ever imposed in the United States on a banking institution for money laundering. The bank was disclosed to have laundered money for the dictator of Equatorial Guinea and for former President Pinochet of Chile, and some of the accounts of the Saudi embassy may have facilitated the financing of terrorism. The ease with which Riggs Bank continued to engage in this activity even after the Patriot Act was initiated is indicative of the relative ease with which it is still possible to launder money in the United States.[51] But increasingly the money is laundered outside of the banking system, where there is less risk of detection.

Most of the proceeds of the drug trade have gone into the national treasuries of the countries where they have been seized. In Italy, unique legislation authorizes the use of seized assets for community development and drug treatment.[52]

Corruption

Corruption is an important tool for organized crime, and transnational organized crime groups have exploited such relationships with politicians and government officials. Put broadly, corruption is "the misuse of office for personal gain" and "means charging an illicit price for a service or using the power of office to further illicit aims."[53] Corruption differs from clientelism in that the latter retains a vertical separation between the patron and client, and is based on an exchange for unspecified services. Corruption blurs the line between the state and transnational criminal organizations. Some states are so thoroughly corrupt that scholars refer to them as criminal states.

Two significant and related phenomena are important for our purposes— political and economic corruption. Political corruption has received strong consideration in the literature. Only recently, however, have the links between political corruption and organized crime been analyzed—for example, the differing views on the connections between corruption[54] and political parties.[55]

Economic corruption hinges on the desire for industries to collude and establish cartels within markets, as when firms use organized crime to organize and maintain cartels among them.[56] Still, virtually no study has tackled the thorny issue of corruption within the sector of international development aid—a significant oversight, given recent scandals involving skimming from aid contracts.[57]

For what ends does organized crime engage in corruption? To answer this question, we refer to the triangular relationship between organized crime, the state (i.e., government), and firms.[58] Organized crime provides electoral support and intimidation powers to politicians in return for protection and legitimization of its activities. Likewise, organized crime provides protection and assistance with cartels in return for money. Finally, an important part of this equation is public contracts, which politicians can use to seek rents from both firms and criminal organizations. In turn, these contracts are a major source of mafia profits. Hence, corruption is a key factor to consider when we analyze the behavior of transnational criminal organizations.

Along with the necessity to understand the relationship between organized crime and corruption is the need to fully address the broader complex that brings these together in association with terrorism and insurgency. Recent studies addressing post–conflict environments and organized crime suggest the merging of these efforts is often found in areas poorly governed or still under the informal control of a faction.[59] The post–Yugoslav conflicts still suffer from the rule of informal political control that finds its support in its ability to generate much-needed funds, employment, and political influence through illicit activities. Often this is a continuation of business as conducted during conflict, as the primary way to obtain materials and personnel and move these in a clandestine manner.[60] Post-conflict Iraq and Afghanistan demonstrate a high correlation with these findings and have given rise to a broader research program—ranging from a postmortem of past conflicts to those only recently coming to an end or protracted pause. Despite the fact that these conflicts are often contained within discrete regions, their impact with regard to transnational organized crime transcends the bounds of the physical conflict.

EXPLAINING TRANSNATIONAL ORGANIZED CRIME

Transnational crime, once neglected in the study of international relations, is now studied in different parts of the discipline because of its far-reaching effects on political systems, national sovereignty, and international political economy. The relationship between transnational crime and the state is central to this entire analysis. The following section surveys some of the approaches to studying transnational crime. Such crime can be considered from two levels of analysis: the community level and the international level with globalization.

A significant difference exists between the strategic studies literature that identifies transnational organized crime as a threat to the industrialized world and world order and the literature that focuses on the societal level at which transnational organized crime operates, shaped by the local community. Whereas organized crime has proliferated with globalization, many of the groups are still deeply entrenched in their home societies where their effects are particularly strong. It is important to consider both aspects when calculating effective responses.

Internal Analysis: Trust and Civil Society

Organized crime usually develops and operates in areas where civil society is weak or nonexistent. For example, in a landmark study, Robert Putnam describes how civil society arose in northern Italy but failed to take hold in southern regions where four organized crime groups are based.[61] In another example, Russian-speaking organized crime has emerged with potency in the states of the former Soviet Union where the communists wiped out all elements of civil society.[62]

Other related factors are trust in intrapersonal societal relations and the effects of trust on governance.[63] Weak states have poorly formed civil societies, which leads to a lack of trust in the state and a dependence on surrogate actors to address civic needs. For example, organized crime in Sicily arose when state control was absent; organized crime substituted itself for the state and provided the protection that substituted for trust in society.[64]

Trust and civil society factors help explain how transnational criminal organizations embed themselves within societal structures. A successful response must consider the societal context within which crime groups operate, particularly within the state, and at the local level where they are based. For example, Sicilian society has mobilized against the Mafia for the past century.[65] In recent decades, the movement has mobilized all levels of society simultaneously and has attempted to reeducate citizens at the local level on the need for alternatives to the Mafia. The primary objective of nearly all the anti–Mafia associations is to educate children to know and respect the law and to prevent them from acquiring a "Mafia mentality" of distrust and antagonism towards public institutions—which may lead to a life of crime.[66] Such programs were introduced in the early 1980s by the first anti–Mafia groups but obtained additional impetus in the early 1990s in response to the Anti–Mafia Commission and the pressures of the mass anti–Mafia organizations of civil society. Libera, the umbrella of 800 nationwide anti–Mafia organizations, works with urban communities, schools, and the Church to implement anti–Mafia curricula.[67]

External Analysis: Globalization

Globalization is a key factor in the rise of transnational organized crime. There are several competing notions regarding how to theorize transnationality, marking a different way to configure social spaces.[68] Transnational organized crime cuts across the globalization discourse, ranging from notions of informal markets and new authoritarianism to ideas about global criminal networks.[69] The majority of the globalization literature captures transnational phenomena as dynamic, cross-sectoral, and embedded in global markets, making the concept more than a new level of analysis.

Globalization provides a theoretical boost to historical notions of national or international organized crime, emphasizing the ascendance of nonstate actors as legitimate objects of political inquiry. However, the concept of globalization is far from a settled theory and stirs great debate, ranging from downplay, through social transformation, to near chaos or turbulence.[70]

The categories of state, economics, and institutional structures are useful for capturing the majority of analysis on transnational organized crime in the globalization context. Globalization benefits the capabilities, resources, and strategies that are available to transnational organized crime.

The neoliberal understanding of globalization stresses the role played by global free market capitalism and representative democracy in making the world richer, more connected, and peaceful, as represented in the writings of Francis Fukuyama and traditional political economic interpretations.[71] In this light, transnational organized crime and other similar issues often are seen as the last vestiges of resistance to this "new world order" that eventually will be brought under control.[72]

THE ROLE OF THE STATE

What effects are globalization processes having on the modern state? These academic discussions directly affect our consideration of transnational organized crime. For example, Saskia Sassen posits that globalization is transforming the logic of sovereignty without eliminating the role of the state,[73] a view shared by James Mittelman and James Rosenau. Combined with weak state scenarios, such as Robert Jackson's concept of "negative sovereignty" and Susan Strange's "retreat of the state," these provide the theoretical backbone for analyzing transnational organized crime and corruption in the globalization context.[74]

Most often, scholars have posited that the weakening of state structures, either caused or enhanced through globalization processes, has created spaces that have allowed transnational organized crime to flourish.[75] Louise Shelley has examined the interplay of weakened states, civil society, and transnational organized crime, viewing criminal groups as taking advantage of new technologies and global opportunities to amplify the weakening of states.[76] Nikos Passas finds that the demise of states is a necessary part of the globalization of organized crime because it erodes the bonds of trust between state and citizenry and provides transnational organized crime with the opportunity to play surrogate for the state.[77] Peter Andreas points out how globalization processes, embodied in the form of NAFTA, directly affected the increase of transnational organized crime in Mexico by liberalizing markets without sufficient regulation and oversight.[78]

THE ROLE OF THE ECONOMY

The political economic approach addresses how the "illicit global economy" affects the state and the licit economy.[79] For example, the illicit Colombian economy distorts the legal economy.[80] Economic markets shape transnational organized crime, taking organizational form based on the economic context.[81] Transnational business strategies of the illicit actors increasingly mirror those in the licit economy. Specialists such as lawyers, accountants, and transportation experts now work for organized crime as they do for the legitimate economy.[82]

As the share of the international economy controlled by organized crime increases, there will necessarily be more attention to the political economy of the drug trade and other diverse forms of illicit activity. Especially since September 11, the interaction of the illicit and licit economies is receiving greater attention.

HYBRID ANALYSIS: SECURITY STUDIES

The security studies literature views organized crime as a threat. Its involvement in the weapons trade, its deleterious effects on state sovereignty, and its corruption of state structures are seen as serious threats to individual states, regional stability, and the international order. Security scholars have used several methods to explore the threat transnational organized crime poses to people, the nation-state, and global stability. Researchers of the "Copenhagen School" focus on how threats are formed and the effects they have across the social experience,[83] providing a flexible approach for looking at a broader spectrum of threats.[84] The military and state continue to be an important sector, but they are evaluated in conjunction with the economic, societal, and environmental sectors. Transnational organized crime and other negative consequences of globalization are seen as a cross sectoral threat. Buzan and Waever take this analytic a step further in their recent monograph, breaking out regions and conflicts and applying the analytic to demonstrate its power in helping to understand and explain security complexes.[85]

However, security experts are increasingly growing concerned about the linkages between organized crime and other threats like terrorism and proliferation—a view that has obtained more currency since September 11, 2001. A recent study has concluded that the range of potential cooperation between crime and terror groups is much broader than security planners had once considered.[86] Recent analysis of crime and terror groups demonstrates the spectrum of potential interactions between crime and terror groups as well.[87] Other analyses of these alliances focus on the capacity to acquire and deploy weapons of mass destruction.[88] Others have addressed the growing links between organized crime and terrorist groups.

MULTIPLE APPROACHES ARE NEEDED

Transnational crime operates on the global level but is embedded in many societies at the local level. International policies that address transnational crime at only a single level are doomed to failure. As the previous analysis has indicated, a multidisciplinary perspective is needed to understand transnational crime—one that incorporates economic, social, political, and strategic studies analyses. Yet these perspectives must also include an understanding of the historical and cultural context that led to the rise of organized crime groups in particular locales. Transnational crime has local and global, societal and state components. Effective responses to manage transnational crime must deal with each of these elements.

Globalization helps to turn once locally and regionally contained phenomena into transnational crime problems. The profits and effects of these
groups are so significant in some regions that they pose threats to nation-states
and undermine the national sovereignty of many countries. The global illicit
trade has assumed massive proportions, and its effects are particularly great in
smaller economies where the profits of this illegal trade can undermine and
distort the economy. Likely the epitome of this asymmetry is found in
Afghanistan, where the narcotics trade represents some 60 percent of the economy and, as the opening anecdote attests, continues to undermine the process
of democratization and state-building. For example, tax rates escalate as the size
of the illegal economy grows. Because less economic activity is conducted in
the sphere where states can levy taxes, states raise rates on the remaining licit
economy to recoup lost tax income and sustain government budgets. In a
vicious circle, government's attempts to sustain its revenue base can push more
businesses into the illicit economy (through fraud, tax evasion, and transfer
pricing) to avoid the high tax rates in the licit economy. Weakened state treasuries reduce the resources that are available to states to fight organized crime.

Organized crime is necessarily, in part, a covert phenomenon. Therefore,
analysis and information on the phenomenon is partial and often misinter-
preted by individuals who do not understand the context in which it
functions. Policy makers from one arena—law enforcement, economics, or
security studies—often believe that their perspective holds the "answer"
without understanding that a multidisciplinary approach is needed.

Effective strategies to control and contain transnational crime cannot
address only one aspect. For example, as peacekeepers have discovered in the
Balkans, Colombia, and elsewhere, transnational crime groups are now the
defining actors in the political environment. Traditional military strategies
cannot be used to contain their activities. As anti-Mafia activists have discovered in Sicily, the legal system can prosecute and isolate the Mafia bosses, but
civil society must change community attitudes toward organized crime and
must prove to the citizens of their island that there are tangible benefits for
them in fighting organized crime.

CONCLUSION: A WAY AHEAD?

We propose the following framework for addressing the transnational organized crime problem through a dynamic and multidisciplinary perspective.
First, any serious researcher or policy maker must ask the following questions
before developing a policy. What is the process of social transformation at
play? What unique and general aspects of a particular manifestation of

transnational organized crime are present in the local context, and how are they embedded within it? How does the transnational crime group connect with regional, international, and multilateral actors of the legitimate and illegitimate economy? To what extent does the community understand the problems of transnational crime and have the willingness and the capacity to help address the problem? What are the costs on the local, regional, and national level of the group's continued criminality?

Because globalization reshapes both international dynamics and the local community, attempts to manage transnational organized crime must acknowledge both levels. Part of this process of social transformation is that time, space, and boundaries are collapsed or compacted. Relationships on an international scale occur more rapidly and commercial relations are more frequent. The illicit can be facilitated and more easily commingled with the licit. On the local level, culture, ideas and society are affected. Local control can be challenged in weak states (places where significant social upheaval exists), which leads to deeper divisions. Therefore, transnational groups face fewer obstacles on the local level and more ability to operate in the global economic environment.

Individual states cannot solve their problems alone. Whether one considers the rise of the European Union, the collapse of border controls of the once territorially immense Soviet state, or the rise of regional conflicts that blur national distinctions, states alone are less important. All of these changes have provided opportunities for transnational crime to work and to expand its operations. With globalization, the central state in many countries has become a less effective institution of control. It cannot sufficiently absorb the shocks, limit the dislocations, or regulate the transformation. Deepening local insecurity further strains the bonds of trust between state and citizen.

Under these circumstances, resistance to social transformation, like that found within globalization, can create the space for the proliferation of organized crime and corruption in a given locale. Local control is assumed, and services are rendered through an informal transaction between people playing the roles of criminal and citizen in exchange for certain rents and permissions. Crime groups based in the local community are not impervious to the logic of global social transformation, which changes the organization and its methods of operation. The transformation of organized criminality into a transnational phenomenon is often a logical response to the effects of globalization on the local level.

Understanding transnational crime at the different levels at which it operates requires the engagement of many different sectors of the policy and legal communities, civil society, and the media. Transnational crime groups often provide services at the local level and fulfill demands for illicit commodities and cheap services at the international level. Therefore, any strategy to address transnational crime must convince individuals that it is not in their interest to support or be complicit in its operations. To achieve this objective, media must be mobilized, independent, and supported in their efforts to report on this phenomenon. Civil society must be mobilized to address transnational crime, a mobilization that often comes only with enormous personal loss and even tragedy. Finally, legal measures must be harmonized. This includes both the criminal codes and the procedures needed to combat transnational crime. For example, much has been achieved in this area in money laundering, but the passage of needed legislation is not sufficient. Unless implementation strategies are achieved, laws remain on the books and have no practical effects.

A resource and intelligence gap divides the capacity of developed and developing and transitional countries from addressing the range of problems caused by organized crime. Affluent societies have the legal tools, personnel, and intelligence resources to pursue transnational criminals. Less affluent societies that are faced with critical health, social welfare, and other concerns often cannot allocate the financial and human resources to address transnational organized crime. Unless strategies address the enormous capacity gaps that exist between developed countries and the rest of the world, there can be little success in achieving a global effort to address this issue.

Transnational crime groups are major actors in areas with significant regional conflicts. The demand for arms and quick profits and the lack of territorial control are fertile grounds for the rise of organized crime. Unless military and peacekeepers begin to integrate the problem of transnational crime into their strategies for conflict management, the problem will undermine conflict resolution and postconflict stability.

Organized crime and corruption issues have not traditionally been part of the discourse of international relations, strategic studies, or economic development. Until these elements are integrated into these disciplines and policy planning, organized crime will continue to proliferate. Incorporating these problems into the needed framework is not a guarantee of success, but the failure to address them ensures their continued growth.

Since September 11, 2001, terrorism has received enormous attention in the United States and transnational crime has received much less attention from governmental authorities. In Europe, transnational crime continues to receive more attention and terrorism less. For Europeans, the pressing problems of illegal migration, human trafficking and the consequences of opening their borders have made them much more sensitive to the problems of transnational crime and the implications for the European Union and their individual countries. In the international context, transnational crime and terrorism are major problems of international concern, especially in countries where citizens are most affected by their prevalence. Recent analysis has shown that transnational crime and terrorism are more closely linked than many acknowledged. The relationship is more complex than the ability of terrorists to support themselves through transnational criminal activity. Therefore, transnational crime has repercussions that far exceed the individual crimes of document fraud, criminal abuse of the Internet, or trafficking in small arms. These issues merit far more attention in all spheres of education, research, and policy in the international community.

ENDNOTES

1. Torcuil Crichton, "To Die For," *The Sunday Herald* 13 (March 13, 2005): 15.
2. United Nations Drug Control Program (UNDCP), *Global Impact of the Ban on Opium Production in Afghanistan (Second Update),* Vienna, 2001; United Nations Office on Drugs and Crime (UNODC), *The Opium Economy in Afghanistan,* New York, Vienna: UNODC, 2003.
3. Alain Labrousse, "The FARC and the Taliban's connections to drugs," *Journal of Drug Issues* 35 (Winter 2005): 169–184.
4. As of the date of this writing the MacQueen case remains open with few solid leads reported. However, Kabul-based international officials and the press regularly express their certainty that this issue is not only linked to the drug trade, but also demonstrates the depth of narco-corruption in Afghanistan.
5. See Gerhard O.W. Mueller, "Transnational Crime: Definitions and Concepts," *Transnational Organized Crime* 4(3–4): 13–21.
6. National Security Council, International Crime Threat Assessment Web site, <www.terrorism.com/documents/pub45270/pub45270chap1.html>.
7. Phil Williams, "Transnational Criminal Organizations and International Security," *Survival* 36(1): 96–113.
8. Ibid., 97.
9. UN General Assembly, "Convention against Transnational Organized Crime," Nov. 2, 2001 (New York: United Nations Publications), 25–26.
10. Pino Arlacchi, *Mafia Business: The Mafia Ethic and the Spirit of Capitalism* (London: Verso, 1986), 187–210.
11. See U.S. Department of State, *Trafficking in Persons Report,* June 2005, pp. 13–14, available at <http://www.state.gov/documents/organization/47255.pdf>. The source or methodology used to produce this estimate is unstated.
12. Amy O'Neill, *International Trafficking in Women to the United States: A Contemporary Manifestation of Slavery* (Washington, DC: Center for the Study of Intelligence, 1999), 55–62; Donna Hughes, "The 'Natasha' Trade: The Transnational Shadow Market of Trafficking in Women" (available at <www.uri.edu/artsci/wms/hughes/natasha.htm>); James O. Finckenauer, "Russian Transnational Organized Crime and Human Trafficking," in Kyle and Koslowski (Eds.), *Global Human Smuggling,* 166–186; Pasuk Phongpaichit, "Trafficking in People in Thailand," *Transnational Organized Crime,* 3(4): 74–104; U.S. Department of State, *Trafficking in Persons Report 2005.*

13. Louise Shelley, "Trafficking in Women: The Business Model Approach," *The Brown Journal of World Affairs* 10(1) (Summer/Fall 2003): 119–133; Andreas Schloenhardt, "Organized Crime and the Business of Migrant Trafficking," *Crime, Law and Social Change* 32(3) (Oct. 1999): 203–233.

14. Kevin Bales, *Disposable People* (Berkeley: University of California Press, 1999), 50.

15. See World Bank, "Understanding Civil War, Crime and Violence through Economic Research" (at <www.worldbank.org/research/conflict>) for research papers that discuss this relationship.

16. Graham Turbiville, Jr., "Organized Crime and the Russian Armed Forces," *Transnational Organized Crime* 1(4): 57–104 (quote on 62–63).

17. CNN, "Italy Cracks Arms Smuggling Network," broadcast April 19, 2001.

18. Jon Swain and John Follain, "Sierra Leone Arms Ring Broken," *Sunday Times* (UK) (July 8, 2001): N24.

19. Alexandre Kukhianidze, Alexandre Kupatadze, and Roman Gotsiridze, "Smuggling through Abkhazia and Tskinvali Region of Georgia, <http://www.traccc.cdn.ge/publications/kukhianidze>, accessed August 17, 2005.

20. Rensselaer Lee, III, *Smuggling Armageddon* (New York: St. Martin's Griffin, 1998), 47–72. See also Phil Williams and Paul Woessner, "Nuclear Material Trafficking: An Interim Assessment," *Transnational Organized Crime* 1(2): 206–238.

21. See *Guardian,* "BAT Exposé" (special report) (available at <www.guardian.co.uk/bat/0,2759,191282,00.html>); and the International Consortium for Investigative Journalists, "Tobacco Companies Linked to Criminal Organizations in Lucrative Cigarette Smuggling" (available at <www.public-i.org/story_01_030301.htm>).

22. Criminal Intelligence Service Canada, "Contraband Smuggling" (2001 annual report) (available at <www.cisc.gc.ca/AnnualReport2001/Cisc2001/contraband2001.html>).

23. Svend Søyland, "Criminal Organizations and Crimes against the Environment," report for the UN Interregional Crime & Justice Research Institute, June 2000; available at <www.unicri.it/pdf/cocae.pdf>.

24. Lauren L. Bernick, "Art and Antiquities Theft," *Transnational Organized Crime* 4(2): 91–116.

25. Elizabeth Olson, "Sending the F.B.I. to Art School," *New York Times* (March 30, 2005): E2.

26. Royal Canadian Mounted Police, "Organized Crime and Automobile Theft," Sept. 1, 1998 (available at <www.rcmp-grc.gc.ca/crim_int/sparkplugeng.html>); Rosalva Resendiz and David M. Neal, "International Auto Theft: The Illegal Export of American Vehicles to Mexico," in Delbert Rounds (Ed.), *International Criminal Justice: Issues in a Global Perspective* (Boston: Allyn & Bacon, 1998), 7–18; Interpol, "Vehicle Crime Profits Can Be Used to Support Terrorist Organizations, Interpol's Chief Says," Nov. 19, 2001 (available at <www.interpol.int/Public/ICPO/PressReleases/PR2001/PR200136.asp>).

27. Anthony Lake, *Six Nightmares: Real Threats in a Dangerous World and How America Can Meet Them* (New York: Little, Brown, 2000), 46.

28. Nomokonov, V.A, and Y.A. Aminyeva, "Two Aspects of the Interrelation of Migration and Crime in the Russian Far East and the Primorya" (Два аспекта взаимосвязи миграции и преступности на Дальнем Востоке России и в Приморье). <http://www.crime.vl.ru/docs/stats/stat_121.htm>. Accessed 10-05-2005 (it was posted on the Web 10/27/04).

29. Kevin Sullivan and Mary Jordan, "High Tech Pirates Ravage Asian Seas," *Washington Post* (July 5, 1999): A18.

30. International Chamber of Commerce, "Piracy Attacks Rise to Alarming New Levels, ICC Report Reveals," Feb. 1, 2001; available at <www.iccwbo.org/ccs/news_archives/2001/piracy_report.asp>.

31. "Overview of Maritime Crime," *Trends in Organized Crime* 3(4): 68–71.

32. Julie Salzano and Stephen Hartman, "Cargo Crime," *Transnational Organized Crime* 3(1): 39–49.

33. John T. Picarelli and Louise Shelley, "Methods, Not Motives: Implications of the Convergence of International Organized Crime and Terrorism," *Police Practice and Research* 3(4) (2002): 305–318.

34. U.S. Department of State, Bureau of International Narcotics and Law Enforcement, "Before You Go" (information on Nigerian advanced fee fraud), April 1997; available at <www.state.gov/www/regions/africa/naffpub.pdf>.

35. "Spain Arrests Members of Terrorist Cell," *The New York Times* (Sept. 26, 2001): B4.

36. Karen Zekan, "Chinese Crime Ring Ripping off Strip," *Las Vegas Sun* (Jan. 21, 1999); available at <www.lasvegassun.com/sunbin/stories/text/1999/jan/21/508304597.html>.

37. Nichole Christian, "Officials Say Stock Scheme Raised Money for the Mob," *The New York Times* (March 9, 2001): B3; Thomas V. Fuentes, "Organized Crime: Statement on the Record) Before House Subcommittee on Finance and Hazardous Materials," Sept. 13, 2000 (available at <www.fbi.gov/congress/congress00/fuentes.htm>).

38. James O. Finckenauer, "Chinese Transnational Organized Crime: The Fuk Ching" (report to the UN National Institute of Justice, International Center); available at <www.ojp.usdoj.gov/nij/international/chinese.html>.

39. Robert I. Friedman, *Red Mafiya* (Boston: Little, Brown, 2000), 173–201.

40. P.N. Grabosky and Russell Smith, *Crime in the Digital Age: Controlling Telecommunications and Cyberspace Illegalities* (Brunswick, NJ: Transaction, 1998).

41. John Picarelli and Phil Williams, "Information Technologies and Transnational Organized Crime," in David Alberts and Dan Papp (Eds.), *Information Age Anthology: National Security Implications of the Information Age,* Vol. II (Washington, DC: NDU Press, 2000), 365–402.

42. Transnational Crime and Corruption Center, *Transnational Crime, Corruption, and Information Technology* (2000 Annual Conference Report), 4–5; available at <www.american.edu/transcrime/pdfs/TC&IT_2000_Report.PDF>.

43. Raymond Baker, "The Biggest Loophole in the Free Market System," *Washington Quarterly* 22(4): 30.

44. Financial Action Task Force on Money Laundering, "1996–1997 Report on Money Laundering Typologies," Feb. 1997, 3; available at <www1.oecd.org/fatf/pdf/ TY1997_en.pdf>.

45. Samuel Porteous, *Organized Crime Impact Study Highlights* (Ottawa: Public Works and Government Services of Canada, 1998); available at <www.sgc.gc.ca/EPub/Pol/e1998orgcrim/e1998orgcrim.htm>.

46. Nikos Passas, *Informal Value Transfer Systems and Criminal Organizations* (The Hague, Netherlands: Netherlands Ministry of Justice Research and Documentation Center, 1999), 13–16.

47. Kathleen Day, "U.S. Islamic Cash Outlets Investigated: 'Hawalas' Suspected in Terror Funding," *Washington Post* (Nov. 7, 2001): A1; and Vincent Schodolski, "Terror Networks Rely on 'Hawala,'" *Chicago Tribune* (Sept. 26, 2001): 10.

48. Peter Quirk, "Money Laundering: Muddying the Macroeconomy," *Finance and Development,* 34(1); available at <www.worldbank.org/fandd/english/0397/articles/0110397.htm>.

49. Vito Tanzi, "Macroeconomic Implications to Money Laundering," in Ernesto Savona (Ed.), *Responding to Money Laundering: International Perspectives* (Netherlands: Harwood Academic, 1997), 91–106.

50. International Narcotics Control Strategy Report 2005, Volume II: Money Laundering and Financial Crimes Country Reports—Georgia, available at <http://www.state.gov/p/inl/rls/nrcrpt/2005/vol2/html/42394.htm>.

51. For a fuller discussion of this topic, see Peter Reuter and Edwin Truman, *Chasing Dirty Money: The Fight Against Money Laundering* (Washington, DC: International Institute for Economics, 2004), 135.

52. Alison Jamieson, *The Antimafia: Italy's Fight Against Organized Crime* (London: Macmillan, 2000), 128–129, 144.

53. Robert Klitgaard, R. Maclean-Abaroa, and H. L. Parris, *Corrupt Cities: A Practical Guide to Cure and Prevention* (Oakland, CA: Institute for Contemporary Studies, 2000), 2.

54. Samuel Huntington, *Political Order in Changing Societies* (New Haven, CT: Yale University Press, 1969), 59–71.

55. Donnatella Della Porta and Yves Meny, "Conclusion," in Donnatella Della Porta and Yves Meny (Eds.), *Democracy and Corruption in Europe* (London: Pinter, 1997), 166–180.

56. Diego Gambetta and Peter Reuter, "Conspiracy among the Many: The Mafia in Legitimate Business," in Gianluca Fiorentini and Sam Peltzman (Eds.), *The Economics of Organized Crime* (Cambridge, UK: Cambridge University Press, 1995), 116–135.

57. Karen DeYoung and Kevin Sullivan, "Bush Urges Nations to Use Aid as Tool against Corruption," *Washington Post* (March 23, 2002): A14; Neil Levine, "Fighting Corruption in Foreign Aid," speech at Second Global Forum on Fighting Corruption and Safeguarding Integrity, The Hague, Netherlands, May 29, 2001.

58. The concept is taken from Donnatella Della Porta and Alberto Vannucci, *Corrupt Exchanges: Actors, Resources, and Mechanisms of Political Corruption* (New York: Aldine de Gruyter, 1999), 236–240.

59. Mats Berdal and Monica Serrano, *Transnational Organized Crime and International Security: Business as Usual?* (Boulder: Lynne Rienner, 2002); Peter Andreas, "The Clandestine Political Economy of War in Bosnia," *International Studies Quarterly* 48(1): 29–52.

60. Three distinct trends in this literature have emerged. First, the results-oriented track, exemplified by the writings of Michael Dzeidzic and Phil Williams, takes a direct rule of law and legal institutional approach to addressing this problem. The clandestine political economy approach, best demonstrated through the recent writings of Peter Andreas and captured in the Mats Berdal and Monica Serrano edited volume, focuses on discovering and understanding the range and scope of the association. Finally the European peace approach, highlighted by the work of Michael Pugh, suggests early detection of these illicit alliances could curb the chances for regional conflict. In each case, the three approaches provide a useful web for understanding and dissecting the relationship between conflict, post-conflict, and organized crime, marking one of the newer and intellectually vibrant tracks in the study of the issue.

61. Robert Putnam, Robert Leonardi, and Raffaella Y. Nanetti, *Making Democracy Work* (Princeton, NJ: Princeton University Press, 1993).

62. Louise Shelley, "Post-Soviet Organized Crime," *Demokratizatsiya* 2(3): 354–355.

63. See Valerie Braithewaite and Margaret Levi (Eds.), *Trust and Governance* (New York: Russell Sage Foundation, 1998); and Francis Fukuyama, *Trust: The Social Virtues and the Creation of Prosperity* (New York: The Free Press, 1995).

64. Louise Shelley, "Mafia and the Italian State: The Historical Roots of the Current Crisis," *Sociological Forum* 9(4): 661–672. For more, see Raimondo Catanzaro, *Men of Respect: A Social History of the Sicilian Mafia* (New York: The Free Press, 1992), and Diego Gambetta, *The Sicilian Mafia: The Business of Private Protection* (Cambridge: Harvard University Press, 1993).

65. Umberto Santino, *Storia del movimento antimafia* (Rome: Editori Riuniti, 2000).

66. Jamieson, *The Antimafia,* 148.

67. Rita Borsellino, "In Spite of Everything: The Popular Anti-Mafia Commitment in Sicily," *Trends in Organized Crime* 5(3): 58–63.

68. For a representation of the treatment of complexity, see Saskia Sassen, *Globalization and Its Discontents* (New York: New Press, 1998); Gwyn Prins, "Notes Toward the Definition of Global Security," *American Behavioral Scientist* (May 1995): 820–821; Robert D. Kaplan, "The Coming Anarchy: How Scarcity, Crime, Overpopulation, Tribalism, and Disease Are Destroying the Social Fabric of Our Planet," *Atlantic Monthly* (Feb. 1994): 44–76.

69. Sassen, *Globalization,* 153–158; Louise I. Shelley, "Transnational Organized Crime: The New Authoritarianism," in H. Richard Friman and Peter Andreas (Eds.), *The Illicit Global Economy and State Power* (Lanham, MD: Rowman & Littlefield, 1999), 26–33; Phil Williams, "The Nature of Drug Trafficking Networks," *Current History* 97(618): 155.

70. The globalization debate is wide, contentious, and marked by a variety of skeptics and believers. For further treatment, see Paul Hirst and Grahame Thompson, *Globalization in Question* (Oxford, UK: Blackwell, 1996); James Mittelman, *The Globalization Syndrome: Transformation and Resistance* (Princeton, NJ: Princeton University Press, 2000); James Rosenau, *Along the Domestic-Foreign Frontier: Exploring Governance in a Turbulent World* (Cambridge, UK: Cambridge University Press, 1997); David Harvey, *The Condition of Postmodernity* (Oxford, UK: Blackwell, 1989); Richard Falk, *Predatory Globalization: A Critique* (Cambridge, UK: Polity Press, 1999); Thomas Friedman, *The Lexus and the Olive Tree* (New York: Farrar, Straus & Giroux, 1999).

71. Francis Fukuyama, *The End of History and the Last Man* (New York: Avon Books, 1992), 39–51.

72. In this regard, power is understood as an act of will that manifests itself through material and ideational expressions: coercion and knowledge. For an articulation of complex power along these lines, see Robert Cox, "Social Forces, States, and World Orders: Beyond International Relations Theory" in Robert Keohane (Ed.), *Neorealism and Its Critics* (New York: Columbia University Press, 1986), 204–254.

73. Sassen, *Globalization,* 81–82, 87–90, 92–97.

74. Robert Jackson, *Quasi-States: Sovereignty, International Relations and the Third World* (Cambridge, UK: Cambridge University Press, 1989); Susan Strange, *The Retreat of the State* (Cambridge, UK: Cambridge University Press, 1986).

75. Rosenau, *Along the Domestic-Foreign Frontier,* 114–117, 349–358.

76. Shelley, "Mafia and the Italian State," 664–669. It is important to note that Shelley's work approaches this triad from the perspective of each place, allowing for a multispectral analysis that can be tested in a variety of empirical contexts. Most recently, Shelley used this framework to investigate and comment on human trafficking, especially in conjunction with the global sex trade. In this same vein, Sassen (*Globalization*) examines the woman and immigrant as "undervalorized" in the globalization dynamic.

77. Nikos Passas, "Global Anomie, Dysanomie, and Economic Crime: Hidden Consequences of Neoliberalism and Globalization in Russia and Around the World," *Social Justice* 27(2): 19–24. Passas's construction is similar to Pino Arlacchi's and Raimondo Catanzarro's, each of whom find the Sicilian Mafia a direct result of weak central authority and poor land reform. In essence, the landowners looked for protection, creating a historical link between legitimate business and organized crime, and thus creating the Mafia.

78. Peter Andreas, "The Political Economy of Narco-Corruption in Mexico," *Current History* 97(618): 162–164.

79. Most of this scholarship owes and pays homage to the work of Susan Strange, namely, *Casino Capitalism* (Oxford, UK: Blackwell, 1986) and *The Retreat of the State,* and a handful of scholarly essays that challenged the mainstream notion of international relations that the state is the only or best legitimate object of inquiry.

80. Francisco E. Thoumi, *Political Economy and Illegal Drugs in Colombia* (Boulder, CO: Lynne Rienner, 1995).

81. Gambetta and Reuter, "Conspiracy among the Many," 118, 121–123.
82. Friman and Andreas (Eds.), *The Illicit Global Economy and State Power,* 7.
83. Bill McSweeney, "Identity and Security: Buzan and the Copenhagen School," *Review of International Studies* 22(1): 81–93.
84. Barry Buzan, Ole Waever, and Jaap de Wilde, *Security: A New Framework for Analysis* (Boulder, CO: Lynne Rienner, 1998); Barry Buzan, *People, States, and Fear* (Boulder, CO: Lynne Rienner, 1990).
85. Buzan and Waever, *Regions and Powers: The Structure of International Security* (Cambridge: Cambridge University Press, 2003).
86. Louise Shelley and John Picarelli, "Methods, Not Motives: Implications of the Convergence of International Organized Crime and Terrorism," *Police Practice and Research* 3 (2002): 305–318.
87. Shelley and Picarelli; Phil Williams, "Terrorism and Organized Crime: Convergence, Nexus or Transformation?" in Jervas (Ed.), *FOA Report on Terrorism* (Stockholm, Defence Research Establishment), 69–92; Makarenko, Tamara, "'The Ties that Bind': Uncovering the Relationship Between Organized Crime and Terrorism," in Dina Siegel et al. (Eds.), *Global Organized Crime: Trends and Developments* (Dordrecht: Kluwer Academic Publishers, 2003), 159–170; Chris Dishman, "Terrorism, Crime and Transformation," *Studies in Conflict and Terrorism* 24(1) (2001): 43–58.
88. Lake, *Six Nightmares,* 1–32.

CHAPTER SEVEN

The Global Drug Trade vs. the Nation-State:

Why the Thugs Keep Winning

Stephen E. Flynn*

For U.S. border control agents, intercepting the ripples of danger in the tidal wave of commerce is like trying to win a lottery. In 2004, 476 million people arrived at the borders of the United States on 675,000 commercial and private flights, on 90,000 merchant and passenger vessels, and in 116 million passenger vehicles, and the majority of this traffic was concentrated in just a handful of ports and border crossings. One third of all the trucks that enter the United States annually, for example, traverse just four international bridges between the province of Ontario and the states of Michigan and New York. At the bi-national Ambassador Bridge between Detroit and Windsor, 6,000 trucks entered the United States each day in 2005. With only 8 primary inspection

*Stephen E. Flynn is the Jeane J. Kirkpatrick Senior Fellow for National Security Studies at the Council on Foreign Relations and a retired Commander in the United States Coast Guard. The views expressed are those of the author and do not reflect the official policy or position of the Council on Foreign Relations. The author is grateful to Andrea Walters for her research support in updating many of the facts that appeared in the earlier version of this chapter published in 2002.

lanes and a parking lot that can hold just 90 tractor-trailers at a time for secondary or tertiary inspections, trucks carrying up to 15 tons of goods must be cleared for entry at an average pace of no more than 2 minutes per truck. If border inspectors fall behind, the parking lot would fill up, trucks would back up onto the bridge and the resulting pileup could cost the U.S. automotive industry $1 million in loss of production per hour per assembly plant.

The persistent growth and dramatic spread of illicit drug markets, most notably for heroin, cocaine, and synthetic drugs, is a disturbing trend. Since 1990, the production of opium poppies has grown by 250 percent in the impoverished and poorly governed regions of Southwest Asia and Latin America. Despite more than a decade of U.S.-sponsored eradication programs and aggressive enforcement efforts, there has been only a marginal reduction in the cultivation of coca in the Andean region. Initial success in eliminating cultivation within one area has only pushed it to another.[1] Internet users can readily surf the Net for formulas for preparing controlled substances and then order up the chemical ingredients from a growing menu of online suppliers. The result: synthetic drugs like methamphetamine and LSD can be concocted by kitchen chemists around the globe[2] The clandestine trafficking organizations that have evolved to link producers with distant consumers have also grown in sophistication. Drug abuse and addiction, particularly near production areas and along the growing array of transit routes, has expanded into areas that had hitherto remained largely unscathed.

This growth in the drug phenomenon has taken place despite a nearly century-old international prohibitionary regime designed to contain it. In the United States, even with a one-quarter-trillion-dollar investment in drug control programs by the federal government since 1981,[3] the drug business continues to thrive. Indeed, for more than ten years suppliers have been compelled to lower wholesale and retail prices of cocaine and heroin and improve the street-level purity in order to stay competitive.[4] Around the world, drugs have become more available and affordable despite a rash of new multilateral initiatives that target not only illicit drugs, but the precursor chemicals and money connected with them.

Today, drugs represent one of the world's largest—and perhaps most lucrative—commodity trades. As an illicit enterprise, it is impossible to establish its total value with any precision. The United Nations Drug Control Program estimates of the annual revenues at the production, retail, and wholesale levels equaled $439 billion in 2003. That value is higher than the Gross Domestic Product (GDP) of 163 out of 184 countries in the world.[5]

That the marketing of drugs has become truly global is illustrated by the fact that the majority of drugs are consumed outside of North America.[6]

In 2003, the overwhelming majority of interdictions of opiates outside the production areas took place in Europe, with U.S. seizures equal to less than 1 percent of the world total.[7] Virtually every country is reporting that drugs are far more available today than at any time in recent history.[8]

WHY STATE-CENTRIC APPROACHES TO DRUG TRAFFICKING ARE INSUFFICIENT

Why is the war on drugs going so badly? The answer lies with the fact that we continue to rely on stepped-up versions of a state-centric approach to confront what is an inherently global problem that thrives in the dark corners of the international systems where traditional sovereign controls are weak or nonexistent. The end of the Cold War dramatically expanded the realm where the writ of the state does not run. Thus enforcement authorities intent on stemming the production, trafficking, and consumption of drugs often find themselves all dressed up with nowhere to go. Since most of the world's illicit drug supply is cultivated within states that are weak or failing, international source control is a house built on the sand of local enforcement bodies that are too primitive or corrupt to take the actions to stop the cultivation of drug raw materials within their borders. Interdiction efforts face the improbable task of sifting contraband from the rising tide of legitimate goods, services, and people that now wash across national borders as a result of the explosive growth of the global economy and the twin trends of liberalization and privatization. Finally, as democratization has taken root around the planet, the ability of police authorities to intrude into the lives of citizens has been properly reined in, leaving people with greater freedom to do more of what they please—including, inevitably, socially sanctioned activities like buying and consuming drugs—outside of the watchful eye of the state.

In short, the explosive rise of the global drug trade in the post–Cold War era highlights the fiction that the international system is the sum of its nation states. Drugs are produced and trafficked by non-state actors who find borders essentially meaningless. In fact, the bad guys find the remaining vestiges of sovereignty to be largely an ally in their global enterprise. Since each state reserves for itself the right to draft laws, to establish rules and procedures for operating its criminal justice system, and to establish public policy priorities, drug control must be pursued against a backdrop of widely differing national jurisdictions. This lack of harmonization muddies the prospect for seamless multilateral cooperation among enforcement authorities. Whenever there is friction, there are "no-man's lands" which drug traffickers can occupy. The bottom line is that while states must still be mindful of the sensibilities of their fellow sovereigns, traffickers need not. As a result, the legal barriers whose aim is to prevent chemicals, drugs, and profits from circulating around the globe leak like a sieve.

The expansion of the drug trade not only reflects the unsteady state of states, but in growing measure, the trade is contributing to the turbulence. The enormous profits generated by drugs provide terrorists and insurgents with hard currency to purchase weapons. Drug money also makes it possible for international criminal organizations to corrupt officials at every level of government, thereby undermining the legitimacy of political and judicial institutions. Since the billions of dollars associated with the global drug trade are illegitimate, they are circulated within the shadow economy, providing a substantial impetus for its growth. Finally, a rise in participation in drug-related activities, particularly when concentrated among youth and minority ethnic populations, accentuates social cleavages that are being fueled already by the pain and dislocations connected with modernization, post-communist, and post-industrial societal transitions.

Acknowledging drugs as a phenomenon that lies *beyond sovereignty* achieves two ends. First, it helps explain why current U.S. and international drug control exertions are not working. Second, it points a way to a better approach. Ultimately states must turn to the primary beneficiaries of globalization to redress its dark side. Since states have a declining presence in the economic and social spheres where the drug trade thrives, ultimately it is non-governmental organizations, businesses, and community activists who are best positioned to create a climate less conducive to the rapid growth of drug supply and demand. In the end it is not states, but non-state actors, who must be enlisted to temper the forces that are motivating and facilitating drug-related activities.

THE RISE OF THE GLOBAL DRUG TRADE

The production and global distribution of drugs is by no means a new phenomenon. Turkish and Persian opium were traded for centuries throughout the Middle East and in parts of Asia. By the latter part of the eighteenth century and throughout the nineteenth, large-scale production and worldwide distribution of opiates became systematically organized, often with the official sanction if not direct involvement of the governments of the major powers. On the eve of the twentieth century, legal markets in cocaine and opiates were flourishing within the United States, Europe, and the Far East, and the global drug trade could be characterized as a widely accepted sector of international commerce.

This would change beginning with the 1909 conference in Shanghai of the International Opium Commission. Growing concern over widespread drug abuse and addiction, voiced primarily by religious missionaries serving overseas and a growing number of physicians and temperance organizations at home,[9] led the U.S. government to sponsor the Shanghai conference with the objective of convincing the principal producer countries to curtail the opium trade.[10] While this drug control agenda was slow to take root, following World War I the League of Nations did create mandatory international controls supervised by a newly created Opium Control Board. The opium trade was to be eliminated within fifteen years and restricted to government monopolies during the interim period. This regulatory body was later reconstituted as the Permanent Central Board and charged with creating a tighter world system of controls over a wider range of drugs to include cocaine and cannabis.

Resting as they did on the power and legitimacy of state authorities to enforce them, these initial steps towards developing a global prohibition regime had the unsettling effect of displacing drug trafficking, production, and consumption toward places where state sovereignty was weakest if not non-existent.[11] Criminal suppliers stepped into the void left by long-standing government monopolies, initially basing their black market activities out of the cities of Istanbul and Shanghai. Thus began a development that would gather force over the next five decades—the tendency for the chemicals, drugs, and money that sustain the drug trade to be concentrated in areas in the international system that offered the lowest level of regulatory resistance to international trade flows. During World War II there were few such locales and the illicit traffic in drugs practically disappeared.[12] But following the war, as the number of these areas grew, so would the drug trade. Havana before Castro was the gateway to the Western Hemisphere. Marseilles served as a base for the famous French Connection until the early 1970s. Today, transnational drug criminals have a vast array of havens for their activities, most notably Caracas, Bogota, Panama City, Karachi, Bangkok, Lagos, Nairobi, Sofia, Moscow, St. Petersburg, and Warsaw.[13]

The tendency for trafficking activities to move toward cities where governmental authority is weakest paralleled a similar kind of shift in production of the botanical ingredients. Over time, traditional cultivation areas once controlled by colonial monopolies were largely abandoned in favor of territories effectively not under the control of any state authority. Today, nearly all coca is cultivated in rebel-controlled areas of Colombia and other remote, rural locations in Colombia, Peru, and Bolivia while Burma, Afghanistan, and Laos together account for 92 percent of opium poppy cultivation.[14] Newly emerging producers such as Kazakhstan, Kyrgyzstan, Uzbekistan, Turkmenistan,

Tajikistan, Ukraine, Azerbaijan, Georgia, Nigeria, Kenya, and Vietnam all share common ingredients, seemingly validating the inverse relationship between production and viable national sovereignty. These countries share three characteristics: (1) a weak central government or widespread corruption among governmental authorities, (2) recently established or enhanced ties to regional or global markets, and (3) vast, remote areas where cultivation can take place largely undetected. Additionally, in several instances, production activities have been directly sponsored or protected by insurgent groups who resist, by force of arms, encroachments by the state into production regions.

While production and trafficking activities have increasingly been concentrated in the largely lawless corners of the global community, for much of the latter half of the twentieth century the end users of illicit drugs have resided largely in developed countries with the United States serving as the primary market. Given the size and resources of the U.S. government, it would appear at first glance that if properly committed, the United States could insulate itself from the wholesale and retail activities of drug traffickers. But upon closer examination, it becomes clear that the government is not well positioned to do so. First, efforts to prevent retail transactions are necessarily hindered by basic civil liberty protections. While these protections obviously apply to all criminal investigations, what make drug crimes particularly difficult for law enforcement officials to pursue is that they rarely receive the cooperation of the victim. This is because, unlike crimes such as burglary or rape, the "victim" in a drug transaction (the consumer) does not file a police report or make evidence available because he or she is also an accomplice. Detecting a drug retail crime, therefore, generally must be accomplished unilaterally by state authorities. At the same time, these authorities must always be mindful not to interfere with the freedoms Americans enjoy to move when and where they please, to possess unfettered control over their disposable incomes, and most importantly, to be secure from the intrusiveness of the state in their private lives. In short, as an essentially free and democratic society, Americans have imposed formidable constitutional limits on the sovereign prerogatives of their government to control wholesale or retail drug-related activities within U.S. borders.

LIBERALIZATION AND THE DRUG TRADE: UNINTENDED CONSEQUENCES

It is not only *within* their societies that advanced democratic countries are confronted with serious limits to their power to pursue drug crimes. The United States and Western European states are also finding that they have a shrinking capacity to detect drug trafficking activities along their borders.

This is in part due to conscious choices by governments to remove restrictions on cross-border flows of a growing volume of legal goods, capital, and services. Beginning in the 1970s, for instance, the U.S. Customs Service (now the U.S. Customs and Border Protection Agency) stopped stationing customs officers at American shipping piers and terminals where imported cargo is discharged, and it removed customs storekeepers from bonded warehouses. These traditional inspection controls were replaced with automated systems and post-audits in response to growing private-sector calls for reductions in domestic barriers to international commerce. Imported goods often transit throughout the United States without undergoing any physical inspection by customs inspectors. The carrier needs only to assure customs authorities that it will maintain custody over these imports until the goods reach their final destination. Officials then authorize release upon receipt of accounting and importers' documentation. In recent years, the requirements on labeling, cords, and seals have been relaxed, and spot inspections of bonded goods in transit are very rare.[15]

The member states of the European Union have gone even further than the United States in adopting new rules that have substantially liberalized their national transportation sectors. Beginning in 1988, for instance, quotas and permits for transporters operating in a member country other than the hauler's own were removed. In March 1991, the EU removed all restrictions on air cargo capacity, and authorized a carrier based in one country to pick up goods in another and deliver them to a third. Finally, on January 1, 1993, the community granted all EU shippers moving cargo by road, free access to any other EU country.[16] The Schengen Agreements took the ultimate liberalization step by eliminating controls on the movement of people within the European Union.[17]

These trends have not been restricted to the United States and Western Europe. Colombia, Venezuela, and Brazil have all engaged in efforts to deregulate maritime and land transport.[18] Mexico dramatically liberalized its regulations governing the trucking industry in June 1989, allowing any licensed truck to move freely within the country and to load and unload in any city, port, or railway station.[19] In May 2002, Mexican truckers were allowed access to the highways of the United States and Canada as part of implementing the final arrangements of NAFTA.[20] "Free trade zones" have proliferated throughout the Caribbean and Central America as a part of a competitive effort to attract direct foreign investment and to facilitate the flow of trade. In the face of this trend, customs agents who inspect cargo entering or leaving their jurisdictions are seen as increasingly undesirable sources of friction that should be marginalized, minimized, or eliminated wherever possible.

Global transportation and logistics trends are also complicating the lives of border control agents. Increasingly, containerized cargo move through hub ports where cascading volumes and the imperative of rapid processing render impractical traditional efforts to examine these shipments.

The challenge of filtering the bad from the good among the cross-border flows of people and goods is clearly daunting. But tracking and freezing illicit money flows represents an even more Herculean task. This is because advanced capitalist societies have undertaken a number of steps to minimize the barriers to international capital movements. Governments began to surrender regulatory control over cross-border investments with the creation of the Eurodollar market and off-shore banking centers in the late 1960s. The trend was given added impetus by the enactment of new laws that lowered the restrictions on foreign investment by pension funds, insurance companies, unit trusts and mutual funds, giving rise to a proliferation of new players in international financial markets.[21] These concessions were inspired in part by the fallout from expansionary policies in the 1980s that produced large deficits in the Group of 7 countries. Confronted by the need to court foreign investors to help them finance bond issues, governments were inclined to eliminate barriers that might discourage would-be creditors. Pressures to ease reporting requirements and other controls came also from the banking and non-banking industries. Given the volatility of exchange rates, competitive global bidding, and the explosive growth in clients attempting to make time-sensitive deals, financial institutions are finding that their survival is dependent on their ability to conclude transactions rapidly. They therefore tend to see government regulators almost exclusively in adversarial terms.

The deregulation of the transportation and financial sectors has been in part a reaction to the dictates of a global marketplace that has been transformed by the extraordinary impact of the communications revolution. The power of computers, computer software, satellites, fiber-optic cables, facsimile machines, modems, and wireless technology has effectively overcome most of the practical limitations connected with geographical distances. Communications technology has made it possible for financial markets to be truly globalized with around-the-clock trading in bonds, stocks and exchanges conducted over hundreds of thousands of electronic monitors linked together in trading rooms all over the world. Communications technology also provides manufacturers with the means to remotely coordinate distant operations, allowing them to disperse production activities to wherever the greatest value can be added to each stage of production. As these multinational corporations deepen these international production-based linkages, their success in turn becomes increasingly tied to their access to open capital markets and a low-cost and smoothly functioning transportation and communications infrastructure. Thus, governments face nearly irresistible pressure to deregulate their financial, transportation, and communications sectors in order to compete within an increasing integrated and time-sensitive global economy.

There is little question that these liberalization trends have served to stimulate the growth in world trade and investment over the past ten years. Since the early 1980s, world merchandise exports have grown in volume at twice the rate of gross domestic product. But these widely heralded outcomes have come at a cost—international markets have been made almost as accessible to illicit commercial activities as licit. This fact has certainly not been lost on the more sophisticated drug trafficking organizations who have increasingly shifted away from low-flying Cessnas and fast-moving "cigarette" boats popularized in action-films, into more stodgy but reliable conveyances such as the millions of commercial containers that move cargo around the planet. Cocaine is inserted inside legitimate cargo or in the floor or walls of containers originating from international shipping centers in Central and South America, particularly in Brazil, Venezuela, Surinam, and Panama. By land, most cocaine crosses the U.S.-Mexican border in the hidden compartments of tractor trailers and other vehicles or in commercial cargo itself. When commercial airlines are used, the drug is hidden on the plane among perishable cargoes such as cut flowers or fruit pulp, or among passengers who conceal it by placing it in luggage with false bottoms or in hollowed-out sneakers, by taping it to their bodies, or by swallowing condoms filled with cocaine. Sometimes it is converted to liquid and smuggled in bottles of shampoo, mouthwash, baby formula, and liquor. In most instances, these shipments are accompanied by complete documentation from licensed companies with legitimate destinations.

DRUG TRAFFICKERS USE THE TOOLS OF MODERN BUSINESSES

Once the cocaine arrives in the United States, it must be distributed to the millions of drug consumers. Given the lucrative nature of this enterprise, it should come as little surprise that this is by no means an amateurish operation. Documents seized during a successful raid on a wholesale distribution network in New York, operated by a Cali-based organization, exposed just how sophisticated these criminals are.[22]

In its prime, the Cali cartel operated dozens of distribution cells throughout the country, with each cell made up of ten to fifteen Colombian employees who earned monthly salaries ranging from $2000 to $7500. They conducted as much as $25 million of business each month. Each cell was self-contained, with information tightly compartmentalized. Only a handful of managers knew all the operatives. The cell typically had a head, bookkeeper, money handler, cocaine handler, motor pool, and ten to fifteen apartments serving as stash houses.

Communications were conducted in code over facsimile machines, cellular phones, and pay phones. To eliminate any risk of interception, cellular phones were purchased and discarded, often weekly. When a wholesale customer wanted to make a purchase, a cell member was notified by a pager system. That cell member would proceed to a public phone and arrange a rendezvous site. He would then get, from the motor pool, a rental car that would be returned to the rental agency after the transaction. The transaction itself, including travel receipts, was logged by the bookkeeper and the money turned over to the money handler to be shipped to the financial network set up by the cartel to hide and invest it. One favored way to ship cash within the United States was by way of the U.S. Postal Service's "Express Mail." There was plenty of cash to ship—up to $200 million each year per cell.

Money laundering typically involves three independent phases. First, drug proceeds are "placed"—that is, deposited in banks or used to purchase monetary instruments or securities that can be turned into cash elsewhere. This is often done by hiring individuals known as "smurfs" to deposit the money in small denominations in as many banks and financial institutions as possible so as to defeat currency reporting requirements.[23] Second, the money is "layered," or sent through multiple electronic transfers or other transactions to make it difficult to track and blur its illicit origin.[24] Finally, the source of the money disappears as it is "integrated," that is, invested into seemingly legitimate accounts and enterprises. To lower their exposure to law enforcement yet further, drug trafficking organizations often contract out these last two phases, getting money handlers to provide them the money upfront, less a 15- to 25-percent commission, in return for providing these handlers the opportunity to launder and keep the full amount.[25]

Today, the notorious Medellin and Cali cartels have been largely dismantled, but the cocaine trade has not. A number of smaller organizations, many with ties to Colombia's guerrilla insurgency and paramilitary groups, have been the beneficiaries of the drug kingpin strategy that was the heart of U.S.-Colombian enforcement efforts during the 1990s. To a large extent, these smaller trafficking organizations mirror the behaviors of successful modern global corporations. They have developed network structures that successfully support vertical and horizontal relationships with "contractors" across borders. They have invested into the most advanced information technologies to maintain secure, real-time links over long distances, in order to coordinate production and distribution activities under rapidly changing conditions and in a potentially adversarial environment. Most importantly, they have immersed their activities within parts of the global infrastructure that are virtually unregulated—commercial containers, air cargo, overland freight, rental cars, cellular phones, overnight mail, and electronic transfers.

The Southeast Asian heroin trade mirrors the sophistication of the Latin American cocaine industry. Heroin produced in the Golden Triangle of Burma, Laos, and Thailand is typically smuggled overland to seaports in Burma, China, Thailand, Malaysia, and Vietnam where it is packed into containers with legitimate cargo before being sent to its intended markets in Europe, Australia, Canada, and the United States. In this "transshipment" process, new bills of lading are produced that mask the origin and nature of the container's contents. After leaving the mainland ports, the container will make an intermediary stop at one of the regional hub ports like Hong Kong or Singapore where every *month* each port handles more than 1 million maritime containers. In Singapore, the average time between discharge and reloading an entire ship requiring as many as 2000 container moves is under 10 hours, giving little time for Singaporean authorities to inspect or audit the cargo.[26] There are tens of thousands of importers, some of which are actually front companies that hide drug shipments within legitimate cargo.[27] There is no shortage of places to hide, with 1.2 trillion metric tons of international waterborne trade arriving at or departing from U.S. ports in 2004. And the volume of containerized cargo is growing rapidly, up 86 percent between 2000 and 2004.[28]

GOVERNMENT RESPONSES

Monitoring and inspecting commercial air traffic has become an equally formidable task for government agents. When these flights arrive in the United States, they are likely to land in a busy airport like Miami where more than 88 airlines moved 30.2 million passengers and 1.96 million tons of air cargo in 2004.[29] Frequently the goods moved by air are perishable.[30] In Houston, for example, inspectors are confronted with shipments of 2 million plants from South America each month, which they must process swiftly or risk generating huge spoilage losses for importers.

Along the land borders of the United States, customs inspectors can find no relief for their overwhelming task of filtering the illicit traffic from the licit. A substantial proportion of the more than 489 million people that enter the United States each year do so in one of the 128 million automobiles that cross American borders.[31] The rule of thumb in the border inspection business is that it takes five inspectors three hours to conduct a thorough physical inspection of a loaded 40-foot container or an 18-wheel truck. Even with the assistance of new high-tech sensors, inspectors have nowhere near the amount of time, space, or manpower to inspect all the cargo arriving.

A case in point is the Ambassador Bridge between Detroit, Michigan, and Windsor, Ontario. There, at the world's busiest commercial land-border crossing, the huge volume means that U.S. Customs officers must average no more than 2 minutes for each truck. If they fall behind, the parking lot fills, trucks back up onto the bridge and the resulting pileup virtually closes the border, generating roadway chaos throughout metropolitan Windsor and Detroit. Prior to the terrorist attacks on September 11, 2001, U.S. customs officials operating at busy commercial border crossings were subject to performance sanctions if they disrupted the flow of commerce by making anything more involved than token, random spot-checks.[32] Since September 11, the business communities in Texas and Michigan have been busy documenting the disruption to the border economies associated with added delays connected with stepped-up border security measures.[33]

Given what are quite clearly horrendous and diminishing odds for successfully discovering drugs based on random border inspections, intelligence to support law enforcement operations would appear crucial to successful interdiction of drugs along U.S. borders and in U.S. streets. Here, however, the traffickers' investment in state-of-the-art communications hardware and software has effectively defeated any hope of successful electronic surveillance by law enforcement officials. Communications via pagers and pay phones are, for all practical purposes, impossible to monitor. While it is possible to listen in on a cellular phone conversation, the interception technology is scarce and expensive. Further, a court order for electronic surveillance also takes time—generally longer than the very brief time span that a trafficker will use the phone before dumping it and getting a new one. Finally, the Internet makes it possible for traffickers to conduct completely secure communications. If the traffickers break their messages up into multiple sub-units, send each unit through anonymous re-mailers that move the message through a large number of "routers" before it arrives at its final destination, and use widely available 128-bit encryption technology such as PGP (Pretty Good Privacy), they can operate with virtually no risk from surveillance efforts by the law enforcement community.[34]

Since the prospects of interdicting drugs or investigating the trafficking organizations that move them appear to be so grim, one final temptation would be to target the money derived from this illicit business. The logic here is that since retail drug sales must be made in cash and the cash is actually far bulkier than the drugs for which it is sold, law enforcement should focus on keeping the money from finding its way back to Colombia or the other trafficking home bases. Unfortunately, given the liquidity of money and the globalization trends outlined above, this strategy too is destined to prove unworkable. There simply is no shortage of ways in which the money can be placed within the economy. Money launderers can and do use non-bank financial institutions such as exchange houses, check cashing services, and credit unions. They purchase instruments like postal money orders, cashier's checks, certificates of deposit, and even securities such as stocks and bonds. Proceeds are invested into legitimate businesses such as travel agencies, construction companies, casinos, securities dealers, real estate agencies, jewelry shops, and antique dealers—that is, businesses with a high volume of cash transactions. Money managers may soon use microchip-based electronic money or cybercurrency, giving them the ability to make instant and anonymous transfers of money around the globe.[35]

RECONSIDERING DRUG CONTROL[36]

In sum, the drug trade has grown in recent years because changes within the international system have raised the fortunes of transsovereign actors while eroding the position of states. Since the beginning of the post-colonial era, there has been an unparalleled growth in the number of state actors in the international system that lack the institutional capacity to exercise sovereignty over much of their national territories. Actors within these new states have virtually unrestricted access to the global economy as a result of the worldwide trend toward economic liberalization. Wholesale privatization and deregulation within national economies has diminished the capacity of all states—developing, post-communist, and developed—to exercise control over production and distribution activities within and across their borders. As a result, the global economy has slid increasingly into a status of *laissez faire,* creating little practical distinction between engaging in legitimate and illegitimate commercial activities. Traffickers in illicit narcotics merely merge with the legitimate flows of goods, capital, and services within the global marketplace, comfortable in the realization that governments have a shrinking capacity to separate the bad from the good.

The manifold factors influencing the growth of the global drug trade render impractical traditional supply-side policies. The drug problem cannot be solved by simply working harder to eliminate drugs at their source or to seize them prior to their arrival in the United States. Policies enacted with these objectives in mind are fatally flawed for two reasons. First, the centrality of enforcement makes them an inherently reactive approach to an extremely dynamic phenomenon. Law enforcement by definition cannot be preemptive—rules must be broken *before* the legitimate coercive authority of the state can be brought to bear to impose sanctions. Second, these policies rest on the fallacious notion that drug production and trafficking activities can somehow be readily rooted out from the context in which they exist.

By defining drugs as "bad," drug control policies rest upon the normative presumption that the phenomenon is alien and "normalcy" can be restored by isolating and exorcising it from the body politic. But the drug phenomenon cannot be exorcised precisely because it is deeply entrenched in so many of the activities that underlie modern life. Further, there is little agreement over exactly what constitutes the evil to be eradicated. While there is nearly universal acknowledgment that the abuse of drugs such as heroin and cocaine is a bad thing, it is difficult to formulate similar tidy judgments about the array of interwoven activities that ultimately supply the addict with his fix. Farmers, chemists, shippers, and bankers who are directly or indirectly involved in the drug trade rarely see themselves as criminals, but instead characterize themselves as "good" businessmen striving to embrace one of capitalism's chief tenets—a commitment to maximizing profits. The inventors and suppliers of new technologies that are exploited by organized criminal networks do not see themselves as accomplices to crime, but as purveyors of progress. Importers, exporters, tourists, and commercial carriers are acting in concert with the principles of economic liberalization when they strongly oppose the use of intrusive border controls governments have traditionally relied upon to detect and stop contraband. Finally, civil libertarians are embracing the core ideals of democratic society when they fight to restrict the intrusiveness of governmental authority into the individual lives of their citizenry, even if it means that some drug crimes will go undetected.

So where does this leave policy makers committed to stemming the burgeoning global drug trade? Obviously it presents them with a far more complicated challenge than the one they have been willing to acknowledge—at least publicly—up to this point, for it is a challenge that cannot be reduced to a state-centric crusade against evil drug producers, traffickers, and consumers. Instead it represents a vexing global problem of the first order.

By outlining the factors that are motivating and facilitating drug production, it becomes self-evident why American and United Nations funded crop eradication, crop substitution, and alternative development programs are not working. Such programs are premised on the notion that if existing growers can be either coerced or enticed to end drug cultivation, the void will remain unfilled. But it takes the prevalence of only three very rudimentary conditions to render this approach unworkable: (1) the existence of suitable alternative sites for cultivation; (2) the greater appeal of profits from drug production vis-à-vis those of the competing agricultural alternatives; and (3) the existence of jurisdictions where drug production can take place because the host governments lack either the means or the will to end it. The first condition is a function of geography; vast tracks of the global landscape are well suited to drug production. The second is a function of market demand that shows no signs of diminishing. And the third is dependent on political legitimacy and the effectiveness of regulatory and enforcement mechanisms, all of which are under significant strain in the post–Cold War era.

Similarly it should be clear why interdiction initiatives that aim to stem the cross-border flows of processing chemicals, drugs, and drug moneys are ineffectual. As long as these activities can blend within the increasingly unregulated movements of people, goods, and services associated with an open global economy, these enforcement efforts are reduced to a futile "needle-in-the-haystack" exercise.

While begrudgingly acknowledging the dim prospect for real achievement, some might argue that these supply-side initiatives serve an important symbolic role, providing a tangible demonstration of national and international support for anti-drug norms. This rationale is found wanting, however, once the costs of undertaking this essentially normative effort are considered. For example, crop eradication programs typically end up displacing production into more remote areas that are often environmentally sensitive public lands. Since farmers neither own the land nor expect that their activities will go undetected over the long term, they clear it with highly destructive "slash-and-burn" practices, plant and harvest a crop, and then move on. If these cultivation activities take place on mountainous terrain as is commonly the case in Southeast Asia and Latin America, erosion can produce irreversible harm to the surrounding area.[37] In addition to displacement, some alternative development programs actually inadvertently facilitate the drug trade. This happens when assistance is provided to enhance the infrastructure of a drug-producing region so as to make the cultivation of other legitimate crops viable, but the farmers secretly continue to engage in illicit cultivation. The net result of these generous investments in new infrastructure is to lower the costs of moving chemicals and fertilizers into the region, and to ease the transportation burden of moving drugs to their downstream markets.

Nowhere are the potential costs associated with aggressive supply-reduction efforts likely to be more painful than in Colombia. After the

Colombian government rolled out "Plan Colombia" in 2000, the United States government committed to becoming the largest donor in a multi-billion-dollar plan to rein in the recent surge in coca cultivation in that long-troubled nation.[38] It is easy to predict what intensified efforts to combat drug cultivation and trafficking, particularly in the remote, guerilla-controlled region of Putamayo, will do. Reports documenting the spillover of kidnappings, crime, violence, and refugees into Ecuador, Venezuela, Brazil, and Panama are multiplying.[39] Unfortunately, none of these countries are in a position to cope with these problems, particularly Ecuador and Panama. Throughout this region there are few resources and little in the way of infrastructure for promoting the rule of law or advancing economic development in the areas most susceptible to the dollars and intimidation drug traffickers can bring to bear. Nowhere is there the capacity to absorb the potential for millions of refugees from Colombia's civil war. Even if Brazilian, Venezuelan, and Ecuadorian police and soldiers are moved into the areas so as to harden the borders with southern Colombia, the costs are likely to be prohibitively high in economic and diplomatic terms. Militarizing the border regions will inevitably compromise the cross-border flow of trade and likely sour diplomatic relations among the neighboring countries.

Stepped-up efforts to disrupt drug trafficking activities in Colombia may also produce harmful unintended consequences. Such efforts inevitably spawn greater innovation on the part of the drug barons. The drug enforcement community often touts this result as progress since it presumably "raises the cost of doing business."[40] This may sound like a worthy objective, but it can in fact prove to be counterproductive if enforcement ends up only taking out the low-lying fruit. More specifically, if "raising costs" only applies to entry-level competitors, the result may mean that more sophisticated trafficking organizations actually benefit from enforcement activities since these activities can have the result of eliminating those who might otherwise threaten their market share.

Enforcement-generated innovation that leads traffickers to move from traditional non-commercial smuggling activities to more sophisticated schemes involving manufacturers, commercial carriers, exporters, and financiers can also prove to be a cure worse than the disease. This is because of the corrosive effect drug money can have across the entire commercial sector, undermining confidence in the private sector and the regulators charged with policing it. In addition, as legitimate trade becomes increasingly contaminated with illicit narcotics, it elevates the risk that all exports will be subject to delays and added costs associated with closer inspections and destructive searches.

Perhaps the most disturbing consequence of more aggressive attacks on Colombian drug traffickers is that the most likely beneficiaries will be Mexican trafficking organizations. For some time Mexican traffickers have benefited from the disruption of the cocaine trade in the Caribbean that led the Colombians to seek out an alternative route to the United States via its southwest border. Mexican narco-traffickers have benefited from the aggressive enforcement efforts against the Medellin and Cali cartels, because of the opportunities those efforts have afforded them to move into the wholesale cocaine distribution business in the United States.[41] If the Colombian drug supplies begin to dry up, there is little to prevent Mexican organizations from sponsoring coca production and refinement in Peru and Bolivia or elsewhere in the Andean region, emulating the example of the Colombian drug barons in the 1970s.

It should require little in the way of elaboration to explain why a transfer of control over the cocaine trade to Mexican traffickers would be so disastrous. Mexico is the United States' second largest trading partner. At just over 100 million, its population is nearly two and one-half that of Colombia. Arguably, its institutions may prove less resilient than those in Colombia to the corrosive threat of "plata o plomo" (silver or lead).[42] Its historic movement away from a one-party state has just begun. Political power in Mexico is more decentralized, with governors possessing a great deal of autonomy. Corruption within the police forces and some elements of the military is rampant. Like Colombia, Mexico has its own problems with insurgencies, particularly in the Chiapas. If Mexico were to become the hemisphere's new capital of drug trade, scarring its fragile political and economic institutions in ways similar to those that have afflicted Colombia, the repercussions for U.S. domestic and regional interests would be enormous.

WHAT CAN BE DONE?

We need to rethink the drug war in light of the qualities of the drug trade illuminated by considering it a transsovereign problem. By overlooking its inherently transnational character, we overlook both a threat and an opportunity. When we pursue policies that treat the drug phenomenon primarily as an enforcement problem, we end up seeing only the proverbial tip of the iceberg. The drug issue inevitably complicates the process of modernization in the developing world; the painful political, economic, and social adjustments now underway in the post-communist world; and the difficult post-industrial transition in the developed world. While clearly not a causal variable, the drug issue also contributes to the challenges of ethnic conflict and civil war, weapons proliferation, and environmental devastation. To try and tackle all these problems without acknowledging the direct or indirect relationship of the burgeoning global drug trade seems wrong-minded at best and possibly self-defeating at worst.

Ultimately, the first step requires moving from rhetoric to reality in addressing demand reduction, which means the United States and other advanced societies must place primary emphasis on providing adequate medical and social services for treating drug addicts. The strategic rationale for this is straightforward. Of the estimated 77 million Americans who have experimented with drugs at least once in their lifetime, the overwhelming majority of drugs are consumed by the 5 million frequent drug users.[43] The 50-percent decline in casual use in the United States during the 1990s was a very positive development. But from a drug market standpoint, the fact that there has been virtually no change in the number of drug addicts means that this drop in recreational drug use has had virtually no effect on the overall demand for cocaine and heroin. Thanks to drug abuse prevention programs, the cocaine industry may not be a growth business in the United States, but the demand for coca and poppies will be unchanged as long as Americans refuse to invest in long-term drug treatment.

Second, we need to recognize that the narcotics trade and the illicit dollars that go with it cannot be divorced from the informal economy that is burgeoning within the region and around the world. Trade fraud, tax evasion, sweatshops that thrive off underground labor, and the smuggling of licit products from DVDs to cigarettes all provide a growing haystack within which drugs and money laundering activities can hide. To a large extent, we should look at the drug trade as something akin to the dye cardiologists use to detect blockages in the circulatory system. It highlights the gaping holes in the international economic system that have facilitated the unsettling growth of what Susan Strange has called "casino capitalism."[44] If we are serious about stemming the scourge of drugs, we must get serious about closing these holes by advancing (1) the adoption of a regional business, transportation and logistics, and investment code that bring transparency in cross-border activities, and (2) providing the means to enforce it.

Particular attention should be paid to developing meaningful and binding guidelines for trade, transshipment, and financial record-keeping. Commercial records should be transmitted electronically at or as near to the point of origin as possible so enforcement and regulatory authorities can more effectively target their inspections. Also, regional organizations such as the Organization of American States could be tasked and resourced to regularly publish an "Accessories to Transnational Crime Report" that spotlights business institutions or individuals who routinely fail to abide by the established codes. The goal should be to shame the participants in the underground economy and to throw light on its shadows, thereby enhancing the risk of detection for criminals or terrorists who are attempting to capitalize on the legitimate flow of commerce to move contraband, weapons, or money.

Third, we need to develop and execute a comprehensive organized crime strategy that strives to deter and disrupt the ability of criminal networks to form, corrupt governments, and prosper from their ill-begotten gains as opposed to placing primary emphasis on securing prosecutions.[45] The counter-terrorism tactics that have been developed over the past two decades provide a more promising model for how to confront organized crime than does the Colombian kingpin strategy of the 1990s. There will always be a new face to fill a vacancy on the "10 Most Wanted List." Initiatives may include establishing a designated Organized Crime Intelligence Unit within each cooperating country that is assigned the responsibility for coordinating crime intelligence collection and analysis within its borders and working with the intelligence units from the other countries.

Finally, we must be mindful of the human dimension associated with any effort to work internationally in attacking a global challenge like the drug trade. An ongoing effort must be made to improve cultural understanding and linguistic abilities among agencies cooperating in multilateral efforts. Journalists and investigative reporters who write stories on crime and corruption, often at significant personal risk, deserve greater support from the international community. Efforts to intimidate media professionals or to undermine a free press should be condemned in the strongest possible terms and, when government officials are involved, subjected to sanctions. A common fund should be established to train journalists, intelligence, judicial, financial, and law enforcement representatives, and to support exchange programs.

Many may see policy initiatives such as these as impractical within the current political and budgetary environment. But if the skeptics ultimately carry the day, what alternatives remain? One option that is unacceptable is continuing business as usual. Sticking to an approach that narrowly focuses on drug control as if it can be divorced from the wider political, economic, and social context in which it rests practically assures that drugs will continue to be widely available, and concurrently, that the criminal organizations that advance the trade will remain powerful and corrosive—they will just operate out of different locales. The only remaining logical course to pursue if we are unable to muster the political will to undertake the ambitious proposals outlined above would be to consider dismantling the prohibitionary regime.

This is because in the final analysis, a failed prohibitionary approach to drug control does more harm than good, for it ends up serving the interests of organized crime, terrorist organizations, and insurgents who benefit from the trade to a far greater extent than the national and international public welfare. If the United States and the global community are unprepared to redress the systemic weaknesses that are facilitating and motivating drug production, trafficking, and consumption, it should begin to accommodate itself to the fact that widespread drug use and its harmful social consequences are an unfortunate fact of life that is an inevitable byproduct of living in an open global capitalist system that promotes the values of self-indulgence and instant gratification to a far greater extent than those of community and self-sacrifice.

BEYOND SOVEREIGNTY TOWARD COOPERATIVE ENGAGEMENT

The persistent growth of the illicit drug trade, despite the long-standing national and international enforcement regimes designed to contain them, offers a compelling case study in the precarious status of national sovereignty. The production of illicit narcotics has gravitated to areas within the region where the writ of the state is weakest. Drug traffickers have benefited from the same revolution in communications, transportation, trade, and finance that has made it possible for so many global businesses to pursue their ends with little concern for the traditional prerogatives of nation-states. Current and potential consumers of drugs are now free to use drugs with little or no risk of state intervention in a growing number of locales where there have been dramatic reductions in authoritarian social controls.

Too, the success of drug traffickers reveals that there are widening holes within the global economy that are facilitating the free trade of an array of nefarious "commodities" of which drugs only rank among the more prominent. High-grade plutonium, hazardous waste, counterfeit credit cards and documents, pirated copyrighted materials, stolen vehicles, child pornography, aliens, and indentured teenage prostitutes can be found on that list. More and more the global marketplace has come to resemble the kind of capitalism familiar to industrialized countries at the turn of the century. Then, as today, governments found themselves witnessing explosive economic growth largely from the sidelines. But the growth unleashed by the industrial revolution came at the cost of macroeconomic stability and led to widespread abuse of the environment, labor, and consumers. Today, such negative externalities of capitalist activity cannot be absorbed as "the cost of doing business" without producing profound global dislocations.

There is a curious paradox embedded in the predicament of declining sovereignty that is fueling the drug trade. In order to strengthen the role of the states in the international system, states must agree to act less and less like states. That is, they must agree to embrace universal norms and empower an array of nonstate actors to advance common interests even though these actions ultimately may limit their capacity to act independently in the pursuit of their own national interests, narrowly defined. If they delay acknowledging this Faustian bargain and sovereignty continues to erode to the benefit of nonstate actors such as organized criminal organizations, the ailment may become terminal. The critical turning point will come when the power of criminal elements with a vested interest in an anarchical status quo co-opt some states altogether. Once that happens, the co-opted states will use their sovereign prerogatives to resist any meaningful multilateral regime that would endanger their nefarious interests.

Taking the necessary steps to prevent an irreversible erosion of the role of sovereign governments in the international system will require that the United States play a leadership role in promoting strategies of cooperative engagement that includes a broadly based alliance of international, regional, nongovernmental organizations and the private sector. In the wake of the tragic events of September 11, 2001, the linkage between the illicit drug trade and international terrorism should provide the impetus for advancing just this kind of approach. The interconnectedness of drug profits, the illicit market in weapons, money laundering, and the operations of terrorist organizations like Al Qaeda has raised the stakes associated with persisting with a fatally flawed national drug strategy. For too long, politicians in Washington have succumbed to the temptation to pander to an American public that craves simplistic answers to complex global problems. Now, more than ever, resisting that impulse is a matter of life and death.

ENDNOTES

1. More than twenty countries are now involved in the production of coca and opium. Total estimated worldwide opium gum production climbed from 3,257 metric tons in 1990 to 5,004 metric tons in 2000. Total coca leaf production grew from 306,170 metric tons to 650,800 metric tons. [U.S. Department of State, International Narcotics Control Strategy Report (INCSR)-March 1, 2001 (Washington: Government Printing Office, 2001): II – 26–27.

2. "The Lycaeum" at www.lycaeum.org, "Erowid" at www.erowid.com, and "ecstasy.org" at http://ecstasy.org are three such sites that provide information on optimal drug dosages and "safe" administration methods, stories on drug experiences, and technical guidance on making drugs.

3. The federal drug budget has grown from $1.5 billion in 1981 to $12.2 billion in FY2005, bringing total federal outlays to just over $250 billion for that period.

(Office of National Drug Control Policy, *Summary: FY 2005 National Drug Control Budget,* February 2005).

4. In most major American cities, heroin for a single "fix" can be purchased for ten to twenty dollars per bag, and a bag of crack can be had in New York City for three dollars. [Office of National Drug Control Policy, *Pulse Check: National Trends in Drug Abuse—November 2001* (Washington: Government Printing Office, 1995), 11, 31]. In 1999, the average purity for retail heroin was 38.2 percent nationwide, up from an average of 7 percent two decades ago. In 2000, a kilogram of cocaine had purity levels of 75 percent (Drug Enforcement Administration, "Drug Trafficking in the United States," September 2001, DEA-01020: 6, 9).

5. United Nations Office of Drug Control (UNODC) World Drug Report 2005, <www.unodc.org/unodc/world_drug_report.html>.

6. North America is estimated to account for 44 percent of world's total drug sales at the retail level. Ibid.

7. The total amount of opiate seizures in North and South America was just 632.9 kg in 2003 out of a worldwide total of 133,706 kg. Ibid.

8. For a country-by-country breakdown, see INCSR:IV 1 – X 80.

9. There was a substantial American missionary presence in China where, by 1906, more than a quarter of all adult males in China were estimated to be regular opium smokers. See Arnold H. Taylor, *American Diplomacy and the Narcotics Traffic, 1900–1939* (Durham: Duke University Press, 1969), 6. The advent of organic chemistry in the 1800s, along with the perfection of the hypodermic needle, made it possible to isolate the active agents from drug plants and transform use patterns. By the mid-1890s, the United States was importing nearly 8 pounds of opium per 1000 people to be placed in a vast array of remedies ranging from cough syrup to pain relievers, mass produced by an astonishing growth in the pharmaceutical industry, and marketed aggressively through advertising. For example, the Bayer Company maintained that its heroin cough syrup, developed in 1898, "will suit the palate of the most exacting adult or the most capricious child" David F. Musto, "Opium, Cocaine, and Marijuana in American History," *Scientific American* (July 1991): 40–47.

10. Peter D. Lowes, *The Genesis of International Narcotics Control* (New York: Arno Press, 1981): 199; and David F. Musto, *The American Disease: Origins of Narcotic Control* (New York: Oxford University Press, 1987), 35–37.

11. For a discussion of the evolution of global prohibition regimes and an evaluation of their successes and failures, see Ethan A. Nadelmann, "Global Prohibition Regimes: The Evolution of Norms in International Society," *International Organization* 44: 4 (Autumn 1990): 479–526.

12. A *Time* editorial remarked in 1942, "The war is probably the best thing that ever happened to U.S. drug addicts." Quoted in James A. Inciardi, *The War on Drugs II: The Continuing Epic of Heroin, Cocaine, Crack, Crime, AIDS, and Public Policy* (Mountain View, CA: Mayfield, 1992): 24.

13. National Narcotics Intelligence Consumers Committee, The Supply of Illicit Drugs to the United States—August 1995 (Washington: Drug Enforcement Administration Pub. #95051, 1995): 3, 32.

14. UNODC World Drug Report 2005, <www.unodc.org/unodc/world_drug_report. html>, 177, 207.

15. Kevin Monroy, "Customs Automation Captures the Imagination but not the Crooks," *American Shipper* 35 (2) (Feb. 1993): 42. These details were also drawn from site visits and interviews by the author with U.S. Customs inspectors at the Port of Newark, April 9, 1992.

16. Marcia MacLeod, "New Markets in the Old World," *Air Cargo World* 82:7 (July 1992): 20.

17. For a detailed analysis of Schengen and other initiatives, see *Free Movement of Persons in the European Union: Specific Issues, a Working Document of the Directorate General for Research,* European Parliament, 05-1999.

18. *Latin America and the Caribbean: A Decade After the Debt Crisis* (Washington: World Bank, 1993): 90.

19. Latin America, 89–90.

20. Joe Cantlupe, "Congressional investigators fault DOT on Mexican truck safety," Copley News Service, Jan. 8, 2002.

21. "In 1998, in a survey under the auspices of the Bank for International Settlements (BIS), global turnover of reporting dealers was estimated at about $1.49 trillion per day for the traditional products, plus an additional $97 billion for over-the-counter currency options and currency swaps, and a further $12 billion for currency instruments traded on the organized exchanges," Sam Y. Cross, *The Foreign Exchange Market in the United States,* The Federal Reserve Bank of New York, 1998: 5.

22. The details on the organization and operation of the Cali distribution cells were provided in a briefing to the author at Drug Enforcement Administration Headquarters on February 12, 1992 and a subsequent DEA briefing on May 18, 1994. These details were discovered after the arrest of an entire cell in New York City and the seizures of their records in December 1991. The narrative on the Cali organization draws heavily from my "Worldwide Drug Scourge: The Expanding Trade in Illicit Drugs," *The Brookings Review* 11: 1 (Winter 1993): 9–10.

23. In one scheme, for instance, Cali cartel operatives recruit middle-aged Colombian couples to travel to Miami for short stays, provide them housing and a vehicle, and then send them on daily rounds to deposit money into banks in varying and uneven amounts under $5000. On an average day, these couples may visit ten different branch offices, making deposits in the lobby in the morning and then making deposits using the "drive-through" windows in the afternoon. Briefing to the author by DEA Field Office Miami, January 11, 1994. For a description of this and other "smurfing" activities run out of New York City, see Fredric Dannen, "Colombian Gold," *The New Yorker* (Aug. 15, 1994): 26–31.

24. For a description of how globalization combined with technological change has facilitated the ease with which illegal drug profits can be laundered, see Jack A. Blum, *Enterprise Crime: Financial Fraud in International Interspace,* Working Group on Organized Crime (WGOC) Monograph Series (Washington: National Strategy Information Center, 1997). One example of layering practices was cited by the State Department in its 1994 International Narcotics Report: "An Asian trafficker operated more than 300 bank accounts in Hong Kong, the United States, and elsewhere in Asia. A number of these accounts were acquired when he purchased an established import/export firm, licensed in Africa, through a New York bank operating in Hong Kong. Because the shares were not publicly traded, there was no requirement to register the shares as sold, and as long as he used the same account signatories, usually nominees, none of the banks needed to be told of the change in ownership." U.S. Department of State, *International Narcotics Control Strategy Report–April 1994* (Washington: U.S. Government Printing Office, 1994): 473.

25. Douglas Forsh and Steve Coll, "Cocaine Dollars Flow Via New Networks," *Washington Post* (September 19, 1993).

26. In July 1995, the Port of Singapore's main port operator PSA set the world record in the loading and unloading of containers, achieving 229 moves per hour on the 4,000-TEU Mette-Maersk NG (Haw Cheng, "Port Facilities, Singapore, Industry Sector Analysis," U.S. & Foreign Commercial Service and U.S. Department of State, 1999: 2.

27. The details for this section were drawn from the U.S. Drug Enforcement Administration, "Drug Intelligence Brief: Southeast Asian Heroin Smuggling Methods: Containerized Cargo," September 2001.

28. <www.worldshipping.org/liner_shipping-facts&figures.pdf>.

29. Miami International Airport, <www.miami_airport.com>.

30. Drug traffickers are fully aware of the enormous pressure U.S. inspectors are under to facilitate the movement of goods, particularly seasonal, agricultural, and animal merchandise. One tactic they use is to smuggle the drugs inside live animals. The U.S. Fish and Wildlife Administration upset one of these plans when an agent discovered 36 kg of cocaine inside the stomachs of several dozen living boa constrictors shipped through Miami International Airport (ABC World News Tonight, Nov. 11, 1994).

31. Figures on truck, train, and passenger vehicle crossings were provided by the Bureau of Transportation Statistics. People, vessel and plane statistics are based on FY00 CLEAR and OMR Data as displayed at <www.customs.gov/about/about.htm>. Container statistic provided by MARAD, Office of Statistical and Economic Analysis.

32. Stephen E. Flynn, "America the Vulnerable," *Foreign Affairs* (Jan.–Feb. 2002): 66–67.

33. Retail sales for "cross-border shoppers" have dropped by 30 to 55 percent in U.S. cities along the border (Global News Service, "El Paso Businessmen Bemoan Tough Security at Border Crossings," January 17, 2002).

34. PGP is based on the RSA (Rivest-Shamir-Adleman) algorithm. "The basic mathematical idea behind public-key systems is that of the 'one-way function.' One-way functions are those that are much easier to perform in one direction than the other. . . . The simplest calculator can determine almost instantaneously that $987 \times 1{,}013 = 999{,}831$. But if a computer starts with the number 999,831, it will take time for the machine to determine, through trial and error, that the number can be evenly divided by 987 and 1,013. As numbers become larger, this period of time becomes significant. . . . Finding the factors of a 200-digit number on a modern top-speed computer would require not milliseconds or minutes but at least several centuries. The task is, in computer terms, 'computationally unfeasible'" (James Fallows, "Open Secrets," *Atlantic Monthly,* June 1994: 48).

35. INCSR: 512–527.

36. Portions of this section of the chapter are drawn from my article, "Asian Drugs, Crime, and Control: Rethinking the War on the Far Eastern Front," in *New Issues for Asia,* ed. James Shinn (New York: Council on Foreign Relations, 1997).

37. For an overview of the pernicious environmental effects of drug cultivation, see UN Drug Control Programme, *Illicit Narcotics Cultivation and Processing: The Ignored Environmental Drama,* Vienna: UN Drug Control Programme, 1992.

38. This critique of "Plan Colombia" draws from my *U.S. Support of Plan Colombia: Rethinking the Ends and Means,* which was published by the Strategic Studies Institute as a part of its monograph series on "Implementing Plan Colombia" (Carlisle, PA: U.S. Army War College, 2001).

39. Suzanne Timmons in Bogota, "The War on Coca: How Far Will the U.S. Go?" *Business Week* (Nov. 20, 2000).

40. Testimony of Barry McCaffrey, Director, Office of National Drug Control Policy before the House Government Reform and Oversight Committee, Subcommittee on Criminal Justice, Drug Policy and Human Resources, "The Drug Legalization Movement in America," June 16, 1999.

41. Testimony of Donnie R. Marshall, Acting Administrator, Drug Enforcement Administration, before the Senate Drug Caucus on International Narcotics Control, March 21, 2000.

42. "Silver or lead"—i.e., officials are confronted by traffickers with the choice of accepting a bribe or being gunned down by a bullet.
43. According to the White House's Office of National Drug Control Policy's *U.S. National Drug Control Strategy: 2001,* there are approximately 5 million drug abusers who need immediate treatment.
44. See Susan Strange, *Casino Capitalism* (Manchester, UK: Manchester University Press, 1997).
45. In this regard, the White House's *International Crime Control Strategy, June 1998,* and its *International Crime Assessment, December 2000* offer a useful stepping-off point.

CHAPTER EIGHT

People on the Move

Refugees, IDPs, and Migrants

Maryann Cusimano Love and Dorle Hellmuth*

Denisa Baransata is a refugee in the Jesuit Refugee Services camp in Zimbabwe. Like many from the Great Lakes region in Central Africa of Burundi, Rwanda, and the Congo, she bundled up her family and fled the violence. As she describes her experience, "The war in Burundi is a war against civilians... when I saw a group of soldiers coming towards our home, I knew this would not be the only visit. I left immediately, carrying my two-year-old baby on my back. I took nothing else with me, no clothes, no shoes, nothing. After walking for some time, I arrived at the outskirts of a town called Gasamanzuki, where I met so many people in distress. We stayed there without aid of any sort. We could not sleep, our children were crying because of hunger, cold, and rain. People died, especially children and pregnant women during delivery as there was no one to assist them... After some days, the area was attacked by soldiers, and many people were killed. Some parents escaped without their children, some women who had twins took one and

*Special thanks to Rosa Ko and Leila Piran for research assistance.

left the other behind. It was very painful. The survivors of the attack were marched by the armed forces into camps where they could be more effectively controlled, and subject to extensive rape and beating. People who resisted entering the camps were killed. . . I decided to flee the country. On my way out, I saw bodies lying on the roadside, many of women and children. Today, I am a refugee in Harare, Zimbabwe. I have bad memories, it may be too hard for me to go back home. I do not even know if my husband is alive or dead. I prefer to have nothing, to be destitute, but to live in peace."[1]

While Denisa crossed an international border fleeing war and ethnic cleansing, many more people cross borders in search of economic opportunities. Looking for jobs, education, and a better life for themselves and their families, immigrants from Muslim and Arab countries came to Europe as part of post–World War II guest worker reconstruction programs. People from these countries continue to be the majority of immigrants to Europe today. Approximately 20 million Muslim immigrants now make Europe their home, accounting for about 5 percent of the total population.[2] According to the UN Arab Human Development Report, Arab countries are the youngest on the globe, with almost 38 percent of the population under the age of 14, significantly younger than the global average. Income and jobs are not growing commensurate with the population, however; more than half of Arab young people surveyed said that they wanted to emigrate outside the region.[3]

In contrast to this steady migration for economic reasons, others hastily flee natural disasters, often with only the clothes on their backs and without knowing the whereabouts of other family members and friends. Aminah and her five children survived the tsunami that killed 280,000 in South and Southeast Asia and washed away their Breuh Island home in Aceh, Indonesia, in December 2004. They are now living on Sumatra Island, Indonesia, in a camp with 3,000 other storm survivors, sponsored by the NGO Catholic Relief Services. "Although we have nothing, we want to go back," said Aminah, but for now there is nothing to go back to.[4] Rebuilding so many homes and infrastructure after such total devastation takes time, and until the work is completed most remain scattered in temporary housing or camps. Millions living in the Himalayan Kashmir region, controlled by both Pakistan and India, suffered an earthquake and mudslides October 8–10, 2005. Some 20,000 are estimated dead, and another 2.5 million have been left homeless. "Kashmir has turned into a graveyard," said Sikander Hayat Khan, the highest elected official in Pakistani-controlled Kashmir, awaiting much-needed international assistance.[5] Similarly, a million people fled the path of Hurricane Katrina along the Gulf Coast of the United States in the final days of August 2005, in the largest sudden displacement of Americans since the U.S. civil war. Neither the San Francisco fire of 1906 nor the Dust Bowl in the 1930s forced as many people out of their homes.[6] The news media referred to this as an exodus of U.S. refugees.

But of the preceding examples, only Denisa from Burundi is a refugee. Those who fled the tsunami or the earthquake and mudslides in Kashmir or Hurricane Katrina are not refugees but internally displaced persons, never crossing an international border. The millions who emigrate to find a better life are migrants, not refugees; they cross an international border but are not fleeing because of a well-founded fear of persecution.

According to international law, the 1951 UN Convention on Refugees defines a refugee as any person who "owing to well-founded fear of being persecuted for reasons of race, religion, nationality, membership of a particular social group, or political opinion, is outside the country of his nationality, and is unable to return to it." Those escaping natural or economic disasters, and those displaced within their countries, are not refugees. Consider the musical "The Sound of Music." The Von Trapp family, on the run from the Nazis, certainly were fleeing a well-founded fear of political persecution. But while they were hiding in the nunnery or climbing the Alps, they were not yet refugees but internally displaced persons. Only when they crossed an international border did they satisfy the international legal definition of refugee, and qualify for asylum status in the country they entered.

WHY DOES IT MATTER HOW REFUGEES ARE DEFINED?

For people on the move, the legal definition of refugee seems full of arbitrary distinctions that only lawyers understand or love. People move to save their lives from a variety of threats to their survival: war, famine, violence, persecution, natural disasters, failed economies. But only some death threats count in international law as a "well-founded fear of persecution," and only some of those who are fleeing qualify for asylum and for international protections as refugees.

The refugee definition matters because 134 countries are signatories to the UN Convention and thus by international law are not supposed to turn away refugees but are expected to offer them asylum. The Convention commits the signatories not to return someone to a country where s/he would be in danger, in addition to offering protection to refugees by granting them the same rights as other foreigners living in their society. It also stipulates that states should not impose penalties on refugees when they have entered the country illegally or return a refugee to a country "where his life or freedom would be threatened on account of his race, religion, nationality, membership of a political social group or political opinion."[7] This does not mean that receiving countries are obligated to offer refugees citizenship. The law states only that host countries are not allowed to forcibly return refugees to their countries of origin, since to do so would be serving as an accomplice to murder, akin to sending Jewish refugees back to the Nazis during the Holocaust.

Based on the definition of a refugee as a person with a "well-founded fear of persecution" for reasons of race, religion, nationality, political opinion, or membership in a particular social group, the refugee definition is commonly understood to include three essential elements: (1) there must be a form of harm rising to the level of *persecution,* inflicted by a government or by individuals or a group that the government cannot or will not control; (2) the person's fear of such harm must be *well-founded*—the U.S. Supreme Court has ruled that a fear can be well-founded if there is a one-in-ten likelihood of its occurring; (3) the harm, or persecution, must be inflicted upon the person for reasons related to the person's race, religion, nationality, political opinion, or membership in a particular social group.[8]

The international definition of "refugee" has been interpreted primarily in the context of male asylum-seekers, to the prejudice of women refugees. Male political dissident Andrei Sakharov of the former Soviet Union, who was persecuted for denouncing totalitarianism, was the classic image of a refugee. In these Cold War cases, an adjudicator had little difficulty recognizing that the harm suffered amounted to persecution, forming the basis for refugee protection.

But women and children make up 80 percent of refugee and internally displaced populations, and the claims of women asylum-seekers often differ from those of men. "First, women often suffer harms which are either unique to their gender, such as female genital mutilation or forcible abortion, or which are more commonly inflicted upon women than men, such as rape or domestic violence. Second, women's claims differ from those of men in that they may suffer harms solely or exclusively because they are women, such as the policies of the Taliban in Afghanistan. And third, women often suffer harm at the hands of private individuals such as family members who threaten them with 'honor killings' or abusive spouses who batter them, rather than government actors."[9]

Do women fleeing female genital mutilation[10] qualify as refugees? They are fleeing a well-founded fear of persecution due to membership in a social group (their gender), and they cross international borders and cannot return. But the UN Convention does not mention gender specifically, and various courts have ruled differently. International law cases are generally heard by domestic systems and courts, so each country (and sometimes different courts within the same country) can apply or interpret the law differently, and there is no "International Supreme Court" to appeal to for final decision or arbitration among conflicting decisions by lower courts. Some judges, concerned that allowing refugee status to women fleeing female genital mutilation would open up the floodgates to new refugee claims, have argued that female genital mutilation is an accepted "cultural practice" and does not rise to the threat status protected by the UN Convention. Others have ruled that the practice threatens the life and health of women due only to their membership in a social group (their gender), and therefore constitutes a well-founded fear of persecution as covered by the UN Convention.

What about women fleeing domestic violence? Should they be accorded refugee status? Rodi Alverado was 16 when she married Francisco Osorio in Guatemala. Her husband brutally beat her and vowed to kill her. "Osorio raped and sodomized Rodi, broke windows and mirrors with her head, dislocated her jaw, and tried to abort her child by kicking her violently in the spine. Besides using his hands and his feet against her, he also resorted to weapons—pistol-whipping her and terrorizing her with his machete." Rodi's repeated attempts to obtain protection failed. The police and the courts refused to intervene because it was a "domestic matter" and because her husband was a former army soldier. Rosa fled to the United States, where her case has been unresolved for the past ten years. Under the Clinton administration she was granted asylum, and the government "issued proposed regulations clarifying that victims of domestic violence and other gender-related persecution are eligible for asylum. However, these proposed regulations never became final."[11] Bush administration attorney general John Ashcroft considered deporting Ms. Alverado back to Guatemala, but Justice Department attorneys prevailed and the case still awaits decision.

Unfortunately, Ms. Alverado's case is not an exception. "Honor killings" are the practice of murdering a woman in order to reclaim the family's "honor." A woman who is accused of socially unacceptable behaviors may be killed or brutally mutilated in order to wipe out the "blemish" on a family's good name. Offenses include walking without a male relative escort, being a victim of rape, kissing or engaging in sexual behavior out of wedlock, flirting, failing to serve a meal on time, seeking divorce, or seeking to choose one's own marriage partner rather than accede to an arranged marriage. In one case, "a husband murdered his wife based on a dream that she had betrayed him. In Turkey, a young woman's throat was slit in the town square because a love ballad had been dedicated to her over the radio. . . . a 16-year-old mentally retarded girl who was raped in the Northwest Frontier province of Pakistan was turned over to her tribe's judicial council. Even though the crime was reported to the police and the perpetrator was arrested, the Pathan tribesmen decided that she had brought shame to her tribe and she was killed in front of a tribal gathering."[12] In some countries the practice is legal; in others, the law looks the other way as vigilante practice takes over. Estimates are that 5,000 women are killed in honor killings each year, but as the crime is generally unreported and unprosecuted, firm statistics are scarce. In India alone, for example, the UN cites that 5,000 women are murdered each year because their bridal dowries are deemed insufficient. Honor killings have been reported to the UN in Afghanistan, Bangladesh, Great Britain, Brazil, Ecuador, Egypt, India, Iraq, Iran, Israel, Italy, Jordan, Pakistan, Morocco, Sweden, Turkey, and Uganda.

Slaves and victims of human trafficking are other people on the move who are accorded little protection. There are 27 million slaves in the world today, more than ever before in human history. Slavery is nowhere legal, but the practice persists. Seventeenth-century slaves were considered valuable property to be defended, but twenty-first century slaves are primarily women and children; they cost little and are easy to replace and thus are considered disposable.[13] Eighty percent of people trafficked are women and girls, and more than 50 percent are minors. Human traffickers use a variety of methods. Children are kidnapped to work as child soldiers, as laborers in the Indian carpet industry, and as camel jockeys in the Gulf states. Women and girls in poor countries answer employment ads for legal jobs in developed countries as domestic workers, waitresses, and so on. When they report to the employer, they hand over their passports and ID so the employer can supposedly photocopy and verify the information, and use the documents to arrange border crossings. The girls soon learn they have been enslaved into the sex trade. They have no documents, are moved illegally across borders and sold in slave markets, are brutally beaten, and are told that if they work hard they can pay back their debt to the brothel owners for room and board and earn their freedom. Many do not know their whereabouts, do not speak the language to be able to ask for help, are incarcerated in the brothels, and report that the police are often customers, not would-be rescuers. Those that do risk beatings or death and are able to escape may find themselves imprisoned for prostitution and illegal immigration (even though they were forced into both). If deported back to their home countries, they are often ostracized by their families and communities for being prostitutes (and/or for being infected with HIV/AIDS, a common fate of those in the sex industry), and are then vulnerable to fall back into the hands of traffickers. Whereas the victims of trafficking are too-often prosecuted rather than protected, traffickers often bribe local law enforcement and avoid prosecution. The U.S. works to pressure foreign governments to do more to prosecute human trafficking and protect victims through the Trafficking Victims Protection Reauthorization Act of 2003. But even the U.S. government, which reports spending $82 million a year to aid anti-trafficking efforts internationally, has an estimated 14,500 victims of trafficking, and has only issued temporary visas to 700 trafficking victims.[14]

While human rights groups argue that women fleeing honor killings, domestic violence, genital mutilation, or human trafficking meet the standard of "a well-founded fear of persecution," many governments have disagreed. An Afghan woman fleeing the abusive practices of the Taliban government, a Jordanian woman fleeing the practice of honor killing, and a Somali woman fleeing genital mutilation were all denied political asylum and refugee status and were ordered returned to their persecutors.[15] The legal definition of refugee matters quite intimately to people on the move.

GLOBALIZATION HELPS PEOPLE MOVE

Today there are more than 40 million refugees and displaced people[16] around the world. With an estimated 25 million IDPs in at least 49 countries, there are almost twice as many IDPs as refugees, which are estimated at 13.2 million.[17] Eighty percent of refugees are women and children. Many are victims of protracted conflicts and have not been able to return home for several years or even decades.

People are pushed into leaving home by war, violence, persecution, disease, environmental degradation, famine, economic crises, and natural disasters. People are pulled into leaving home by more attractive circumstances elsewhere (peace, jobs, and educational opportunities), compared to less promising conditions at home. Countries court rich or educated workers from abroad. But countries resist foreign population flows of refugees and economic migrants, viewing poor and more vulnerable populations as a liability, a strain on public services and budgets, and a source of societal instability and violence. Trying to prevent population flows, many countries keep refugees warehoused in camps, separated from society, unable to farm or work or return to normal social patterns. Food to the camps may be rationed or cut back to encourage refugees to return home (whether or not conditions are safe for them at home). Families may be separated in camps, crime and rape too often occur, and the armies or militants who chased refugees from their homes may enter the camps and continue their violence.

Refugee flows mostly originate in the developing world. Sadly, the top ten sending countries reads like a Who's Who of conflict and instability:

Afghanistan, Sudan, Burundi, DR Congo, Somalia, Palestinians, Vietnam, Liberia, Iraq, and Serbia and Montenegro. More than 20 percent of all refugees in 2004 were from Afghanistan.[18] Those seeking refuge are either headed for neighboring countries, or, whenever possible, Western Europe and the United States. Regionally, close to one third of all the world's refugees are hosted in Asia. The largest receiving countries in the world are Iran and Pakistan; in Africa, Tanzania has traditionally taken in large refugee contingents. While only one fourth of all refugees are hosted in Europe, Germany is home to the third largest refugee group in the world. Other main countries of asylum include the United States, China, and the United Kingdom.

In addition to these continual refugee flows there are an estimated 175 million migrants around the world, and their numbers are expected to continue rising rapidly.[19] Migrant flows usually are headed toward developed countries and facilitated by open societies, open economies, and open technologies. As many state borders and trade barriers have been removed to encourage the free exchange of goods and services, information technologies facilitate digital communications and transactions beyond borders. Due to labor shortages in the information technology and health care sectors, many Western countries have practiced selective recruitment of skilled migrant workers; many other immigrants have made their way illegally into Europe and the United States.

Developed states have resorted to ever-new technologies and strategies intended to deter, divert, and preempt migrant flows along their porous borders. Aiming to detect illegal "human freight," British border authorities in Calais send trucks through X-ray scanners and use carbon monoxide tests to identify breathing inside freight containers.[20] In a highly publicized example of extraterritorial "preemption," Australian soldiers in 2001 intercepted boats with Afghan refugees to prevent them from coming ashore. Similarly, Italy and England have reviewed proposals for the extraterritorial processing of asylum seekers that would require moving refugee reception centers to the African coast of the Mediterranean or back to the country of origin.[21] In theory, the creation of a new frontier would thus add to the protection of the host country's borders, because asylum seekers would have to overcome an additional geographical barrier. Critics note that moving the processing centers to the places people are trying to escape from undermines the very concept of asylum. Additionally, these measures are no guarantee for keeping people out. Thousands risk their lives every year by crossing the Mediterranean Sea in rubber boats, walking across the Mexican desert, or jumping onto Eurochunnel trains; it is far from clear that new frontiers will deter people from coming. Located at the coast of Morocco, the Spanish enclave Ceuta has served as the "southernmost gateway" to Europe for thousands of asylum seekers who manage to overcome barbed wire fences with sensory lights and 24-hour guards.[22] Even after the French government complied with British demands to close the refugee reception center near the Eurochunnel, refugees continued to pour into the French frontier town of Calais.[23]

Sovereign borders do not keep out people flows. As it has become both more cumbersome and costly to distinguish between wanted and unwanted border flows, migrants and asylum seekers often benefit from the same information, technology, and dwindling transportation costs that made globalization possible in the first place. They can resort to services provided by illegal smuggling networks that specialize in human trafficking via air and road transportation, or global container trade.[24] And they can "get lost among thousands of other undocumented immigrants."[25]

Sovereign institutions are unwilling or slow to respond to the needs of migratory populations. Plagued by application backlogs, the often-inefficient systems have created a general "impression of governmental incompetence and incapacity."[26] Applications might take years to process—in 2005, Australia's longest-detained asylum-seeker Peter Qasim was granted refugee status after seven years[27]—but asylum seekers and migrants do not have a voice or a vote in the democratic politics of their host countries.[28]

Economic migrants, however, are becoming increasingly powerful in the political systems of the countries they left. Monies sent home from emigrants are "one of the most visible manifestations of today's migration,"[29] and have become a huge income source in many developing countries. Remittances to Latin America and the Caribbean average over $26 billion a year (although that estimate may be low).[30] Mexico is the world's largest recipient of remittances, receiving more than $20 billion dollars per year.[31] Behind foreign direct investment, it is the second largest component of external financing in the region, and the largest form of income for countries such as El Salvador and Honduras.[32] While "las remesas" have turned Central and Latin America into the largest remittance market in the world, most of the money is still sent by mail or through informal agents.[33] Governments and financial institutions are increasingly paying attention to this growing market, mainly because it appears to hold large dividends in the form of human and financial capital.

"Remittance management" serves as an example for an emerging public-private partnership beyond sovereignty, involving the governments and the private sector in both home and host countries. As remittances have been surpassing official development assistance since 1996, Western governments like to think of the monies sent to local communities as development aid that can alleviate poverty in developing countries.[34] Because these flows could be even higher if the transfer was handled more efficiently, the U.S. government is working to cut transfer costs by reducing exchange rates in receiving countries and fostering competition between banks.[35] Banks, too, are eager to increase their share in a market that has been dominated by transfer agencies like Western Union and informal operators; currently banks handle only about 5 percent of the transfers.[36] Banks in origin and receiving countries have started joining forces so both can profit from a greater network and visibility.[37] While both parties are interested in improving existing channeling structures, Western governments are also seeking to stop informal and anonymous money transactions beyond sovereignty. Known as black market peso exchange in Latin America and hawala in the Islamic world, these transactions are impossible to track and usually take place in venues used by money laundering and other organized crime networks.[38] On the receiving end, Latin American governments and banks have designed remittance plans that can be used to secure long-term loans and credit, and even home ownership in Peru. In Ecuador, people can use remittances to qualify for mortgages and to build education and retirement funds.[39] Guatemalan, Mexican, and Salvadoran expatriates have formed hometown associations through which remittances are pooled and eventually used for local community projects in their respective home countries, provinces, and villages.[40] Programs have been largely successful, and according to the World Bank, monies "appear to be a more stable source of external financing and to be more evenly distributed among and within countries" than other foreign investment sources.[41]

Once they are registered voters in their home countries, many migrants retain voting rights in sending countries and are a powerful and much sought after constituency. Elections now go beyond sovereignty, as Mexican President Vincente Fox in 2000 campaigned in California, Texas, and Florida to earn the votes of Mexicans who had emigrated to the United States.[42] Until June 2005, the ballot system required a physical presence of voters. While this prevented many from casting their own vote, emigrants still played a key role in mobilizing votes of family members back in Mexico and influencing them to vote for certain candidates.[43] In the 2006 national elections, Mexican emigrants are expected to play an even more decisive role: for the first time they can cast absentee votes by mail.[44] Similarly, presidential candidates from the Philippines made sure to extend their 2004 election campaign to visit with thousands of migrant workers and potential voters in Hong Kong, because a new law had been passed in 2003 that allowed overseas citizens to vote in state and federal elections.[45]

NGOs SERVING PEOPLE ON THE MOVE

NGO numbers and capabilities to serve as advocates and provide services for the displaced have increased as a result of the expanded communications and networking capacities allowed by globalization. On the pro side, NGOs provide much-needed services to vulnerable populations who are truly beyond sovereignty, often not served well by either the governments of sending countries or host countries. NGOs can be powerful advocates and watchdogs for the rights of people on the move, providing a voice for those who otherwise would have no voice in international politics, and bringing attention and pressure on abusive and corrupt governments and policies. On the con side, NGOs operate at the intersection between the global and the local, and are challenged to walk on that fault line when international practices or concerns do not match local ones. Do international NGOs impose one-size-fits-all packages of services, or do the people served have an ability to articulate and participate in meeting their own needs, both short- and long-term? Are the practices of NGOs transparent and accountable? When governments are corrupt or abusive, do NGOs have the ability to challenge this, or must they "go along to get along," looking the other way or participating in corrupt practices in order to be able to do their jobs and serve people on the move?

NGOs provide services for people on the move at all stages of their movements: NGOs provide instant emergency relief and everyday food, clothing, shelter, medical, legal, and educational services to refugee settlements and IDP camps, assist in post-conflict resettlement and reconstruction efforts once they can return home, as well as guide them through the complex asylum jungle in receiving countries. Suffering from budget cuts, the UNHCR (the Office of the United Nations High Commissioner for Refugees, traditionally the lead agency for refugee relief) increasingly relies on NGOs for the work on the ground. At the same time, donor governments have shown a tendency to directly contact and work through NGOs, which are frequently viewed as a more flexible and cheaper alternative to working through governments.[46] Unlike the UNHCR, NGOs also do not need the permission of sovereign governments to assist IDPs in relief efforts that go beyond sovereignty.[47]

Field NGOs, both indigenous and international, play a crucial role in the "on-site" assistance of refugees and IDPs. Their very presence can be essential for the safety of displaced people, as they serve as a deterrent against violent attacks inside and outside the confinements of their camps.[48] Basic on-site services generally include the distribution of food rations and provision of health care to meet everyday needs. NGOs may provide trauma and psychological counseling, human rights education, and legal assistance.

Other NGO activities are geared toward the future and designed to increase the self-reliance and dignity of displaced persons. Jesuit Refugee Services offers education, sewing, carpentry, farming, small business, and handicraft opportunities to help refugees return to work and become self-sufficient. In Tanzanian camps, NGOs offer workshops so refugees can develop baking, weaving, and carpentry skills.[49] Refugees in Guinean camps received loan services and business training. The American Refugee Committee managed to continue this service even after the refugees had returned to their homes in Sierra Leone so their credit history would not get lost.[50] In Mozambique and Rwanda, World Relief has successfully introduced microfinance programs, allowing refugees and displaced persons to take out loans, keep savings accounts for remittances, or even transfer money between camps.[51] NGO work on the ground often involves long-term development projects as well. While assisting in the resettlement of refugees in Ethiopia, environmental protection, including reforestation and soil conservation, is a core responsibility of local NGOs.[52] NGO projects involving the construction of roads, schools and health centers improve local infrastructures and have "strategic" implications, as the facilities benefit displaced and local populations alike.[53]

While many of these initiatives can revive local economies and reduce strains between local and refugee populations, NGO supply structures can also have detrimental effects. NGO services may undermine state structures that are already too weak to perform these functions and provide for their own people. In the case of Tanzania, the local benefits of NGO services were so dramatic that the UN called the full repatriation of the refugees to their home countries "the worst-case scenario for the [nearby villages] in terms of access to services utilized in the camps for local populations who have no other facilities to turn to."[54] Governments are not oblivious to the possible effects of these parallel NGO structures. For example, government agencies closely monitor NGOs in Eastern Tigray because "their population usually feels more related to (foreign) NGOs, who are, after all, their main service providers, than to their government. This erodes the government's base of support."[55] The Ethiopian government has also been suspicious of any NGO projects involving civic or human rights education, fearing that it might lead people to question the ruling elite.[56]

NGO relationships with local governments are usually complicated. NGOs walk a fine line: cooperation with local governments may be necessary to help provide refugees with security and access local economic systems. However, NGOs serve as watchdogs and advocates for refugees, and must be accountable to their donors, so NGOs are often critical of government actions. In countries where corruption is widespread, NGOs are viewed as "cash cows" and government officials expect to "cash in on approach," which is often the only way to get project assessment reports approved.[57] Field NGOs might also decide to follow local rules out of fear that governments might take revenge and close them down.[58] In these situations, international NGOs have an advantage over indigenous NGOs because it is easier for them to join forces with human rights agencies, publicizing and decrying abuses and fraud without revealing sources.[59] The collaboration between Jesuit Refugee Services and Human Rights Watch is an example of this kind of symbiosis.

The sheer number of different NGOs, both local and international, creates competition between NGOs and poses challenges for the coordination of relief efforts and long-term development.[60] NGOs need to coordinate their activities among themselves and with fellow international actors. In times of emergency, local organizations may be "pushed aside" and "cannibalized" by larger and better-equipped international NGOs, which might also seek to recruit their personnel.[61] Sometimes collaboration between NGOs is further complicated by the fact that some NGOs have become hybrid organizations with diffuse agendas, and might also be accountable to their donors (DONGOs) or the local government (GONGOs).[62] As field NGOs are attuned to their community's needs and problems, their "embeddedness" can also affect their "objectivity." There is a risk that NGOs might become entangled in power politics as humanitarian operations can be used to justify foreign interventions and facilitate convenient supply lines for troops and warring factions.

Conversely, critics argue that NGOs (as the operational arm of the international donor community) too often acquiesce to local practices and fail to use the "power of the purse" to ensure basic rights of those refugees whose status has remained in limbo for sometimes whole generations. In 2004, the U.S. Committee for Refugees started a campaign against "refugee warehousing," which refers to refugees who have been living in refugee camps for five or more years and are deprived of the right to work or move freely.[63] Host governments often isolate refugees, who remain cut off from local markets and dependent on international aid, in an attempt to reduce the attractiveness of their country as a permanent resettlement site. As conflicts in Somalia, Burundi, or Myanmar have dragged on for more than a century, these camps have served as recruitment centers for future generations of soldiers and terrorists who are interested in perpetuating the conflict that caused the displacement in the first place.[64] The camps can serve as a breeding ground for conflicts to spill over into the host country and destabilize an entire region, as the example of Rwandan refugee camps in Zaire illustrated in the 1990s. IDP camps breed similar problems. Acknowledging the link between regional instability, failed states, and large numbers of displaced people, USAID in 2004 issued a policy detailing a coordinated approach to international IDP assistance in affected countries.[65]

NGOs face a number of "balancing act" challenges: short- vs. long-term activities; relief and development vs. justice and peacebuilding activities; activities that address symptoms or underlying causes. For example, Catholic Relief Services had been active in relief, development, refugee and IDP work in Rwanda for more than three decades when the Rwandan genocide broke out in April 1994, killing 800,000 and displacing over a million more. CRS had known of the underlying fault lines in Rwandan society but had not attempted to resolve them, instead working around them to deliver relief and development services. As Fr. Bill Headley of CRS describes it, "Peace had not been part of the mission of CRS. It had not been part of what we did. We had competencies in agriculture, health, education and a number of other social service disciplines. . . And so, CRS did its development work and did it well. What we were not prepared to do was make peace. When the genocide occurred, CRS' projects were wiped out in days; many of the people we had served became the 'well-fed dead.' After and partly because of the genocide, CRS took a hard look at itself. This introspection called us to realize that we could no longer just address the symptoms of conflict-stimulated crisis: burned out houses, food shortages and refugee movements. We also had to attack the systems and structures that underlie oppression and poverty. . . Today, peacebuilding is an agency-wide priority for CRS. We have 75 staff dedicated to this service. There is a team of regional advisors and a headquarters-based technical staff to work with partners. Presently, CRS has better than 100 peace projects in 50 countries. In 2003, we spent $20 million on justice and peace activities. . . In the spring of 2004, aided by U.S. government funding, CRS brought a group of 21 Burundians, including bishops, priests, sisters and a range of lay leaders, to the Baltimore area. They were offered three weeks of joint planning and preparation for practical peacebuilding back in Burundi. It was reasoned that in a predominantly Catholic country, where a decade-old conflict still smolders, the church with its array of institutions could play a critical role."[66]

CRS's story is not unique among NGOs. All organizations must balance concerns over mission-creep with questions of long-term effect and sustainability. Is success providing emergency food assistance reliably for years to refugees who are in limbo, restricted to camps, not allowed to move forward or move back? Or is success helping refugees to make new lives abroad and resolving conflicts so they may repatriate back home, creating sustainable livelihoods so they will not need future emergency food aid? Organizations created to address one set of problems may find they must adjust as circumstances change.

NEVER AGAIN: THE HISTORY OF THE UNHCR

The United Nations High Commissioner for Refugees is one such agency. On May 13, 1939, the *S. S. St. Louis* passenger ship set sail from Hamburg, Germany. Nine hundred of its 937 passengers were German Jews fleeing Hitler's Nazi regime to join relatives or start new lives in the Americas. But when the ship arrived in Havana, the Cuban government refused entry to the passengers. The captain then sailed the ship to Florida, but the U.S. government also refused to admit the refugees; the Coast Guard even fired a warning shot to turn the ship away from the U.S. coastline. The ship's passengers, dubbed "the Voyage of the Damned," then appealed to other countries to save them from the certain death awaiting should they be returned to Nazi Germany. Belgium, Holland, France, and England eventually admitted the refugees, but the first three countries were overrun by the Nazis within months. The *St. Louis* passengers died in the Holocaust along with other European Jews who were unable to escape. Only the few passengers admitted into England survived.[67]

After the Nazi regime's ouster and the end of World War II, memory of the Holocaust galvanized international human rights groups. The establishment of the Universal Declaration of Human Rights, the International Convention to Prevent Genocide, and the United Nations High Commissioner for Refugees were all informed by the Holocaust and the motto "Never again." The 1951 UN Convention on Refugees' definition of a refugee as any person who "owing to well-founded fear of being persecuted for reasons of race, religion, nationality, membership in a particular social group, or political opinion, is outside the country of his nationality, and is unable to return to it," becomes more understandable in the context of the Holocaust. Had this treaty been in force before World War II, the thinking went, countries would not have been allowed to turn away Jews fleeing Nazi persecution. People fleeing persecution, refugees, ought to be allowed protected status and not be forcibly returned to their home countries and the peril that awaits them there.

The Cold War then left its mark on the Refugee Convention. As the world became split into the Communist East and the Democratic West, the refugee definition was used to embarrass the Soviet Union and Eastern bloc countries. Defectors leaving the Soviet bloc by definition were welcomed into the West as refugees. They did not have to prove that they particularly or personally had a well-founded fear of persecution, as did those coming from Africa or other regions. Soviet defectors were welcomed as refugees simply because they hailed from a communist state, and the existence of these defectors was used in the propaganda war between East and West to show the deficiencies of the communist system (how good could the communist dream really be if people were fleeing it?). This policy was abruptly changed when the Berlin Wall fell in 1989 and the USSR dissolved in 1991. The reversal shocked many defecting from Russia shortly after the political changeover, who were surprised to find they no longer had special treatment, and had to show a well-founded threat of persecution to themselves particularly, as did any other asylum applicant.

The UNHCR began in this climate after World War II. With a three-year mandate, it was believed to be a temporary agency that would close its doors after having resettled those people displaced by World War II. Unfortunately, wars and persecution continued. The UNHCR mandate was extended every five years to serve the growing number of people that were displaced in the wars of colonial independence in Asia and Africa during the 1950s, '60s and '70s.[68] As an international agency of the United Nations, the UNHCR dealt with refugees displaced across borders, tending to refugees' needs in the relatively sheltered environment of their new host countries. Toward the end of the Cold War, the increase in civil wars in which civilians were a common target of violence brought new challenges to the UN relief agency. Originally with a mandate to serve only refugees, the UN extended the organization's mission to also serve IDPs (the internally displaced) in 1992 in response to the war in Bosnia Herzegovina, and appointed Francis Deng as the Representative on Internally Displaced Persons.[69] The decision heralded the beginning of a new era in which the UNHCR's mandate of assisting and protecting refugees was expanded to include IDPs, thus going beyond sovereignty.

As the former state of Yugoslavia broke apart in civil wars in the Balkans, the problems associated with only helping refugees became apparent. Slobodan Milosevic, President of the former Republic of Yugoslavia and head of its armed forces, is now on trial for crimes against humanity and violations of the Geneva Conventions and the laws of war.[70] Milosevic's charges are due to his acts of ethnic cleansing, attempting to force ethnic Bosnians, Croatians, and Albanians out of lands he wanted to claim for Serbia. In this case, if the UNHCR only tended to people's needs after they left their homes and crossed an international border, was the UNHCR in some way aiding and abetting ethnic cleansing? Some argued that the UNHCR should attend to the needs of internally displaced persons before they crossed international borders and became refugees. It was not enough to help refugees after the fact; UNHCR should be working to prevent the dire circumstances that caused people to flee. More narrow political interests were also in play. Western European countries were interested in preventing refugee flows. If people could be encouraged to stay in their home countries, it would relieve the strain on host countries caused by refugee flows.[71] In Bosnia, the UNHCR was thus tasked with creating safe areas of "humanitarian space" for civilians so they would not have to leave. Once the fighting broke out, however, the UNHCR faced an impossible mission. As the conflict moved, previously "safe areas" became areas of war. UNHCR often had to negotiate with the warring parties in order to get aid shipments through to the civilian population, and the UNHCR could not protect civilians from hostile factions determined to implement ethnic cleansing.[72] The UN introduced peacekeeping troops, UNPROFOR, to try to stabilize the situation. But the introduction of UN peacekeeping troops undermined UNHCR's role as a neutral provider of humanitarian aid, and the peacekeepers' limited mandate made them ineffective and unable to provide the support UNHCR needed.[73] A mission to save people from refugee miseries thus "took on the characteristics of preventing flight rather than changing conditions."[74]

The case of the former Yugoslavia illustrates the ongoing difficulties the UN and relief agencies face in trying to deliver humanitarian assistance in the midst of conflict. It also shows that while people and relief agencies move beyond sovereign borders, state actors can undermine attempts to help IDPs and refugees. States pushing people out may not want outsiders "meddling" in their affairs, and states receiving refugees may not want them and may try, despite the refugee convention, to make it difficult for refugees to enter their countries and unattractive for them to stay.

MIGRATION TRENDS AFTER SEPTEMBER 11

Not one of the September 11 bombers entered the U.S. as a refugee claiming asylum. The London and Madrid bombers appear to have been British and Spanish citizens, respectively. Nevertheless, after September 11 and other attacks, refugee and asylum and immigration programs came under increased scrutiny and anti-immigration platforms thrived in the politics of Western countries. The U.S. government initially placed a moratorium on refugee admissions while a comprehensive review of procedures was undertaken and new security measures were developed and implemented. As Arthur Dewey, then Assistant Secretary of State for Population, Refugees, and Migration, noted, "demented individuals" might use the U.S. refugee admissions program as "a soft underbelly for such entry."[75] Refugee admissions dropped precipitously. A decade ago, the United States typically allowed about 130,000 refugees into the country each year. In 2001, the U.S. admitted 69,304. This fell to 27,110 in 2002 and 28,422 in 2003, even though the Presidential authorization for 70,000 refugees had not changed.[76]

Even after new security screening procedures were in place, many previously approved refugees remained frozen out of the U.S., in limbo. A group of 230 Lebanese approved for refugee resettlement into the U.S., and a group of Iraqi refugees waiting to be processed, were shut out for several years. Statistics cannot do justice to the suffering that is behind these cases, notes Lavinia Limon, executive director of Immigration and Refugee Services of America and the U.S. Committee for Refugees, a non-profit resettlement agency in Washington, DC. Limon expressed grave concern about many refugees who were murdered, who died of diseases, who were raped, deported, or incarcerated because they were kept in limbo in the aftermath of the September 11 attacks. In spite of years of delays and detailed background checks, not a single refugee applicant has turned out to be a security threat, said a State Department official, speaking on condition of anonymity. That does not surprise people like Limon who believes that no terrorist would waste his or her time sitting for ten years in a refugee camp waiting to win the lottery for resettlement into the U.S. Furthermore, Limon thinks that the plummeting rate of refugees has been triggered by "bureaucratic inertia... or perhaps even more scary is the fact that people are more comfortable saying nothing than saying yes, because everyone is so afraid they are going to be the one to sign the visa for someone who might turn out to be a terrorist."[77]

Initially bureaucratic inertia seemed to be the stumbling block for resumption of the U.S. refugee resettlement program. Then the program was underfunded. Today refugee admissions are again creeping upward, although they still fall far short of the 70,000 ceiling; 52,868 were admitted in 2004 and more than 50,000 were on track for admission in 2005.[78] But today the USA PATRIOT anti-terrorism law itself is an obstacle to legitimate refugees. A provision of the Patriot Act excludes from refugee admission anyone who has provided "material support" to any organization involved in terrorist activities. Unfortunately this clause has been broadly interpreted without exceptions for "support" forced at gunpoint or under duress, or for minimal or unknowing support. This means that Colombian families forced to pay ransom for the return of kidnapped loved ones are deemed to be terrorist supporters rather than being recognized as victims of terrorism. Most Colombians identified by the UNHCR as in need of resettlement are thus excluded, as extortion by paramilitary forces is routine. Similarly the Burmese Chin in Malaysia and other Burmese Christian groups facing religious persecution are also excluded by this law that was intended to catch terrorists.

PROSPECTS FOR THE FUTURE

People are hardwired to survive. Thus people have always moved to flee violence, persecution, disease, famine, disaster, and to find a better place in the world for themselves and their families. The modern period of globalization makes it easier than ever before for people to move across sovereign borders. The challenges presented by people on the move will not go away on their own, but will only intensify.

The push factors of war, violence, persecution, disease, environmental degradation, famine, economic crises, and "natural" disasters show no signs of abating. In fact quite the opposite has been true: as people build large and permanent non-sustainable settlements (in coastal areas, flood plains, cliffs, earthquake zones, wild fire plains, mud slide areas, deserts, and barrier islands, using inexpensive and impermanent building materials and techniques) weather cycles are ever more deadly and costly. As global warming increases, so does the intensity of storms.

The 24/7 information environment gives pull factors a loud megaphone with global reach. There has always been inequality in the world. But people today are more likely to know that there are places in the world where people don't suffer from war, violence, persecution, disease, environmental degradation, famine, economic crises, and disaster, and to know how to get there. Demographic trends ensure that pull factors will be with us for some time. Developed countries are graying, while developing countries have majorities of young people of working age. Developed countries need to import labor to sustain their economies, lifestyles, and aging populations.

Alleviating push factors addresses the root causes that force people unwillingly out of their homes. To protect people in their home communities from forced dispersion, governments and the private sector must work together to foster peace, build sustainable economies and stable environments, and protect human rights. Catholic Relief Services and Mennonite peace-building activities are examples of public-private partnerships to address underlying causes that force people from their homes.

Stopping and prosecuting practices such as female genital mutilation, honor killings, human trafficking, and other violence against women, will help protect women and allow them and their children to remain in their homes. Some progress has been made,[79] as the U.S. and the UN have enacted anti-trafficking laws and conventions that pressure action by other states.[80] Much work remains to be done, however, as millions are still victims of these practices, in developed and developing countries alike.

These issues are linked. For example, people may be forced from their homes due to food shortages, but famines are political rather than natural disasters; no democracy with a free press has ever suffered a major famine. Even when crops fail or drought prevails, food is generally available in other parts of the country or region, but food is not distributed to vulnerable populations for political reasons. Food may be used as a weapon by conflicting sides, as in the Somali famine of 1992.[81] Starvation may be used to punish rebels, to achieve ethnic cleansing, to make a population docile or to weed out insurgents, as in Sudan, or the Irish potato famine of 1846–1850. And refugee camps may be deprived of food in order to push refugees out of host countries. Alleviating the underlying conflicts that cause food shortages prevents not only starvation, malnutrition, and the related diseases that prey on compromised immune systems, but it also prevents refugee flows.

Lessening push factors also decreases pull factors, which are often a matter of relative gains. Leaving home is never easy and extracts a host of social, political, economic, emotional, familial, and spiritual costs. These costs loom larger and life abroad looks less attractive when life at home holds more promise.

But minimizing push and pull factors will not eradicate them. People will vote with their feet as long as global inequalities persist in human security; political and religious rights and freedoms; education, job, and economic opportunities; and safe environments. Personal security will always trump deference to sovereignty. As long as people continue to move, and governments respond insufficiently to the needs of people on the move, NGOs and IGOs will continue to step into the gap, serving in critical capacities and at times challenging states. Larger networks of people, money, and services exist and work in these gaps of sovereignty.

Previous forms of political organization took a more flexible approach toward migratory populations. As sovereignty tied territory to jurisdiction, people were no longer defined as "children of God" or other more mobile identities, but primarily as citizens of a particular geographic space. Civic rights and governmental responsibilities depended on where you lived. Counterintuitively, today attempts to harden and militarize borders against population flows have the unintended consequence of increasing the number of permanent illegal aliens resident in developed countries. When borders are more permeable, people prefer to move back and forth with circumstances or with the employment market, retaining their homes abroad. But as immigration becomes more restrictive, the cost and danger of border crossings make trips back and forth too difficult and risky. Families become split, and efforts to keep out illegal aliens work perversely to wall them in. Attempts to manage population flows must begin with the recognition that developed economies critically depend on imported labor and will continue to do so as their populations age. A globalization that protects and defends capital flows but not people flows is highly problematic, leads to pernicious injustices, and fuels security problems. The growth of al Qaeda in Europe is fueled by resentments of Muslims whose parents emigrated to Europe via guest worker programs. These Muslims are European citizens who feel they have not been respected, welcomed, or fairly treated by other Europeans. From Burundi and Rwanda to Europe, improperly handled population flows can lay the groundwork for conflicts to come.

The growth of international humanitarian law, such as the International Conventions on Refugees and Human Rights, and the practices of NGOs and IGOs, are expanding the notions of human rights and governmental responsibilities regardless of a person's residence or country of origin. As states increasingly contract out aid and social service functions to NGOs, they aid the growth of non-state actors, which work to promote ideas of portable human rights regardless of geographic borders. People have fundamental human rights regardless of the countries they find themselves in. States and MNCs have an interest in expanding human rights beyond sovereign borders, if only to protect their own industries and populations from conflict and instability. We need to move from reactive responses to flows of people after the fact, to more proactive responses to the underlying causes that force people to move.

ENDNOTES

1. Jesuit Refugee Services, *War Has Changed Our Life, Not Our Spirit: Experiences of Forcibly Displaced Women,* Rome, Italy, 2001, <www.jrs.net/jrs/>.
2. Robert S. Leiken, "Europe's Angry Muslims," *Foreign Affairs* (July/August 2005).
3. United Nations, "Arab Human Development Report," 2003, <www.undp.org/rbas/ahdr/englishpresskit2003.html>.
4. Catholic Relief Services, "Rebuilding After the Tsunami," *The Wooden Bell,* 16 (5) (Aug. 2005): 3.
5. John Lancaster, "Overwhelmed at Quake's Ground Zero," *The Washington Post* (Oct. 11, 2005): A13.
6. David Von Drehle and Jacqueline Salmon, "The Refugees: Displacement of Historic Proportions," *The Washington Post* (Sept. 2, 2005): A1.
7. United Nations Conference of Plenipotentiaries on the Status of Refugees, 04/22/1954, Preamble, available at <http://www.refugee.net/legal/un.html>.

8. UNESCO (United States Educational, Scientific, and Cultural Organization) 2004, [Convention of 1951, Article 1A (2)] The United Nations High Commissioner for Refugees (UNHCR) and the Executive Committee of the High Commissioners Programme, <http://portal.unesco.org/shs/en/ev.php-URL_ID=3138&URL_DO =DO_TOPIC&URL_SECTION=201.html>.

9. Karen Musalo, Director, "Gender Asylum Facts: Background on Gender and Asylum," Center for Gender & Refugee Studies (CGRS), <http://cgrs.uchastings.edu/about/ facts.php>.

10. Robin M. Maher, "Female Genital Mutilation: The Modern Day Struggle to Eradicate a Torturous Rite of Passage," *Human Rights* 23 (4) (Fall 1996). Maher suggests that the term "female genital mutilation" generally describes three different forms of genital mutilation. The most common form is female circumcision, in which the clitoris is partially or completely cut away, often with razor blades or broken glass, and rarely with anesthesia. The most extreme form of FGM is infibulation, in which the entire genital area and outer tissues are cut away. The external sides of the vagina are then sewn together using catgut or thorns, leaving only a tiny opening for the passage of urine and for menstruation. The procedure, often performed by female family members, is carried out in non-sterile conditions and frequently results in serious and sometimes fatal infections. In some areas in West Africa, dirt, ashes or pulverized animal feces are thrown into the wound to stop the bleeding, which contributes to the opportunity for infection, shock, and uncontrolled hemorrhaging. Following the procedure, the girl's legs are bound together for as long as forty days, during which time (if she survives) her wound heals and scars. The long-term effects of this procedure include complications and pain with menstruation, urination, intercourse, and childbirth. The association suggests that it is no coincidence that the highest maternal and infant mortality rates in the world are recorded in regions where FGM is practiced. The scarring and complications associated with FGM frequently result in delayed and obstructed labor, tearing, and hemorrhaging. Unassisted childbirth is impossible following infibulation; many women and infants die during childbirth as a consequence of the procedure.

11. Karen Musalo, "Gender Asylum Facts: Background on Gender and Asylum," Center for Gender & Refugee Studies (CGRS), <http://cgrs.uchastings.edu/about/facts.php>.

12. Hillary Mayell, "Thousands of Women Killed for Family 'Honor,'" *National Geographic* (Feb. 12, 2002), <http://news.nationalgeographic.com/news/2002/02/0212_020212 _honorkilling.html>.

13. Kevin Bales, "Modern-Day Slavery," Testimony Before the Congressional Human Rights Caucus, June 17, 2003, <www.house.gov/lantos/caucus/TestimonyBales061703.htm>; Kevin Bales, "How We Can End Slavery," *National Geographic* (Sept. 2003), <http://magma. nationalgeographic.com/ngm/0309/feature1/online_extra.html>; Andrew Cockburn, "Twenty-First Century Slaves," *National Geographic* (Sept. 2003), <http://magma. nationalgeographic.com/ngm/0309/feature1/index.html>.

14. Ambassador John R. Miller, "Release of the Fifth Annual Trafficking in Persons Report," U.S. Department of State Briefing, Washington, DC, June 3, 2005, <http://www. state.gov/g/tip/rls/rm/2005/47210.htm>.

15. Karen Musalo, "Gender Asylum Facts: Background on Gender and Asylum," Center for Gender and Refugee Studies (CGRS), <http://cgrs.uchastings.edu/about/mission. php>.

16. These figures include the UNHCR numbers plus 4 million Palestinian refugees from UNRWA numbers. The total population of concern to the UNHCR includes refugees, asylum-seekers, returnees (returned refugees), Internally Displaced Persons (IDPs), Returned IDP's, and Stateless persons. UNHCR, *2004 Global Refugee Trends* (June 17, 2005), 2.

17. Global IDP Project/Norwegian Research Council, *Internal Displacement: Global Overview of Trends and Developments in 2004* (Geneva: Global IDP Project, March 2005), 9.
18. All figures taken from UNHCR, *2004 Global Refugee Trends* (Geneva: UNHCR, June 17, 2005).
19. International Organization for Migration, *World Migration 2005* (Geneva: IMO, 2004), 13.
20. Charles M. Sennott, "An Immigrant Rush Stirs British-French Friction Eurotunnel Lure Draws Foreigners," *The Boston Globe* (June 9, 2002): A6.
21. Ian Fisher and Richard Bernstein, "On Italian Isle, Migrant Plight Draws Scrutiny," *The New York Times* (Oct. 5, 2004): 1. See also Jeff Crisp, "Global Politics of Asylum," in Sarah Spencer (Ed.), *The Politics of Migration* (Malden, MA: Blackwell Publishing, 2003), 85–86.
22. Sara B. Miller, "Migration Station," *Christian Science Monitor* (June 26, 2003): 11.
23. Lara Marlowe, "The Refugees Stranded at the Last Post of Call. The Closure of the Sangatte Centre Near the Channel Tunnel Hasn't Stopped the Influx of Refugees, Reports Lara Marlowe from Calais," *The Irish Times* (Aug. 23, 2003): 53.
24. Richard Bernstein, "One African's Ten-Year Odyssey Reflects a Growing European Concern," *The New York Times* (Dec. 5, 2004): 10.
25. Miller, "Migration Station." See also Crisp, "Politics of Asylum," 83.
26. Crisp, "Politics of Asylum," 83.
27. "Home at Last," *Economist* (June 25, 2005): 42.
28. UNHCR, *2004 Global Refugee Trends,* 5.
29. The United Nations Economic Commission for Latin America and the Caribbean (ECLAC), *Productive Development in Open Economies* (June 18, 2004): 53.
30. United Nations Department of Economic and Social Affairs, *World Economic and Social Survey 2004* (New York, 2004), 108, <www.un.org/esa/policy/wess/wess2004files/part2web/chap4.pdf>.
31. Krissah Williams, "U.S. Banks Hope Money Transfers Attract Hispanics," *Washington Post* (Oct. 6, 2005): D5; United Nations Department of Economic and Social Affairs, *World Economic and Social Survey 2004* (New York, 2004), 108, <www.un.org/esa/policy/wess/wess2004files/part2web/chap4.pdf>.
32. ECLAC, *Productive Development,* 93. See also Richard Lapper, "For a Few Dollars More, A Better Life Back Home," *Financial Times* (April 13, 2005), 2.
33. Manuel Orozco, *Workers Remittances: The Human Face of Globalization* (Washington, DC: Multilateral Investment Fund, Inter-American Development Bank, 2002).
34. UN, *World Economic Survey 2004,* 105, 111; "Dollars Without Borders," *The New York Times* (May 13, 2004): 26; Peter Wise, "A Mainstay of the Economy: Portugal's Banks Have Been Singled Out as Model for How Remittances Can Be Used to Build National Wealth," *Financial Times* (Oct. 20, 2004): 3.
35. Krissah Williams, "U.S. Banks Hope Money Transfers Attract Hispanics," *Washington Post* (Oct. 6, 2005): D5; Christopher Swann, "Helping More Cash Reach the Families Back Home: The US Treasury Is Encouraging Cheaper and Easier Methods for Foreign Workers to Send Remittances," *Financial Times* (June 10, 2004): 11.
36. Krissah Williams, "U.S. Banks Hope Money Transfers Attract Hispanics," *Washington Post* (Oct. 6, 2005): D5.
37. John Authers, "Mexican Wave of Remittances for US Banks: Big Four Target the Tide of Money Sent Home by Migrant Workers," *Financial Times* (June 18, 2004): 29; Betsy Cummings, "Cash Flow Across Border Starts to Get More Savvy," *The New York Times* (July 28, 2005): 6.
38. Motoo Noguchi, "Help Needed for the 'Unbanked,'" *Washington Post* (March 26, 2004): A23; Elizabeth Becker, "Adding Value to Immigrants' Cash," *The New York Times* (June 6, 2004): 4; Bei Hu, "Remittance Firms Wary of Backdoor Channels; Competition

Concerns Foreign Money-Movers As They Eye Larger Share of Transfers," *South China Morning Post* (Aug. 11, 2005): 2.

39. Lucien O. Chauvin, "With Money Sent from US, Peruvians Buy Homes," *Christian Science Monitor* (July 13, 2005): 4.

40. UN, *World Economic Survey,* 109.

41. UN, *World Economic Survey,* 105.

42. "Mexico in US Politics," *Christian Science Monitor* (March 8, 2004): 8.

43. John Authers and Sara Silver, "Migrants Make Their Mark in Mexico Poll State Elections," *Financial Times* (July 6, 2004): 2.

44. Benedict Mander, "Mexicans Abroad Win the Right to Vote by Post," *Financial Times* (June 30, 2005): 6.

45. Roel Landingin and Justine Lau, "Philippine Presidential Race Moves Overseas," *Financial Times* (Feb. 16, 2004): 2; Simon Montlake, "Filipinos Abroad Get Vote," *Christian Science Monitor* (March 17, 2004): 7.

46. Mark Raper, "Changing Role of NGOs in Refugee Assistance," in Leonore Loeb Adler and Uwe P. Gielen (Eds.), *Migration: Immigration and Emigration in International Perspective* (Westport, CT: Greenwood Publishing Group, 2003), 355; Lubkemann, "Refugees," 531.

47. Raper, "Changing Role," 359.

48. Ibid, 356–357.

49. Gregory Chen, "Confinement and Dependency: The Decline of Refugee Rights in Tanzania," in U.S. Committee for Refugees and Immigrants, *World Refugees Survey 2005,* 3, <www.refugees.org/uploadedFiles/Investigate/Publications_&_Archives/WRS _Archives/2005/gregory_chen.pdf>.

50. Karen Jacobsen, *The Economic Life of Refugees* (Bloomfield, CT: Kumarian Press, 2005), 80–81.

51. Jacobsen, *Economic Life,* 77–78.

52. Benjamin Gidron, Phillip Quarles van Ufford, and Abdulhamid Bedri Kello, *NGOs Dealing with Refugee Resettlement in Ethiopia,* NIRP Research for Policy Series 12 (Amsterdam, NE: Royal Tropical Institute, 2002), Netherlands-Israel Development Research Programme (NIRP), 24–25.

53. Chen, "Confinement and Dependency," 9–10.

54. Quoted in Chen, "Confinement and Dependency," 10.

55. Benjamin Gidron, Phillip Quarles van Ufford and Abdulhamid Bedri Kello, *NGOs Dealing with Refugee Resettlement in Ethiopia,* NIRP Research for Policy Series 12 (Amsterdam, NE: Royal Tropical Institute, 2002), 40.

56. Gidron et al., *NGOs in Ethopia,* 19.

57. Ibid., 27–28.

58. Chen, "Confinement and Dependency," 7–8.

59. Raper, "Changing Role," 358.

60. Ibid., 360.

61. Ibid., 352.

62. Gidron et al., *NGOs in Ethiopia,* 41.

63. U.S. Committee for Refuges, World Refugee Survey 2004—Warehousing Issue, May 2004, <www.refugees.org/data/refugee_reports/archives/2004/0504.pdf>; "Warehouses for Refugees," *The New York Times* (Sept. 28, 2004): 24.

64. See, for example, Gil Loescher and James Milner, *Protracted Refugee Situations: Domestic and International Security Implications,* Adelphi Paper 375 (International Institute for Strategic Studies, London: 2005).

65. U.S. Agency for International Development, *USAID Assistance to Internally Displaced Persons Policy,* USAID Policy (October 2004).

66. Fr. William Headley, "Catholic Relief Services, Caritas Internationalis and Catholic Peacebuilding Network as 'Practical Peacebuilders,' San Diego, CA, June 9, 2005, available at <http://cpn.nd.edu/beyond_merton.htm>.

67. U.S. Holocaust Memorial Exhibit, and Frank Davies, "Ill-Fated WWII Voyage Created a Mini Holocaust," *The Miami Herald* (June 1, 1999).

68. In 2003, more than fifty years after the UNHCR was founded, the UN General Assembly decided to change it into a permanent mandate until the resolution of all refugee problems was achieved. UNHCR, *Basic Facts: Helping Refugees*, <www.unhcr.ch/cgibin/texis/vtx/basics/opendoc.htm?tbl=BASICS&id=420cc0432>.

69. Stephen C. Lubkemann, "Refugees," in *World at Risk: A Global Issues Source Book* (Washington, DC: CQ Press, 2002), 530.

70. United Nations, "Milosevic Case Information Sheet," April 5, 2005, <www.un.org/icty/glance/milosevic.htm>.

71. Jolene Kay Jesse, "Humanitarian Relief in the Midst of Conflict: The UN High Commissioner for Refugees in the Former Yugoslavia," Institute for the Study of Diplomacy, Case 471 (Georgetown University, 1996), 1–7.

72. Jesse, 6–7.

73. Ibid.

74. Ibid., 8.

75. Arthur E. Dewey, "Remarks to the American Society for International Law," April 3, 2003, <www.state.gov> (Sept. 13, 2005), 1.

76. U.S. Department of State, Bureau of Population, Refugees, and Migration, "Refugee Admissions and Resettlement," June 2005, <www.state.gov/g/prm/refadm/rls/c13006.htm>.

77. Hendrix, 3.

78. U.S. Department of State, Bureau of Population, Refugees, and Migration, "Refugee Admissions and Resettlement," June 2005, <www.state.gov/g/prm/refadm/rls/c13006.htm>.

79. "The developing international human rights and refugee norms provide a basis for extending protection to women asylum-seekers. The United Nations High Commissioner for Refugees (UNHCR) has provided guidance in cases of women asylum-seekers, and immigration authorities in Canada, the United States and Australia have all issued guidelines for adjudicators. However, notwithstanding these developments, the claims of women asylum-seekers continue to meet denials due to erroneous interpretations of the refugee definition by decision-makers, as well as a fundamental lack of understanding of the applicable human rights norms and the relevant country conditions," Karen Musalo, Director of the Center for Gender and Refugee Studies (CGRS), "Gender Asylum Facts: Background on Gender and Asylum," <http://cgrs.uchastings.edu/about/facts.php>.

80. White House, "Presidential Determination with Respect to Foreign Governments' Efforts Regarding Trafficking in Persons," September 21, 2005, <www.state.gov/g/tip/rls/prsrl/2005/53777.htm>; U.S. Department of State, "2005 Report: Victims of Trafficking and Violence Protection Act of 2000: Trafficking in Persons Report," June 2005, <www.state.gov/g/tip/rls/tiprpt/2005/>; UN Global Programme against Trafficking in Human Beings, <www.unodc.org/unodc/en/trafficking_human_beings.html>.

81. Maryann Cusimano, "Operation Restore Hope: The Bush Administration's Decision to Intervene in Somalia," Pew case study published by the Institute for the Study of Diplomacy, Georgetown University, 1995, <www.guisd.org>.

CHAPTER NINE

The Cyberthreat Continuum

Richard A. Love*

Coinciding with the September 11 terrorist attacks, the rate of cyberattacks in the United States—that is, computer-to-computer attacks over the Internet—increased by an estimated 79 percent in late 2001.[1] In February 2005, the President's Information Technology Advisory Committee reported that the rate of attacks, which include viruses, worms, cyber fraud, and insider attacks in companies, is rising by more than 20 percent annually.[2] Worldwide, in the first six months of 2002, cyberattacks grew at an annual rate of 64 percent, with more than 1 million suspected attempted attacks and 180,000 confirmed successful attacks.[3] Within the first six months of 2005, there had already been more than 237 million security attacks worldwide, with a 50 percent increase in attacks on governments, financial services, manufacturing, and health care industries.[4] Attackers are targeting government agencies more than any other business sector, and the U.S. Government is the main target, with more than 54 million attacks in the first half of 2005.

*The author wishes to express his thanks to Ms. Karin Lion, Research Associate at National Defense University, who provided important research for this chapter.

Cyberthreats may appear in various forms. Before the September 11 attacks, law enforcement officials knew that terrorist organizations used communications technology to further their objectives. Sheik Ahmed Yassin, founder of Hamas, once stated, "We will use whatever tools we can—e-mails, the Internet—to facilitate jihad against the (Israeli) occupiers and their supporters."[5] Osama bin Laden and the al Qaeda network, Hezbollah, and Hamas use computerized files, e-mail, and encryption to facilitate terrorist activities. These organizations make use of the Internet's distributive nature to organize, plan, and conduct their operations, thereby engaging in an "e-jihad," or holy war online. Captured al Qaeda computers revealed the group had been planning to destroy physical critical infrastructure such as dams and electric power grids by attacking the computer systems that control them. More recently, in June 2003, e-jihadists, spotted by IDefense, a cyber security firm, unsuccessfully attempted to take down the Bank of Israel's Web site.[6]

On January 25, 2003, the Slammer worm began infecting Microsoft's database software worldwide, causing cash machines to stop issuing money, taking most of South Korea offline, and slowing down the Internet. The virus, considered the fastest spreading worm in history, spread to most of the vulnerable hosts that could be found within ten minutes.[7] One of the vulnerable hosts it penetrated was a private computer network at Ohio's Davis-Besse nuclear power plant. The Slammer infected the plant's computer system and disabled a safety monitoring system for nearly five hours, despite a belief by plant personnel that the network was protected by a firewall.[8] The plant was offline at the time of the attack, but the ability to tamper with a nuclear plant's monitoring system could have had disastrous effects if the plant had been operating.

Computer hackers in St. Petersburg, Russia, broke into Citibank's electronic money transfer system and attempted to steal more than $10 million by making wire transfers to accounts throughout the world.[9] Citibank later recovered all except $500,000 of the funds.[10] The leader, Vladimir Levin, was not subject to extradition to the United States because wire and computer fraud and abuse was not a violation of Russian law. However, when Levin left the safety of Russia two years later, Scotland Yard and the FBI arrested him at an airport outside London and extradited him to the United States. He pled guilty to transferring $3.7 million from Citibank customer accounts to accounts he controlled, and in 1998 a U.S. Court sentenced him to a three-year prison term and ordered him to make $240,015 restitution to Citibank.[11]

The ILoveYou computer virus first appeared in an e-mail attachment named Love-Letter-For-You that, when activated, produced an e-mail worm that overwrote files on hard drives and then mailed itself to every e-mail address contained in an infected Microsoft Outlook address book.[12] The virus spread its damage internationally, but when U.S. law enforcement officials located the suspected hacker in the Philippines, he could not be prosecuted. No antihacking law was yet in place in the Philippines. Following the incident, the Philippines moved quickly to pass legislation and now has an antihacking law.

Computer operators at the Lawrence Livermore National Laboratory in California (operated by the University of California at Berkeley) discovered that unknown attackers were infiltrating their computer systems. Law enforcement authorities determined that because nothing of value seemed to have been stolen, no violations of law had occurred. The officials shelved the investigation. Cliff Stoll, a graduate student in astronomy, was not satisfied and conducted his own investigation. His research over two years concluded that the intruders had obtained sensitive information, including weapons and munitions data, from the laboratory's computers. Authorities later learned that the hackers sold this information to the KGB. Stoll's investigation eventually led to Hanover, Germany, where a German court tried and convicted three hackers of espionage, later placing all three on probation.[13]

As California suffered through a power crisis that included rolling blackouts, a hacker conducted a computer attack against a server under development at the California Independent System Operator electricity exchange. The attacker, who was apparently attempting to gain control of the server, went undetected for 17 days. The hacker was not able to access key operational systems, but if he had managed to gain control, the power crisis could have been significantly worse. The California Independent System Operator electricity exchange discovered the hacking and reported the intrusion to authorities, but local law enforcement officials treated the incident as an isolated event. The FBI, however, recognized the potential for catastrophic and cascading damage to already strained infrastructure and began an investigation.[14]

These cases illustrate the wide cyberthreat continuum we face today. The e-jihad example demonstrates the ability of adversaries to use asymmetric capabilities provided by information technology to attack opponents who otherwise could not be confronted conventionally. The Citibank case demonstrates the difficulty in coordinating law enforcement activities globally and the vulnerability of commercial entities to planned cyberattacks. The ILoveYou virus example represents the mutual vulnerabilities that users share in the interconnected environment.[15] The Lawrence Livermore National Laboratory case shows how difficult it is to quickly and correctly characterize the nature of an attack. Authorities first considered this attack a mere intrusion but were later convinced it was a concerted espionage conspiracy and a serious threat to national security. Finally, the California power case and the Ohio nuclear plant case illustrate the potential for catastrophic and widespread damage to infrastructure, industry, and ordinary lives. Each example also reveals, to some degree, the difficulty faced by commercial and government entities in understanding and defending against cyberthreats, and it demonstrates how those attacked—even after a close call—tend to dismiss the event as mere nuisance.

THREATS AND INTERDEPENDENCE

Computer threats are a reality in our private lives, corporate boardrooms, and government planning offices. Concern over the threat is well justified. As communications technologies converge and computer capabilities expand, it is as easy to manipulate the networks, systems, and computers that carry and compute data for good as for illegal purposes. This is true for several reasons.

Developers created the open architecture of the World Wide Web for efficiency, not security. Although the open nature of the Web allows for easy user access, it is difficult to control or exclude wrongdoers from committing illegal acts. The anonymity of the Internet allows both honest citizens and criminals the opportunity to act unnoticed. Both use the same infrastructure and enjoy protection of the same rights. Criminals can develop viruses, plan attacks, and organize complex fraud schemes in secret and in isolation and unleash their plans instantaneously or in stages if they choose, all at the touch of a few keystrokes. Criminals also have the ability to act globally, irrespective of territorial and jurisdictional boundaries that constrain state-based law enforcement. The absence of effectively trained law enforcement and substantial international coordination to combat cyberthreats is an invitation to criminals and adversaries. There is also an absence of cyber security specialists to manage the consequences of a cyber-attack. In U.S. academic institutions alone, there are fewer than 250 active cybersecurity or cyberassurance specialists, many of whom lack either formal training or extensive professional experience in the field.[16]

Cyberattackers can choose the time and place of an attack, but those on the receiving end must respond reactively; except in the infrequent case of a tip, they rarely have the ability to proactively pursue their cyberattackers. In addition, attacks are not always limited to the intended targets. They are difficult to contain and often have unintended consequences that may lead to cascading failures among other systems. Finally, states, corporations, and individuals are mutually vulnerable. In many respects, the interconnected world is only as strong as its weakest states and private computer systems. Often states and corporations assumed to have adequate protection do not. For example, the U.S. Defense Intelligence Agency estimated that 80 percent of attacks on U.S. computer networks and systems originate or pass through Canada, which has been described as a virtual "hacker haven."[17]

The growth of the World Wide Web also has greatly expanded the ability of individuals, states, and nonstate groups to commit crimes, challenge or undermine the national security of other states, and attack key infrastructures. Today's information technology is expanding the divide between our vulnerabilities and our ability to respond to threats. As individuals, corporations, states, and civil society are increasingly interconnected, the near future is likely to witness an increase in this divide. According to Forrester Research, electronic commerce generated sales worth US $12.2 billion in 2003.[18] The number of people using the Internet for business transactions is increasing. From May 2004 to May 2005, approximately 77 percent of Americans shopped online, 73 percent regularly logged on to banking accounts, and 63 percent paid bills online.[19] Maintaining security in the exponentially expanding wired environment presents a supreme challenge. More than 1 billion people are currently connected to the Internet, a number that is only growing.[20] How can policy makers modify or adjust the technology that propels the benefits of globalization (while at the same time exposing us to greater vulnerabilities) to minimize the unwanted costs?

The cyberthreat environment has prompted new thinking over how to craft solutions across the cyberthreat continuum. For example, critical infrastructures—those determined essential to the preservation of state interests—now include telecommunications networks, banking and finance operations, and access to resources in addition to traditional roads, ports, and rail lines. Private and governmental actors are working to forge partnerships to effectively combat cyberthreats, and they are organizing across borders to ease cross-jurisdictional challenges.

Since the events of September 11, 2001, security concerns over physical and cyberthreats have gained new emphasis as states struggle to develop plans and implementation regimes to enhance security. The terrorist attacks underline the fact that many threats today are regional, and global concerns that blur public–private distinctions may not be amenable to "go it alone" solutions. In the United States, 85 percent of critical infrastructure is privately owned, rendering government solutions without private cooperation hollow and likely to fail.[21] Foreign private ownership of domestic critical infrastructures increases the level of difficulty in crafting solutions.

Much of the critical information infrastructure in place today was developed with efficiency and cost concerns at the forefront of planning and development. With the current emphasis on security, is it time to rethink basic planning assumptions that focus on guaranteeing profits and efficiency? Many people are asking not only what can be done to patch the current system, but also whether the overwhelming need for enhancing security warrants a wholesale reevaluation and replacement of more vulnerable systems. Some of the most important players in the information technology industry now acknowledge the need for added security. Bill Gates has repeatedly made clear that he will make Microsoft's software less vulnerable to cyberthreats even if that means delaying the development of new applications.[22] Larry Ellison promised that iOracle was unbreakable, and has since built the broadest set of security features into Oracle's technology stack, such as encryption for securing data and intrusion detection for preventing unauthorized access to applications.[23] John Chambers of Cisco Systems has stated that he no longer regards security enhancements on Internet routers as extras but as necessities.[24] Governments have also recognized the need to protect against cyberthreats. In the United States, President Bush released the National Strategy to Secure Cyberspace in February 2003, as an implementing component of the National Strategy for Homeland Security. The purpose of the document is "to engage and empower Americans to secure the portions of cyberspace that they own, operate, control, or with which they interact."[25] It gives direction to the federal government and agencies, state and local officials, private companies and organizations, and individual Americans on how to improve collective cybersecurity.

Decision makers in both industry and government face significant challenges in light of the cyberthreat continuum. Policy makers must balance the need for new laws and regulations to ensure security with the need to provide users access and privacy, all without putting unwarranted restraint on innovation and promising technology. Industry will not partner with government if security concerns are not balanced with maintaining open markets and allowing firms to remain globally competitive. The global nature of the technology and the fact that it spans public and private boundaries not only complicates the picture for leaders, but also offers potential opportunities if effective public–private relationships can be forged. Neither government nor industry alone has the means to solve the challenges posed by cyberthreats.

The comparative technological advantages once enjoyed by developed states are eroding as essential technology is developed not by government research labs but increasingly by the private sector and is available "off the shelf." As a consequence, new, state-of-the-art technology such as sophisti-cated encryption is available globally, enabling everyone including money launderers, rogue states, and terrorists to enjoy an asymmetric capability without the heavy research and development budgets of the past. States are interdependent, as are government and industry, and must rely on each other for an effective international response to cyberthreats.

CYBERTHREATS AND NATIONAL SECURITY

In 2000, a Japanese investigation revealed that the government was using software developed by computer companies affiliated with Aum Shinrikyo, the doomsday sect responsible for the sarin gas attack on the Tokyo subway system in 1995.[26] "The government found 100 types of software programs used by at least 10 Japanese government agencies, including the Defense Ministry, and more than 80 major Japanese companies, including Nippon Telegraph and Telephone."[27] Following the discovery, the Japanese govern-ment suspended use of Aum Shinrikyo–developed programs out of concern that Aum-related companies may have compromised security by breaching firewalls, gaining access to sensitive systems or information, allowing invasion by outsiders, planting viruses that could be set off later, or planting malicious code that could cripple computer systems and key data systems.[28]

From these facts, is it clear that the suspects were likely to attempt to overthrow the Japanese government? Had they engaged in espionage, crim-inal violations, or possible terrorism? Was this a threat to national security? Was Aum Shinrikyo conducting a legitimate commercial enterprise? Is it possible to tell? Clearly, considering the cult's history, the Japanese govern-ment proceeded under the assumption that this was a serious state-level threat. The example highlights the key challenges posed by cyberthreats: determining intent and determining the level and nature of the threat quickly and accurately.

Cyberthreats place enormous stress on security and criminal systems that rely on proving intent to secure a criminal conviction. Computer attacks can be instantaneous, time-delayed, or staged in waves. They can be anony-mous or falsely attributed to unsuspecting users. It is difficult to identify with a high degree of certainty exactly who committed an act.[29] This is precisely why U.S. law enforcement solves only 2 percent of hacker cases, as compared to 80 to 90 percent of all homicides.[30] There is also no way to know for certain an attacker's exact motives or to quickly determine whether the attacker is part of a wider conspiracy. In a broader context, while authorities can identify individual hacks or intrusions, it is much more difficult to quickly judge whether individual attacks are part of a wider series of attacks. Even if a state recognizes that a concerted attack is underway, an attack is not likely to have purely military objectives. The military–civilian distinction breaks down, requiring government responders to alert and work with private infrastructure and systems owners to safeguard against the attack.

Both the security apparatus that developed to pursue Cold War security objectives and sovereign law enforcement organizations are struggling to adapt to new threats ushered in by globalization. Traditional responses to new security challenges such as cybercrime and cyberterrorism are failing to keep up with the methods and tactics that are available to state and non-state actors alike.[31]

Because developed states, and most notably the United States, enjoy preeminent conventional and strategic military power, adversaries are seeking ways in which to inflict indirect or asymmetric harm on strong states and their interests abroad. Developed countries are reliant on information technology. Therefore, one area for exploitation by adversaries is attack on critical computer networks.[32]

A few examples illustrate the level to which developed states rely on computer networks and technology. The U.S. Department of Defense infrastructure consists of more than 2.1 million computers, with 10,000 local area networks and 1,000 long-distance networks.[33] These figures do not even account for the millions of computer users who regularly do business with the DOD. In addition, GAO revealed that DOD computer users reported only a small fraction of systems attacks, and the number of annual attacks was much higher than reported.[34] A computer network attack has the potential for causing catastrophic injury to security and could have a strategic reach that would affect cultural sensibilities, including confidence in the government's ability to protect against threats and safeguard personal and commercial interests.[35]

In the United Kingdom, there is growing concern over the threat of computer-based attack and cyberterrorism. In 2001, former Foreign Secretary Robin Cook warned that hacking could cripple Britain faster than a military strike because computers are managing most of the country's infrastructure.[36] The United Kingdom thus signed the first-ever bilateral Science and Technology Agreement on Homeland Security with the United States in late 2004, in the hopes of closer collaboration in security-related science such as cybersecurity.[37]

Japan also took the first steps toward combating cyberterrorism. Japan issued special legislation with the specific purpose of combating cyberattacks and protecting network communications systems.[38] The Japanese government also began the first formal discussions of cybersecurity with the United States in June 2002 and continued the talks throughout 2004.[39]

Adversaries are developing the tools and doctrine necessary to conduct offensive cyberwarfare programs. A major challenge will be to find ways to defend infrastructure and protect commerce while maintaining an open society. Openness and ease of connectivity promote efficiency, but these attributes also make information infrastructures vulnerable to attack. Unlike the threats of the Cold War, which required state-sponsored infrastructures and installations, cyberthreats are strategically asymmetric, require no state sponsorship, and use commercially available equipment and facilities. A computer in a basement hardly qualifies as a weapons site. These threats can affect systems anywhere in the world, disguise origins and travel routes, and do it all instantaneously.[40]

Despite the potential magnitude of the harm and the strategic nature of the threat, many states—including the United States—continue to characterize cyberthreats as a law enforcement issue with possible national security consequences rather than as a frontline national security issue. As such, a foreign or domestic adversary that develops the ability to interrupt the flow of data will have the potential to weaken any entity that is incapable of responding.

The characterization of the cyberthreat—criminal versus national security threat—is important. The law enforcement community is fundamentally concerned with trials, convictions, and punishing wrongdoers who run afoul of criminal law. Thus, it is bound by statutory authority and concerned with evidentiary trails, burdens of proof, and expert testimony. However, democracies did not develop criminal law based on principles of efficiency. It was based on the understanding that law enforcement needed to afford certain principles, rights, and protections to the accused. Criminal law generally requires both criminal intent and a criminal act. Proving intent, however, is difficult in many computer-related crimes.

Issues that fall under national security, on the other hand, often focus solely on the act's illegality. Representing a threat to national security is sufficient for liability. An example may help illustrate this point. If a computer emergency response team detects a hacker, then the FBI may want the hacker to continue his or her activities in order to trace the hacker and develop an evidentiary trail. By following and monitoring the hacker's moves, his or her intent may become apparent. However, if such an intrusion were to occur against the military's Central Command in Tampa, Florida, during a deployment (the command is responsible for U.S. military operations in the Middle East and South Asia), the military may wish to immediately terminate the hack and even strike back or "hack back" at the attacker.

But what if the attack is coming not from a single hacker but is being orchestrated by a state? Many countries are developing doctrines of computer attack and defense. The United States bases its information operations doctrine on its ability to attack an adversary's information and information systems while defending its own. The U.S. approach is to blind an adversary and keep it confused over the "ground truth" of the battlefield, thus interfering with the opposing senior leadership's ability to make sound decisions.

The Russian Federation is also developing information warfare strategy and doctrine. The Russian concept of information warfare includes computer network attack and defense but is more expansive than the U.S. concept and includes the use of information to break down the ability of the human mind and body to function effectively. China is currently developing a unique information warfare strategy based on information weapons as unconventional warfare weapons and battlefield force multipliers.[41]

What state-sponsored information warfare operations have in common is the use of information technology to achieve strategic (national-level) or tactical (battlefield-level) effects in order to achieve political or military objectives. Essentially, it is the conduct of warfare through the use of information technology. Specifically, the United States defines information operations as

> The integrated employment of the specified core capabilities of Electronic Warfare [EW], Computer Network Operations (CNO), PSYOP [psychological operations], Military Deception [MILDEC], and Operations Security [OPSEC], in concert with specified supporting and related capabilities, to influence, disrupt, corrupt, or usurp adversarial human and automated decisionmaking, while protecting our own.[42]

If an incident appears to have the characteristics of a computer attack, then just what options are available to the government? Pursuant to the UN Charter specifically and the body of law known as the Law of Armed Conflict in general,[43] a state can use military force only when responding to an armed attack on its own territory. In addition, customary international law holds that a state must retaliate in self-defense and only to the extent necessary to terminate the initial attack and to prevent further intrusions.[44] Where does this leave a state after a cyberattack? The answer depends on the level and degree of damage caused by an attack. If a cyberattack causes physical damage or death to citizens by, for example, causing a dam to fail, then certainly a cyber-response would be warranted and probably a use of force would be justified. If, however, a hacker takes down a banking system, a state is not permitted the use of force and a cyber-response might or might not be justified. In this case, considering the potential for unintended consequences that a response might cause, decision makers may want to find other alternatives. International practice recognizes that states may inflict great hardship on each other and their respective citizenry without such activity constituting the use of force or a violation of international law.[45] This is significant because information attacks will certainly create harm and hardship but may never constitute aggression or rise to the level of an armed attack. Law and policy have yet to evolve fully so that they can answer many of the questions posed by cyberthreats. The February 2003 U.S. National Strategy to Secure Cyberspace makes clear that the U.S. Government reserves the right to respond "in an appropriate manner" if the United States comes under computer attack, including the use of cyber weapons. That same month, the president announced plans under National Security Presidential Directive 16 to develop national-level guidance for determining when and how the United States would launch computer network attacks against foreign adversary computer systems.[46] However, a global consensus on how to effectively deal with cyberthreats still does not exist.

CYBERTERRORISM

Cyberterrorism presents a definitional problem. There is no recognized international definition for cyberterrorism. Each country has its own cyberterrorism rules. For example, the special legislation enacted by Japan to combat cyberterrorism defines it as the unauthorized entry into computer systems through communications networks such as the Internet and the damage caused to those systems as a result of the unauthorized access.[47] This expansive definition would constitute computer fraud and abuse in other states such as the United States, and such activities would not rise to the level of cyberterrorism. In the United States, the FBI defines cyberterrorism as a "premeditated, politically motivated attack against information, computer systems, computer programs, and data which results in violence against noncombatant targets by sub-national groups or clandestine agents."[48]

Perhaps the best way to understand cyberterrorism is to view it as an extension of age-old terrorist principles adapted for use in the new high-tech environment. Using violence against noncombatants to cause fear, terrorists' activities are politically motivated and seek to coerce governments or civilians in furtherance of the terrorists' political agenda. Cyberterrorists are thus politically motivated but make use of information technology and networks to further their agendas. Clearly, disrupting communications, airport, and utilities systems for the purpose of inflicting damage to achieve a political end are all cyberterrorist activities, capabilities al Qaeda is developing. In one example, a suspected terrorist group calling itself the Internet Black Tigers attacked Sri Lankan government computers with "suicide e-mail bombings" in an effort to overwhelm and disable government information systems, embarrass the Sri Lankan government, and draw attention to the cause of Tamil separatism in northern and eastern Sri Lanka.[49] Incidents such as this may become increasingly familiar as marginalized groups without political voices learn how to exploit Internet technology for their political ends.

Using the Internet to facilitate terrorist activities is another aspect of cyberterrorism. For example, Wadih el Hage, a prime suspect in the 1998 U.S. embassy bombings in Africa, sent encrypted e-mails under alias names to al Qaeda "associates." Ramzi Yousef, the planner of the 1993 attack on the World Trade Center, used encrypted files to hide details of a plot to destroy eleven U.S. jetliners. Philippine officials discovered Yousef's computer and sent it to the FBI for analysis. Two of the files took more than a year to decrypt.[50] U.S. officials also believe that alleged terrorist-sponsoring countries such as Iran and North Korea, and even Russia and China, have trained hackers in Internet warfare.[51]

For terrorists, cyber-based attacks have distinct advantages over physical attacks. They can be conducted remotely, anonymously, and relatively cheaply, and they do not require significant investments in weapons, explosives, and personnel. The effects can still be widespread and profound. Consider the effects and publicity that followed when the message "Hacked by Chinese" appeared on government and corporate computers as communications networks were shut down because of the Code Red virus in July 2001.[52]

Incidents of cyberterrorism are likely to increase. They will be conducted through denial-of-service attacks that overload servers, worms and viruses, unauthorized intrusions, Web-site defacements, attacks on network infrastructures, and other methods that we are unable to envision today. The former National Infrastructure Protection Center concluded that the potential for compound cyber and physical attacks, referred to as "swarming attacks," is an increasing threat to the United States.[53]

So why does the vulnerability persist? Commercial off-the-shelf operating systems and applications are widely shared, and their vulnerabilities are widely known. In addition, because many technology developers and producers contract out work and services, often to overseas partners, there is opportunity for mischief whenever controls and quality-assurance procedures are not in place. The Internet is also a target-rich environment in which not all systems can be protected. Finally, cultural sensitivities, such as privacy rights, preclude intrusive security measures.

CYBERCRIME

A hacker used a U.S.-based Web site to gain unlimited access to multiple U.S. military, university, and private computer systems in 1995–1996. The FBI tracked the hacker to Argentina and notified a local telecommunications carrier, which in turn notified local law enforcement. An Argentinean investigating judge authorized a search of the hacker's apartment and the seizure of his computer. Argentinean officials investigated Julio Cesar Ardita for intrusions into an Argentinean telecommunications system, but Argentine law did not cover hacking systems in the United States, and the judge ruled that only the United States could prosecute him for these crimes. In the absence of an extradition treaty, Ardita agreed in May 1998 to come to the United States and plead guilty to felony charges of unlawfully intercepting communications and damaging Department of Defense files and NASA computers. U.S. authorities fined Ardita $5,000 and sentenced him to three years' probation.[54]

This example illustrates many of the challenges that law enforcement faces in overcoming cyber-related crimes. Authorities must address jurisdictional, substantive, and cultural issues. Information technologies pose a variety of challenges to criminal law and procedure. Many age-old crimes, such as fraud, theft, and money laundering, have qualitatively changed because of the new cybermedium. With the aid of computers and the Web, wrongdoers can perpetrate crimes with greater ease, speed, and anonymity. Individuals can easily copy and steal information, interfere with or co-opt commercial and public assets, and gain illegal access to private information. New criminal activity, such as computer network attacks, virus disseminations, and hacking, likewise pose significant challenges because of the speed at which they take place and the magnitude of damage they can create.[55]

Cybercrime and cyberterrorism are not mutually exclusive because both are intent-based. For most crimes, a state prosecutor must prove that the suspect intended to commit the crime and indeed did so.

Cybercrime is the commission of illegal acts through the use of communications and information-based technology. Cybercrime includes fraudulent activities such as e-mail schemes, identity theft, and credit card fraud, as well as theft crimes such as electronic espionage, corporate espionage, and money laundering.[56] It also includes nuisance crimes, including transmission of viruses, system shutdowns, interference with network systems, denial-of-service attacks, and Web site defacements.

Cybercrime is also a tax because it increases the costs of doing business and passes those costs on to consumers.[57] Estimated worldwide losses to cybercrime were $50 billion in 2002, with the United States, specifically, losing $5 billion.[58] The full extent of the damage, though, cannot possibly be known because of the fact that victims report only about 10 percent of all committed cybercrimes, with fewer than 2 percent resulting in a conviction.[59]

A FRAMEWORK FOR ADDRESSING THE PROBLEM

States, corporations, and industry are mutually vulnerable and interdependent with regard to cyberthreats. States and citizens must recognize that their own self-interests lie in multinational cooperation and the development of global information-related standards and practices. The challenges posed by cyberthreats cannot be overcome by the developed world acting alone. All states are stakeholders in combating cyberthreats. However, because of the informational advantages enjoyed by developed states and the costs associated with enhancing the information infrastructures of developing states, there is some reluctance to support open and multilateral solutions. For example, even though it is vulnerable to computer network attacks, the United States enjoys superiority if not dominance in the realm of information operations and information warfare. This dominance is perpetuated by U.S. attempts to limit the ability of other states to gain information capabilities via dual-use technology or anti-encryption limitations.

A more robust understanding of the vulnerabilities and advantages posed by cyberthreats must be developed before we can develop a cogent strategy that aligns domestic and global policy. The rise in cyberincidents warrants a more coordinated global response.[60] In analyses of how law and public policy can be used to combat cyberthreats, solutions often suffer from a lack of practicality and applicability to real-world circumstances. Therefore, in determining the proper policy course to pursue, states and private parties must first address whether there is a need for additional public–private cooperation or regulation. In other words, is the current system working? A state must then, in coordination with industry, consider whether the nature of the threat in light of the security requirements necessitates a coordinated international approach. Finally, if international harmonization is warranted, an international framework will have to be developed.

One attempt to forge a public–private partnership was the creation of a new U.S. government agency in 1998: the National Infrastructure Protection Center (NIPC), an interagency unit within the Department of Justice (DOJ). NIPC provided cyberthreat assessments, warnings, and vulnerability assessments and shared this information with industry and the public. For example, three days after the September 11 attacks, NIPC issued an advisory that warned of an expected increase in computer-related incidents as a result of the terrorist attacks.[61] NIPC has had some successes in fostering incident reporting and information sharing, such as the speedy notice and containment of the Melissa computer virus in 1999. NIPC was the U.S. government's first attempt to cooperate and collaborate with industry to reduce cyberthreats, but there were limitations to its success. Though NIPC did issue advisories to the public, the link to industry was modest and lacked the breadth and depth that both government officials and corporate leaders had originally anticipated. Why the lack of success when both the government and industry acknowledged the need for cooperation? In organizing NIPC, the government did what governments do best. It organized an interagency group and identified key government officials to lead the new center. It put in place policies and procedures and drafted a mission statement. Then the NIPC "rolled out" its policies and procedures to industry. Industry then did what it does best: It evaluated the costs of partnering with NIPC, asked why it was not consulted before, and ignored the agency.

The reason for the failure thus lay in a lack of coordination from the beginning and in difficulties in overcoming mistrust. For public–private partnerships to work, neither side can come to the other and roll out a program with all the answers. Government and industry are organized to achieve vastly different objectives, and points of view must be aired and procedures negotiated. The government also failed to appreciate how its NIPC programs would affect industry. A one-size-fits-all approach cannot work to combat cyberthreats that cross vastly different industries. For example, NIPC provided for no Freedom of Information Act (FOIA) exemption or exclusion, meaning that any information turned over to the government could be subject to a FOIA request and wind up in the public domain. This raised concerns that information volunteered to help contain computer threats could be used against companies. Would government warnings undermine confidence in the banking industry or a specific company, for example, if the government made public the total amount of money electronically stolen from banks? Furthermore, NIPC initially mandated that failure to provide the information requested could lead to fines and liability.

Due to the challenges facing NIPC, in March 2003, the Department of Homeland Security (DHS) integrated NIPC into its new Directorate for Information Analysis and Infrastructure Protection, along with a number of other agencies, including the Department of Commerce's Critical Infrastructure Assurance Office and the General Services Administration's Federal Computer Incident Response Center. This integration attempted to remove many of the obstacles to a cooperative relationship between government and industry. The new directorate established the Protected Critical Infrastructure Information (PCII) Program in February 2004 to specifically encourage private industry to voluntarily share their sensitive and proprietary business information with the Federal Government. Unlike NIPC, the Critical Infrastructure Information Act of 2002 (CII Act) exempted any information shared with the PCII from public FOIA disclosure.[62]

Though progress has been made, more needs to be done. Although better public–private cooperation is needed, should governments enact additional domestic laws to combat cyberthreats? The answer changes, depending on the state in question. In many developed states, comprehensive laws are on the books to punish wrongdoers; in others, no such prohibitions exist. Therefore, a case can be made for seeking international agreements on legal harmonization. The global community should pursue international agreements when a challenge has transboundary effects, represents an extraterritorial threat, produces a failure in effective enforcement in response to a threat, or where there are highly divergent state practices and a need to harmonize law to increase effectiveness. Cyberthreats satisfy each criterion. So what are the options?

States and private-sector actors may rely on the ongoing development of international policy and law to combat cyberthreats. Although detractors term this the "do-nothing" approach, it has the advantage of a more stable and arguably more gradual and balanced development because it builds on current structures. Another approach is to clarify legal ambiguities at the margin, modifying current policy and adapting it to information technology and computer threats. This affords policy makers the chance to develop a strategy that fosters individual and specific critical information technology structures. These efforts may proceed through the United Nations or may concentrate on lower-level, bilateral, or multilateral agreements. This approach favors formalizing agreements where agreement can be found.

Finally, in a more comprehensive fashion, global leaders could seek to harmonize domestic laws and expand criminal liability in a coordinated way for agreed-upon cyberthreats. This approach relies on promoting cooperation in investigations and prosecutions. Because of the inherent importance of information infrastructures globally, the international community could condemn certain actions and, considering today's environment, perhaps outlaw them as acts of terrorism or egregious cybercrimes.[63]

Policy makers should not construe the options above as either–or solutions but should consider them as appropriate responses to different challenges along the threat continuum. For example, cybercrime and anti-cyberterrorism laws may require a wider and more comprehensive approach, while criminal liability for fraud and hacking may better evolve at the margin.

In evaluating specific initiatives, global leaders should craft new international agreements to ensure that they are flexible enough to adapt to the changing technological environment, are tailored and scaled to the challenge, are reasonable and proportional to the threat they seek to overcome, and consider the unique values of the states involved (to use the U.S. example, consider the liberal democratic principles based on underlying constitutional rights).

While assessing the current global policy on cyberthreats, its successes and failures in the past, and the economic and structural importance of information infrastructures, policy makers should consider the option to clarify legal ambiguity at the margin highly attractive and able to generate consensus on key issues. It provides flexibility to respond to technological changes and takes advantage of existing laws. This is particularly true for cyberthreats, where the relative potential harm is great and the measures that could be used to combat the threat are so potentially sweeping.

A MULTILATERAL APPROACH

The effort by the Council of Europe to combat cybercrime provides an interesting case study in how to pursue cyber-related solutions. As an intergovernmental organization, the Council of Europe seeks to shape common European legislation for its member states. Among the council's stated purposes is

> to modernize and harmonize national legislation with a view to democracy, human rights and the rule of law; to make justice more effective by proposing simpler, more flexible judicial procedures; to find shared solutions to the new legal and ethical problems which scientific and technological progress is causing for modern societies.[64]

In 1989, seeing the need for consistent computer-related legislation, the Council of Europe issued a recommendation on computer-related crime.[65] This was the first step in unifying European computer law. It proposed required minimum standards and activities that member countries must criminalize, and another set of options that member states might wish to criminalize. Building on the success of its recommendations, the Council of Europe spent four years working on a Convention on Cybercrime, with help from the United States, Canada, Japan, and other non-members of the organization. The document opened up for signature to EU and non-EU members alike on November 23, 2001, and entered into force on July 1, 2004. Today 11 countries have ratified it and 31 more have signed the treaty, including the United States.[66] The treaty proposes common definitions of computer-related offenses and content-related offenses.[67] It also names four types of cybercrime: confidentiality offenses, notably breaking into computers; fraud and forgery; content violations, such as child pornography and racism; and copyright offenses.[68] The convention has the full effect of a multilateral treaty with the force of law, but only among the ratifying countries.[69]

Among its provisions, the convention makes it a crime to create, download, or post on a Web site any computer program that is "designed or adapted" primarily to gain access to a computer system without permission. It also prohibits the development of software designed to interfere with the "functioning of a computer system" by deleting or altering data, and it allows authorities to order someone to reveal his or her passwords or phrases used in an encryption key.[70] The convention also requires Web sites and Internet providers to collect information about their users, a rule that would potentially limit anonymous remailers.

The Convention on Cybercrime raises many issues. For example, many in the United States accustomed to protection of privacy rights are skeptical because the convention favors law enforcement capabilities over U.S. privacy rights. Privacy advocates are concerned that the convention may interfere with the ability of online users to speak anonymously and that anonymous remailers may be outlawed. The convention also may interfere with the ability of everyone from corporations to hackers to test the security of their own information infrastructures. Internet service providers claim the draft makes unfair demands on them by asking them to track Web users' online movements.

The Convention on Cybercrime illustrates how good ideas can become controversial when they move from the drawing board to implementation. As early as 1989, the Council of Europe recognized that domestic regulation alone was insufficient to overcome the cybercrime threat in Europe. There was widespread industry support and both the public and private sector recognized the need for legal harmonization. The threat posed by cybercrime is clearly an extraterritorial threat, effective enforcement is lacking, and there are highly divergent state laws and practices on cybercrime. So why is there controversy? New laws, particularly regional agreements, tend to establish legal norms for the largely unregulated realm of cyberspace. Regional agreements often become customary international law that may ultimately evolve into formalized treaties. In effect, Europe wrote the first international code of conduct and criminal code that a multilateral body accepted.

By setting this benchmark, states and industries that did not have a voice in the process may find the European convention an attack on the unique values of other countries. Finally, and perhaps most significantly, the Council of Europe is a state-centric organization. Although industry applauded the council's efforts early on, the lack of transparency increased as the release date for the draft neared. The draft convention may be ratified by the member states, but industry has resisted it and will continue to resist. The lack of industry buy-in across the entire life cycle of the convention may render it a blunt and ineffective tool.

TOWARD CYBERTHREAT SOLUTIONS

Cyberthreats come in a variety of forms, including hacking, cybercrime, cyberterrorism, information warfare, and information operations. Information technology allows a wide range of actors to cause a wide range of damage and chaos across the cyberthreat continuum. To understand and overcome cyberthreats, policy makers must make two assumptions. First, states, industry, and individuals are mutually vulnerable and interdependent. Second, neither states nor industry alone has the authority or capability to solve the problems posed by cyberthreats. Much of the key technology and infrastructure lies in the private sector, while the authority to create and enforce laws and the legitimacy to enter into international agreements resides with states. Recognizing these two key assumptions and embedding them in planning and policy will go a long way toward developing cyberthreat solutions.

ENDNOTES

1. "Riptech Releases Ground Breaking Internet Security Threat Report" (press release), Jan. 28, 2002. Available at <www.riptech.com/newsevents/release020127.html>; "Riptech Internet Security Threat Report Volume II Quantifies Rise in Internet Attacks" (press release), July 8, 2002, <www.riptech.com/newsevents/release020708.html>.
2. <www.nitrd.gov/pitac/reports/20050301_cybersecurity/cybersecurity.pdf >
3. Riptech, an Alexandria, Virginia, firm that tracks computer intrusions, discovered at least 180,000 cyberattacks from January through June 2002 for its more than 400 clients across the world ("Riptech Internet Security Threat Report").
4. <www.csmonitor.com/2005/0816/p01s02-stct.html>
5. Barton Gellman, "Cyber-Attacks by Al Qaeda Feared: Terrorists at Threshold of Using Internet as Tool of Bloodshed, Experts Say," *Washington Post* (June 27, 2002): A1; Jack Kelley, "Terrorist Instructions Hidden Online," *USA Today* (April 14, 2001). Operational details of future targets are hidden in plain view. As Kelley writes, "We recognize that cyber tools offer them new, low-cost, easily hidden means to inflict damage. Terrorists and

extremists already use the Internet to communicate, to raise funds, recruit, and gather intelligence. They may even launch attacks remotely from countries where their actions are not illegal or with whom we have no extradition agreements."

6. <www.forbes.com/business/forbes/2004/0920/070sidebar.html>

7. <www.caida.org/analysis/security/sapphire/>

8. <www.securityfocus.com/news/6767>

9. The accounts were global indeed and included Finland, Russia, Germany, the Netherlands, the United States, Israel, and Switzerland.

10. <http://news.com.com/2009-12-956901.html>

11. Dorothy Denning, *Information Warfare and Security* (New York: ACM Press, 1999), 55.

12. A description of the ILoveYou virus can be found at <http://getvirushelp.com/iloveyou/>.

13. Denning, *Information Warfare and Security,* 206–207.

14. Charles Bickers, "Combat on the Web," *Far Eastern Economic Review* (Aug. 16, 2001).

15. Referred to as *cyberplagues* by Dorothy Denning. See *Information Warfare and Security,* 269–281.

16. <http://www.nitrd.gov/pitac/reports/20050301_cybersecurity/cybersecurity.pdf>, 4.

17. Apparently, Canada is a "hacker haven" because of its large number of computers, high percentage of residents who own computers, and the heavy integration between U.S. and Canadian computer infrastructure and systems. See David Pugliese, "Blame Canada for 80% of Cyberattacks: Country's 'Zone of Vulnerability,' U.S. Military Report Warns," *Ottawa Citizen* (March 25, 2000).

18. <http://en.wikipedia.org/wiki/Electronic_commerce>

19. <www.gartner.com/press_releases/asset_129754_11.html>

20. <www.cnn.com/2005/TECH/internet/06/23/evolution.main/>

21. <www.dhs.gov/dhspublic/interapp/press_release/press_release_0350.xml>

22. Ariana Eunjung Cha, "Cybersecurity a Top Priority: White House Adviser Presses Computer Industry to Do More," *Washington Post* (Feb. 8, 2002): E1. Also see <http://www.microsoft.com/industry/government/csisiti.mspx> from 2003.

23. <http://issj.sys-con.com/read/133719.htm>

24. Cha (see note 22 above).

25. <http://www.whitehouse.gov/pcipb/cyberspace_strategy.pdf>, 8.

26. Maryann Cusimano Love, *Public-Private Partnerships and Global Problems: Y2K and Cybercrime.* Paper presented at the International Studies Association, Hong Kong, July 2001.

27. Ibid. Cusimano Love adds, "The Japanese defense ministry used Aum-developed communications programs at 20 ground bases across Japan to gain more rapid access to the Internet. Aum programs were also used for airline route management and mainframe computer operations. The software companies earned the business through indirect subcontracting relationships, underbidding competitors by 30 to 40% because their employees, all Aum members, worked for virtually no pay."

28. Calvin Sims, "Japan Software Suppliers Linked to Sect," *The New York Times* (March 2, 2000): A6.

29. This is true even if the specific terminal from which the attack originated can be identified, because it may be difficult to say exactly who was at the terminal when the attack was planned and executed.

30. <www.microsoft.com/industry/government/csisiti.mspx>

31. Virtually every benefit of the global era in some way poses a challenge to security. For example, the cheap cost of technology facilitates the rise of computer-related crime and cyberterrorism. The rapid transit of goods and people now challenges the ability of

states to secure their borders. The free flow of data, people, and ideas makes it difficult to conduct intelligence gathering without running afoul of First Amendment guarantees. The growth of world markets and international investment aids in financing terrorism and engaging in money laundering.

32. But are the most technologically advanced states also the most vulnerable? According to Bangladeshi Deputy Prime Minister Datuk Seri Abdullah Ahmad Badawi, "Technologically superior states can also cripple the defenses and economies of victim states at will, again placing developing states at a disadvantage. . . . It would cost the average Bangladeshi more than eight years' income to buy a computer, whereas it would cost the average American just one month's wage. And what would this repository of information, in which more than 80 percent of the content is in English, mean to 90 percent of the people worldwide who do not speak it?" See "Internet Widening Gap Between Haves, Have Nots," *New Straits Times Press* (June 5, 2000).

33. <www.csmonitor.com/2004/0415/p06s02-woeu.html?s=widep>

34. <http://www.gcn.com/16_32/news/32050-1.html>

35. A comprehensive list of potential computer network attacks is beyond the scope of this paper, but a few to mention are using computers to reroute trains, corrupt databases, impose information blockades in or out of computers, alter traffic control systems, interfere with law enforcement emergency response systems, and corrupt key utilities. See Roger C. Molander, Andrew S. Riddile, and Peter A. Wilson, *Strategic Information Warfare: A New Face of War* (New York: Rand Corp., 1996); and the President's Commission on Critical Infrastructure Protection, *Critical Foundations: Protecting America's Infrastructures* (Washington, DC: U.S. Government Printing Office, Oct. 1997).

36. Nick Hopkins, "Cyber Terror Threatens UK's Biggest Companies," *Guardian* (April 3, 2001).

37. <www.publictechnology.net/modules.php?op=modload&name=News&file=article&sid=2638>

38. "Japan Special Legislation to Combat Cyberterrorism," *Yomiuri Shimbun* (Nov. 30, 2000).

39. <www.crime-research.org/news/02.12.2004/822/>

40. John C. Gannon, "Intelligence Challenges through 2015." Remarks to Columbus Council on World Affairs, April 27, 2000, <www.cia.gov/cia/public_affairs/speeches/archives/2000/gannon_speech_05022000.html>. Gannon is chairman of the National Intelligence Council.

41. James Mulvenon, *China and Cyberwar*. Presentation to "Information Warfare Post Y2K: A National Security Perspective," Jane's Conference, Washington, DC, May 12, 2000.

42. <www.prwatch.org/node/4040>

43. The Law of Armed Conflict (LOAC) is a body of international law that attempts to regulate conduct during armed hostilities in a manner that minimizes savagery but does not impede the ability of states and factions to enter into and carry out conflict. The rules and general principles of the LOAC are applicable to all conflicts, including those conducted in cyberspace.

44. Humanitarian law limits how much a state may punish an enemy. The most significant principles—to protect citizens and noncombatants—require a state to weigh the prospect of gain through military attack against harm. This principle, derived from customary law, essentially establishes that a response must be appropriate to a grievance and must be considered in light of objectives and possible casualties. See Martens Clause, 1899 Hague Peace Conference (attacks will be judged by effects rather than by methods).

45. Examples include boycotts and withholding medical aid or other needed resources.

46. <www.fas.org/irp/crs/RL32114.pdf>, 15.

47. "Government Drafts Plan to Combat Cyberterrorism," *Yomiuri Shimbun* (Nov. 30, 2000).

48. <www.crime-research.org/articles/Cyber_Terrorism_new_kind_Terrorism>

49. Jim Wolf, "Cyber Terrorism," *Scotsman* (May 13, 1998): 3.

50. Jack Kelley, "Terror Groups Hide Behind Web Encryption," *USA Today* (April 13, 2001).

51. <www.forbes.com/global/2004/0920/104_2.html>

52. "'Chinese' Virus Targets Microsoft Security Hole," CNN, July 20, 2001; available at <www.cnn.com/2001/BUSINESS/asia/07/20/hk.codered/>. Update: <www.gao.gov/htext/d03715t.html> from 2003.

53. <www.gao.gov/htext/d03715t.html>

54. David Goldstone and Betty-Ellen Shave, "International Dimensions of Crimes in Cyberspace," *Fordham International Law Journal* (June 1999): 1924, 1928.

55. In many respects, the realm of cyberspace represents the ultimate potential of economic liberalism: private self-regulation of human interaction, unfettered and instantaneous free flows of capital, and trade in a new, borderless space unconstrained by sovereign institutions.

56. Money laundering facilitates much illegal activity worldwide. However, it can also be seen as a theft crime that deprives the legitimate owners of resources the benefit of their property.

57. Anthony Lake, *Six Nightmares: Real Threats in a Dangerous World and How America Can Meet Them* (New York: Little, Brown, 2000), 46.

58. Chris Hale, "Cybercrime: Facts and Figures Concerning the Global Dilemma," *Crime & Justice International* 18 (65) (Sept. 2002): 5–6.

59. Ibid, 24–26.

60. Attacks on computers are on the rise. Notable cyberattacks and viruses include the attack on the CIA on September 19, 1996; the attack on the U.S. Department of Justice in August 1996; the attack on *The New York Times* in September 1998; the Melissa virus in 1999; the Naked Wife virus on March 7, 2001; and the Matcher virus on April 19, 2001.

61. NIPC Advisory 01-020, Sept. 14, 2001, <www.infragard.net/warnings/ 01_020.htm>.

62. <www.dhs.gov/dhspublic/interapp/press_release/press_release_0350.xml>

63. Perhaps hijacking agreements could serve as a useful and instructive model.

64. Information obtained from the Council of Europe Web site, <www.coe.int/portalT.asp>.

65. Council of Europe, "Computer-Related Crime," Recommendation No. R (89) 9; <http://europa.eu.int/ISPO/eif/InternetPoliciesSite/Crime/crime1.html>.

66. <http://conventions.coe.int/Treaty/Commun/ChercheSig.asp?NT=185& CM=8&DF =&CL=ENG

67. For a discussion of the history of the Convention on Cybercrime, see Goldstone and Shave, "International Dimensions of Crimes in Cyberspace," 1945.

68. <http://www.cbsnews.com/stories/2004/09/16/tech/main643897.shtml>

69. These efforts involve only developed countries; multilateral efforts in the developing world lag. It's not easy to persuade countries where Internet use is not yet pervasive to see cybercrime as an urgent problem. But an attack can be launched as easily from the Third World as from Europe or the United States, and the network will only be as strong as its weakest links.

70. Only Singapore and Malaysia have enacted such a requirement into law. This requirement may pose a substantial problem for the United States because it runs counter to the constitutional protection against self-incrimination.

CHAPTER TEN

Ecological Interdependence and the Spread of Infectious Disease

Dennis Pirages and Paul Runci

The disease outbreak began in a remote region of Guangdong Province in China sometime in the autumn of 2002, when a previously unknown virus jumped from either horseshoe bats or masked palm civet cats to people. The virus quickly spread throughout the region, but news about the new disease was kept under wraps by the Chinese government, which considered the matter to be "top secret." In February 2003 the disease made its way to Hong Kong, carried by a physician from Guangdong province who had been treating patients afflicted by this mysterious disease. From there the virus quickly spread to much of the rest of Asia, and eventually to thirty countries. The most affected Asian economies lost tens of billions of dollars as trade dropped off, tourists shunned the region, air traffic was dramatically curtailed, and hotel rooms remained empty. By the time this new disease had been brought under control in June 2003, more than 8,000 people had been sickened and more than 900 had died. Quick action by the world health community stopped this SARS outbreak in its tracks. But other diseases, such as a modified form of avian flu (H5N1), could spread more rapidly around our shrinking planet, thus endangering the lives of tens of millions of people.

Viruses, bacteria, and other pathogens have never respected national borders. Throughout history microbes have moved across frontiers, carried by wind, water, explorers, migrants, merchants, and mercenaries. Most of the time, these unauthorized crossings have had little impact, but occasionally whole societies have been reshaped because of them. Deepening globalization is now causing growing concern over the potential development and spread of new and resurgent diseases across increasingly porous state borders.

Over the course of history, populations of human beings have coevolved with millions of other animal and plant species as well as a host of pathogens. Only during the last century did technological innovation give *Homo sapiens* a clear, but perhaps temporary, edge in this struggle. There is now growing evidence that an array of pathogens is making a comeback in an increasingly interdependent and urbanized global system. In addition, various plant and animal species, having been introduced to new environments through expanded trade and transportation, are wreaking ecological havoc in many countries. The changes associated with increasingly open societies, open economies, and deployment of new technologies—growing economic integration, gradual disappearance of national borders, more rapid movement of people and goods among regions, weakening of the authority of the state, and changing patterns of human settlements and behavior—are combining to make the resurgence of pathogenic microorganisms, as well as the worldwide spread of various kinds of other potentially destructive species, an important threat to future human security and well-being.[1]

Globalization has been quietly underway for some time. The first modern humans lived some 100,000 years ago and inhabited areas that spanned eastern Africa and the Middle East. From there, a series of expansions and migrations moved outward until most of the habitable world had been at least loosely settled 15,000 years ago.[2] Since then, there has been a slow but accelerating reintegration of these previously scattered and mostly isolated human populations into larger units. Thus, the Roman Empire, the Mongol empires, and European colonialism are all examples of the ways in which previously isolated human populations have been absorbed into much larger administrative units. This long-term reintegration process is expected to culminate in the emergence of an immense global city over the next few decades. But each step in this reintegration of human populations has had significant ecological, political, and socioeconomic consequences, not the least of which has been the insecurity associated with the emergence and rapid spread of disease.

INTEGRATION AND DISEASE IN HISTORY

Homo sapiens is one species among millions that share the global ecosystem. Like most other species, *Homo sapiens* lives in and identifies with basic biological units called *populations.* Populations of any species are "dynamic systems of interacting individuals . . . that are potentially capable of interbreeding with each other."[3] The boundaries of human populations, which social scientists call *societies* or *ethnic groups,* could theoretically be located by mapping subtle genetic differences that result from generations of reproduction within populations. But it is easier to identify the boundaries of populations or societies through marked gaps in communication efficiency. These communication gaps and inefficiencies both help to maintain and are maintained by so-called ethnic differences that are reflected in different languages, behavior, values, and beliefs.[4] Throughout much of human history, the boundaries of these human populations, their political administrative units, and the local ecosystems in which they have been embedded have coincided. The early great outward dispersals of the earth's human populations resulted in a world inhabited by thousands of geographically isolated human populations that were administered as clans, tribes, and kingdoms. These societies coevolved with other species and microorganisms within the constraints of shared local ecosystems. It was only with the emergence of larger administrative units, such as empires, that the large-scale mingling of previously isolated human populations and the microorganisms they carried began.

The integration of previously small and isolated populations of human beings into empires and more densely populated cities was accompanied by a tragic death toll from disease. William McNeill has observed that the Roman Empire was repeatedly wracked by the scourge of strange diseases. There were at least eleven microbial disasters in republican times. A major epidemic struck the densely packed city of Rome in 65 A.D., but that paled in comparison with a more widespread pandemic that began to sweep the empire in 165 A.D. Mortality as a result of this latter plague was heavy: One-quarter to one-third of those exposed to the disease died.[5]

In more recent history, the integration of growing European populations into a nascent global community has had similar disease ramifications. By the year 1350, the various kingdoms of Western Europe had become large and densely populated enough to press against the carrying capacities of relevant ecosystems and even against each other. Such pressures led to local European famines in most years between 1290 and 1350 A.D.[6] At the same time, contacts and commerce between West and East were increasing, manifest in the growth of lengthy trade routes between Europe and China.

The intensification of caravan traffic across Asia and contact among previously separated peoples surged under the Mongol empires. At the height of Mongol power, the empires embraced nearly all of China and Russia as well as Central Asia, Iran, and Iraq.[7]

During this period of European population increase, urban growth, and expanded commerce, messengers, merchants and mercenaries, among others, increased their travel and came into contact with new peoples. This increased contact resulted in an enhanced exchange of pathogens between Europe and Asia. From the European point of view the most infamous was *Yersinia pestis,* the cause of the deadly Black Death. The arrival of the plague in Europe in 1346 began a lengthy pruning process during which successive waves of disease trimmed the region's population by nearly 40 percent, the highest mortality rates being in the urban areas.[8]

Contact among previously separated peoples took another leap forward during the age of European exploration and colonization. The ships of Christopher Columbus, which arrived in the Caribbean in 1492, were the first of a wave of European vessels that eventually brought the Europeans into contact with numerous indigenous peoples. This contact not only eventually resulted in the absorption of this territory into Spanish, Portuguese, British, and French empires, but also was responsible for pathogens that accompanied the conquerors wiping out a significant portion of these indigenous peoples. The military history of the period is replete with tales of miraculous conquests of huge numbers of indigenous peoples by mere handfuls of European troops. But, in reality, there were few bona fide miracles. Diseases unwittingly spread by the invaders, particularly smallpox, killed approximately two-thirds of the indigenous populations, leaving them in disarray and unable to muster a decent defense of their territories. As William McNeill has put it, "From the Amerindian point of view, stunned acquiescence to Spanish superiority was the only possible response. . . . Native authority structures crumbled; the old gods seemed to have abdicated. The situation was ripe for the mass conversions recorded so proudly by Christian missionaries."[9] The spread of smallpox was followed by measles and eventually by typhus, with such diseases from Africa as malaria and yellow fever being transplanted into the American tropics. By the time these transplanted diseases had run their course, only an estimated one in twenty Amerindians in the affected areas had survived.[10] Indeed, as the European colonial networks expanded to embrace much of the world, an unequal exchange of diseases took place, with the bulk of the disease casualties being among the conquered.

More recently, another spurt of disease accompanied the large-scale movement of military personnel during World War I. While the eyes of the world were focused on battlefield casualties, a deadly influenza pandemic spread quickly around the world, often moving with the troops. By the time the casualties began to taper off, this unexpected spin-off from the war resulted in the greatest pandemic in world history. Estimates of the magnitude of this catastrophe vary, but somewhere between 30 and 40 million people died, many times the number of battlefield casualties.[11]

AN EVOLUTIONARY PERSPECTIVE

Since World War II there has been a tremendous acceleration in the pace of globalization and urbanization. The historical record makes it clear that such periods of growing interactions among previously separated populations are often punctuated by serious outbreaks of disease. The last fifty years has witnessed the spread of exotic and lethal diseases in tropical areas of the world, several deadly worldwide influenza epidemics, and an HIV/AIDS pandemic that continues to spread slowly around the world. There is heightened fear that environmental change, more frequent international travel, growing bacterial resistance to antibiotics, and changing human behavior and settlement patterns are leading to outbreaks of new kinds of deadly diseases and a resurgence of others.[12] In spite of the development of a broad spectrum of antibiotics and new medical technologies, the world remains a biologically dangerous place. "At the root of the resurgence of old infectious diseases is an evolutionary paradox: The more vigorously we have assailed the world of microorganisms, the more varied the repertoire of bacterial and viral strains thrown up against us."[13]

The key to comprehending why there are so many new challenges to human microsecurity is to understand the nature and evolution of ecological interdependence. Populations of *Homo sapiens* have coevolved with other species and a variety of microorganisms within ever-changing physical environments. Ecological interdependence refers to the growth and maintenance of a delicate network of relationships among these organisms and between them and the sustaining physical environments. Rapid changes in any of these relationships can rebound to the detriment of human beings, other creatures, microorganisms, and even the ecosystem itself. Thus, a mutation in a potentially pathogenic microorganism, a rapid increase in populations of voracious pests, or even a change in rainfall can destabilize an ecosystem with unfortunate results for all the creatures that share it.

For most of history, this coevolution has been occurring within local and isolated ecosystems. Because of mutual adaptation processes that involve the human immune system, localized bouts of nonfatal diseases have been common. But as previously separated peoples are now being brought into more frequent contact by the pressures of globalization, there are complex and unforeseen consequences. The world is now experiencing much deeper ecological interdependence. The complicated network of interdependence between human populations, other species, and various microorganisms is moving to the global level.

The human immune system, which protects the body against diseases, is the product of countless generations of interactions between people and disease organisms. Natural-selection processes, which shape these immune systems, represent learning by bitter experience. People with weak immune systems often succumb to deadly diseases and do not live to reproduce. People with stronger immune systems are more likely to survive, have children, and to pass on their genes to future generations.

Epidemics can develop when biologically naive human populations come into contact with new pathogens. Obviously, people who move into new environments are at substantial risk of contracting new illnesses. This is why traveling businesspeople or scholars attending international conferences often come down with influenza or similar illnesses on their return, or why people who move from one coast of the United States to the other are frequently ill during their first year of residence. Likewise, people or animals moving into new environments can bring new pathogens with them. And many diseases, such as HIV/AIDS and SARS (Severe Acute Respiratory Syndrome) jump from animals to people. Social and cultural practices can often accelerate the spread of disease. For example, among certain African tribes, marrying and supporting a widow becomes the responsibility of a dead husband's brother. Because many African males have recently died of HIV/AIDS, this custom has accelerated the spread of the virus from widows of HIV/AIDS victims to the dead man's extended family.[14]

Problems can also arise when changes take place in pathogens, sometimes making them more lethal to human beings. For various reasons, including environmental changes, exposure to chemicals or radiation, widespread use of antibiotics and antivirals, or interactions with other microorganisms, dangerous changes can occur in pathogens, potentially confronting immune systems with additional challenges.

Pathogens can also be liberated by people moving into previously unpopulated forest areas. Population growth in tropical areas of the world often forces people to clear land for settlements at the edges of rain forests, thereby liberating various kinds of microorganisms from their forest animal hosts. Thus, the human immunodeficiency virus (HIV, the proximate cause of AIDS) and Ebola, Marburg, and yellow fever viruses were probably first found in monkeys; Rift Valley fever in cattle, sheep, and mosquitoes; and Hantaan virus in rodents. "These pathogens probably lurked relatively undisturbed in their animal hosts in the tropics, jumping to humans only on rare occasions. They had little opportunity to adapt to humans, who usually were 'dead end' host species, because the viruses would fizzle out once they rapidly swept through a small population at the edge of the forest."[15] But these and other viruses now can make successful leaps from animals to denser human populations, thus putting deadly new diseases in motion. In late 1997 and early 1998, for example, viruses made leaps from monkeys to humans in Congo (monkeypox) and from chickens to humans in Hong Kong. And in late 2006 scientists were carefully scrutinizing an outbreak of avian flu among birds in Asia, fearing that as the virus (H5N1) would move westward into Europe that the deadly pathogen would change into a form that could pass readily among people. In a similar process, plant and animal species can wreak havoc when they jump from their home ecosystems to ecosystems that have had no previous contact with them. Historically, plants and animals native to Europe had both positive and negative effects as they moved around the world with colonists.[16] In the contemporary world, it is often the unintended movement of plants and animals, largely as a result of expanded trade and travel, that can have devastating effects. In the United States, for example, species ranging from the blue water hyacinths of South America that now clog Florida's waterways to the Africanized honeybee, an aggressive stinger that was brought to Brazil in 1959 and then escaped North, are now having significant economic and environmental effects.[17]

In summary, the major disease outbreaks and epidemics that often have transformed the nature of societies have occurred when human immune systems have encountered pathogenic microorganisms with which they have had little experience. When the Black Death arrived in Europe from Asia, nearly half the population was wiped out in many areas, thus leading to major sociopolitical transformations. Similarly, the "conquest" of the Americas was aided and abetted by European pathogens transplanted into biologically naive human populations. This is one reason for the current concern about the disappearance of borders, state failures, civil wars, large-scale migrations and the rapid integration of previously separated peoples into an emerging global city. Rapid movement of people, produce, animals and microorganisms around the world raises concerns about the resurgence of old diseases, the appearance of new ones, and economic and environmental damage from hitchhiking creatures great and small.

ECOLOGICAL INTERDEPENDENCE: SOME EVIDENCE

Governments have been slow to react to the challenges associated with rapidly growing ecological interdependence. The current concern about nonhuman immigrants in the United States remains much the same as it was in the 1870s when Spencer Fullerton Baird of the U.S. Fish Commission attempted to improve his dining experiences by bringing a new, tasty species of Eurasian carp into the United States. His venture was a great economic success and the fish became the culinary craze of the nation. But ever since then, the carp have been reproducing prolifically in U.S. waters, destroying habitats and crowding out native fish. The legacy of these attempts to make nature more productive through the introduction of new species lingers on in U.S. regulations. There is rigorous screening to catch potentially dangerous agricultural pests, but much less attention is paid to imported species that do not directly threaten to ravage crops. For example, state governments can allow the import of exotic fish species from other countries or regions without even consulting their neighboring states.[18]

Until quite recently, the potential spread of infectious diseases was similarly treated. The development and large-scale use of antibiotics and other pharmaceuticals fostered complacency in the face of growing global disease challenges. In 1969, for example, the U.S. surgeon general declared that infectious diseases had been conquered and that the time had come to focus on chronic diseases such as cancer and heart disease.[19] But things have been changing, and in 1995 the World Health Organization (WHO) felt it necessary to reemphasize that infectious diseases are still the world's leading cause of death.[20] The former Clinton administration went so far as to declare HIV/AIDS a threat to U.S. national security in April 2000. And the technological optimism of an earlier era is beginning to fade in the face of the seemingly incurable HIV/AIDS virus and the resurgence of several diseases in antibiotic-resistant form. More than one-tenth of the new cases of tuberculosis (TB) worldwide are now resistant to at least one of the drugs commonly used to treat the disease. And between 1 percent and 2 percent of all new cases are resistant to multiple drugs. In addition, other serious diseases are also developing drug resistance.[21]

There is now ample evidence of the increasing threat of infectious diseases, but changes over time in the personal and economic impacts of various diseases are difficult to quantify for several reasons. First, it is not necessary for people to die from an infectious disease for the disease to affect their quality of life. Various debilitating diseases can disable large numbers of people for considerable periods of time without actually making them into mortality statistics. Second, infectious-disease statistics are often deliberately manipulated downward by some countries as a matter of national pride or economics. Tourists prefer not to travel to countries known to be experiencing plagues. Finally, there are few reliable historical data to use as a baseline for assessing the extent to which disease has increased or decreased in many areas of the world, particularly in the most poverty-stricken countries where infectious diseases are likely to be most prevalent.

Given these caveats, in recent years about 15 million people have died annually from communicable diseases. Respiratory infection—mostly influenza and pneumonia—have accounted for about 4 million of these deaths, HIV/AIDS for nearly 3 million deaths, and diarrhea, tuberculosis, and malaria, taken together, have accounted for another 5 million deaths.[22] Approximately 40 million people now live with HIV/AIDS worldwide, some 5 million are newly infected each year, and about 3 million die from AIDS annually. In sub-Saharan Africa 25 million people are now stricken with HIV/AIDS.[23]

Fifty years ago, many of these diseases surely afflicted human beings. But it is unclear how much globalization and urbanization have affected their geographic scope and prevalence. What is clear is that these diseases now move much more rapidly along with the large flow of travelers and agricultural commodities in the contemporary world. There is thus growing worry about a potential worldwide spread of killer viruses. In the 1990s, outbreaks of pneumonic plague, which can be spread through the air, killed hundreds of people in India and disrupted air travel in the region.[24] Airports as far away as Kennedy in New York City were screening dozens of flights daily for potential carriers. Also in the late 1990s, an outbreak of bird flu in Hong Kong caused a major drop-off in tourism and led to the execution of 1.5 million chickens and other birds in an attempt to stop the spread of the virus. In 2002–2003 an outbreak of SARS, a previously unknown virus, sickened more than 8,000 people and killed more than 900 as it rapidly moved from Southern China into 30 countries. And in 2005 the avian flu returned to Asia and moved into Eastern Europe. As a result, hundreds of millions of chickens and ducks were slaughtered and several dozen people died when they contracted the disease from contact with fowl.[25]

Although the many exotic species of flora and fauna that now travel around the world rarely kill people, they often do extensive damage to the recipient economies. In the United States, it is estimated that more than 4,000 exotic species of flora and fauna have become naturalized (able to survive without human help) over the past century. Just 79 of those species cost the nation an estimated $97 billion between 1906 and 1991 in damage to agriculture, ecosystems, industry, and health. Most of the species brought into the United States unintentionally have been the inadvertent by-products of commerce, tourism, or travel.[26] It is difficult to estimate the toll from invasive species on the global level, but one recent estimate of the damage to crops from nonindigenous pests put the figure somewhere between $55 billion and $247 billion per year.[27]

Many new species make their way into the United States and other countries along with other imported commodities. Agricultural products, nursery stock, cut flowers, and timber often harbor insects, plant diseases, and snails, while bulk commodities such as gravel, sand, and wool often contain hidden seeds. Ballast water on commercial ships, taken on to provide stability at sea and often dumped when ships load at different ports, is also a major transport medium for spreading nonindigenous species around the world.

ECOLOGICAL SECURITY: CONTEMPORARY CHALLENGES

The ongoing globalization process represents a growing challenge to human health as well as ecological stability. Although ecological interdependence grew at a gradual pace for some time, it is only recently that a confluence of change drivers—rapid technological innovation and the broad, worldwide diffusion of liberal ideology—has created a historically unique climate that has accelerated these change processes.[28] As globalization proceeds in tandem with human disturbances of remote ecosystems where many previously unknown pathogens reside, the likelihood of new disease outbreaks grows. Pathogens that have previously been restricted to isolated geographic locations have spread rapidly and with relative ease to other areas as the world's transportation networks have expanded.[29]

Diseases are currently being spread more rapidly and widely in two obvious ways: by increased travel and contact among people and by integration of the world's food markets. More frequent contacts are now occurring in densely populated cities and among human populations across political boundaries that once served as relatively impermeable barriers. Spatial separation in general has become a far less significant hindrance to human interaction as technological advances have accelerated and expanded the possibilities for transnational flows of information, money, goods, and people.

Professional journals and the mass media now carry accounts of globalization-related public health incidents with alarming regularity as pathogens old and new move worldwide along with the rising volume of trade and travel. More than 2 million people now cross an international border each day, up from only 69,000 in 1950. Since 1950, the number of passenger kilometers flown internationally has increased by nearly one hundred fold.[30] Commercial air travel has been implicated in the transmission of TB among airline passengers and the reintroduction of dengue fever to the United States through cargo containing hitchhiking Asian mosquitoes.[31]

A second set of health risk factors emerges from the growth and deeper integration of the world food market. Like other economic sectors, agriculture and food production became increasingly globalized in the 1990s. Since the 1980s, food imports to the United States have more than doubled, and more than 30 percent of the fruits and vegetables the nation consumes now originate in other countries.[32] The growing cross-border traffic in food and agricultural products increases the risks to human health by creating more opportunities for pathogens to migrate from their native environments in food shipments and cause disease outbreaks among people in other countries. This traffic also increases the likelihood of plant and animal diseases moving from one part of the world to another. In 2001, for example, a strain of hoof-and-mouth disease that was discovered in India in 1990 made its way to England and eventually to the European continent, resulting in the slaughter of hundreds of thousands of animals to prevent the further spread of the disease.

Part of the emerging food-safety problem results from trade liberalization. Although tariff and trade barriers in the agricultural sector have been reduced and better transportation means that food products move more rapidly from farm to market, health and food-safety standards and practices in many exporting countries remain poor. Thus, the risk of exposure to food-borne disease is rising as more countries pursue export-oriented agricultural production under various worldwide and regional free trade regimes.[33] Moreover, the tension between food safety and free trade grows more acute when it becomes a matter of international economic diplomacy. This occurs, for instance, when more stringent food safety standards in importing countries are attacked as non-tariff barriers to trade. Such conflicts highlight the challenges that increased economic interdependence poses to state sovereignty. Trade disagreements are increasingly likely to be settled by the dispute resolution bodies of free trade regimes such as the WTO or NAFTA, rather than by the actions of national governments. Consequently, the limitations that trading regimes place on state sovereignty conceivably make it more difficult for countries to deal effectively with growing risks to public health.

MIGRATION, URBANIZATION, AND DISEASE

While there is currently much greater contact among the various neighbor-hoods of the nascent global city, the neighborhoods themselves are becoming more densely packed and prone to the spread of disease. People are migrating much more freely among and within countries, often carrying pathogens with them. The United Nations has estimated that by the year 2015 there will be 33 urban areas called *megacities,* having 8 million inhabitants or more. Twenty-seven of these will be in less-industrialized countries. The fact that the most rapid urban growth is occurring in the cities of the poor and politically unstable less-industrialized world raises additional health concerns given the limited resources, shaky health infrastructures, and inadequate institutional arrangements available to governments in these countries.[34] Because greater human population densities mean more fre-quent interaction, urbanization creates the conditions necessary for the rapid spread of infectious disease. Just as ancient Rome was prone to rapidly spreading epidemics, the rise of megacities in impoverished countries, increasingly linked to each other by rapid transportation, presents growing challenges to public health.

Several forces are driving this unhealthy urbanization trend. Environ-mental decay in rural areas of poorer countries is a major contributor to the growing rural-to-urban migration. Degradation of the agricultural resource base is driven by a complex interplay of population pressures, desertifica-tion, deforestation, droughts, and salinization of soils because of irrigation. These problems have contributed directly to increases in the number of migrating rural poor in many regions of Africa, Asia, and Latin America, as well as to declines in agricultural productivity, particularly in marginal areas. Compounding matters, throughout the developing world population growth rates in rural areas are particularly high and numbers often exceed the sustaining capabilities of local ecosystems. The lure of urban areas, where industry and related economic opportunities are perceived to be growing, becomes almost irresistible to many in the countryside for whom living conditions have grown increasingly difficult. Thus, the migration of marginalized rural residents to urban centers is propelled by a complex set of ecological and economic push and pull factors.[35]

The prevalence of unemployment, poverty, pollution from municipal and industrial wastes, poor nutrition, and an inadequate public health infrastruc-ture (particularly sanitation and sewers) in urban areas means that the urban poor of these growing megacities in less-industrialized countries frequently encounter and carry a host of maladies. They experience the problems characteristic of poverty (for example, deaths from infectious disease and higher infant mortality rates) and those characteristic of wealth (higher rates of death from heart disease, cancer, and accidents). Nonetheless, many migrants in the developing world still regard themselves as better off in cities than in the countryside, where economic circumstances are often worse.[36]

This urbanization trend is now especially troubling for human health because of the rising incidence of infectious waterborne diseases (such as cholera, typhoid, and hepatitis A and E) and vector-borne diseases such as malaria that thrive around stagnant water, particularly in cities of the less-industrialized world. The ever-increasing numbers and densities of the urban poor also help to create conditions for the occurrence of serious disease outbreaks as well as for the persistence of endemic infectious disease.

Health threats associated with megacities are not limited to the less-industrialized world. Recent viral and bacterial challenges in New York illustrate the emerging threats that infectious diseases pose to urban populations, even in the industrialized world. New York witnessed a rebirth of TB in the 1990s facilitated by the convergence of at least three key trends: the spread of HIV/AIDS, the economic recession of the late 1980s, and budgetary reductions in public health programs. In the early 1970s, when TB appeared to be under control, programs in the United States aimed at detecting and controlling the disease were downsized and phased out. But HIV/AIDS began its spread into segments of the urban population in the 1980s, creating ideal hosts within which TB could make a comeback. Unchallenged by the defenses of a healthy human immune system, TB found hospitable conditions in weakened HIV/AIDS victims. When the economic recession of the late 1980s hit, it left poorer, TB-infected HIV/AIDS victims in New York and elsewhere unable to gain access to adequate medical care. As a result, many of the urban poor with active TB cases did not complete the necessary six-month regimen of antibiotics, thereby helping the surviving bacteria become drug-resistant.[37]

POLICY RESPONSES TO EMERGING HEALTH RISKS

These emerging health threats are symptomatic of the new challenges raised by deepening globalization and increasing urbanization, and dealing with them requires comprehensive, sustained policy responses at both the national and international levels. But governments have been very lax in responding to the challenges of infectious disease, and persisting sovereignty claims have impeded development of effective international institutions with the power to deal with disease outbreaks wherever they occur. Until the SARS outbreak in 2003 illustrated how rapidly a deadly virus can spread in the contemporary world and how economically damaging such an outbreak can be, there was only modest concern about this disease threat to human well-being. The persisting threat that avian flu could change into a form easily passed from person to person coupled with the specter of bioterrorism have galvanized public concern about infectious diseases and spurred greater international cooperation in attempting to contain them.

Surveillance, diagnosis, and response capability are key elements in preventing disease outbreaks and epidemics. The global revolution in telecommunications has greatly increased surveillance capabilities. The growth of the Internet has facilitated the development of two global surveillance and diagnosis operations. The first, the Program for Monitoring Infectious Diseases (Pro Med-Mail), now links more than 30,000 subscribers in 150 countries. It uses the Internet to circulate information about outbreaks of human, animal, and plant diseases from correspondents around the world. The World Health Organization uses the Internet to support communications within its Global Outbreak Alert and Response Network (GOARN). This network links laboratories around the world that identify pathogens likely to cause disease outbreaks and ensures the rapid arrival of technical assistance when outbreaks take place. But the WHO has a limited budget and must tap into a network of other organizations to provide personnel and resources to fight disease.

There are many other governmental and non-governmental organizations that are frequently mobilized in attempts to stem disease outbreaks. Among the most important of these is the Centers for Disease Control and Prevention (CDC) in the United States, which has several hundred personnel focusing specifically on international health issues. Doctors Without Borders (Medecins Sans Frontiers) is an important private-sector organization that provides medical assistance and disaster relief to those in greatest need. In a typical year its volunteer staff embarks on nearly 3,500 aid missions. And the Bill and Melinda Gates foundation has been very active in disease prevention in the less-industrialized world, including a major HIV/AIDS prevention effort in India.

These efforts, however, are subject to significant limitations. Surveillance efforts require transparency (openness) in order to detect disease outbreaks, but politicians often prefer less candor. Disease outbreaks can exact a significant economic toll from lost revenue due to cutbacks in tourism and trade. Furthermore, telecommunications and medical research capabilities are rudimentary in remote parts of poorer countries, where new diseases often emerge. Even in the United States reporting of diseases to the CDC is somewhat haphazard and, due to inadequate funding, some state public health infrastructures have deteriorated to the extent that detection of diseases cannot be assured.[38]

But it is of little use to report on disease outbreaks if adequate in-country or international response capabilities do not exist. In the absence of such capabilities, local doctors, scientists, and public health officials have little reason to participate in reporting networks. The CDC and other organizations do deploy teams of epidemiologists to various parts of the world to assist communities where outbreaks occur, but they must be invited by affected countries. Sufficient international response demands the creation of a more powerful and centralized agency with access to state-of-the-art laboratories, world-class staff, sufficient funding, and a political mandate to take the lead in responding to the threat of emerging or reemerging diseases. The WHO would appear to be the logical choice, given its established role as the coordinator of international health programs. Yet the WHO now lacks many of the necessary elements—authority, mandate, funding, staff, and facilities—sufficient for the task at hand.

This lack of a robust global program for responding to emerging disease threats highlights important political dilemmas that are characteristic of global ecopolitics. For example, the current U.S. disposition to minimize involvement in international organizations flies in the face of a growing need for its leadership and assistance in dealing with many undesirable side effects of globalization. Moreover, the greatest threats to world health frequently originate in poor countries and failing states, which have limited capabilities for managing them. And countries with the resources necessary to address such problems often lack the political will to use them in the absence of an imminent crisis. From the perspective of U.S. policy makers, for example, there is little apparent political gain and much potential damage associated with sponsoring costly new international programs designed to combat disease threats that are not yet perceived to be serious biosecurity concerns by the American public.

There are additional issues involved in attempting to curtail the potential spread of infectious diseases. For instance, some governments are reluctant to report on disease outbreaks for fear of serious economic fallout. Thus, when India experienced its outbreaks of pneumonic plague in the 1990s, the government at first failed to provide information to the international medical community, anticipating de facto quarantines and declines in trade and tourism. Similarly, the outbreak of bird flu in Hong Kong not only resulted in economic damage from a loss of tourism, but also damaged the political fortunes of a new government. And initially China tried to cover up the extent of the SARS outbreak in late 2002, understandable since the disease outbreak eventually cost China tens of billions of dollars in lost tourism and trade. If reporting is perceived as unlikely to muster assistance in combating disease outbreaks but highly likely to result in economic losses of various sorts, then denial rules and there is no advantage to reporting.

Finally, the dilemmas associated with international policy responses to emerging disease threats are indicative of some of the broader tensions incumbent in the process of globalization. In an increasingly integrated, interdependent, and technologically advanced world, the power of the sovereign state to control its own affairs is becoming more ambiguous. A revolution in telecommunications and information technologies, for example, has given more power to the international medical community by facilitating much more effective global surveillance of infectious diseases. While governments may attempt to resist this growing transparency, they are increasingly fighting a losing battle.

In effect, technology is now enhancing the ability of nonstate actors to play a key role in areas where governance is now lacking. The technologically augmented power of international professional networks might, on the one hand, be viewed as enhancing the authority and legitimacy of government by helping to fill significant vacuums in government functions, particularly in poor countries. But, on the other hand, this power might as easily be viewed as weakening conventional governmental authority by expropriating some of the traditional responsibilities of government in the public health arena. The nascent responses to emerging disease threats, like the threats themselves, raise questions about the future of state sovereignty in an increasingly global system.

Thus, infectious diseases, many of which have played a major role in shaping societies throughout history, continue to exert a strong influence on the welfare of people and governments in the first decade of the Third Millennium. The complex interactions of technological advances in medicine and the growing levels of interdependence among the regions of the world are creating both new pathways for the transmission of disease and new weapons in the struggle against them. In the long run, however, one of the casualties of growing ecological interdependence might well be globalization itself as the increasingly rapid worldwide spread of human, animal, and plant diseases could create conditions that would provoke a reaction against globalization, dramatically slowing, or even reversing, the process.

ENDNOTES

1. See Dennis Pirages, "Microsecurity: Disease Organisms and Human Well-Being," *Washington Quarterly* (Autumn 1995).

2. Luigi Cavalli-Sforza and Francesco Cavalli-Sforza, *The Great Human Diasporas* (Reading, MA: Addison-Wesley, 1995), 157–159.

3. Kenneth Watt, *Principles of Environmental Science* (New York: McGraw-Hill, 1973), 1.

4. Karl Deutsch, *Nationalism and Social Communication* (Cambridge: MIT Press, 1964), 100.

5. William McNeill, *Plagues and Peoples* (Garden City, NY: Anchor Press, 1976), 115–117.

6. Henry Hobhouse, *Forces of Change: An Unorthodox View of History* (New York: Arcade, 1990).

7. See McNeill, *Plagues and Peoples,* Ch. 4.

8. Hobhouse, *Forces of Change,* 11–23.

9. McNeill, *Plagues and Peoples,* 208.

10. Ibid., 215 and references cited therein.

11. See Alfred Crosby, *America's Forgotten Pandemic: The Influenza Epidemic of 1918* (Cambridge, UK: Cambridge University Press, 1990).

12. See Laurie Garrett, *The Coming Plague: Newly Emerging Diseases in a World Out of Balance* (New York: Farrar, Straus & Giroux, 1994); Stephen S. Morse (Ed.), *Emerging Viruses* (New York: Oxford University Press, 1993); Tony McMichael, *Human Frontiers, Environments and Disease* (Cambridge, UK: Cambridge University Press, 2001).

13. Marc Lappe, *Evolutionary Medicine: Rethinking the Origins of Disease* (San Francisco: Sierra Club Books, 1994), 8.

14. See Stephen Buckley, "Wife Inheritance Spurs AIDS Rise in Kenya," *Washington Post* (Nov. 8, 1997).

15. Ann Gibbons, "Where Are 'New' Diseases Born?" *Science* (Aug. 6, 1993): 680.

16. See Alfred W. Crosby, *Ecological Imperialism: The Biological Expansion of Europe, 900–1900* (Cambridge, UK: Cambridge University Press, 1986).

17. See Elizabeth Culotta, "Biological Immigrants under Fire," *Science* (Dec. 6, 1991): 1444–1447.

18. Ibid., 1444.

19. Cited in David P. Fidler, "Return of the Fourth Horseman: Emerging Infectious Diseases and International Law," *Minnesota Law Review* (April 1997): 773.

20. World Health Organization (WHO), *The World Health Report 1995* (Geneva: WHO, 1995).

21. David Brown, "One in Ten TB Cases Worldwide Resist Common Treatment, Survey Shows," *Washington Post* (Oct. 23, 1997); WHO, "The Big Guns of Resistance," Ch. 4 in *Overcoming Antimicrobial Resistance* (Geneva: WHO, 2000), <www.who.int/infectious-disease-report/2000/>.

22. Data from World Health Organization, *The World Health Report 2004* (Geneva: WHO, 2004), Annex Table 2; World Health Organization, *The World Health Report 2001* (Geneva: WHO, 2001), Annex Table 2.

23. UNAIDS and World Health Organization, *AIDS Epidemic Update,* December 2004, <www.unaids.org/wad2004/EPIupdate2004_html_en/Epi04_13_en.htm>.

24. See Laurie Garrett, *Betrayal of Trust: The Collapse of Global Public Health* (New York: Hyperion, 2000), Ch. 1.

25. See David Brown, "World Responds Swiftly to Track 'Bird Flu' Spread," *Washington Post* (Jan. 11, 1998); David P. Fidler, *SARS, Governance and the Globalization of Disease* (New York: Palgrave, 2004); Guy Chazan, "Threat of Bird Flu Spreads to Europe," *Wall Street Journal* (Aug. 18, 2005).

26. See U.S. Congress, Office of Technology Assessment, *Harmful Non-Indigenous Species in the United States* (publication no. OTA-F-565) (Washington, DC: U.S. Government Printing Office, Sept. 1993), 69, 92; available at <www.wws.princeton.edu/~ota/disk1/1993/9325_n.html>.

27. Chris Bright, *Life Out of Bounds: Bioinvasion in a Borderless World* (New York: W. W. Norton, 1998), 176.

28. See James N. Rosenau, "The Complexities and Contradictions of Globalization," *Current History* (Nov. 1997): 360–364.

29. See Stephen S. Morse, "Regulating Viral Traffic," *Issues in Science and Technology* (Fall 1990): 81–82.

30. Hilary French, *Vanishing Borders: Protecting the Planet in an Age of Globalization* (New York: W. W. Norton, 2000), Table 1-1.

31. See, for example, Ellen Ruppel Shell, "Resurgence of a Deadly Disease," *Atlantic Monthly* (August 1997): 45–60 (available at <www.theatlantic.com/issues/97aug/malaria.htm>); Thomas A. Kenyon, Sarah E. Valway, Walter W. Ihle, Ida M. Onorato, and Kenneth G. Castro, "Transmission of a Multidrug-Resistant Mycobacterium Tuberculosis During a Long Airplane Flight," *New England Journal of Medicine* 334 (1996): 933–938 (available at <http://wonder.cdc.gov/wonder/prevguid/p0000436/p0000436.asp>); "E. Coli Is Found in Shipment of IBP Frozen Beef to Korea," *Wall Street Journal* (Sept. 29, 1997); Jeff Gerth and Tim Weiner, "U.S. Food Safety System Swamped by Booming Global Imports," *The New York Times* (Sept. 29, 1997); Rachel Nowak, "WHO Calls for Action against TB," *Science* (March 24, 1995).

32. Gerth and Weiner, "U.S. Food Safety System Swamped."

33. Ibid.

34. United Nations Centre for Human Settlements, *An Urbanizing World: Global Report on Human Settlements 1996* (New York: Oxford University Press, 1996), 6.

35. World Commission on Environment and Development, *Our Common Future* (Oxford, UK: Oxford University Press, 1987), 95–102.

36. World Bank, *Urban Policy and Economic Development: An Agenda for the 1990s* (Washington, DC: World Bank, 1991), 51; Mike Parnwell, *Population Movements in the Third World* (London: Routledge, 1993), 18–24.

37. Clark Merrill and Dennis Pirages, "Ecological Security: Micro-Threats to Human Well-Being," *Futures Research Quarterly* (Spring 1997): 49–50; Richard M. Krause, "The Origin of Plagues: Old and New," *Science* (Aug. 21, 1992): 1074.

38. See Merrill and Pirages, "Ecological Security," 59–60; and Garrett, *Betrayal of Trust,* Ch. 4.

CHAPTER ELEVEN

Combating the Proliferation of Weapons of Mass Destruction

Richard A. Love*

"Six decades later [following Hiroshima & Nagasaki], our world has been reawakened to nuclear dangers. Nuclear proliferation remains one of the most pressing problems confronting our world. Tens of thousands of nuclear weapons remain, many of them on 'hair-trigger' alert. The emergence of a nuclear black market and attempts by terrorists to acquire nuclear weapons and materials have compounded the nuclear threat."

—United Nations Secretary General Kofi Annan (2004)[1]

"The gravest danger our Nation faces lies at the crossroads of radicalism and technology. Our enemies have openly declared that they are seeking weapons of mass destruction, and evidence indicates that they are doing so with determination. The United States will not allow these efforts to succeed. . . . History will judge harshly those who saw this coming danger but failed to act. In the new world we have entered, the only path to peace and security is the path of action."

—President George Bush (2002)[2]

In 2003, the *BBC China,* a German-owned freighter, was intercepted by Italian authorities on the high seas as it made its way from Dubai in the Middle East bound for Libya. The ship's cargo included centrifuge components and exposed a global network—a nuclear black market—operated by the Pakistani engineer Abdul Qadeer Khan. A. Q. Khan is the revered "father" of the Pakistani nuclear program that successfully conducted up to six nuclear tests in 1998. The *BBC China* intercept also pegged him as the principal supplier of Libya's still-embryonic uranium enrichment effort, and the greatest trafficker in nuclear technology yet known to the world. While the interception of the *BBC China* was a forcing function that prompted Libyan leader Qadhafi to abandon efforts to develop weapons of mass destruction (WMD), the scope and global reach of the Khan network

*This chapter builds on research the author conducts at the Center for the Study of Weapons of Mass Destruction at National Defense University. The author can be contacted via e-mail at LoveR@ndu.edu.

illustrate the challenges of private global networks to traditional state-based solutions in combating the spread of weapons of mass destruction.

As a result of the information gathered on board the *BBC China* and the subsequent investigation, intelligence agencies worldwide expanded their understanding of this clandestine procurement network—a global enterprise that for well over a decade provided "one-stop shopping" for nuclear fuel, uranium enrichment technology, and even nuclear weapons design.[3] Regardless of whether Khan was a rogue actor or an instrument of Pakistani state policy (or, as is most likely, something in between), the revelations of his activities carry important lessons.[4] First, in an environment of technology diffusion, global markets and networks, and open borders, the efforts and ambitions of one individual can make a difference. Whether in the development of state nuclear, biological, and chemical (NBC) weapons programs, or in transferring knowledge, technologies and know-how to the highest bidder, individuals can influence regional and even the global security environment. Secondly, the A. Q. Khan network exposes major gaps in the state-based nuclear technology control regime. "Secondary proliferation" by non-state actors (entrepreneurs in this case) remains largely outside the reach and capacity of existing international control mechanisms, and to some extent is a problem that the states—parties that created the Nuclear Nonproliferation Treaty (NPT) and associated agreements—simply never anticipated. In many respects, international control mechanisms remain mired in a Cold War mentality and lack the flexibility to adapt to the emergent threat environment. Indeed, as with the A. Q. Khan network, if there is a willing and politically unconstrained single source for virtually an entire nuclear fuel cycle, then the very premise of supply controls—that slowing the transfer of critical technologies buys time for diplomacy and politics to address proliferation incentives—is fatally undermined.

To the degree that private procurement networks persist, they hamper the ability of intelligence agencies to assess and warn about covert WMD programs. Despite the *BBC China* success, the United States and its allies still lack a complete picture of the entire Khan enterprise, even as they work to "roll-up" the network. Parties to the NPT regime, including the U.S., must face the reality that today's threats occur in a post-proliferated world and acknowledge that significant and sensitive nuclear, chemical, and biological technical *information* is globally dispersed and available for a price. The international community must also acknowledge that the model of the "loose nukes" problem is incomplete. The post–Cold War strategy pursued by the West, in large measure, focuses on containing nuclear "leakage" from the former Soviet Union states. And while the West and particularly the

U.S. continues to devote resources to cooperative threat reduction to address and minimize this important risk in the former Soviet states, from Libya to North Korea to countries and individuals yet unknown, the fact remains that the A. Q. Khan network profited from selling nuclear technology from an entirely different source—indeed, from a country that is an ally of the United States and key partner in the global war on terror.

THE WMD THREAT ENVIRONMENT

The WMD threat environment is dynamic, driven by increasingly available technology and evolving quickly in ways that are difficult to predict. To confront that threat, innovative policy and flexible operational concepts that meet today's challenges and anticipate those over-the-horizon threats need to be pursued and implemented. The greatest threat facing the U.S., according to President Bush, is WMD in the hands of rogue states and terrorists.[5] But what are weapons of mass destruction? Is the definition effects based on characteristics, or is it convenient shorthand for policy makers? Before addressing strategies and tools to combat the proliferation of WMD, a few thoughts on WMD are in order. We tend to lump nuclear, radiological, chemical, and biological weapons together under the term "weapons of mass destruction." While convenient, it is misleading since each weapon represents vastly different underlying technologies for development, weaponization, and delivery. Different concepts of operation apply to each, and countermeasures and consequence management procedures are implemented differently depending on the weapon used. With this in mind, a short review of the current status of nuclear, radiological, biological, and chemical weapons is required.

Nuclear Weapons

Nuclear weapons are, in a sense, the only "true" mass-destructive weapons. Motivations for developing nuclear weapons are varied, ranging from their unique destructive potential and perceived deterrence value to their utility as instruments of coercion or blackmail, or as a means of advancing regional or geopolitical objectives, international prestige, or perhaps for domestic political motivations. Potential proliferators benefit from the fact that most of the basic research, as well as the basics of weapons design, are completed and widely disseminated via the Internet and other sources. This does not mean that the process is easy. Would-be nuclear powers were traditionally constrained by financial considerations or the time-consuming, labor-intensive nature of the development process. The key hurdle in developing nuclear weapons is the acquisition of fissile material—plutonium or highly enriched uranium (HEU)—for use in a weapon. While states traditionally sought to reprocess plutonium or produce HEU themselves, the potential for black market procurement as a cost-efficient alternative is highly attractive.

As seen in the A. Q. Khan network, nuclear weapons technology and knowledge are spreading. There are five declared nuclear weapons states under the Nuclear Nonproliferation Treaty (the primary international non-proliferation agreement): Russia, the United States, China, France, and the United Kingdom. India and Pakistan are not declared states under the NPT, but both countries—India in 1974 and 1998 and Pakistan in 1998—tested nuclear weapons. Israel has never admitted to having nuclear weapons but is presumed to have between 98 and 172 nuclear weapons.[6] North Korea and Iran are widely suspected of having clandestine nuclear weapons programs, and both are clearly interested in obtaining nuclear technology. It is estimated that the total number of nuclear warheads globally is 31,055.[7] Non-state actors are also interested in acquiring nuclear capabilities. Indeed, al Qaeda leader Osama bin Laden asserted in 2001 that he had acquired nuclear weapons, although he declined to indicate where they came from.[8]

As denial and deception capabilities become more sophisticated, the potential exists for a new or different model of nuclear proliferation: one in which the amount of fissile material required for entry-level weapon designs is significantly reduced, and the facilities and activities required to produce such material are correspondingly smaller and less observable. Under these conditions, it may be possible for many countries to possess a latent capability to produce some number of nuclear weapons over time. Increasingly, "latent proliferation" may fit many states' needs to have access to strategic capabilities without the burdens associated with maintaining large industrial infrastruc-tures or deploying large operational stockpiles. Response times will vary in this model, as countries position themselves relative to their technical capacity and their unique perceived threats. But whether a state seeks to preserve the capability to produce a few weapons very quickly or many weapons over a longer period (or something in between), the spread of relevant technologies is likely to reduce the amount of time required to acquire fissile material and the observable science and engineering of the activity.

This model of future nuclear proliferation is of great concern, since it could lead to rapid, competitive, nuclear proliferation in volatile regions or in response to geopolitical events. It also poses challenges for intelligence and for traditional approaches to nonproliferation that focus on limiting, controlling, or monitoring fissile material and its production. If the amount of fissile material required to create a credible nuclear device is reduced, a strategy premised on fissile material control becomes less credible. A better understanding of these issues is needed. How might this model of proliferation take shape, what choices will nuclear aspirants face, and how can the WMD community understand the technology and political dynamics in key regions?

Radiological Dispersal Devices

Another method for using radiation as a weapon is by means of a radiological dispersal device (RDD), which is "designed to disperse radioactive material to cause destruction, contamination, and injury from the radiation pro-duced by the material."[9] An RDD is not the same as a nuclear weapon, and it does not have the destructive potential of such weapons. For this reason, some refer to RDDs as "weapons of mass disruption" rather than as weapons of mass destruction. There are several types of RDDs, each using a different means of dispersing radioactive elements.[10] Explosive RDDs, popularly known as 'dirty bombs,' use conventional explosives to scatter radioactive material over a wide area, potentially causing contamination and casualties through radiation sickness. Passive RDDs involve simply placing an unshielded radiation source in a location where large numbers of people will be exposed. Atmospheric RDDs convert radioactive materials into a form that is conducive to transportation on air currents.

Although RDDs are not generally seen as militarily effective battlefield weapons, such devices may be a relatively simple and straightforward way for non-state actors to conduct an attack. The most widely reported suspected RDD case involved suspected al-Qaeda operative José Padilla, who was arrested in Chicago's O'Hare International Airport in May 2002. Padilla was transferred from FBI custody to a military brig in Charleston, SC, and accused of planning to set off a dirty bomb. To date, Padilla has not been charged with a crime and is being held as an "illegal enemy combatant" without trial. His legal status is being fought in the courts. One other noteworthy RDD incident occurred in 1995 when Chechen rebels planted an RDD in Moscow's Izmailovo Park. The RDD contained caesium-137 and dynamite; the caesium was likely removed from cancer treatment equipment. After reporters were notified about its location, the RDD was defused and did not detonate.

Unlike nuclear weapons, which require uranium or plutonium, RDDs can use a wide variety of radioactive materials, such as caesium-137 as noted above.[11] These materials are widely used in hospitals, educational and research facilities, industrial and construction sites, and laboratories—places with fewer nuclear controls and security, and more individuals with access, than military complexes.[12] RDDs do not necessarily cause a great deal of blast damage, but they do raise issues regarding potential long-term contamination of targeted sites. Depending on the type of radioactive material used in the device, cleanup and decontamination of target areas could be costly and time-consuming. Such weapons are unlikely to kill large numbers of people, but the presence of radioactive materials is likely to cause panic and apprehension among the population of a targeted area. These devices received considerable media attention post-9/11 with the arrest of that suspected al-Qaeda operative who was charged with plotting an RDD attack.[13]

Biological Weapons

The least-understood element of WMD remains the biological weapons threat. For older, better-understood traditional agents such as anthrax, there still remain important gaps in knowledge such as the ability to accurately model a release within an acceptable margin of error. Increasingly, scientists are developing genetic engineering techniques that eventually will be within the capability of scientists everywhere. This process is fueled by the growing diffusion of advanced biological techniques pursued in a wide variety of settings from pharmaceutical labs to universities to corporate development labs. Indeed, the "biotechnology industrial complex" becomes more global everyday as states make substantial investment to create what in their view is a strategically important industry. These technologies will allow the creation of infrastructures that can support bioweapons programs as well as advance legitimate scientific pursuits such as the development of pharmaceuticals. The net result, however, may well be increased global access to biotechnology by terrorists determined to exploit the expertise and materials needed to execute biological attacks.

Biological weapons (BW) use microorganisms or toxins derived from organisms to cause disease in humans, plants, or animals. They come in many different forms, ranging from viruses to bacteria to rickettsiae to toxins. While there are many uncertainties with biological weapons, they are not new. In the Middle Ages, corpses with plague were catapulted over walls to break sieges, and in the Second World War, the notorious Japanese Unit 731 dropped bombs filled with plague-infected fleas over cities in Manchuria. With effects ranging from lower to higher lethality, they may also pose the risk of contagion. They can be genetically modified to make effects more severe and more difficult to diagnose and treat, as genetically modified pathogens are not found in nature and hence would not have a medical track record or treatment protocol. They may be employed as weapons of terror, or even against agricultural targets to poison food supplies, with potentially devastating economic or psychological effect. Many pathogens are endemic in certain regions of the world and therefore are relatively easy to acquire.

As living organisms, many biological agents are affected by variances in environmental conditions, including the heat caused by an explosion, ultraviolet radiation, and changes in atmospheric conditions such as temperature. Thus the performance of a potential dissemination mechanism must be within certain tolerance levels in order to be effective. The challenge lies in finding a means of dispersal that does not kill the organism while spreading it in a form and in sufficient quantity that will increase the likelihood of infection.

Adversaries may find biological weapons attractive for several reasons. First, they may allow an attack with a low likelihood of discovery, since attribution is difficult. Given the nature of many biological agents, it may be difficult to determine whether or not an attack has occurred, let alone who might be culpable. A case in point is the anthrax attacks that occurred in the United States in the fall of 2001. A series of anthrax-tainted letters were mailed to several media and government targets. At least four anthrax-filled envelopes were sent and twenty-two people were infected with pulmonary or cutaneous anthrax. Five died of pulmonary anthrax. It is estimated that hundreds were exposed and tens of thousands were put on the preventative antibiotics ciprofloxacin (Cipro) and doxycycline (Doxy) in Washington DC, New York, Florida, and Connecticut. Contamination efforts cost millions, not including the loss in productivity. The perpetrator(s) is still at large. Additionally, if the agent used is one that is endemic to the targeted area, an attack may be mistaken for a natural outbreak.

Second, the equipment, technology, and materials needed to produce biological weapons are in many cases quite similar to those used in the production of pharmaceuticals and other commercial products. As a result, the building blocks of a BW program are widely available and relatively easy to obtain. Because of the general availability of many necessary materials, the development of particular biological weapons may represent a relatively low-cost option (compared to nuclear weapons) for states or sub-state groups. Given the dual-use nature of much of the equipment used in the production of biological weapons, easy concealment of a development program is possible. As the Soviet Union's Biopreparat organization demonstrated, it is even possible to hide such a program in "plain sight," collocating BW development facilities with legitimate sites such as pharmaceutical plants.

Third, the expertise needed to produce biological weapons is widespread, and the knowledge base is growing due to scientific advances in biotechnology and genetic engineering. This has led to the concern that state programs and possibly terrorist groups could use these techniques to improve characteristics of existing biological agents or to combine genetic features of several agents to create "designer" pathogens. However, many advanced biotechnologies and techniques are beyond the current capabilities of terrorist groups, and in some cases would provide few advantages over existing "traditional" microbiology techniques. Some recently developed or emerging microbiology techniques require state support and funding of research and development. This may not always be the case. The availability of literature on biological warfare and the growth of "communities of interest" focused on sharing BW information suggest that realistic opportunities for exploitation of new biotechnologies are beginning to grow.

Finally, biological weapons have a wide range of effects and can be used against a wide range of targets. This versatility can make it difficult for states to craft an appropriate response. For example, an anti-crop weapon, while potentially causing a great deal of economic damage, may not necessarily result in the loss of any human life. Similarly, an adversary may opt to use an anti-personnel biological agent that has mass-casualty but not mass-fatality characteristics. The lack of human fatalities (or the absence of massive numbers of fatalities) in such cases could complicate retaliatory efforts by the targeted country—especially if the attacker's identity is uncertain. An attacker could also employ multiple agents simultaneously to cause a range of effects, hampering identification and treatment efforts.

The Intelligence Community assesses that "perhaps" a dozen states today are actively pursuing offensive BW programs.[14] Although the Russian offensive program was ended by presidential decree in 1992, the restrictive nature of the Russian scientific culture and community has brought lingering concerns that prohibited activities may continue. Furthermore, many Russian civilian facilities possess pathogen and toxin collections that lack adequate security or accounting measures. As with nuclear and chemical weapons, there is also the possibility that Russian scientists and technicians with BW knowledge could seek to improve their personal economic status by accepting employment in countries of proliferation concern.

Several other countries are suspected of pursuing offensive BW research, development, and possibly weaponization, including North Korea, China, and Iran.[15] Countries that have the potential to develop offensive biological weapons and that may possibly be conducting limited efforts include Pakistan, Cuba, Israel, India, and Syria.[16] Still other states retain the capacity to rapidly mobilize resources in support of BW programs. Most of these countries are parties to or signatories of the Biological Weapons Convention,[17] which provides that "Each State Party to this Convention undertakes never in any circumstances to develop, produce, stockpile or otherwise acquire or retain: (1) Microbial or other biological agents, or toxins whatever their origin or method of production, of types and in quantities that have no justification for prophylactic, protective or other peaceful purposes; (2) Weapons, equipment or means of delivery designed to use such agents or toxins for hostile purposes or in armed conflict."[18] Consequently, any offensive programs undertaken would violate their obligations under that treaty.

As biotechnology creates more opportunities and a greater array of options for proliferators, what traditionally has been a difficult intelligence target will become even more so, especially if intelligence assessments in the period ahead reflect a greater degree of caution. It will become more challenging to detect and monitor activities that could support proliferation, and almost impossible to predict the full range of options available to groups pursuing BW capability. Even if the West takes significant steps to improve intelligence capabilities in this area, a high degree of uncertainty seems unavoidable, and any future use of biological weapons almost certainly will come as a surprise. Developing countermeasures under these conditions is a major challenge.

Chemical Weapons

Chemical weapons (CW) make use of the toxic properties of various chemical compounds to kill, injure, or incapacitate. These weapons saw extensive use during World War I and were responsible for thousands of injuries and deaths. More recently, chemical weapons were used in the 1980s-era Iran-Iraq war, by the Iraqi government against its Kurdish citizens, and in a 1995 terrorist attack by Aum Shinrikyo on Tokyo subway commuters. Groups have long sought chemical agents for a number of reasons. First, they have been viewed as force multipliers on the battlefield or, more recently, as instruments of terror in urban areas. Second, the wide range of dispersal methods available, from very crude methods (such as that employed by Aum Shinrikyo in Japan) to crop dusters and other aerosol sprayers to sophisticated military munitions, leads to a range of different attack options. Third, some chemical weapons—especially "first-generation" weapons such as chlorine or phosgene—are relatively inexpensive, compared to nuclear weapons. Virtually any country with a reasonably sized industrial base (particularly in the chemical, petroleum, or pesticide industries) has the necessary infrastructure to produce at least first-generation chemical agents. Furthermore, the expertise and equipment for many chemical weapons are easily available, particularly for first-generation chemical weapons that, while no longer widely considered militarily effective, could be valuable to terrorists. Finally, the dual-use nature of much of the materials and equipment needed for the production of chemical weapons, including chemical precursors, allows for easy concealment of a development program.

The Chemical Weapons Convention (CWC) builds on and expands the Geneva Protocol of 1925 for chemical weapons and includes extensive verification measures such as on-site inspections.[19] The Convention is administered by the Organisation for the Prohibition of Chemical Weapons (OPCW), and is charged with conducting inspections of suspect facilities of the member states. According to Article 1 of the Convention, States Parties are obligated

> never under any circumstances:
> (a) To develop, produce, otherwise acquire, stockpile or retain chemical weapons, or transfer, directly or indirectly, chemical weapons to anyone;
> (b) To use chemical weapons;
> (c) To engage in any military preparations to use chemical weapons;
> (d) To assist, encourage or induce, in any way, anyone to engage in any activity prohibited to a State Party under this Convention.

Some states, however, retain active chemical weapons programs.[20] Russia, for example, maintains the largest CW stockpile in the world (approximately 40,000 metric tons), but is in the process of destroying its publicly reported stocks of agents. Many experts have lingering concerns that Russia has not declared its entire stockpile, as required under the CWC, and are concerned that its program has not been terminated.[21] Iran and Syria are believed to hold stockpiles of munitions and are pursuing development of advanced agents with foreign assistance.[22]

Libya's efforts in the chemical weapons arena attracted significant attention in the 1980s, especially with the construction of allegedly CW-related facilities at Rabta and Tarhuna. With the lifting of sanctions in 1999, Libya reportedly began renewing contacts with foreign suppliers to revive its CW efforts.[23] However, in December 2003, Libya publicly renounced its chemical weapons program along with its other WMD programs and has been working with U.S. and international representatives to dismantle its production capabilities.[24] India, as an original signatory to the CWC, declared its CW capabilities, opened related facilities to international inspection, and destroyed its stockpile of agents. China, North Korea, and the Sudan are suspected of having CW programs, with the former two believed to possess moderate to sizeable stockpiles.[25] Pakistan is assessed to have clear potential to develop chemical weapons, although it remains uncertain whether it is pursuing offensive development efforts.[26] Nonstate actors are also suspected of pursuing activities in chemical weapons, although the available evidence is sketchy and sometimes of indeterminate credibility.[27] A videotape was uncovered in Afghanistan that apparently shows dogs exposed to vapors from a "white liquid." Some experts speculate that the gas could be a nerve agent such as sarin.[28] Additionally, Ahmed Ressum, convicted for a millennium bomb plot on the Los Angeles airport, testified that he received instruction from al Qaeda on how to place toxins on doorknobs and that he was part of experiments which injected animals with a mixture containing cyanide and sulphuric acid.

Iraq had an active and advanced chemical weapons program prior to its 1991 defeat at the hands of the U.S.-led coalition. Even after the war, however, Iraq retained a latent capability and possibly hidden munitions stocks. UNSCOM, the UN Special Commission charged with implementing the non-nuclear provisions in Iraq following the first Gulf War, was unable to verify the destruction of several thousand chemical-filled munitions.[29] The U.S.-led coalition began inspections of Iraq's chemical-related facilities after its victory in 2003. The U.S. uncovered evidence that Iraq examined the possibility of resuming production of chemical agents in the 2001–2002 period, and evidence recovered indicated that some proscribed CW-related research could have been conducted by Iraqi scientists.[30] However, no stockpiles of chemical munitions were uncovered, and in January 2004, David Kay, the head of the Iraq Survey Group that investigated Iraqi's WMD programs, testified to the U.S. Senate Armed Services Committee that "We simply have no evidence" that Iraq maintained stockpiles of chemical weapons.[31]

EMERGING WMD-LIKE TECHNOLOGIES

Over the next twenty years, a number of advances in science and technology have the potential to transform major aspects of how people live—extending human life, reshaping the global economy—and how the world wages war. Devastating new weapons are possible through the application of these scientific and technological advances that rival the lethality of existing weapons of mass destruction. Indeed, the definition of what constitutes a weapon of mass destruction increasingly will be open to revision as these applications take shape. Two technology areas have the greatest potential to yield new kinds of WMD: biotechnology and nanotechnology.

A new generation of biological weapons based on genomic research has the potential to create new capabilities not envisioned or restricted by existing arms control treaties. Examples include the following:

❏ *Genetic weapons* that target specific groups based on their genetic characteristics may be possible as an offshoot of ongoing research into assessing human health by reading metabolic signatures in human respiration. Preliminary results suggest that this technology could lead to ways of identifying race and ethnicity.

❏ *Aptamers* are strands of nucleic acid that act in a manner similar to antibodies. They bind and block cell receptors responsible for a variety of life-sustaining biological functions.

❏ *Molecular poisons* are nano-sized, microscopic particles whose size is one-billionth of a meter, capable of working at the subcellular level and engineered to create specialized effects that could cross the blood-brain barrier, disrupt genetic material, or trigger counterproductive immune system responses.

Nanotechnology can be both an enabler of highly lethal effects (e.g., the aforementioned molecular poisons) as well as a discrete form of mass destruction/mass disruption warfare. Current research in nanotechnology includes the development of explosive microdust, an ultra-high-explosive/ultra-incendiary material several times more potent than an equivalent mass of TNT. Visionaries in the field theorize about destructive nanites or "nanobots" programmed to carry out anti-materiel or anti-personnel missions. Recent experiments in the United States have demonstrated that nano-sized carbon particles can introduce respiratory distress or death in mammals.[32] Respected scientific associations in Europe also warned of the potentially toxic effect of existing nano-particle contamination of the biological environment.

WMD TERRORISM

If any one concept has taken hold in the past few years, it may be the "nexus of WMD and terrorism." Experts recognize that jihadist terrorists are seeking such weapons, will not be deterred from using them, and have the potential to wreak catastrophic damage. This truly is the nightmare scenario—one that concentrates the mind on better understanding the nature of this threat. Among decision makers today, there appears to be a working assumption that, with respect to terrorists and WMD, "possession = use," meaning if terrorist groups develop or acquire WMD, they will use them and not merely retain WMD for deterrence purposes. This is undoubtedly a prudent assumption, though as decision makers think more about the terrorist threat the United States faces and as they learn more about al Qaeda in particular, there is an opportunity to refine thinking about the specific dimensions of the "nexus" that defines so many of the worst fears.

Recently, several incidents have spawned growing fears that terrorist organizations or other non-state groups could obtain and use WMD. One of the first of these incidents was the 1995 Tokyo subway sarin attack carried out by the Aum Shinrikyo cult and the subsequent police investigations that uncovered the extent of the group's WMD aspirations. More recent were the October 2001 anthrax attacks in the United States, which resulted in five deaths and seventeen other infections,[33] the discovery of ricin, a deadly BW agent, in a January 2003 anti-terrorist operation in London, and the finding of a ricin-tainted letter in the office of Senator Bill Frist in February 2004. Finally, Osama bin Laden has declared that the acquisition of WMD is a religious duty, and intelligence collected in Afghanistan revealed that al Qaeda was working to acquire nuclear, biological, and chemical weapons as well as a radiological dispersal device.[34] Two Pakistani scientists allegedly shared WMD information with al Qaeda sometime in or prior to 2001 and commented on the viability of a radiological bomb.[35]

Terrorist (and other sub-state groups) interested in such weapons are tied to a perceived shift in the motives and goals of some terrorist organizations. According to one school of thought, religious motivations are complementing or even superseding the political motivations that once drove terrorists. Combined with this motivating force is another perceived shift away from the previously held tenet that terrorists want more people watching an event than they want killed by that event. Indeed, mass-casualty events are becoming more common: globalization broadcasts the psychological shock value of large numbers of fatalities to a wider audience, and allows mass casualties to be inflicted abroad, not undermining local audiences' sympathies for terrorist causes. However, there is a great deal of debate over the extent to which terrorist organizations may possess the necessary technical and financial resources to acquire effective WMD capabilities.[36] In practice, it is not as easy to do as it sounds. Even Aum Shinrikyo, skeptics frequently note, with almost a billion dollars in assets and university-level scientists, was unable to develop biological weapons or a truly effective chemical weapons dissemination capability. At the same time, that group's partial success, coupled with known interest in acquisition and continuing advances in technology (usable for weapons development), suggests that sub-state actors may become increasing capable with respect to WMD.

Indeed, there is a growing prospect that terrorist organizations will acquire WMD, either on their own or with the help of another, be it a country or a smuggling entrepreneur. The intent to acquire these capabilities is clear, the requisite materials and information have never been more readily available, advances in technology will make this job easier over time, and use is likely if these weapons are acquired. Moreover, many proliferators such as Iran, Syria, and North Korea are known or suspected state-sponsors of terrorism, raising the possibility that such states could provide weapons or material/technical assistance to terrorist groups. However, the specific form of WMD-related assistance a state-sponsor would provide to a terrorist organization, and the circumstances under which that assistance would be provided, remain unclear. In addition to support and assistance from a state sponsor, another avenue for sub-state acquisition of WMD lies at the intersection of failing (or failed) states and WMD capabilities. In theory, a terrorist or sub-national group could take advantage of the collapse of a WMD-capable state to seize control over a portion of that state's WMD arsenal. This has been the ongoing concern over the safety of WMD arsenals, materials, and research labs in the successor states to the FSU. That such a situation might occur was a concern with Pakistan in late 2001, when there were serious concerns over the stability of the government and the security of Pakistan's nuclear stockpile.[37] These concerns arose again following two attempts to assassinate Pakistan's president, Pervez Musharraf, in December 2003.

U.S. intelligence agencies have learned much since September 11, 2001, about al Qaeda's interest in and pursuit of nuclear, radiological, chemical, and biological weapons—so much so that it sheds a sobering light on how little the United States knew before that day. Before September 11, intelligence agencies believed al Qaeda was focused primarily on simple chemical warfare agents, guided by an over-inflated sense of what these weapons could accomplish in achieving mass effects. The United States has since learned that they had in fact made a major investment in a range of chemical warfare capabilities, both simple and advanced. Analysis of an al Qaeda document recovered in Afghanistan in 2002 indicates the existence of crude procedures for producing mustard agent, sarin, and VX.[38] In his testimony before the Senate Select Committee on Intelligence in February 2004, former Director of Central Intelligence (DCI) George Tenet spoke of "a heightened risk of poison attacks" and the possibility of increasingly sophisticated delivery methods and tactics, including improvised chemical weapons that could create significant casualties in a crowded, enclosed area.[39]

Al Qaeda's biological weapons effort has been described by senior intelligence officials as sophisticated. In Afghanistan, the group was successful in acquiring the expertise and equipment needed to grow biological agents, including a dedicated laboratory near Kandahar.[40] Anthrax was an area of emphasis, and while U.S. intelligence agencies still lack a comprehensive understanding of this program, the Intelligence Community views this as one of the most immediate terrorist WMD threats the United States is likely to face.[41] It has come to light, for instance, that some of the September 11 hijackers made repeated inquiries regarding cropdusters and that state law enforcement authorities viewed this as sufficiently serious to twice ground cropdusters nationwide in the period after September 11 and to question more than 3,000 pilots and cropduster owners.

And the United States learned more in Afghanistan about al Qaeda's nuclear agenda, which is now described as ambitious in its pursuit of the materials and expertise required to construct a radiological dispersal device and possibly other kinds of nuclear devices. The Intelligence Community believes construction of a "dirty bomb" is well within al-Qaeda's capabilities if it can obtain the radiological material, and terrorists likely understand how such a device could be used.[42]

Among terror groups pursuing chemical, biological, radiological and/or nuclear materials, al Qaeda remains the most advanced and the principal concern. Still, it is vitally important to look beyond al Qaeda, as there are two to three dozen other terrorist organizations believed to be interested in acquiring WMD of some sort, particularly chemical weapons. And their interest may be driven in part not so much by an objective analysis of U.S. vulnerabilities as by the public and open discussions common in the United States about fears of WMD and the relative ease with which terrorists could mount devastating attacks. The al Qaeda leadership shows evidence of this. According to press accounts, an April 1999 memo apparently written by Dr. Ayman al-Zawahri comments on al-Qaeda's decision to acquire chemical and biological weapons: ". . . despite their extreme danger, we only became aware of them when the enemy drew attention to them by repeatedly expressing concern that they can be produced simply."[43] Especially as states move to improve their ability to defend against the classical forms of WMD attack, terrorists increasingly will look to WMD as a way to achieve strategic effects. Along the way, those charged with defending their borders can expect more numerous—and more sophisticated—hoaxes that will command ever-greater response resources.

PROLIFERATION PREVENTION

Proliferation prevention is preventing the spread of weapons of mass destruction and their means of delivery. Traditionally, prevention mechanisms were seen in terms of horizontal and vertical proliferation. Horizontal proliferation seeks to prevent the spread of WMD weapons and technology to states that do not currently possess them. Vertical proliferation, on the other hand, seeks to prevent the increase in the number and destructiveness of weapons within a state already possessing them. In some ways, nonproliferation, the full range of political, economic, and diplomatic tools to prevent, constrain, or reverse the proliferation of NBC weapons and their associated delivery means, represents the concept of horizontal proliferation prevention focused on preventing acquisition. Nonproliferation has a long history and is the traditional focal point for U.S. government efforts. Such efforts include the Nuclear Suppliers Group, the Nuclear Nonproliferation Treaty regime, export controls, and the Cooperative Test Ban Treaty, among others. Nonproliferation controls, such as the Nuclear Nonproliferation Treaty (NPT), rely on state parties to control weapons and technology from spreading outside their borders. For example, the NPT requires the five declared nuclear weapons states to seek disarmament and to share peaceful nuclear technology with non-nuclear declared states. The non-nuclear weapons states in return promise not to seek nuclear technology for military or strategic application. Therefore, nonproliferation relies primarily on diplomacy and is based on the concept that sovereign states will adhere to their treaty commitments.

Counterproliferation is the full range of military preparations and activities to reduce and protect against the threat posed by WMD weapons and delivery means. Counterproliferation is a blend of vertical and horizontal prevention focused on preventing the use of WMD weapons. The concept of counterproliferation grew from a recognition in the early 1990s that nonproliferation geared to Cold War objectives ignored the growing concern over non-state actors. Thus, counterproliferation was envisioned as a tool to be used when diplomacy fails—when there is a threat of use or illicit proliferation.

As demonstrated in the Libya case at the beginning of the chapter, the nuclear black market operated by the Pakistani engineer Abdul Qadeer Khan poses challenges to both nonproliferation (preventing WMD acquisition beforehand) and counterproliferation (stopping the spread of WMD in progress). This points to a larger lesson of the A. Q. Khan experience: that there will always be policy tradeoffs as the world seeks to combat proliferation in a complex and dangerous regional setting. The United States accepted official Pakistani assertions that there was no government involvement in Khan's activities, and did not challenge the pardon Khan received, which immunized him from criminal charges. For now, the war on terror and the search for Osama bin Laden seem to be more important imperatives in U.S.-Pakistan relations than nonproliferation.

Proliferation events are constantly shaping and reshaping the agenda for combating WMD. As decision makers confront a dynamic proliferation environment, policy must respond with agility and innovation. The Proliferation Security Initiative (PSI) is a good example of how a group of like-minded states is attempting to deal with the WMD proliferation threat in today's threat environment. Allies and international institutions are indispensable, whether for strengthening the nonproliferation regime, deepening cooperation on interdiction, or pursuing rollback in specific countries.

STRENGTHENING PREVENTION—CHALLENGES OF INTERNATIONAL COOPERATION

Longstanding weaknesses in the international nonproliferation regime now demand serious attention. In light of the A. Q. Khan revelations, continuing challenges from North Korea and Iran, and the likely consequences of WMD terrorism, gaps in the policy and legal framework for nonproliferation pose an unacceptable risk. President Bush's speech of February 11, 2004, at the National Defense University took direct aim at a number of these problems, particularly in the area of nuclear control mechanisms.[44]

Criminalizing WMD Proliferation

President Bush formally proposed what many observers have long called for: the criminalization by all countries of proliferation and the enactment of strict export control laws. Too few states have domestic laws prohibiting proliferation; those laws that do exist are not reliably enforced. This is part of the larger effort to de-legitimize and stigmatize proliferation, and with the passage of United Nations Security Council Resolution 1540 (2004) on April 28, 2004, the international community now is on record calling on states to refrain from supporting non-state actors in their pursuit of WMD, and to adopt and enforce domestic laws and controls toward this end.[45] The key provisions of the Security Council Resolution 1540 obligate states to keep non-state actors from gaining access to nuclear, biological, and chemical weapons, to enact legislation to prohibit non-state access to those weapons, to adopt and enforce effective domestic controls to prevent WMD weapons proliferation, and to cooperate internationally to prevent illicit trafficking in WMD materials and their means of delivery.

Expanding Threat Reduction

Following the fall of the Soviet Union in 1991, the United States engaged in a program to assist the former Soviet Union states of Russia, Kazakhstan, Belarus, and Ukraine in controlling and protecting their nuclear weapons,

weapons–usable materials, and delivery systems. This effort, called the Cooperative Threat Reduction (CTR) Program, focuses on dismantling and destroying a number of nuclear weapons and their associated delivery systems in accordance with Russia's disarmament treaty obligations. From 2000 to 2010, the United States will spend a projected $1 billion per year on the program. Associated programs were also developed to help hire unemployed and underemployed scientists in the former Soviet Union, in an effort to prevent a "brain drain" of these scientists to would-be proliferators.

The president also called for expanding the scope of international threat reduction efforts as one means to reduce the availability of materials that could support WMD acquisition efforts by states or non–state actors. The functional scope of these activities must extend beyond the former Soviet Union, as there is a growing need to apply this model to other countries and regions, such as Iraq, Libya, and Southwest Asia. And as more countries require this type of assistance, more donor states are required to underwrite the cost. At the June 2004 Group of Eight (G-8) summit at Sea Island, Georgia, seven new countries agreed to contribute funds amounting to 20 billion dollars over ten years to cooperative threat reduction efforts.[46] The president called for more states to contribute to this G-8 Global Partnership Against Catastrophic Terrorism.

This proposal responds to some of the concerns expressed by serious commentators about the priority and resources attached to global threat reduction activities. Unsecured nuclear weapons material anywhere is a threat to all countries.[47] Getting this material under secure control must be a priority, and nowhere more so than in Russia. Decision makers cannot lose sight of the overriding importance of securing Russia's vast arsenals of nuclear weapons and materials. In the post–September 11 world, the stake in this is dramatically increased. Yet today, Russia's nuclear weapons and weapons materials are still no more than 50 percent secure. In 2003, the Russian government, in conjunction with Cooperative Threat Reduction programs, completed comprehensive security and accounting upgrades for an additional thirty-five tons of potentially vulnerable weapons–usable material. But, by the Department of Energy's own accounting, security upgrade work has not even begun on more than one hundred metric tons of plutonium and highly enriched uranium. And while the pace of work has accelerated somewhat, at thirty-five tons per year it will take about thirteen years to complete the job. To be fair, it is important to note that 70 percent of the sites with weapons or weapons material now have upgrades in place, so progress is being made. But this still leaves a significant security gap that some observers believe must be addressed at the highest levels with a greater sense of urgency, especially if bureaucratic battles over taxes, liability, site access, and other issues are to be overcome. Placing the fight against proliferation and catastrophic terrorism at the centerpiece of the U.S.-Russia security relationship, supported by closer presidential involvement, may be the only way to complete the threat reduction mission in Russia in a reasonable period of time.

Unity of effort in threat reduction is an additional concern. If WMD in the hands of terrorists is the single greatest threat, it is possible that more centralized authority may be required to ensure that state and cooperative resources are effectively marshaled.

Closing NPT Loopholes

The challenge posed by North Korea and Iran to the Nuclear Non-Proliferation Treaty regime (NPT), the preeminent global nonproliferation treaty, is a great concern to global peace. The NPT obligates the five acknowledged nuclear-weapon states (the United States, Russian Federation, United Kingdom, France, and China) not to transfer nuclear weapons, other nuclear explosive devices, or their technology to any non–nuclear-weapon state. Non–nuclear-weapon states agree in return not to undertake acquisition or production of nuclear weapons or nuclear explosive devices. Non–nuclear-weapon states are also required to accept safeguards that detect diversions from peaceful activities, such as power generation, to the production of nuclear weapons or other nuclear explosive devices and is done in accordance with an individual safeguards agreement. This agreement is negotiated and concluded between each non–nuclear-weapon State Party and the International Atomic Energy Agency (IAEA), the UN's nuclear watchdog agency. These agreements require that all nuclear materials be declared to the IAEA, whose inspectors have routine access to the facilities for periodic monitoring and inspections. If information from routine inspections is not sufficient to fulfill its responsibilities, the IAEA may consult with the state regarding special inspections within or outside declared facilities.

The actions of Iran and North Korea have created a crisis of confidence in the treaty regime. Effective April 10, 2003, North Korea withdrew from the NPT, threw out IAEA monitors, and is suspected of reconstituting its nuclear weapons development program. The IAEA Board of Governors recently adopted a resolution on September 24, 2005, finding Iran in "non-compliance" with its agency safeguards agreement. The resolution sets the stage for the board to refer the Iranian nuclear issue to the UN Security Council but does not specify when or under what circumstances such a referral would take place.[48] Without substantial progress in these two states, countries that to date have placed their faith in nonproliferation treaties may feel compelled to reconsider the wisdom of abjuring not just nuclear weapons, but possibly chemical and biological weapons as well. A cascade of WMD acquisition decisions resulting from further erosion of the NPT regime cannot be ruled out. In parallel, closing the "loopholes" in the NPT that have allowed countries like Iran to pursue a nuclear weapons capability under the cover of treaty compliance must be a priority for the United States and the international community. Better verification mechanisms and assurance procedures must be put in place to signal to the international community that a state party is in compliance and not seeking nuclear weapons covertly and under the cover of compliance.

Addressing the most important concern regarding the availability of WMD materials, President Bush's National Defense University speech proposed reforms to the NPT designed to make it harder for proliferators to acquire weapons grade nuclear materials under the cover of peaceful nuclear energy programs. Stating that "enrichment and reprocessing are not necessary for nations seeking to harness nuclear energy," the president called for states pursuing civilian nuclear power to renounce enrichment and reprocessing in exchange for the reliable supply of nuclear fuel at reasonable cost. Any country not already possessing full-scale, functioning enrichment and reprocessing plants would not be allowed to acquire the means to develop them through legitimate trade with the forty-four countries of the Nuclear Suppliers Group (NSG). The Nuclear Suppliers Group (NSG) is a widely accepted export-control arrangement that establishes guidelines for control of nuclear and nuclear-related exports. Member states agree to voluntarily adhere to the NSG Guidelines, which are adopted by consensus and through exchanges of information on developments of nuclear proliferation concern. This will make it more difficult for states intent on developing nuclear weapons to manipulate the NPT and acquire the material and information necessary for manufacturing illegal weapons. And only states that have signed the International Atomic Energy Agency's (IAEA) Additional Protocol which allows the IAEA to carry out a range of additional verification measures to ensure there are no undeclared facilities and activities would be allowed to import equipment from NSG countries for their civilian nuclear programs.[49]

With respect to the NPT, it is not an exaggeration to state that the treaty is at a historical juncture that requires a fresh look and decisive action. How hard the world and key players such as the United States, Russia, and China will push what amounts to an ambitious set of treaty reforms remains to be seen.[50] Other challenges face the NPT regime, including the concern by many non-nuclear states that the nuclear powers have shown no movement toward or interest in actually disarming nuclear stockpiles, a condition embedded in the NPT agreement. Indeed, the failure of the NPT review in the summer of 2005 stemmed in large measure from the inability of the NPT signatories to agree on an agenda. Countries such as the United States wanted to focus on preventing WMD terrorism and enhancing procedures to stem illicit WMD trafficking. The non-nuclear powers, led by countries such as Egypt, aggressively sought to put the issue of disarmament squarely on the agenda, seeking assurances and timeframes for the nuclear powers to disarm. The inability to resolve these differences ended the NPT review and plagues negotiations today.

ADVANCING THE PROLIFERATION SECURITY INITIATIVE (PSI)

A growing coalition of like-minded countries today is now planning, exercising, and executing interdiction operations aimed at disrupting the traffic in WMD- and missile-related materials and technologies. On May 31, 2003 in Krakow, Poland, President Bush announced the Proliferation Security Initiative (PSI). The concept was largely developed as a result of the *So San* interdiction incident in 2002. In December 2002, U.S. intelligence assets tracked the unflagged vessel *So San* as it departed from North Korea with an unknown destination but was assumed to be bound for the Middle East. Acting on a request from the U.S., Spanish special operations forces staged from the Spanish frigate *Navarro* intercepted and boarded *So San*. While searchers found a great deal of cement, the declared cargo, they also discovered non-manifested Scud-B missiles, warheads, and fuel oxidizer. The Bush Administration, facing protests from North Korea and Yemen, conceded that the weapons and their components were the legally acquired property of the Yemeni government. Indeed, the Bush Administration during this time complimented Yemen for being a staunch ally in the global war on terror. Subsequently, Spanish forces released the *So San* to deliver its cargo.[51] On December 11, 2002, just days after the U.S. relented to North Korea and Yemen and over *So San* and its cargo, the president unveiled the National Strategy for Combating Weapons of Mass Destruction, which identified aggressive counterproliferation as its principal element.[52]

Applying lessons learned from the embarrassing *So San* incident, the Administration developed and implemented PSI as a multilateral effort based on a statement of interdiction principles. These principles, created within the framework of existing international and state-based agreements and laws, enable partner states to disrupt and interdict the illegal proliferation of WMD. To be successful, PSI requires signatories to work cooperatively to stop the trafficking of WMD-related material and technology to and from states and organizations that present a proliferation risk. PSI partner states commit to interdiction efforts using shared intelligence, timely communication, and multilateral action.[53]

This process was evident in the interception of *BBC China*. The United States shared with Germany and Italy intelligence developed from its operations targeting the A. Q. Kahn network. This intelligence identified the likelihood that a Malaysian company was shipping nuclear technology to Libya via Dubai aboard a German-registered vessel.[54] Acting on that intelligence, and with operational assistance from the U.S. Navy, German and Italian officials coordinated the diversion of the ship to Italy. This operation represents the type of multilateral interdiction effort laid out in PSI. PSI advocates point to the fact that Qadhafi did not make any substantial public moves to initiate WMD rollback until after the interception of *BBC China* and its cargo of centrifuge components.[55]

Today, the original eleven PSI partners have grown to a group of nearly sixty participating and supporting states. As PSI continues to expand its membership and its activities, it is not only complicating the efforts of proliferators, but also strengthening nonproliferation norms, providing a concrete means of security cooperation with allies and friends, and demonstrating that coordinated actions among like-minded states can be achieved without having to create new organizations or bureaucracies.

Progress has been made along several fronts in establishing the PSI global network of partnerships. Countries have committed to a statement of interdiction principles. Guidelines and processes are in place for the collection, analysis, and sharing of intelligence. New shipboarding agreements are extending available legal authorities.[56] Operational experts from participating states meet regularly to develop improved intelligence, military, and law enforcement capabilities to support interdiction activities. These capabilities are being refined in a growing exercise program; nine maritime, air, and ground exercises have been completed to date, and countries have agreed to a systematic exercise program for 2005 based on scenarios that reflect trends of concern in WMD trafficking.

In his speech to the students and faculty of the National Defense University, President Bush advanced broadening the work of PSI to address the problems highlighted by the revelations of the A. Q. Khan nuclear black market:

> . . . I propose that the work of the Proliferation Security Initiative be expanded to address more than shipments and transfers. Building on the tools we've developed to fight terrorists, we can take direct action against proliferation networks. We need greater cooperation not just among

intelligence and military services, but in law enforcement as well. PSI participants and other willing nations should use the Interpol and all other means to bring to justice those who traffic in deadly weapons, to shut down their labs, to seize their materials, to freeze their assets.[57]

Moving forward, the goal is to extend both the functional reach of the PSI framework and the breadth of international participation. In tandem with other elements of the global nonproliferation agenda, the solid diplomatic and operational foundation of the PSI provides a basis for making progress in strengthening prevention efforts. However, there are some concerns regarding the PSI approach to combating WMD. As a coalition of the willing not tethered to an international regime or institution, there is concern about the lack of institutionalization of the program. Whether and how will lessons learned be retained and transmitted over time without an institutional frame-work, and will the "coalition of the willing" approach be durable over time as leaders and administrations change?

ROLLBACKS

Rolling back a nuclear or other WMD program has been part of the combating WMD vocabulary since the Indian nuclear test of 1974. While no longer a realistic policy choice in the near term on the Indian subcontinent, the rollback concept aptly captures what many seek to achieve in Libya, North Korea, and Iran.

Libya

Encouraging Libya to renounce both terrorism and WMD aspirations has been a longstanding global and regional objective. As Colonel Muammar Qadhafi intensified his efforts in recent years to "come in from the cold," the West made clear the central importance of the WMD issue in any process of normalization. While Qadhafi may have believed he could achieve normalized relations and a lifting of U.S. sanctions while still maintaining clandestine WMD programs, this position became increasingly untenable as he witnessed the global reaction to the events of September 11, 2001. The campaigns in Afghanistan and Iraq demonstrated that the United States and allies were prepared to marshal significant force to eliminate terror and WMD threats posed by rogue states. This probably led him to conclude that he too could become a target of coalition military action. The seizure of the *BBC China* in October 2003 demonstrated that his nuclear program was no longer clandestine and that his procurement effort could be penetrated and shut down. And, according to some accounts provided by Libyan officials, the capture of Saddam Hussein in December 2003 underscored to Qadhafi the personal risks associated with rogue status. In considering these factors, one can see how the post–September 11 environment shaped Qadhafi's calculus of the benefits and risks in pursuing WMD and led him openly to renounce WMD and to accept comprehensive disarmament rather than attempt to maintain covert programs.

In this sense, WMD became a source of *insecurity* to Qadhafi and an impediment to his principal goal of reintegrating with the international community in order to address Libya's growing economic and social problems. By tying the removal of sanctions and the prospects for political and economic rehabilitation to Libya's WMD efforts, and by demonstrating a credible threat of military action, U.S. policy presented Qadhafi a powerful set of incentives to disarm. In this "carrot and stick" dynamic it is important to not underestimate the power of the carrot—that is, the promise of significant benefits. Economic sanctions by the U.S. and the UN beginning in the early 1990s hit Libya hard, and the regime's poor economic management compounded their effects. Libyan oil production had fallen by more than half, with lost revenues estimated by the World Bank at \$18 billion.[58] Plagued by outdated technology and mismanagement, the country's oil infrastructure suffered. The rising expectations of an increasingly young population created conditions that demanded a serious program of economic reform critically dependent on opening the Libyan economy to the outside world.

The circumstances of the Libyan case are unique, but the basic logic of rollback is evident: presented with the right mix of pressures and promised benefits, the motivations and behavior of even rogue regimes regarding WMD can change. It is this logic that informs current promotion of the "Libyan model" of disarmament to countries like North Korea and Iran. How viable is this model? Libya is certainly not the first country to give up its WMD program. Brazil, Argentina, South Africa, and three former states of the Soviet Union—Belarus, Kazakhstan, and Ukraine—all renounced and demilitarized their WMD programs. The larger question is how the Libya model fits into the broader context of WMD rollback and what lessons can be learned and applied to states of proliferation concern today.

North Korea

In principle, this same logic of rollback would appear to fit the North Korean case quite well. The basis for any agreement with North Korea is essentially the same—significant economic, political, and security benefits in exchange for comprehensive disarmament (though in North Korea's case, limited to nuclear). And North Korea, in far more dire economic straits than Libya, would seem to have significant incentives to reach an agreement. But in reality, circumstances in Northeast Asia are far different. Unlike Libya, North Korea may be a de facto nuclear weapon state since its withdrawal from the NPT in January 2003. Moreover, intelligence indicates that North Korea is pursuing a clandestine uranium enrichment capability whose scope, maturity, and location are essentially unknown. Pyongyang's failure to acknowledge this program remains an important impediment to progress. Here, rollback is a far more ambitious and complex proposition, further complicated by the regime's hidden and unpredictable behavior coupled with significant gaps in intelligence of North Korean intentions and capabilities.

While Qadhafi's intentions ultimately became quite clear, no one knows whether Pyongyang is prepared to give up its entire nuclear weapons enterprise and submit to a process of complete, verifiable, and irreversible disarmament. The possibility cannot be ruled out that the regime's objective is to achieve normalized relations while retaining a covert stockpile or weapons production capacity. Certainly the regime has demonstrated through word and deed how powerful a lever they view the possession of nuclear weapons and weapons production potential to be, and Kim Jong Il may well see nuclear weapons as key to regime survival. And the intelligence challenges North Korea continues to pose for the West may lead him to believe that a clandestine nuclear program can in fact be maintained.

Testing North Korea's intentions is the objective of the ongoing six-party talks that seek to bring a halt to their nuclear program and ambitions and minimize the prospect of North Korean cheating. The idea of the six-party talks is to engage North Korea in a multinational setting that includes regional powers Russia, Japan, China, and South Korea as well as the United States. By having more parties to the talks, it is hoped that North Korea will be more likely to honor its commitments. By engaging China directly in the negotiating process, the six-party talks give Beijing a significant stake in a successful outcome and leverage China's longstanding relationship with (and knowledge of) Pyongyang.

Can this brand of diplomacy achieve rollback in North Korea? Realistically, there are few attractive alternatives, and policy options that would adopt a more confrontational approach toward North Korea are not likely to succeed without the active participation of the regional actors. While all parties to the talks undoubtedly are frustrated with North Korea's posture, it's highly unlikely that diplomacy will be exhausted any time soon. All parties have much at stake in a peaceful resolution and see the risks associated with confrontation as very high. To be sure, the payoffs for North Korea would be substantial, providing political legitimacy, enhanced security, and the means to revive an utterly failed economy. Viewed through the prism of cold rationality, these payoffs appear compelling. Nonetheless, there clearly are countervailing pressures. Given the value North Korea appears to place on nuclear capability, the progress they appear to have made, and their ability to conceal proscribed activities, an important practical question is whether the states to the six-party talks may be compelled to consider outcomes short of "complete, verifiable, and irreversible disarmament" as the United States defines this goal. Put differently, what degree of ambiguity, if any, are the members to the talks willing to accept in North Korea's nuclear capabilities?[59]

Iran

The case of Iran is different still. Compared to Libya, Iran is much further along in assembling the infrastructure required to enrich uranium and reprocess plutonium on a large scale. It appears committed to closing both these fuel cycles and achieving an independent capability to produce fissile material suitable for making weapons. It claims the right under the NPT to do so, and has made a huge investment over the last two decades to advance this effort. Compared to North Korea, Iran seems to take a less instrumental view of nuclear weapons; that is, they are not fundamentally treated as a bargaining chip but rather are central to the regime's ambitions for regional influence, the requirements of deterrence, safeguarding the Islamic revolution, and balancing Israel's perceived nuclear power. Moreover, while it faces significant economic challenges, Iran's economic vulnerability is far less acute than that of Libya or North Korea, given its indigenous energy resources and robust international trading relations. At the same time, the international community does not believe that Iran possesses nuclear weapons. Iran remains a member of the NPT and to date has worked within the IAEA framework to attempt to resolve compliance issues.

Given these conditions—a highly motivated, committed, and combative proliferator *not* facing dire economic circumstances—is there a credible rollback strategy premised on some achievable set of mutual benefits? The diplomatic track, while far from exhausted, has not yielded a satisfactory outcome to date. Led by France, Germany, and the United Kingdom, this effort has focused on getting Iran to suspend critical activities such as uranium enrichment in exchange for the supply of enriched uranium suitable to fuel power reactors and economic incentives. Tehran does not view this as a compelling trade. Is there a "grander" bargain to be made with Iran, one that gives them a sufficiently powerful incentive to reconsider the nuclear path? There appears to be little official thinking about this, and admittedly it is difficult to map the contours of such a grand bargain. What can Iran be offered that will be of commensurate strategic value to the possession of a nuclear capability? What combination of political, security, and economic benefits could induce them to forego the bomb?[60]

Policy is increasingly characterized in terms of a denial strategy aimed at slowing and disrupting the Iranian program. Through the IAEA and a variety of interdiction activities, the goal is to force Iran to bring more elements of its program under safeguards and prevent outside assistance from reaching the program while raising the costs associated with noncompliance.[61] If successful, such a strategy would complicate, make more costly, and delay Iran's acquisition of nuclear weapons capability. Conceivably, these problems could influence a decision by the Iranian leadership on whether to take the final steps to actually manufacture weapons. Conceivably, the delay imposed by a denial strategy could be long enough to allow a process of internal political change to alter the nature of the Iranian regime and its basic security outlook.

Behind the denial strategy is the threat of punitive action. Pressure is growing on the IAEA to refer this matter to the United Nations Security Council, where Iran would come into direct confrontation with the United States and the threat of sanctions would become manifest. Beyond this, recent statements by U.S. officials have intentionally not ruled out the use of force to prevent Iran from going nuclear. Threats of military action may not compel Iran to give up the bomb, but they could create internal pressures to consider stopping short of manufacturing weapons and developing an operational stockpile. Keeping Iran at "threshold status" may not sound like victory and may not accommodate everyone's view of "rollback," but in the end—short of preventive war to keep Iran from going nuclear—it may turn out to be the least bad outcome.

THINKING ABOUT TERROR CAMPAIGNS

Terrorists think and act in terms of campaigns—an orchestrated series of violent acts intended to advance a strategic objective. It is hard to identify acts of terror that are not somehow part of a campaign, whether the time-span of that campaign is short or long. By contrast, crisis and consequence managers tend to think in terms of single events. Responding effectively to single events is daunting enough; responders have barely begun to think concretely about the challenges posed by multiple events. Yet this challenge must be faced in light of the risks and opportunities it presents.

The risks seem clear enough—a greater chance that policymakers and the responder community will make mistakes that exacerbate rather than ease fear and panic, impair response capability, or undermine the legitimacy of government at all levels. The opportunities presented by terror campaigns are principally to learn and adapt, gain the initiative, and exploit mistakes the terrorists might make. How these possibilities play out will be shaped by a number of factors, such as the speed and degree of simultaneity of attacks and the degree of clarity about the "who, what, when, where, and why" of the attacks. At early points when uncertainty on these questions is greatest, risks are likely to dominate. As terrorist capabilities and intentions become clearer, the prospects for an adaptive response should increase. And it is important they do so, because life under a prolonged state of emergency will undoubtedly create profound stresses to any society so affected.

If decision makers assume, prudently, that after an initial biological or chemical attack terrorists are "re-loading" for follow-on attacks, then it is equally prudent to expect the demands of dealing with the aftermath of an event to grow commensurately—perhaps "only" cumulatively at the local level, but probably exponentially at the country and international level as state leaders confront an overwhelming volume of "day after" demands.[62] At any level, the response to a biological terror campaign in particular will be resource-intensive in ways not fully understood today. Assistance from outside one's own borders almost certainly will be critical. How well a state can respond to an event and how well it can effectively communicate with its people in the face of a terror campaign will be far more challenging, and may lead to a lack of public confidence if not handled professionally and in a timely, accurate manner. All the keys to public information success will be more difficult to achieve when the threat is characterized by multiple events, perhaps with a variety of agents, and perhaps geographically dispersed.

What are the possible elements of a strategy directed at countering and preparing for a biological terror campaign? In the context of an extended terror campaign, states need to demonstrate their ability to adapt and steadily improve their response to multiple attacks, particularly with respect to public health, risk communication, and the maintenance of social order. Strengthening resilience is also an important, if less tangible, imperative here, to include the psychosocial factors relevant to coping with prolonged stress and the ability to respond to incidents both efficiently and compassionately. Just as important is to attack the adversary's ability to adapt—for instance, by denying him information, funding, training capacity, and strategic partners. This may be a more effective strategy against a terrorist organization than a true terrorist network, which is likely to command greater resources and exhibit greater resilience. Additionally, certain topics that generally have been taboo need to be discussed seriously. Confronting issues such as quarantine, triage, and martial law may not be avoidable, however uncomfortable these discussions may be.

CONCLUSION: PROLIFERATION CONTROL MUST GO BEYOND SOVEREIGNTY

The threat from the proliferation of weapons of mass destruction is global, networked, adaptable, and facilitated by private actors like A. Q. Khan who seek to benefit financially by exporting the world's most dangerous technology. Individual states cannot solve the WMD problem single-handedly, let alone hope to safeguard their own borders isolated from important global actors, be they public or private. Because of this, proliferation control regimes premised on state-to-state agreement are likely to fail since they ignore the growing threat posed by non-state actors and the role the private sector plays in proliferation, wittingly or not. It is not enough to wish the NPT were "more verifiable" or to hope difficult states will cooperate more fully with the IAEA in the future. Indeed, the fundamental underpinnings of nonproliferation agreements are that states will fulfill their international commitments and that they have the capacity to do so, retaining the ability to control what goes on within their borders. But is this a viable reality? There are too many failing or failed states; too many opportunities for global networks, designed for speed, efficiency, and security in ways governments are not, to act globally.

To combat weapons of mass destruction, the cost to proliferators for engaging in this illicit activity must be raised exponentially. To do this, traditional nonproliferation activities must be expanded, but the key very well might be found in the private sector. It is on their networks—their ships, planes, and trucks—and through their financial institutions—investment banks, insurance, transshipping concerns—that illegal weapons and components are moved and paid for, and it is here that the process of proliferation, while arguably at its most automatic, may also be most vulnerable.

Certainly, states and corporations have different interests, motivations, and capabilities. But without engaging the private sector and finding mutual areas of interest to combat WMD, state-based initiatives alone are likely to be late and less likely to succeed in today's global threat environment.

ENDNOTES

1. United Nations Secretary General Kofi Annan, Message to the General Conference of the Mayors for Peace commemorating the sixtieth anniversary of the atomic bombings of Hiroshima and Nagasaki, delivered in Hiroshima by Nobuyasu Abe, Under-Secretary General for Disarmament Affairs, August 4, 2005.

2. United States President George W. Bush, Introduction, *The National Security Strategy of the United States of America* (Washington: GPO, 2002).

3. Arrangements for Libya's disarmament involve the United States, the United Kingdom, the International Atomic Energy Agency (IAEA), and the Organization for the Prohibition of Chemical Weapons (OPCW). See "Lessons from Libya and North Korea's Strategic Choice," John R. Bolton, Undersecretary of State for Arms Control and International Security. Remarks presented to Yonsei University Graduate School of International Studies, Seoul, Republic of Korea, July 21, 2004.

4. The Khan network, in addition to laboratories in Pakistan, involved suppliers and middle-men in Dubai, France, Germany, Italy, Japan, Malaysia, The Netherlands, South Africa, Spain, Switzerland, Turkey, United Arab Emirates, and the United Kingdom. The network's business dealings are believed to be valued in the low hundreds of millions of dollars with countries that include Libya, Iran, and North Korea.

5. National Strategy to Combat Weapons of Mass Destruction, *NSPD-17/HSPD 4,* December 2002.

6. Joseph Cirincione, Jon B. Wolfsthal, and Miriam Rajkumar, *Deadly Arsenals,* Carnegie Endowment for International Peace (Washington, DC: The Brookings Institution Press), 43.

7. Ibid.

8. "Bin Laden 'has nuclear weapons,'" BBC, November 10, 2001, <http://news.bbc.co.uk/1/hi/world/south_asia/1648572.stm>.

9. Central Intelligence Agency, "Terrorist CBRN: Materials and Effects," June 2003, 4.

10. Central Intelligence Agency, "Terrorist CBRN: Materials and Effects," June 2003, 4; U.S. Nuclear Regulatory Commission, "Fact Sheet on Dirty Bombs," March 2003.

11. RDDs could use Cesium-137, Strontium-90, or Cobalt-60, for example.

12. Central Intelligence Agency, "Terrorist CBRN: Materials and Effects," June 2003, 4; U.S. Nuclear Regulatory Commission, "Fact Sheet on Dirty Bombs," March 2003.

13. Dan Eggen and Susan Schmidt, "'Dirty Bomb' Plot Uncovered, U.S. Says; Suspected Al Qaeda Operative Held as 'Enemy Combatant,'" *Washington Post*, (June 11, 2002): A1.

14. Thomas R. Wilson, "Statement for the Record to the Senate Armed Services Committee on Global Threats and Challenges," March 19, 2002, 18; Counterproliferation Program Review Committee, *Report on Activities and Programs for Countering Proliferation* (Washington, DC: Department of Defense, May 1995), 8; Barry Erlick, Testimony before the Permanent Subcommittee on Investigations of the Senate Committee on Governmental Affairs, in U.S. Senate, *Global Spread of Chemical and Biological Weapons,* S. Hrg. 101–744 (Washington, DC: U.S. Government Printing Office, 1990), 33.

15. *Proliferation: Threat and Response;* John R. Bolton, "Beyond the Axis of Evil," Remarks Made at the Heritage Foundation, May 6, 2002.

16. See, variously, Central Intelligence Agency, *Unclassified Report to Congress on the Acquisition of Technology Related to Weapons of Mass Destruction and Advanced Chemical Munitions, 1 January Through 30 June 2001,* January 30, 2002; *Proliferation: Threat and Response*; John R. Bolton, "Beyond the Axis of Evil," Remarks Made at the Heritage Foundation, May 6, 2002.

17. The official title of the Biological Weapons Convention is "The Convention on the Prohibition of the Development, Production, and Stockpiling of Bacteriological (Biological) and Toxin Weapons and on Their Destruction." It entered into force on March 26, 1975.

18. Article I, Biological Weapons Convention, is the Convention on the Prohibition of the Development, Production and Stockpiling of Bacteriological (Biological) and Toxin Weapons and on their Destruction, 1975.

19. The official title of the Chemical Weapons Convention is "The Convention on the Prohibition of the Development, Production, Stockpiling and Use of Chemical Weapons and on Their Destruction." It entered into force on April 29, 1997.

20. Lowell E. Jacoby, Statement before the Senate Select Committee on Intelligence, February 11, 2003. In U.S. Congress Senate Select Committee on Intelligence, *Current and Projected National Security Threats to the United States*. 108th Congress, 1st session (Washington, DC: GPO, 2003), 7–8.

21. *Proliferation: Threat and Response,* 57.

22. Central Intelligence Agency, *Unclassified Report to Congress on the Acquisition of Technology Related to Weapons of Mass Destruction and Advanced Chemical Munitions, 1 January Through 30 June 2001,* 30 January 2002; *Proliferation: Threat and Response,* 36, 45.

23. Central Intelligence Agency, *Unclassified Report to Congress on the Acquisition of Technology Related to Weapons of Mass Destruction and Advanced Chemical Munitions, 1 January Through 30 June 2001,* 30 January 2002; *Proliferation: Threat and Response,* 47.

24. See, for example, Patrick E. Tyler, "American and British Weapons Experts Return to Libya," *The New York Times* (January 20, 2004): A3; Anton LaGuardia, "Western Experts Arrive to Begin Disarming Libya," *Daily Telegraph* (London), (January 20, 2004): 11; Stephen Fidler, "Libya to Admit Weapons Inspectors," *Financial Times* (London) (February 3, 2004): 11; and Stephen Fidler, "Libya Had Sizeable Chemical Weapons Programme," *Financial Times* (London), (February 7, 2004): 8.

25. *Proliferation: Threat and Response,* 11, 15.

26. Ibid. 28.

27. Nations in this category could include Egypt, Israel, and Vietnam, among others. For additional information, see, for example, Joseph Cirincione, Jon B. Wolfstahl, and Miriam Rajkumar, *Deadly Arsenals: Tracking Weapons of Mass Destruction* (Washington, DC: Carnegie Endowment for International Peace, 2002), 52; U.S. Congress, Office of Technology Assessment, *Proliferation of Weapons of Mass Destruction: Assessing the Risks,* OTA-ISC-559 (Washington, DC: U.S. Government Printing Office, August 1993), 65, 80–81.

28. "Qaeda Videos Seem to Show Chemical Tests," by Judith Miller, *The New York Times* (August 19, 2002); "Al Qaeda video tapes obtained by CNN," CNN, August 19, 2002.

29. Blix, *An Update on Inspection to the Security Council.*

30. David Kay, Statement on the Interim Progress Report of the Iraq Survey Group, Before the House Permanent Select Committee on Intelligence, the House Appropriations Committee Subcommittee on Defense, and the Senate Select Committee on Intelligence, October 2, 2003, <http://www.cia.gov/cia/public_affairs/speeches/2003/david_kay_10022003.html>.

31. David Kay, Testimony on Iraqi Weapons of Mass Destruction Before the Senate Armed Services Committee, January 28, 2004.

32. "Nanomaterials Show Signs of Toxicity," *Science* 300 (April 11, 2003): 243, <www.ece.neu.edu/edsnu/mcgruer/nano/nanotoxicityscience0304.pdf>.

33. For more information, see Center for Counterproliferation Research, "Anthrax in America: A Chronology and Analysis of the Fall 2001 Attacks," November 2002.

34. See George Tenet, Testimony Before the Senate Select Intelligence Committee on Intelligence on the Worldwide Threat: Converging Dangers in a Post 9/11 World, February 6, 2002.

35. Peter Baker, "Pakistani Scientist Who Met Bin Laden Failed Polygraphs, Renewing Suspicions," *Washington Post* (March 3, 2002).

36. Center for Counterproliferation Research, *CBRN Terrorism: An Annotated Bibliography* (Washington, DC: National Defense University, November 2002), 4–5.

37. Douglas Frantz, "U.S. and Pakistan Discuss Nuclear Security," *The New York Times* (Oct. 1, 2001): A3; John J. Fialka and Scott Neuman, "Will Pakistan's Warheads Stay Secure? If a War Topples Leader, Control Is Uncertain; Some Call Threat Slim," *Wall Street Journal* (Oct. 4, 2001): A17; Paul Richter, "Pakistan's Nuclear Wild Card," *Los Angeles Times* (Sept. 18, 2001): A2; Nigel Hawkes, "Pakistan Could Lose Control of its Arsenal," *Times* (London), September 20, 2001, n.p.

38. "Terrorist CBRN: Materials and Effects," Central Intelligence Agency, Directorate of Intelligence, May 2003, 1.

39. "The Worldwide Threat 2004: Challenges in a Changing Global Context." Testimony of Director of Central Intelligence George J. Tenet before the Senate Select Committee on Intelligence, 24 February 2004 (as prepared for delivery), 4.

40. "The Worldwide Threat 2003: Evolving Dangers in a Complex World." Testimony of Director of Central Intelligence George J. Tenet before the Senate Select Committee on Intelligence, 11 February 2003 (as prepared for delivery), 4.

41. Tenet, 2004, 4.

42. Tenet, 2004, 4.

43. This memo was discovered in 2001 on a computer acquired by the *Wall Street Journal* that had been used by al-Qaeda members in Afghanistan. Government officials are reported to have confirmed the authenticity of the files found on the computer's hard drive, which also contained a table of lethal doses for poisons according to body weight and a list of disease agents, including anthrax. See "Al-Qaeda: New Evidence of Chemical and Biological Weapons Pursuit," *Global Security Newswire,* January 2, 2002.

44. Remarks by the President on Weapons of Mass Destruction Proliferation, National Defense University, February 11, 2004.

45. United Nations Security Council Resolution 1540 (2004) Adopted by the Security Council at its 4956th meeting on April 28, 2004.

46. Informally known as the "10 + 10 over 10" program, the G-8 agreed in 2002 to commit $20 billion over ten years—half from the United States—toward WMD threat reduction in the former Soviet Union. Decisions taken at the 2004 G-8 summit envision more nations contributing to an effort that extends beyond the former Soviet Union.

47. According to the Nuclear Threat Initiative under the Atoms for Peace Program, twenty metric tons of highly enriched uranium was distributed in more than 100 civilian reactors and other facilities in forty countries. While the vast majority of this material is not a security risk, some of it is.

48. Paul Kerr, "IAEA Cites Iran on Safeguards Failures," *Arms Control Today* (Oct. 2005), <www.armscontrol.org/act/2005_10/OCT-IAEAIran.asp>.

49. The Additional Protocol is designed to improve the IAEA's ability to detect clandestine nuclear programs in non-nuclear weapons states by providing the Agency with increased information and expanded access to nuclear fuel cycle activities and sites. The Additional Protocol grants the IAEA the right to conduct no-notice inspections at any facility, declared or not. See "The IAEA 1997 Additional Safeguards Protocol," *Arms Control Association Fact Sheet,* September 1999.

50. The president also proposed the following: creation of a special committee of the IAEA Board of Governors to focus intensively on safeguards and verification, and denying rotating membership on the board (and the special committee) to any state under investigation for proliferation violations.

51. David E. Sanger and Thom Shanker, "Reluctant U.S. Gives Assent for Missiles to Go to Yemen," *The New York Times* (Dec. 12, 2002): A1.

52. Bush, Statement, December 11, 2002, <www.whitehouse.gov/news/releases/2002/12/20021211-8.html>.

53. Bush, Remarks to the People of Poland, May 31, 2003, <www.whitehouse.gov/news/releases/2003/05/20030531-3.html>.
54. Albright, op. cit.
55. John R. Bolton, Keynote Address at The American Enterprise Institute Panel: "The International Atomic Energy Agency: The World's Enforcer or Paper Tiger?" September 28, 2004, <www.aei.org/events/eventID.911,filter./transcript.asp>.
56. On February 11, 2004, the United States signed a shipboarding agreement with Liberia, a major flag of convenience state. This agreement provides authority on a bilateral basis to board vessels suspected of carrying WMD and delivery means materials. Similar agreements are being pursued with other flag of convenience states.
57. President George Bush, Speech to the Students and Faculty of National Defense University, Ft. Leslie McNair, Washington, DC, February 23, 2004.
58. Libya claims losses of only $3 billion.
59. Undersecretary of State John R. Bolton spoke to this point in remarks in July 2004, particularly in reference to North Korea's clandestine uranium program and its insistence on maintaining a "peaceful" nuclear program: "We are interested in a lasting and meaningful solution to the threat posed by North Korea's nuclear weapons program . . . halting ongoing nuclear programs can only make sense when it is explicitly and credibly part of a clear plan leading to rapid dismantlement . . . North Korea's continued denial of its uranium enrichment program precludes a solution . . . [A]nd the United States knows that North Korea's nuclear programs are primarily intended to support its nuclear arms program. This is why we insist that the dismantlement of their programs must be complete, verifiable, and irreversible." "Lessons from Libya and North Korea's Strategic Choice," remarks at Yonsei University, Seoul, South Korea, 21 July 2004.
60. According to British press accounts, in August 2004 Iran issued an extraordinary list of demands to its British, French, and German interlocutors. These demands include access to advanced nuclear technology, provision of conventional weapons, and "security assurances" against nuclear attack (presumably from Israel). What concessions Iran would make on the nuclear issue was not clear. See Anton La Guardia, "Hand Over Nuclear Weapons and Know-How, Iran Tells Britain," August 11, 2004, <www.telegraph.co.uk>.
61. Speaking in August, National Security Adviser Dr. Condoleezza Rice said: "I do think that there are very active efforts underway . . . to undermine the ability of the Iranians under the cover of civilian nuclear cooperation to get the components that would help them for nuclear weapons developments." Meet the Press, August 8, 2004. In the context of the interview, this comment implied that Israel is engaged in such efforts.
62. The "re-load" phenomenon is discussed in Richard Danzig, "Catastrophic Bioterrorism—What Is To Be Done?" A report of the National Defense University Center for Technology and National Security Policy, August 2003. See pp. 1–2.

CHAPTER TWELVE

Globalization and the Environment

Teng Fu

For hydroelectric power companies and local governments in Yunnan, southwest China, the proposal to build thirteen large dams on the Nu/ Salween River was expected to be approved without any complication, as the plan came at an opportune time. China's rapid development and its soaring demand for energy has brought a new wave of enthusiasm for the construction of hydroelectric power plants. Few places are better positioned for hydroelectric development than Yunnan, where rivers and waters have always been abundant, compared to the more populated and dry areas in East and North China. Necessary capital and technology for dam development should be easy to obtain, particularly with the central government's "Go West" development strategy in place, which aims to drive both Chinese and foreign investment for infrastructure projects into western areas of the country. China is keen on large dam construction, and boasts itself as amongst the world leaders in dam civil engineering, especially for undertaking the Three Gorges Dam project, the world's largest.

However, the surprise came when China's Premier Wen Jiabao did not approve the proposal and postponed the project until the environmental impact assessment had been completed. Environmental journalist Wang Yongchen won the Conde Nast Traveler Environmental Award, a prize of $20,000, for her coordination of a massive campaign that temporarily halted the construction of these thirteen dams.[1]

The anti-dam campaign involves Chinese environmental organizations, such as Green Volunteers and Green Watershed; Chinese research institutes, such as the Chinese Academy of Social Sciences; Chinese media; China State Environmental Protection Administration (SEPA); regional and international environmental and anti-dam NGOs and foundations, such as Thai and Burmese NGOs and affected people's organizations, Rivers Watch East and Southeast Asia and International Rivers Network; and UNESCO World Heritage Centre. These transnational actors spoke with one voice, used different channels of communication, and successfully influenced the Chinese government's decision-making on the proposed thirteen large dams on the Nu/Salween River.

The opposition based its advocacy on the norm of "sustainable development" that "meets the needs of the present without compromising the ability of future generations to meet their own needs."[2] Development is not merely an economic issue. Social and environmental dimensions should be integrated in the overall consideration of development. Nine of the thirteen dams proposed would be located in the Three Parallel Rivers World Heritage Site composed of Nu/Salween River, Jinsha (Upper Yangtze), and Lancang (Upper Mekong) Rivers. The site is regarded as one of the richest temperate regions of the world, nurturing more than 6,000 plant species and supporting over 50 percent of China's animal species. Additionally, millions of people from at least twenty ethnic minority groups in Yunnan, China, and downstream riparian communities in Thailand and Myanmar have depended on the watershed for fishing and farming for generations. The 21.32-gigawatt 13-dam project (greater than the scale of the Three Gorges Dam with a capacity of 18.2 gigawatts) would trigger substantial environmental and social impacts, such as biodiversity loss and involuntary resettlement.

This case highlights three main themes that this chapter will explore. First, the causes, effects, and solutions of environmental problems increasingly are moving beyond state sovereignty. One state's behavior can influence the regional and global environment. States are more likely to face transsovereign environmental problems that one state, acting alone, is unable to mitigate. Second, the collision between economic development and environmental protection is real. Globalization exacerbates the conflict between quick development and environmental protection by spreading economic integration based on the principles of market liberation. Third, globalization, at the same time, alleviates global environmental problems by empowering transnational advocacy networks that represent the interests of traditionally weak actors. The emergence and rise of these transnational advocacy networks present hope for a more balanced and environmentally friendly globalization.

OVERVIEW OF GLOBAL ENVIRONMENTAL PROBLEMS

This section first offers a survey of some pressing global environmental problems, including global warming, hazardous wastes, and global biodiversity loss. It then discusses the difficulties involved in solving global environmental problems.

Environmental problems have drawn growing public attention over the last several decades. With the global trend of industrialization and the rise in population, the damaging impact of human activities on the natural environment is startling.

The world population reached more than 6 billion in 2000, up from 2.5 billion in 1950.[3] The earth will need to support another 5 billion people before the human population stabilizes between 10.5 and 11 billion after 2050. Almost all of the future population growth will be in developing states. Feeding, housing, and supporting such a huge population will put enormous stress on land, water, energy, and other natural resources. Due to increasing demand for food and loss of arable land resulting from over-intensive cultivation, the need for agricultural land is expanding, which exerts the greatest threat to forests, wetlands, mountains, and biodiversity. Agriculture also dominates global water use. Nearly half of the world's people will experience water shortages by 2025, as water use increases with economic development, particularly for industrial and municipal use, in addition to agricultural irrigation. Water withdrawals and pollution further degrade natural ecosystems, as about half of all wetlands world-wide have been lost and more than 20 percent of the world's 10,000 known freshwater species are extinct, threatened, or endangered. Most of the increase in energy demand is still served by fossil fuels, although renewable energy usage is growing. As fossil fuel consumption and emissions of carbon dioxide, the major greenhouse gas, continue to rise, the result, according to some researchers, is a warming of the earth's surface at an unprecedented rate. The impacts of climate change could have serious implications for food security, freshwater supplies, human health, and species survival.[4]

Global Warming

Global warming is arguably one of the most pressing and controversial environmental problems. Despite existing scientific complexity and uncertainty in the field, human-induced climate change is identified to be caused by anthropogenic emissions of greenhouse gases such as carbon dioxide and methane. Atmospheric CO_2 concentrations have increased 31 percent since 1750, due primarily to human activities such as fossil fuel combustion and deforestation, according to the Third Assessment Report (2001) of The Intergovernmental Panel on Climate Change (IPCC), established by the World Meteorological Organization and the United Nations Environmental Program in 1988.[5] The assessed signs of climate change include the following:

❑ Global average surface temperatures have increased by about 0.6 degree Celsius since 1900, with the 1990s being the warmest decade on record.

❑ Sea levels are rising by about 1 cm per decade.

❑ Arctic sea ice thickness has declined 40 percent in the past 40 years.

❑ Major glaciers throughout the world are retreating.

❑ Lake ice is forming later in the autumn and melting earlier in the spring.

❑ Precipitation in the Northern Hemisphere has increased, particularly as intense rainfall.

❑ El Nino events have become more common and more intense.[6]

Changes in climate could have major influences on ecosystems, hydrology, water resources, food production, coastal systems, and human health.[7] Global warming would change the rainfall and temperature patterns, increasing the intensity and frequency of severe weather events, such as droughts, hurricanes, and floods. Ecological systems and the mix of species that they contain would have difficulty adapting to the new environment. Such changes would affect soil characteristics and disturbance regimes (e.g., fires, pests, and diseases), favoring some species over others and changing the natural composition of ecosystems. Moreover, whereas periodic and chronic shortfalls of water caused by climate change could impose additional burden on countries located in arid and semi-arid regions, flooding and associated damages, such as dam and levee failures, are likely to become a larger problem in many temperate and humid regions. Furthermore, climate changes would influence the length of growing seasons and the timing of extreme or critical threshold events relative to crop development, impacting agriculture and food production. Potential detrimental changes in diseases, pests, and weeds are suspected as well, though their effects have not yet been quantified in most available studies. Coastal systems will be directly affected through sea-level rise and increase in storm-surge hazards. Currently, an estimated 46 million people live in areas that are at risk of flooding from storm surges. Climate changes will only exacerbate these problems, leading to disastrous impacts on ecosystems and human coastal infrastructure. Climate changes, in all, could affect human health through increases in heat-stress mortality, tropical vector-borne diseases, urban air pollution problems, and decreases in cold-related illnesses. Though it is unclear whether the intensity and frequency of hurricanes along the U.S. coast during the summer of 2005 were caused by climate changes,[8] the aftermath of powerful hurricanes such as Katrina and Rita can demonstrate the potential kinds of damage global warming can cause, especially when these kinds of extreme weather events happen simultaneously on a larger scale.

Hazardous Wastes

Hazardous waste control is another important example of global environmental problems. With industrialization came record high levels of the production of toxic, explosive, flammable, and other types of hazardous wastes. As environmental awareness rose in developed countries during the 1970s, domestic regulations regarding waste disposal became stringent, giving strong incentives for exporting hazardous wastes to developing countries with lower labor costs, less local opposition, and less-strict environmental laws that were often loosely enforced.

The North-South shipments of hazardous wastes drew public attention with several notorious incidents of illegal dumping.[9] In one case, the cargo ship Khian Sea spent almost two years at sea in search of a disposal site for 14,000 tons of incinerator ash containing lead and cadmium that had originated in Philadelphia, PA. Eventually, the ship dumped 4,000 tons of ash on a beach in Haiti and the remaining 10,000 tons somewhere between the Suez Canal and Singapore.[10] Another example was the 1987 Koko, Nigeria case. Toxic industrial wastes from Italy were exported to Nigeria based on a deal struck between an Italian businessman and a Nigerian. The Nigerian resident was told the wastes were merely miscellaneous construction materials, and so he stored them in the backyard of his property. The scandal broke out when barrels of waste began leaking into the surrounding area, causing various health problems for residents and workers exposed to the highly toxic substances.[11]

Loss of Biodiversity

Yet another pressing area demanding environmental protection is species diversity. Recently, the known rate of extinction among mammals and birds has accelerated far beyond the estimated average rate through geological time.[12] Twenty-four percent of mammal species and 12 percent of birds were considered globally threatened in 2000. According to the Living Planet Index (LPI), which measures overall trends in populations of wild species around the world, one third of the world's biodiversity has been lost since 1970.[13]

One of the richest, yet most threatened, sources of biodiversity is the forest, particularly rainforest ecosystems.[14] Rainforests exist mainly in the tropics of Latin America, Africa, and Asia. Besides being home to an incredible amount of biodiversity, including endangered species such as the orangutan, sumatran tiger, and scarlet macaw parrot, rainforests play an important role in regulating climate, conserving soil, and storing and purifying water. Yet, human activities, such as logging, plantation development, cash crop cultivation, urbanization, and construction projects are destroying forests at an unprecedented rate. Every year, an area of rainforest the size of England is cut down.[15]

Another finding of scientists assessing the status of biological diversity is that inland waters are suffering most from human activities at present. "The two major documented extinction events in the twentieth century both took place in inland water ecosystems."[16] The Mobile Bay, Alabama, drainage in the U.S. was one of these events. The drainage basin used to be home for 9 families and around 120 species. However, after extensive dam construction, including 33 major hydroelectric dams and many smaller impoundments, as well as locks and flood control structures, at least 38 species are believed to have become extinct since the 1930s and 1940s. This kind of catastrophic impact on the diversity of freshwater snail fauna is likely to have been repeated at a smaller scale in many other, less well-documented, parts of the world.[17]

Challenges of Environmental Preservation

These international environmental trends are alarming, yet the transsovereign nature of the environmental problems complicates attempts to solve them. While part of the definition of sovereignty is a state's ability to control its land and other natural resources, increasingly natural resources may be degraded by global environmental trends that states are poorly positioned to control or respond to individually. The transboundary causes, effects, and potential solutions of such global problems present great challenges for global environmental protection.

First, global environmental problems are global commons problems. The old story of "the tragedy of the commons" took place in the historic commons, a centrally located pasture open to anyone for grazing livestock.[18] The "tragedy" occurred when each owner increased his or her herds to maximize benefits from the communal pasture. As the pasture was overgrazed, these herdsmen eventually destroyed the commons and their means of survival. Whereas the entire group would likely have benefited from limiting the number of grazing animals, with no institutional mechanism in place, none of the herdsmen had the incentive to limit their consumption of the common good when they were not sure if others would do the same. At the heart of this lack of motivation to cooperate in achieving common interests is the free-rider problem: if people know that they can enjoy benefits without contributing any effort, they choose not to contribute and thus free-ride on others' efforts.

Our natural environment is a global commons that transcends political borders. No single state can own or control air, water, or climate. States must thus share these "free" goods. The problem is that for the sake of development, the natural environment has been bearing the external cost that is not accounted for in the cost-benefit consideration of these economic activities. One country's reckless development may abuse and pollute critical common resources shared by many (as both raw materials and as sinks for pollution). Even worse, the resulting degradation may be disproportionably distributed, damaging other countries more seriously than the polluter state itself. The acid rain problem between Canada and the U.S. illustrates this point. Power plants in the Midwest region of the U.S. emitted pollution that traveled to Canada and caused acid rain damage on lakes and forests. Stricter restrictions on sulfur dioxide emissions in Canada could hardly protect the welfare of its citizens, because the major polluters were in the U.S. The cost and benefit of U.S. power development was asymmetrically distributed between two sovereign states.[19]

Second, the structure of the international political system does not allow the use of third-party enforcement—Hobbes' classic solution to problems of collective action—to protect the global environment. While coercive enforcement can be used by a ruler to obtain taxes, labor, or other resources for the common good of the state, there is no supranational entity or world government with recognized authority to punish violators and maintain order in the global environmental policy area. The anarchic nature of the international system precludes the use of third-party enforcement as a solution to governing the global environment.

Third, the alternative solution of "stable institutions of self-government" is compromised by the uneven economic development of states. The gap between the rich and the poor countries of the world is enormous, and this north–south divide (developed countries versus developing countries) complicates the establishment and functioning of global environmental institutions.[20] Developing countries argue that the developed countries have exploited natural resources for their own purposes in the past and are responsible for most of the world's present pollution and resource depletion, including ozone depletion and climate change. Environmental protection is viewed as an effort by developed countries to forestall the economic growth of the South. While the North emphasizes environmental issues that threaten ecological stability, the South focuses on immediate needs for economic growth to survive and improve standards of living. The difference in the needs and policy agendas of the North and the South makes it difficult to reach consensus on international environmental policies.

Such was the major argument made by the G-77 and China during the international climate negotiations. The resulting principle of "common but differentiated responsibilities" acknowledges that while the protection of climate for present and future generations is an obligation for all members of the international community, industrialized and formerly communist countries with economies in transition have a responsibility to take the lead in addressing climate change.[21] The responsibility comes from their high historical emission of greenhouse gases and the assumption that they possess the financial and technological capabilities to control those emissions.

Fourth, environmental issues often involve scientific complexity and uncertainty that make reaching consensus on environmental protection policy difficult.[22] The lack of certainty on the scope, severity, and time frame of individual problems makes it difficult to infer causation, to attribute responsibility, and to design solutions. More certain economic and political interests often take advantage of this lesser certainty, dominating the policy-making arena. Climate change, biodiversity loss, and ocean fish stocks are examples of issues where scientific uncertainty obstructs progress in international negotiations.

GLOBALIZATION EXACERBATES GLOBAL ENVIRONMENTAL PROBLEMS

Globalization integrates capital and knowledge worldwide. With revolutions in communication and transportation technologies, information, capital, and values are able to travel more rapidly and easily throughout the world. The worldwide division of labor and specialization based on comparative advantage contribute to the increase in efficiency and growth in economies.[23]

These globalizing forces, based on liberal market principles, exacerbate global environmental problems. Market forces unleashed by globalization create various social and environmental concerns. Riding the globalization tide, market and landed private actors have assumed stronger roles in the decision-making process, often dominating social and political outcomes. Unfortunately, in this manner, the opportunities and rewards of globalization often are spread unequally, concentrating power and wealth in a select group of people and marginalizing others.[24] Moreover, to a large number of developing regions and countries, comparative advantages point to natural resources and raw materials. Engaging in global trade for survival and quick development relies on the utilization of these natural resources. As a result, environment and sustainability are put as lower priorities after economic development. Economic development is then expected to benefit the poor and the environment through the "trickle-down effect."

For example, by the 1970s, the dominant industrialization mindset of "first development, then environment" viewed large infrastructure constructions, including dam projects, as the means to achieving fast development. Development was perceived as man's conquest of nature. Dam construction, particularly, symbolized human progress from a life controlled by nature to the triumph of science over nature.

Dam advocates cross borders. They include transnational epistemic communities of engineers and scientists, multinational corporations, international development banks, and national bureaucrats, and economic globalization connects them. The International Commission on Large Dams (ICOLD) was established by a group of engineers, developers, and bureaucrats to collect information and coordinate the exchange of knowledge about big dam construction around the world in 1929. Multinational corporations such as Asea Brown Boveri, Siemens, GEC Alsthom, Kvaerner, Bechtel and others grew rapidly during the 1950s and 1960s. The World Bank, Food and Agriculture Organization, United Nations Development Program, Inter-American and Asian development banks also played major roles in promoting the big dam industry. Bilateral aid agencies, such as the U.S. Agency for International Development and British Overseas Development Administration, were additional sources of funding and planning of these dam projects, in partnership with bureaucratic agencies in the development-oriented countries.[25]

Funding and technologies of large dam building were transferred through "open economies" and "open technologies" to developing countries in Latin America and Asia.[26] But the conventional wisdom of building large-scale dams to generate power and control floods has become suspect in the developed world during the last thirty years. Large dams, in particular, have been blamed for environmental destruction by environmentalists in the North (particularly in the United States, Sweden, and France)—the classic industrialization/modernization without any consideration for sustainability, economic equity, or justice. Therefore, as domestic environmental and social impact regulations in Western developed countries tightened, the large dam industry moved its attention to developing countries where rules were lax.

In this way, globalization potentially creates a "race toward the bottom" in setting environmental standards. Countries with lax environmental standards not only produce pollution and damage the global environment, but also put pressures on countries with high environmental standards in the global market competition.

Differences in the U.S. and Latin American levels of economic development and environmental standards are among the central concerns of critics of the North American Free Trade Agreement (NAFTA), Central American Free Trade Agreement (CAFTA), and the proposed Free Trade Agreement of the Americas (FTAA). With much lower environmental standards and looser enforcement mechanisms, Mexico may receive or "suck" U.S. pollution.[27] Even when local communities realize the environmental injustice and make efforts to reverse the negative impact, free trade requirements provide protection for multinational corporations. Metclad, a U.S. company, took full advantage of the NAFTA free trade agreement in its case against a Mexican municipality. After discovering the dumping site chosen by Metclad was a critical source of ground water that provided drinking water for the community, the Mexican municipality refused to grant a building permit to Metclad. However, the NAFTA Tribunal backed Metclad under a chapter of NAFTA and required compensation for violation of the agreement by the federal government of Mexico.[28] The loss of regulatory power of governments on events that have large social and environmental impact, in the face of free trade agreements, may well open the door for further global environmental abuse.

On the other hand, free trade rules also threaten countries with relatively high environmental standards. Embracing the market liberation principles for economic development, developing countries often view environmental regulations promulgated by environmentalists in developed countries as a new type of trade protectionism scheme, and use market liberation principles to get away with their bad environmental standards. In the 1991 "tuna/dolphin" case,[29] the U.S. Marine Mammal Protection Act required an embargo on Mexican tuna, because fishermen used tuna nets that killed dolphins. Yet, a GATT dispute resolution panel in Geneva declared the embargo illegal under the rules of international trade, which caused environmentalists to condemn the cruelty of trade liberation principles.

GLOBALIZATION ALLEVIATES GLOBAL ENVIRONMENTAL PROBLEMS

Market liberalizing forces spread by economic globalization contribute to a power imbalance between private interests and public interests, and between short-term interests and long-term interests. The state, which used to be considered a vehicle for protection of public interests, is losing both economic and political control, facing the rising power of private-sector and business organizations. The future restoration of the power balance seems to lie in the emergence and growth of transnational advocacy networks that are empowered by globalization as well.

Transnational advocacy networks usually involve international and domestic non-governmental organizations, regional and international inter-governmental organizations, parts of the governments, media, and intellectuals that are bound together by "shared values, a common discourse, and dense exchanges of information and services."[30] These transnational advocacy networks make joint efforts in persuading, socializing, and pressuring states and international organizations to change their norms and behaviors with respect to issues beyond sovereignty, such as the environment. They blur the boundaries between sovereign states by building new links among domestic, regional, and international actors through pursuit of common issues and values. Margaret Keck and Kathryn Sikkink outline a few tactics these networks use:

> (1) *Information politics,* or the ability to quickly and credibly generate politically usable information and move it to where it will have the most impact; (2) *Symbolic politics,* or the ability to call upon symbols, actions, or stories that make sense of a situation for an audience that is frequently far away; (3) *Leverage politics,* or the ability to call upon powerful actors to affect a situation where weaker members of a network are unlikely to have influence; and (4) *Accountability politics,* or the effort to hold powerful actors to their previously stated policies or principles.[31]

So far, such networks have been successful in bringing about discursive and procedural changes by sharing resources and multiplying channels of access to international and domestic systems. They have played an indispensable role in promoting the norm of "sustainable development" and monitoring the implementation of principles and procedures such as environmental impact assessment.

The 1972 and 1992 United Nations Conferences heralded a change in the norm of development. The classic industrialization mindset of "first development, then environment" was gradually replaced by the norm of "sustainable development." Sustainable development was first regularized and institutionalized, at the international level, through the creation of the United Nations Environment Program, the first environmental unit at the World Bank—which eventually became the Office of Environmental and Scientific Affairs (OESA)—and an environmental wing of ICOLD after the 1972 United Nations Conference on the Human Environment in Stockholm, Sweden. It was further affirmed through the formation of the United Nations Commission on Sustainable Development, a Vice-Presidency for Environmentally Sustainable Development at the World Bank, and the Global Environmental Facility after the 1992 United Nations Conference on Environment and Development in Rio de Janeiro, Brazil.[32]

At the national level, the global normative framework of sustainable development was applied through the establishment of national environmental bureaucracies and the institutionalization of procedures such as environmental impact assessment.[33] Not a single national environmental bureaucracy existed before the 1972 U.N. Conference. But environmental agencies and ministries were established at a rapid rate thereafter, with about 60 by 1988, another 40 around 1992, and more than 100 by 1995. Procedures such as environmental impact assessments have spread along with the formal establishment of these bureaucratic agencies, prompting the inclusion of environmental evaluation as an essential part of the planning and implementation of development projects.

First, transnational advocacy networks contribute to the diffusion of these norms and practices by disseminating ideas and information, and soliciting and transferring needed resources across borders through the same technological and economic instruments globalization offers. The "debt for nature swaps" practice exemplifies innovative efforts of transnational environmental networks facilitated by open economies and technologies.[34] The negotiations of the practice usually involve, at a minimum, a sovereign state (the debtor country), a donor organization headquartered in another country, and a private creditor agency. Part of the developing country's debt is redeemed by nongovernmental conservation organizations in return for that country using funds to protect the rainforest or other conservation work. The first case was Conservation International from the U.S. trading Bolivian debt for the expansion and long-term management of the Beni Biosphere Reserve. Though the redemption is usually less than the face value of the debt, private banks are still willing to sell it because of the need to satisfy stockholders and preserve the bank's credit rating. In this way, a win–win situation emerges, as the debtor country is more than willing to shed part of the debt burden and the transnational environmental group is happy to make constructive moves toward the preservation of nature.[35]

Second, transnational environmental networks empowered by globalization challenge international capital markets face to face. Multilateral development banks increasingly claim to address environmental protection objectives in their loans and have eliminated environmental high-risk projects in the project evaluation stage. Aside from the adoption of the discourse on sustainable development, considerable procedural changes have also been implemented. Environmental impact assessments are practiced more seriously at all multilateral banks now.

For example, the transnational anti-dam network has focused on multilateral bank campaigns in pushing forward ideas of environmental protection, social justice, and human rights. A series of anti-dam struggles during the 1980s and 1990s against the World Bank signaled the start of efforts in reforming bank practices in project finances. Campaigns against World Bank-funded dam projects from Nam Choan in Thailand to the Xingu River in Brazil to the Sardar Sarovar Project in India's Narmada Valley played a leading role in restricting the Bank's involvement in large dam projects and adopting new policies regarding resettlement, environmental assessment, effects on indigenous people, and information disclosure.[36]

These policies formed the basis for the Equator Principles, a voluntary initiative launched in 2003. The initiative stipulates environmental and social guidelines for private banks in project financing.[37] A growing number of international banks, including Citigroup, HSBC, and ABN Amro, have agreed to follow these principles, developing guidelines that prevent them from providing loans to projects that cause environmental damage and harm to local people.

Currently, the transnational anti-dam network strives to apply the Equator Principles to indirect financing, including bond issuance.[38] International Rivers Network and Friends of the Earth recently alerted the public that, by coordinating and underwriting bonds for China Export-Import Bank, global banks, including Merrill Lynch, HSBC, Citigroup, BNP Paribas, and Goldman Sachs, helped finance socially and environmentally destructive projects in Sudan and Burma that they could not directly finance under their own environmental policies. When private banks have already made progress in reducing negative impacts of development projects by committing to the Equator Principles in direct loan practices, the challenge from transnational network groups in bond issues demonstrates the continuing efforts of these groups in promoting the norm of sustainable development.

Third, transnational advocacy networks are more likely to influence states' decisions and to discourage behaviors that are potentially destructive to the global environment. The coming-together of domestic, regional, and international groups expands the space of activism and multiplies channels of access to both domestic and international systems. Domestic groups are empowered by the global sharing of information and resources. Meanwhile, international groups, with the linkage to local actors, are able to legitimize their activities and gain better insights on transsovereign issues. With the global spread and institutionalization of such norms as sustainable development, transnational advocacy networks seize and exploit modest political opportunities with enough other resources (strong social networks and powerful symbols). The modest opportunity is widened for more social and environmental changes, when the government makes initial tactical or genuine concessions. Eventually, serious discursive and procedural changes will take place.

The Nu/Salween River case at the beginning of this chapter may display the first transnational advocacy network that successfully affected China's decision-making on matters of internal development. Indeed, during the anti-Three Gorges Dam campaign, international environmental groups were vocally involved. However, there was no cooperation or coordination on the level of a transnational advocacy network. International advocacy groups did successfully dissuade some international banks and associated corporations from joining the construction. Yet, the Chinese government proceeded without significant international investment. Thus, a closer review of the Nu/Salween case offers an important example for understanding how globalization assists the efforts of transnational networks in global environmental protection, especially considering the facts that China is the world's fastest developing state, and economic development has been the paramount priority of the government.

The public campaign to protect the Nu River was arguably initiated by SEPA, a Chinese central government institution. On the Nu River project, poignant disagreement exists between SEPA and the National Development and Reform Commission (NDRC). NDRC approved the proposed project as early as August 2003, while officials from SEPA strongly opposed it. According to Wang Yongchen, the award-winning environmental reporter with the Central People's Radio Station and head of the Chinese environmental group called the Green Earth Volunteers, it was an official with SEPA that called her and requested assistance from more scientists who were familiar with the Nu River. The official hoped to build a strong alliance to reinforce SEPA's battle against NDRC.[39] Indeed, a strong anti-dam alliance was built—one that transcended state boundaries.

In addition to public forums, study tours, photo exhibits, petition letters, and other awareness-raising activities through Web sites and e-mails domestically,[40] Chinese environmental groups, journalists, and scientists built up their connection with downstream anti-dam groups at the Rivers for Life Second International Meeting of Dam-Affected People and Their Allies in Rasi Salai, Thailand, in late November and early December 2003.[41] The meeting was organized by Assembly of the Poor (Thailand), International Rivers Network (USA), and Southeast Asia Rivers Network (Thailand). It was funded by a group of international NGOs and foundations, including Action Aid Asia, the Ford Foundation, Novib, Oxfam America, Siemenpuu Foundation, and the Swedish Society for Nature Conservation. More than 300 activists and dam-affected people from over 62 countries attended the meeting, exchanging ideas and strategies and sharing experiences. It was at this meeting that Chinese activists made the initial contacts with downstream and international anti-dam activist groups and coordinated future campaigns.

Chinese environmental groups' participation in the Rivers Watch East and Southeast Asia consolidated the transnational cooperation on the campaign against the Nu/Salween River dam project. Rivers Watch East and Southeast Asia is a network of NGOs from the region, supported by their international allies, working to stop destructive river development projects in East and Southeast Asia and to restore rivers to the communities that depend on them.[42] During the anti-dam campaign on the Nu/Salween River, the network collects and disseminates updated news on the status of the planned dam project on the Internet and through e-mails. It provides a forum for network actors to learn previous anti-dam experiences in other areas.

Moreover, over 80 people's groups in Thailand and Myanmar, coordinated by the Southeast Asia Rivers Network, wrote a petition to the Ambassador of the Chinese Embassy in Thailand in December 2003, saying that the dams would bring devastating effects for people downstream.[43] Another letter of concern to the President of China, Hu Jintao, was signed by over 76 organizations from 33 countries in March 2004.[44] The letter emphasized that dam projects in the area "risk drastic impacts to all of these (environmental) resources" and that consultations with downstream riparian residents and affected communities need to be conducted according to international standards before any decisions are made.

Meanwhile, the International Rivers Network informed UNESCO, warning them of the possible impacts of the planned 13 dams on the Three Parallel Rivers World Heritage Site. Francesco Bandarin, Director of the UNESCO World Heritage Centre, sent letters of concern to both Tian Xiaogang, Secretary-General, Chinese National Commission for UNESCO, and Zhang Xinsheng, Chairperson of the World Heritage Committee c/o National Commission of the People's Republic of China for UNESCO in February and March 2004, respectively. The letters expressed serious concern about the potential threats such development projects could pose to the World Heritage Site and emphasized the necessity to carry out the environmental impact assessment on such hydropower projects. They also urged the Chinese government to provide information regarding the environmental impact assessment report for review by the World Conservation Union (IUCN), the advisory body to the World Heritage Committee on natural heritage. In addition, the letters brought attention to China's obligations under the World Heritage Convention and requested further information concerning the current policy regarding this World Heritage Site.[45]

Next, Conservation International's China Office coordinated a joint letter to the 28th session of the World Heritage Committee held in July 2004 and the UNESCO World Heritage Centre, calling on them to act on the Nu River dam plan.[46] Conservation International's China Office held a symposium on Southwest Dams and Biodiversity Conservation in June, and gathered 43 representatives from 23 NGOs and research institutes from across China. After the symposium, the letter was drafted and signed by the participants, including Green Watershed, Green Earth Volunteers, scientists from Yunnan University, Sichuan Provincial Academy of Social Science, China Academy of Social Science, and village representatives from Nu River Prefecture and Manwan, Yunnan.

At the 28th session of the World Heritage Committee in July 2004, IUCN's report raised concerns about the potential direct or indirect environmental and social impacts of dam construction in or around the Three Parallel Rivers site. The World Heritage Committee, in turn, expressed its grave concerns and invited the Chinese authorities to respond to the appeals by academics, scientists, and conservationists in China. Since that session, IUCN and UNESCO continued to express serious concerns, seek clarification on the 13-dam hydropower development proposal, and emphasize that the environmental impact assessment should be comprehensive and open to wide participation.[47]

During the anti–dam campaign, the media has also played a significant role in furthering the cause of the campaign. The debates on dam projects and the latest development of the Nu/Salween River project have received considerable coverage from "Green Net" of the *China Youth Daily, South China Morning Post, China Electricity Power Newspaper, China Central TV, Hong Kong Phoenix TV station, China National Geography Magazine, International Herald Tribune, The New York Times,* and other media.[48] Such media reports and broadcasts provide the general public with access to participate in state policy debates. The close monitoring of the media also facilitates the efforts to hold traditionally powerful actors, such as power companies and government officials, accountable to international standards on sustainable development.

CONCLUSION: A MORE BALANCED GLOBALIZATION?

The transnational anti-dam campaign against the Nu/Salween River dam project continues, as the environmental impact assessment remains incomplete. The State Council of China has not approved the project. Regardless of the result, however, the transnational anti-dam network on the Nu/Salween River has already been successful in postponing the planned construction of 13 large dams. With open economies, technologies, and societies, the network has been successful in mobilizing and sustaining the anti-dam campaign over the last couple of years.

Global environmental issues are transsovereign problems by nature. Globalization, with its opening of economies, technologies, and societies, can aggregate the inherent difficulties in solving such transsovereign problems. Unrestrained human activities are the root causes of many environmental problems. Globalization allows the classic dilemma between development and environment to be staged on a larger scale, from national to regional and global.

Fortunately, globalization also empowers traditionally weak actors by connecting them to the world more quickly and easily. The emergence and rise of transnational advocacy networks, such as "debt for nature swaps" and anti-dam coalitions, signal the potential for a more balanced globalization. The capacity of these non-state actors working together on issues beyond sovereignty is built on, and will further contribute to, the global spread and institutionalization of norms such as sustainable development.

ENDNOTES

1. Woodrow Wilson International Center for Scholars, "Environmental Journalist Stops Plans to Dam China's Last Untamed River," October 12, 2004, <www.wilsoncenter .org/index.cfm?fuseaction=events.event_summary&event_id=96093>, accessed on September 20, 2005.
2. United Nations Department of Economic and Social Affairs, Division of Sustainable Development, "About US," <www.un.org/esa/sustdev/about_us/aboutus.htm>, accessed on August 20, 2005.
3. United Nations Department of Economic and Social Affairs, *Global Challenge, Global Opportunity: Trends in Sustainable Development,* Publication for the Johannesburg Summit 2002.

4. Michele M. Betsill, "Global Climate Change Policy: Making Progress or Spinning Wheels?" in Regina S. Axelrod, David Leonard Downie, and Norman J. Vig, (Eds.), *The Global Environment: Institutions, Law, and Policy* (Washington, DC: CQ Press, 2005), 103–124.

5. Contribution of Working Group I to the Third Assessment of Report of the Intergovernmental Panel on Climate Change (IPCC), "Summary for Policymakers," *Climate Change 2001: The Scientific Basis* (Cambridge: Cambridge University Press, 2001), <www.grida.no/climate/ipcc_tar/wg1/006.htm>, accessed September 26, 2005.

6. United Nations Department of Economic and Social Affairs, *Global Challenge, Global Opportunity: Trends in Sustainable Development;* IPCC, *Climate Change 2001: The Scientific Basis.*

7. Robert Watson, Marufu C. Zinyowera and Richard H. Moss, *IPCC Special Report on The Regional Impacts of Climate Change: An Assessment of Vulnerability,* <www.grida.no/climate/ipcc/regional/503.htm#overview>, accessed September 24, 2005.

8. The evidence is mixed; while the frequency of hurricanes appears average, more of those hurricanes are more intense category 4 and 5 storms than ever before.

9. David Downie, Jonathan Krueger, and Henrik Selin, "Global Policy for Hazardous Chemicals," in Regina S. Axelrod, David Leonard Downie and Norman J Vig (Eds.), *The Global Environment: Institutions, Law, and Policy* (Washington, DC: CQ Press, 2005), 128–129.

10. "A Slow Burn," *Philadelphia Inquirer* (April 6, 1998), A14; James Ridgeway and Gaelle Drevet, "Dumping on Haiti: How Thousands of Tons of Philadelphia's Toxic Waste Ended Up on a Haitian Beach, and What the City of New York Is Doing About It," *The Village Voice* (Jan. 13, 1998).

11. "Hazardous Waste Trade, North and South: The Case of Italy and Koko, Nigeria," Pew Case Studies, Georgetown University Institute for the Study of Diplomacy, <www.guisd.org>.

12. *Global Biodiversity Outlook* (Montreal, Canada: Secretariat of the Convention on Biological Diversity, 2001), <www.biodiv.org/gbo/chap-01/chap-01-04.asp>, accessed on September 24, 2005.

13. World Wide Fund for Nature, *Living Planet Report 2004* (Gland, Switzerland: World Wide Fund For Nature, 2004), <www.panda.org/downloads/general/lpr2004.pdf>, accessed on September 24, 2005.

14. Friends of the Earth, "Biodiversity: Disappearing Forests," <www.foe.co.uk/campaigns/biodiversity/issues/disappearing_forests/>, accessed on September 26, 2005.

15. World Resources Institute, "Global Forest Watch," <http://forests.wri.org/globalforestwatch-project-58.html>; Rainforest Action Network, "Rates of Rainforest Loss," <www.ran.org/info_center/factsheets/04b.html>.

16. *Global Biodiversity Outlook.*

17. Ibid. The other one is "Lake Victoria, shared by Kenya, Tanzania and Uganda, was until recently the home of a species flock of around 300 halpochromine cichlid fishes, of exceptional scientific interest, as well as of a number of other fish species. Following introduction of the Nile Perch *Lates niloticus,* and possibly also as a result of a range of other factors, at least half and up to two-thirds of the native species are now believed extinct or nearly so, with virtually no chance of recovery."

18. Garrett Hardin, "The Tragedy of the Commons," *Science* (Dec. 13, 1968): 1243–1248.

19. Dr. Vicki Golich, "United States-Canadian Negotiations for Acid Rain Controls," Pew Case 452, Georgetown University Institute for the Study of Diplomacy, available online at <www.guisd.org>.

20. Norman J. Vig, "Introduction: Governing the International Environment," in Regina S. Axelrod, David Leonard Downie and Norman J. Vig (Eds.), *The Global Environment: Institutions, Law, and Policy* (Washington, DC: CQ Press, 2005), 5.

21. Michele M. Betsill, "Global Climate Change Policy: Making Progress or Spinning Wheels?" in Regina S. Axelrod, David Leonard Downie, and Norman J. Vig, (Eds.), *The Global Environment: Institutions, Law, and Policy* (Washington, DC: CQ Press, 2005), 108–109.

22. David Leonard Downie, "Global Environmental Policy: Governance through Regimes," in Regina S. Axelrod, et al. (Eds.), *The Global Environment*, 74.

23. Maryann K. Cusimano, "Globalization: A Virtue or a Vice?" in Siamack Shojai (Ed.), *Globalization: A Virtue or A Vice?* (New York: Praeger Publishers, 2000).

24. U.N. Development Program, *Human Development Report 1999* (New York: Oxford University Press, 1999), 1–8; Ignacio Ramonet, "Dueling Globalization: Let Them Eat Big Macs," *Foreign Policy* (Fall 1999): 126.

25. Patrick McCully, *Silenced Rivers: The Ecology and Politics of Large Dams* (London: Zed Books, 1996).

26. For a detailed description of the changing dynamics of dam buildings in these countries, see Sanjeev Khagram, *Dams, Democracy, and Development: Transnational Struggles for Power and Water,* Ph.D. dissertation, Stanford University, August 1999, 3.

27. Ross Perot, *Save Your Job, Save Our Country: Why NAFTA Must Be Stopped—Now!* (New York: Hyperion, 1993).

28. Maryann Cusimano Love and Richard Love, "Multinational Corporations: Power and Responsibility," Chapter 5 in *Beyond Sovereignty* (Belmont, CA: Wadsworth/Thomas Learning, 2006).

29. Daniel C. Esty, *Greening the GATT: Trade, Environment, and the Future* (Washington, DC: Institute for International Economics, 1994), 34.

30. Margaret Keck and Kathryn Sikkink, *Activists Beyond Borders: Advocacy Networks in International Politics* (Ithaca, NY: Cornell University Press, 1998).

31. Ibid.

32. Sanjeev Khagram, *Dams, Democracy, and Development: Transnational Struggles for Power and Water,* 25.

33. Ibid.

34. Vicki Golich, "The Nature of the Nature Problem: Environmental Interdependencies," in Maryann Cusimano Love (Ed.), *Beyond Sovereignty: Issues for a Global Agenda* (Belmont, CA: Wadsworth/Thomson Learning, 2003), 288–289.

35. Ibid.

36. Sanjeev Khagram, *Dams, Democracy, and Development: Transnational Struggles for Power and Water,* 275; Robert Wade, "Greening the Bank: The Struggle over the Environment, 1970–1995," in Davesh Kapur, John P. Lewis, and Richard Webb (Eds.), *The World Bank: Its First Half Century* (Washington DC: The Brookings Institution, 1997), Volume 2.

37. Megan Rowling, "Bond Issue Sounds Ethical Alarm," BBC, August 9, 2005.

38. Ibid.

39. Deng Jin, "Huanbao Xinliliang Dengtai de Taiqian Muhou" (Background of the Emergence of New Environmental Protection Force), *Nanfang Weekend,* (Jan. 27, 2005), <www.nanfangdaily.com.cn/zm/20050127/jj/jjxw/200501270033.asp>.

40. Yang Guobin, "Is There an Environmental Movement in China? Beware of the 'River of Anger,'" *Active Society in Formation: Environmentalism, Labor, and the Underworld in China,* Woodrow Wilson International Center for Scholars Asia Program Special Report (Sept. 2004), 4.

41. Aviva Imhof, Campaigns Director, International Rivers Network, phone interview, August 18, 2005.

42. Rivers Watch East and Southeast Asia, <www.rwesa.org/>.

43. Southeast Asia Rivers Network, "Petition to China from 83 organizations from Thailand/Burma on Upper Salween Dam," <www.searin.org/Th/SWD/SWDletE2.htm>.

44. Doris Shen, "Letter to President Hu Jintao," International Rivers Network, March 4, 2004, <www.irn.org/programs/nujiang/nu_hujintao_letter.pdf>.

45. Paragraph 56 of the Operational Guidelines for the Implementation of the World Heritage Convention states, "The World Heritage Committee invites the States Parties to inform the Committee, through the UNESCO Secretariat, of their intention to undertake or to authorize in an area protected under the Convention, major restorations or new constructions which may affect the World Heritage value of the property. Notice should be given as soon as possible (for instance, before drafting basic documents for specific projects) and before making any decisions that would be difficult to reverse, so that the World Heritage Committee may assist in seeking appropriate solutions to ensure that the World Heritage value of the site is fully preserved." Letters on file with author.

46. "23 Chinese groups write to World Heritage Committee over Nu River dam plan," e-mail communication on file with author.

47. IUCN Letter to Kevin Yuk-shing Li, February 25, 2005.

48. Wang Luxiang, "Da Jiangtang: Nujiang Shuidian Kaifa de Weixie" (Threats from the Nu River Hydropower Construction), *Phoenix TV,* June 28, 2004, <http://210.51.8.60/home/zhuanti/fhxd/sjdjt/200406/28/282671.html>; Jim Yardley, "Beijing Suspends Plan for Large Dam," *The New York Times* (April 8, 2004), <www.irn.org/programs/nujiang/index.php?id=041304_ihtnyt.html>; Jim Yardley, "Dam Building Threatens China's Grand Canyon," *The New York Times* (March 10, 2004), <www.irn.org/programs/nujiang/index.php?id=041304_nyt.html>.

CHAPTER THIRTEEN

Mind the Gaps

Global Problems Outpace Institutions

Maryann Cusimano Love

"The human family is a dysfunctional family. What is needed is a network of structures, institutions, principles and elements of law to help manage in the best possible way the world's common good, which cannot be protected only by individual governments."[1]

—Archbishop Diarmuid Martin, Archbishop of Dublin and Former Vatican Representative to the United Nations and Specialized Agencies in Geneva

"A world connected by trade and technology must be bound by common values."[2]

—Mary Robinson, Executive Director, Realizing Rights: The Ethical Globalization Initiative; UN High Commissioner for Human Rights, 1997–2002; President of Ireland, 1992–1997

Every year, 8 million people die of AIDS, tuberculosis, and malaria, primarily in poor countries—approximately one Holocaust each year.[3] In one hospital in Malawi, a trickle of patients with money come in one end of the building, pay $1 a day, and receive the life-saving triple cocktail medication that manages their HIV and AIDS. The other end of the hospital corridor is where most of Malawi's AIDS patients go. Too poor to afford the $1 treatment, they are brought to the hospital not for medicine or care but to die. They are warehoused four to a bed, two head to foot on the mattress, and two on the floor below. Families gather to say goodbye, and the hospital waits for the disease to run its deadly course as other patients are treated just steps away.

This scenario is repeated every day throughout sub-Saharan Africa and developing countries in a life-and-death example of institutional gaps. The public health and government institutions of these regions do not have the capacity to save their citizens. Other countries have public health institutions with greater capacity, but Malawi's problems are beyond their jurisdiction.

Because of sovereign jurisdictions, other governments do not regard it as their responsibility to help the dying. Governments have promised more funds to the Global Fund to Treat AIDS, Tuberculosis, and Malaria than they have delivered.[4] Until the Doha meeting, World Trade Organization (WTO) rules protected the profits of pharmaceutical companies more forcefully than they protected the lives of the sick and poor—and denied affordable generic drugs because of WTO rules that protected pharmaceutical patents.[5] Today, more lenient WTO rules allow governments to license generic production of essential medicines to fight public health emergencies. But this does little to aid the sick in Malawi, where the average life expectancy is thirty-seven years and more than half the population lives below the poverty line.[6] Malawi is too poor to produce generic drugs locally. Although a few multinational corporations (MNCs) have pledged to sell their medications at reduced prices, these prices are still beyond the purchasing power of the poor in Malawi. Millennium Development Goal 6 aims to combat HIV/AIDS, to stop the spread of HIV/AIDS by 2015 and begin reversing it, but according to the WHO, developing countries are not on track to meet these targets. Eighty-eight percent of those needing antiretroviral drugs in developing countries receive no treatment.[7] Less than 1 percent of those needing HIV/AIDS drugs in Africa receive treatment.[8]

As a heavily indebted, poor country, Malawi has implemented structural adjustment programs required by the international financial institutions (IFIs) since the 1980s, cutting public spending internally (including on health care and education needed for HIV and AIDS treatment) in order to increase external debt repayment.[9] Such actions have led to legitimacy gaps as the poor of the world question whether the WTO and other IFIs rightly represent their interests. It also is evidence of an ethical or values gap, as the market values pursued by pharmaceutical companies, governments, and IFIs are at odds with the important societal value of saving human life. UN Secretary-General Kofi Annan notes, "It is a shocking fact that, out of the 1,233 drugs licensed in the world between 1975 and 1997, only 13 were for tropical diseases, and only four were commercially developed specifically for tropical diseases suffered by human beings."[10] At the same time, many more drugs were created for developed markets for non–life threatening afflictions such as acne. The disparity results from market assessments of who can pay rather than from medical assessments of pressing human needs. Efficiently functioning markets can still allow millions to die. Markets create profits. They do not solve all human problems.

INSTITUTIONAL GAPS

Global economic and technological change is fast, while government, legal, and intergovernmental responses are slow. This creates institutional gaps between the problems of globalization and attempts to manage them.[11] These institutional gaps are growing, tall enough to swallow the twin towers of the World Trade Center and wide enough to make the Pentagon a quadrangle for a time. As on September 11, governments are often surprised by these gaps. For example, when the governments of the Philippines, Britain, and Japan wanted to combat problems of cyberthreats, they found they had neither the organizational nor the legal tools to do so.[12] They had to create new institutions.

Institutions range from "formal organizations, which have explicit rules and forms of administration and enforcement, to any stabilized pattern of human relationships and actions."[13] Generally agreed-upon societal norms and specific treaties or organizations with a routine way of doing business may be referred to as institutions. The institutions considered here, however, are a much narrower group: the organizations (whether unilateral or multilateral) that carry out foreign policy. By taking a narrower focus, we can examine theories of bureaucratic organizations as well as institutions writ large. Unlike the broader definition of institution (which can incorporate ideas, behavioral patterns, roles, and even ceremonies such as marriage), the institutions addressed in this chapter are specific in time and space. They have addresses. They are organizations that are generally arranged bureaucratically and hierarchically.

Existing states and international regimes are having difficulties coping with the challenges globalization brings because globalization creates and exacerbates institutional gaps. These institutional gaps fall into several categories: capacity, jurisdictional, participation, legitimacy, and ethical value. Capacity gaps are shortfalls in organizations or organizational strength, resources, personnel, competence, or standard operating procedures that hinder a state's ability to effectively respond to problems of globalization. Jurisdiction gaps are found when the writ of the problem extends farther than the authority of the institutions charged with responding to the problem. Participation gaps exist when people affected by globalization are excluded from partaking in the decision processes of managing or guiding globalization, earlier described as "democracy deficits." Legitimacy gaps are found when the institutions that manage or regulate globalization are not perceived by society as rightfully representing them. Ethical or values gaps arise when globalization is perceived either to have no ethical base or to promulgate values that are at odds with societal values or the common good.

All of the preceding chapters discussed capacity gaps, ways in which global problems challenge institutions' abilities to effectively respond. From containing terrorism to containing disease, capacity gaps vex state, multilateral, and private-sector institutions. Besides the problem of speed (institutions moving slower than global problems), there are other reasons why governments alone cannot effectively respond to globalization's problems. Many regimes have only shaky control over their respective territories. The last decade has seen an increase in the number of failed states and states destabilized by democratic and market transitions and internal conflict. Lack of institutional capacity and resources hamstrings many governments' abilities to respond to global problems.

Comparatively speaking, developed democracies are better equipped to meet the challenges of globalization because they have adaptive and well-resourced political and economic institutions that are capable of responding to the dislocations, disruptions, and unintended consequences that globaliza-tion brings. States with adequate educational and public health systems and access to technology, coupled with stable governance, allow people access, an on-ramp to the globalization highway. But for many developing and newly democratizing states, rule of law and political and economic institutions are weak; they lack the capacity and resources to respond to globalization's challenges. Even strong states may lack capacity, as growth in the private sector (legal and illegal) has outpaced growth in the public sector by design. Weak and strong states both have capacity gaps, as evidenced by the September 11 attacks. They are more severe for developing states, collapsing states, and states undergoing transitions.

Yet even strong states cannot manage global problems alone because the issues cross jurisdictional and territorial boundaries. Jurisdiction gaps are described throughout this book, arising when problems cross borders but governments are still constrained by borders in their abilities to respond. Cybercriminals and international terrorists attack from a distance. Bringing them to justice is complicated by these jurisdictional gaps. In addition, the private sector often has better information and technology for containing global problems, while public-sector capabilities lag behind. For example, the transportation and financial infrastructures exploited by the September 11 terrorists were all privately owned and operated, further complicating govern-ment's jurisdictional reach. Terrorism crosses international and public–private jurisdictions, making governmental responses necessary but insufficient to successfully manage these problems. As democratization and the Washington consensus spread liberal political and economic systems globally, more states find themselves constitutionally limited in what interventions they may undertake in the private sphere. IGOs are also increasing in number, resources, functions, and power, but IGOs and states alone cannot solve globalization problems because many of the factors that constrain individual states also constrain collections of states. This again creates gaps between what institutions can do and what they are needed to do.

Institutional gaps also exist between rich and poor. Generally, the wealthy have institutions with more capabilities to act on their behalf; the poor often do not.[14] The rural poor have less opportunity to access globalization's benefits. Poor countries and peoples face institutional gaps that fuel the increasing backlash against globalization. Lacking resources, the institutions of poor countries are disadvantaged when bargaining with more powerful countries' institutions over the rules and regimes that govern globalization. For example, although most of the planet's populations are poor people living in developing countries, multilateral institutions such as the WTO and WIPO often favor the intellectual property rights and profits of MNCs at the expense of the poor (through TRIPS and TRIMS).[15] In what developing countries refer to as "biopiracy," local farmers are being told they cannot continue practices of creating seed banks or certain traditional medicines without paying fees to MNCs who now own the intellectual property, patents, and copyrights for these. Although multinational pharmaceutical companies use the populations of developing countries for human testing of potential medicines in the research and development phases, these poor people and countries often do not share in the benefits of these medicines once they are approved because the poor cannot afford the cure.

Poor peoples and countries do not have adequate participation in the decision-making processes that channel globalization, from corporate boardrooms to annual World Economic Forum summits to the Group of Eight meetings. The thirty poorest member states of the WTO cannot afford to send delegations to represent and negotiate on their own behalf in Geneva. The participation gaps, capacity gaps, and asymmetric distribution of costs and benefits intensify dissatisfaction and backlash against globalization. Institutions that do not adequately protect developing countries and those that exclude them from decision-making processes are increasingly seen as illegitimate by those who are excluded. These various institutional gaps are self-reinforcing. Institutions must be perceived as legitimate to be effective, and participation gaps exacerbate legitimacy gaps, which in turn intensify capacity gaps.

The participation and legitimacy gaps also further the ethical and values gap. Many observers believe that corporations rule the world[16] and that globalization puts profits ahead of people. Although powerful multinational corporations seek profits, states seek wealth and development in globalization.

Many decry the degree to which rich states, particularly the United States, drive globalization, putting market values ahead of other values. Most of the world's poor are not citizens of the developed states, leaving rich states with no jurisdictional or perceived ethical obligations to the world's dispossessed. Thus, whether driven by powerful companies or powerful states, many observers decry the ethical basis of globalization, believing globalization is driven by an ethic of crass materialism and consumption or Western (especially U.S.) cultural imperialism.[17] To the extent that this ethos pervades globalization, many people suggest that the violence and backlash against globalization will increase, producing a world in which the benefits of globalization reach too few people and countries, making the dynamics of globalization politically unsustainable.[18]

The ethical gaps are large and growing. Today, more than half of the world's citizens are not receiving the benefits of globalization, either because they are not plugged into the global economy or because they do not have institutions that can advance or protect their interests as participants in the global economy. Human life is lost, human development unfulfilled, and creation destroyed. This disparity between those who benefit from globalization and those who are left behind or vulnerable to its challenges is increasing. The world's poorest populations are growing, while the populations of developed countries are stable or slightly declining with the graying of the baby boomers. For example, world population is expected to grow from its current 6 billion to 7.2 billion in the next fifteen years. Ninety-five percent of that population growth will occur in developing countries and in already stressed urban areas—megacities such as Lagos and Mexico City.[19] Therefore, globalization's moral and ethical problems will only intensify. The values gap is exacerbated by the legitimacy, jurisdictional, and participation gaps. As Benjamin Barber notes, we must combat a malevolent interdependence (of terrorists and human smugglers, etc.) with a benevolent "democratic architecture of interdependence."[20]

POLITICAL SCIENCE AND OBSTACLES TO ORGANIZATIONAL CHANGE

How can we build institutions that better address global problems and better protect and promote peace and prosperity for more people on the planet? How can we change institutions to address the institutional gaps exacerbated by globalization? Political scientists have many theories about institutional change, but most of them tend to be pessimistic, emphasizing the obstacles to changing institutions. This chapter will consider five approaches in the political science literature on institutional change, those of rationalists, reflectivists, institutionalists, bureaucratic and organizational theorists, and political psychologists.[21]

Rationalists

Rationalists stress that institutions are rational reactions to the environments that states face. States create institutions because it is in their interest to do so. They expect that benefits will flow to them from the institutional arrangements that will be worth the cost.[22] Institutions reflect the power, resources, and interests of states at the time of their creation (which is why Germany and Japan, defeated powers when the UN Security Council was created, do not have veto power or status as permanent members of the Security Council). States create institutions, and thus states can change institutions whenever they want, which usually occurs when the distribution of power or resources has changed.

Sunk costs are an obstacle to institutional change, however. States are attentive to how much time, attention, and resources they have already poured into an institution, and thus they are not likely to change institutions quickly or lightly. The other permanent members of the Security Council have few incentives to change the institution to now include Germany and Japan.

Reflectivists

Reflectivists emphasize that institutions are constructed based on ideas, norms, values, culture, and history.[23] For example, although the structure of the United Nations represented the interests of the World War II victors, it also reflected the lessons learned from the failure of the League of Nations. The structure of NATO represented not only the interest of containing the USSR's power, but also ideas about promoting democracy in Western Europe and cooperation among democratic states. States are not billiard balls moved only by power dynamics, and institutions are not mere puppets of states. An institution can assume a life of its own. Actors often do not know exactly what outcomes they want in advance, and value-based institutions help shape and create their interests. Ideas and norms change, and so institutions can change. But existing institutions will affect and constrain change.[24]

Institutionalists

Institutionalists stress the importance of history, path dependency, and chance. Actors never have the entire universe of possible organizational varieties from which to choose. They must choose from the options that are available to them; earlier selections narrow the options.[25] Even if another choice later appears more efficient, changeover costs may wipe out any gains. Gatekeeping and self-censorship are also obstacles to change. Dominant forms may actively work to keep out alternative forms, or alternatives may try to make themselves resemble the dominant form so they will be accepted into the system. People conceive of the world and themselves within current institutional frameworks (vertical linkages), and existing organizations have many standardized ways of doing business with other organizations (horizontal linkages). Vertical and horizontal linkages (concepts and relations with others) allow institutional structures to persist even after the circumstances created to deal with them have changed and institutions have become inefficient or outmoded. These links create formidable obstacles to institutional change.[26]

Change happens in fits and starts (punctuated equilibrium) and is constrained by the weight of existing organizational structures. Rapid change can occur unexpectedly if "a stable structure is stressed beyond its buffering capacity to resist and absorb [change],"[27] but such examples are rare because institutions actively influence the environment to promote their own survival. More often, old institutions are retrofitted to do new tasks. Even though these structures may not be the most efficient or logical way to tackle a new problem, the existing structure has the advantage of being available: "Credit cards can be used to open doors."[28] UN peacekeeping troops may be used to fight famine in Somalia; commercial airlines may be used as weapons. Having the tool often leads to its use.

Bureaucratic and Organizational Theorists

The bureaucratic and organizational approach stresses the role and effect of domestic and internal politics on institutional structures. Many theorists of this approach are "in-and-outers" in government service, so they focus on characteristics that policy makers and practitioners believe are important.[29] They describe bureaucratic organizations as semifeudal agencies, each fighting to protect its turf and to guard its missions, budgets, functions, personnel, resources, and autonomy. Internal conflicts may exist in organizations between bureaucratic chiefs and followers, but in general personnel are socialized (through training, standard operating procedures, and advancement incentives) into certain shared organizational viewpoints (vertical linkages).[30] Bureaucratic organizations may engage in strategic bargains with others. Agencies may give up subsidiary functions in order to protect primary ones. They may bow out of fights with more powerful agencies if they believe they cannot win and want to survive and preserve resources. But regardless of the specific strategy, organizations will seek to promote their own survival—and change will come slowly, in an incremental fashion, and when viewed as necessary to organizational survival. Change that is seen as threatening to the organization's missions, functions, budgets, autonomy, or personnel will be resisted.

Much of what is perceived as bureaucratic waste and inefficiency is actually the result of conflicting purposes given to public-sector organizations. Different expectations exist for public and private organizations. As Milton Friedman put it, "the moral responsibility of business is to make a profit."[31] Government organizations raise different expectations. We care about what they produce as well as how they produce it. In some cases, what is produced is so nebulous (national security, for example) and hard to measure that greater emphasis and constraints are placed on the process (which can be seen and measured). We may not be entirely sure what we want the military to do or how it may best produce national security, but we know a lot about how we expect the military to operate. For example, the U.S. military was under strict orders to integrate the armed services decades before the rest of American society integrated. We expect the marketplace to offer better treatment to those who can pay more. We expect the government to treat all citizens equally.

Because government bureaucracies face greater operational constraints than private bureaucracies, it is unrealistic to expect them to operate as efficiently as their private counterparts, but many organizational reform proposals are based entirely on this flawed premise. Proposals for UN and IMF reform focus on downsizing, defunding, and privatizing the existing machine for budgetary purposes (less is more, according to this view). Although cost savings, organizational efficiency, and simplified chains of command are all laudable goals, these reforms are not aimed at making the organization better able to manage global issues. Focusing exclusively on cutting budgets and bodies may actually hamper the United Nations' capacities to respond to global problems. Scholar James Q. Wilson is skeptical of trying to change organizations through additional regulations or external reorganization plans without parallel changes in internal incentives. If executives favor change, if they change the incentive structure (through training and promotion opportunities) to reward innovation and encourage the rank and file to innovate, then organizations may change—but such change will not be quick or easy.

Institutions are inherently political animals. Every organizational structure was created as a result of political negotiation enacted into law. Thus, every organization is based on the political coalitions that won out or the compromise that was reached in order to create an institutional structure. Powerful actors rarely get what they want because institutional structures represent compromise and bargaining among groups. In addition, institutions are not particularly adaptive or efficient in response to changes in the external environment:

> The choices about structure that are made in the first period, when the agency is designed and empowered with a mandate, are normally far more enduring and consequential than those that will be made later. . . . Most of the pushing and hauling in subsequent years is likely to produce only incremental change. This, obviously, is very much on everyone's minds in the first period.[32]

Structures may be quite ill-suited to organizational goals by design. In democracies, organizational structures were created by groups who wanted to address particular needs, curry favor with political constituents, or wrest power or functions from existing organizations. Controlling mechanisms were foisted on organizations by opponents who either did not want particular issue areas addressed or did not want the new organization to succeed or become too powerful, or sometimes by proponents of the original organization who, fearful that political opponents would control the organization at some future point, wanted to limit the damage the opponents could do. Changing institutions is therefore not about making more efficient structures, but about changing political balances. There are no easy answers—if they existed, they would have been implemented long ago:

> It would be nice to say that there is an easy way out of all this, that the nation can have an effective public bureaucracy if only it wants one. But this is probably not so. A bureaucracy that is structurally unsuited for effective action is precisely the kind of bureaucracy that interest groups and politicians routinely and deliberately create . . . [B]ecause they are forced to design bureaucracy through a democratic process, their structural choices turn out to be very different indeed from those intended to promote effective organization.[33]

Moe expects bureaucratic structures to be "grotesque" and "bizarre," not efficient or easily adapted. Ironically, this point is lost on many think tanks that produce many ideas of how to reform specific foreign policy organizations for greater efficiency and effectiveness without attention to changing the underlying political coalitions. Without the political support to bring them to fruition, these ideas often die on the vine.

Political Psychologists

Another helpful academic approach to understanding institutional change has been undertaken by political psychologists. These authors also stress the difficulty of changing conceptual or belief systems, and the ways in which outmoded beliefs can persist despite changes in external circumstances. Individual decision makers and small decision-making groups are important in international politics. People make policy, and people create and lead institutions, so people can bring about change. Conceptual change is necessary for institutions to change, but it does not come easily or precipitously, because change in beliefs is "gradual and ragged."[34]

For example, Deborah Larson studied the origins of Cold War ideas and institutions. For an extended period, policy makers themselves did not know what course of action to pursue and what to think about Soviet behavior and the nature of the new postwar world. They did not develop new beliefs in the abstract, but they were forced by circumstances to deal with the changed environment. They improvised and developed ad hoc policy responses, tinkering with a variety of sometimes contradictory approaches. Policy makers often knew their old ideas were inadequate, but they did not discard them quickly because they had no replacement theory. Decision makers were forced to act, and out of those actions they gradually developed new ideas, which they then used to justify their past and subsequent actions and to create new organizations. "Forged in the fires" of action and crisis, "ideology leads to the development of policy doctrines that become institutionalized through the creation of bureaucracies. In particular, the Cold War ideology underlay a vast expansion of the power and resources of the executive branch of the U.S. government."[35] Changing ideas made organizational change possible. Larson's account parallels our current period of institutional tinkering.

The literature agrees that change is difficult. It will be resisted by bureaucracies that see change as threatening to their missions, functions, budgets, personnel, autonomy, or standard operating procedures. Peripheral tasks will be easier to change than core tasks. In democratic systems, change can be initiated by legislators, prime ministers or presidents, interest groups, and voters, but even externally imposed changes need some degree of internal support if the proposed changes are to be carried out in accordance with the spirit of the law and not just its letter. Ideas may need to change before organizations can change, and they may change only through hands-on experience in grappling with a changed environment. Leadership, concepts, and coalitions are needed for change.

MACHIAVELLI WAS RIGHT: CHANGE IS THE ONLY CONSTANT

What is often overlooked in the literature's emphasis on the obstacles to organizational change are the facts that (1) change does occur, and (2) sometimes the same characteristics of bureaucratic and organizational behavior that are cited as obstacles to change can be marshaled to promote institutional change. It seems, after all these years, that Machiavelli is still right. Change is the only constant in politics. Perhaps the only thing organizations fear and resist more than change is their own obsolescence or threats to their survival. If organizations are seen as ineffective, outdated anachronisms, then they may have powerful incentives for reinventing themselves to survive with the changing times. It is not merely a matter of cosmetics. Organizations do not want to put their personnel or resources at risk. If older standard operating procedures are seen as no longer being able to protect personnel or resources, then organizations will have powerful incentives to change the way they do business. After September 11, there was little argument that institutions must change to better contain the threats of terrorism. The only debates have been over how best to do so.

Organizations do not want to appear outdated—and not just because they want to convince political decision makers of their validity, necessity, and fiscal worth. Although some bureaucrats may be concerned only with maintaining their paychecks, many others want to use their organizations to effectively perform tasks. Most bureaucrats consider themselves members of some profession, and their professional ethics prompt them to want to pursue effective action in their field. Thus, there will always be advocates for change within any institution: people who see better ways to do their jobs or who want to improve their institutions' abilities in a changing world.

Once these agents for change begin interacting with the environment, the results may be unpredictable. Gorbachev did not set out to dismantle the USSR. He tried to improve worker productivity and cut down on alcohol abuse on the job in an attempt to improve the performance of Soviet institutions. But the changes he unleashed had the unintended but eventual consequence of ending the Soviet empire.

As people engage in the process of changing institutions, the process may change the people as well. Perhaps you can't always get what you want in institutional structure. But if Larson is correct about how people revise their belief systems, then we may not know what we want until we engage in the process and begin to learn from experience. Thus, although action for change may come from individuals or political coalitions in alliance with reformers within institutions, the process may change as the institutions interact with the agents for change and vice versa.

Institutional change is occurring in fits and starts. As we experience the institutional gaps posed by globalization, new concepts for change, leaders, and coalitions are emerging to address globalization's gaps with the aid of reformers within organizations. Governments, multilateral institutions, and private institutions are hard at work, especially in addressing capacity gaps.

Developed country governments address capacity gaps by creating new bureaucratic organizations or changing old ones, changing laws and policies that direct these institutions, and adding resources. Poor countries have fewer resources to address their governments' capacity gaps, so IGOs and NGOs also work to bridge them. Multilateral organizations and NGOs address capacity gaps of state institutions in developing countries by offering technological assistance or training, for example, to bridge the digital divide. Although some businesses exploit low capacity in developing governments, most MNCs desire greater capacity in developing countries' institutions in order to have a stable and predictable business environment governed by rule of law. But poorer countries will always have fewer resources to fund their institutions, and in an effort to attract foreign direct investment may even forgo further tax revenues, further exacerbating capacity gaps.

State and multilateral institutions are increasingly trying to borrow or buy capacity from the private sector. Whether in deterring cyberthreats or terrorism, protection of critical infrastructure (largely privately owned and operated) requires the cooperation of the private sector. Governments and IGOs increasingly contract out to the private sector to provide key capacities. The Australian government, for example, hires a private company to run refugee camps. Private companies are de-mining Afghanistan and de-nuclearizing the arsenals of the former Soviet Union on behalf of the U.S. government. Through the voluntary Global Compact, Kofi Annan and the United Nations work to harness the capacity of businesses to fight environmental, human rights, and labor abuses. Working with the private sector has meant forming new collaborative networks to help monitor, report, and share information on problems; contribute to policy solutions; and implement policy to manage global problems. Across a variety of issue areas, diverse foreign policy institutions are widening their contacts and partnerships with the private sector.

Rather than creating entirely new state agencies to deal with global problems, existing institutions are developing new integrating and coordinating mechanisms that cross agency and public–private sector boundaries. For example, to avert Y2K-related problems globally, unprecedented public–private partnerships shared information about problems and best practices for solutions. Governments had neither the resources nor the know-how to tackle the problem, and most of the infrastructure to be protected was in the private sector. The private sector had selected sets of information but no forum by which to share that information across organizations and internationally. The costs of Y2K-related repairs were estimated at between $300 billion and $500 billion internationally. Problems still occurred. Some Italian prisoners had a century added to or subtracted from their jail sentences. France lost satellite communications with its troops in Bosnia. Four thousand U.S. small businesses failed to download Y2K compliant credit-card billing software and lost business while banks reversed erroneous double and triple credit-card charges to more than 40,000 customers who made purchases in the first days after the date change to 2000. But Russian nuclear missiles were not accidentally fired, air traffic control systems generally worked, and many other Y2K-related concerns were averted.[36]

Borrowing ideas from the private sector and from computer technology about connectivity, institutions are generally not trying to create large, new federal bureaucracies that attempt to control activities and impose policy solutions from the top down (as was done after World War II). Instead, state institutions are trying to serve as better facilitators, coordinators, and integrators of information and action across a wide variety of actors and issues. Networking may be difficult for government organizations because they are organized as hierarchical bureaucracies, whereas NGOs and other nonstate actors may not be. State institutions' roles, missions, functions, procedures, authority, accountability, and chains of command are often more clearly demarcated than those of nonstate actors. NGOs often have flatter and looser organizations, and bureaucratic government organizations may find it difficult to determine who's in charge. When a bureaucratically organized institution attempts to coordinate and integrate information and action with a less hierarchically organized institution, they may "talk past each other." The bureaucratic organization wonders how anyone can function in such fluid chaos without standardized ways of doing business. The nonbureaucratic organization wonders why the bureaucracy cannot be more flexible to the nuances of the emerging situation. Differences in communication, culture, and organization make networking difficult but not impossible, as when international bankers in the IFIs try to reach out more systematically to the NGO community.

To create new institutions or adapt existing institutions to better leverage the resources of the private sector, institutions must increasingly go not just beyond sovereignty but also beyond bureaucracy. Called *postbureaucratic organizations,* these organizational forms stress integrative and interactive networks that are based on ideas drawn from successful entrepreneurs and technologies.[37] Often when government reformers talk of moving beyond bureaucracy and "reinventing government," what they really mean is cleaning up bureaucracy and making government more like a business.[38] Despite the grandiose language of a "paradigm shift,"[39] these reforms really do not demolish bureaucracy but streamline and downsize overgrown and inefficient bureaucracy. Although it has some advantages, this approach is limited in how far it can go given the differences discussed earlier between businesses and governments. But some of the current reforms break down or circumvent bureaucracy's formal, rule-bound structures based on clear demarcations of hierarchy and office.

These postbureaucratic organizational forms are flatter and more adaptive, based not on hierarchical chains of command but on interdependent webs of actors.[40] The benefits of this type of structure are increased flexibility, increased information sharing regardless of rank or organizational affiliation, a greater emphasis on the job to be done than on bureaucratic rules or routines, and more fluid boundaries. These trends are facilitated by career patterns that no longer assume people will spend entire careers in one organization, and information technologies that allow the building of temporary networks of people who work together virtually on specific problems and may never meet face-to-face.[41] The problems are challenges in coordination, greater complexity, and questions of transparency and accountability.

These changes in organizational forms may help combat global problems. When the models of organization from business were large, cookie-cutter bureaucracies such as IBM, and when the external threat was a stable, monolithic, universal, hegemonic Cold War adversary, foreign policy organizations responded with large, bureaucratic, and hierarchical structures that heavily emphasized stable routines, rules, and standard operating procedures. Change makes sense now that external threats come from diffuse and decentralized networks such as terrorism and international crime. Institutions need to be organized as networks to better fight networks. Yet sustained leadership, fresh concepts, and new political coalitions are necessary to make these changes.

MIND THE GAPS: BRIDGING INSTITUTIONAL GAPS

Globalization is intensifying institutional gaps, and there are many obstacles to institutional change. Yet change *is* occurring. To address capacity gaps, states and nonstate actors are partnering in new ways and using new, more networked institutional forms. To address jurisdiction gaps, governments harmonize laws and develop new or strengthen existing international regimes to better manage problems that go beyond state borders and juris-dictions. To address participation gaps, IGOs try to include NGOs in some manner in their activities. To address ethical gaps, some IGOs, NGOs, and MNCs adopt voluntary codes of conduct. To address legitimacy gaps, IGOs are increasing transparency, primarily by posting information about their activities on Web sites. But Web sites and ad hoc codes of conduct and NGO forums are not enough to bridge these gaps. Powerful political coalitions continue to obstruct efforts to better address participation, legitimacy, and ethical gaps. NGOs often work to build new political coalitions to bridge these gaps through organizing grassroots support and direct-media cam-paigns that pressure democratic governments internally and externally, as well as applying direct pressure on MNCs to better address pressing global issues. Governments and IGOs are more concerned with capacity and juris-diction gaps than legitimacy, participation, and ethical gaps, but IGOs cannot be effective or sustainable if these other gaps are not addressed. Powerful governments and IGOs will be increasingly targeted for sometimes violent protests as long as these gaps worsen or go unaddressed.

In Lewis Carroll's classic story *Alice in Wonderland,* the white queen chastises Alice for an insufficient imagination and tells her that expanding her imagination requires daily practice. "My dear, sometimes I think six impossible thoughts before breakfast."

Perhaps during the stability of the nearly fifty-year Cold War period, our imaginations atrophied. We did not give our imaginations much practice, as indicated by an exchange in 1986 between then-director of the CIA Richard Gates and Senator Daniel Patrick Moynihan. The senator, a former academic, had noticed that all economic indicators from the Soviet Union seemed to be pointing to an end to the Soviet empire. No one in Washington agreed with Moynihan's analysis because the Reagan adminis-tration and Congress were involved in unprecedented peacetime defense spending levels in order to combat the "evil empire" of the Soviet threat. In a Senate Intelligence Committee hearing, Moynihan asked Gates what plans the agency was making for how to deal with a post-Soviet world.[42] Gates responded, "[M]y resources do not permit me the luxury of sort of just idly speculating on what a different kind of Soviet Union might look like."[43] He did not see the point of making plans for the impossible.

Today we find that the impossible has occurred. The Soviet empire col-lapsed, and a small band of nonstate actors brought thousands of deaths and billions in damages to the world's most powerful state.[44] Our thoughts have not caught up with the impossible. Like Alice, we have not figured out how to think about the strange new world into which we have unexpectedly fallen.

Markets and global problems are moving faster than institutional and conceptual responses to the challenges of globalization. Of all the obstacles to organizational change, the biggest one appears to be ourselves and our limited ways of thinking about our changed world. Too often the debates over globalization are portrayed as a choice between a globalization that puts profits over people versus no globalization at all. In reality, there are more choices than that. We do not have to choose between the current form of globalization, with its mix of benefits along with its excesses and problems, or a return to a more closed, isolated, and less interdependent world. Instead of debating over false choices, we can build institutions that better represent important values; better distribute the benefits of globalization; better mitigate the problems of open economies, open societies, and open technologies; and better protect and promote the common good, building a global infrastructure that advances more authentic human development.

Change is not easy, direct, or logical, and institutions created by democracies will not be efficient in the narrow economic sense. But these observations about the obstacles to change should not obscure the fact that change is occurring, even if it is hard-fought, long in coming, constrained by political parameters, and occurring unevenly in fits and starts. Institutions are minding globalization's capacity and jurisdictional gaps, though much work remains, especially with gaps in legitimacy, participation, ethics and values. If we learn by doing and we change our ideas about the world as a result of our actions in the world (not before our actions), then we will see greater change as a result of our experiences in the changed international environment. Attention to global issues can bring increased leadership, awareness, urgency, and changed concepts and coalitions toward the problem of institutional gaps, bringing more communication, cooperation, and coordination among a wide variety of public and private actors.

ENDNOTES

1. Archbishop Diarmuid Martin, speech to the "Humanizing the Global Economy" conference of the Catholic bishops of Latin America, Canada, and the United States, Catholic University, Washington, DC, January 28, 2002.
2. Mary Robinson, "The Ethical Globalization Initiative: Realizing Rights," <www.realizingrights.org/>; <www.eginitiative.org/>.
3. Jeffrey Sachs, *The End of Poverty* (New York: Penguin Press, 2005); Sachs, speech to the "Humanizing the Global Economy" conference of the Catholic bishops of Latin America, Canada, and the United States, Catholic University, Washington, DC, January 31, 2002.
4. The Global Fund to Fight AIDS, Malaria, and Tuberculosis, "Funding Gap 2005," <www.theglobalfund.org/en/funds_raised/funding_gap/>.

5. World Trade Organization (WTO), *Declaration on the Trips Agreement and Public Health,* November 14, 2001 (Doha), <http://docsonline.wto.org/> (search for "Declaration on the Trips Agreement and Public Health").

6. Central Intelligence Agency, "The World Factbook 2005," <www.odci.gov/cia/publications/factbook> (check under Malawi).

7. United Nations, September 2005, <http://unstats.un.org/unsd/mi/pdf/MDG%20 Book.pdf>.

8. WHO, Measuring Progress toward the Millennium Health Goals, September 2005, <www.who.int/mdg/measuring_progress/progress/en/index.html>.

9. WTO, "Trade Policy Reviews: Summaries and Conclusions," <www.wto.org/english/tratop_e/tpr_e/tp_rep_e.htm#malawi2002>.

10. UN Secretary-General Kofi Annan, address to the World Economic Forum, February 4, 2002.

11. Maryann Cusimano Love, "Globalization and Religion," International Studies Association annual meeting, Chicago, February 24, 2001; Maryann Cusimano Love, "Bridging the Gap: Globalization and Religion, and the Institutions of the U.S. Catholic Church," American Academy of Religions annual conference, Denver, CO, November 20, 2001; Maryann Cusimano Love, "Globalization and Religion," *Journal of Social Thought.*

12. Maryann Cusimano Love, *Public–Private Partnerships and Global Problems: Y2K and Cybercrime.* Paper delivered to the International Studies Association, Hong Kong meeting, July 2001.

13. Jack Knight, *Institutions and Social Conflict* (Cambridge, UK: Cambridge University Press, 1996), 2.

14. World Bank, "World Development Report 2006: Equity and Development," <http://wdsbeta.worldbank.org/external/default/WDSContentServer/IW3P/IB/2005/09/20/000112742_20050920110826/additional/841401968_200508263002017.pdf>.

15. WIPO is the World Intellectual Property Organization. TRIPS are Trade-Related Intellectual Property Rights, and TRIMS are Trade-Related Investment Measures.

16. David C. Korten, *When Corporations Rule the World* (West Hartford, CT: Kumarian Press, 1995); Richard Falk, *Predatory Globalization: A Critique* (Malden, MA: Blackwell, 1999); John Gray, *False Dawn: The Delusions of Global Capitalism* (New York: New Press, 1998).

17. Joseph E. Stiglitz, *Globalization and Its Discontents* (New York: W. W. Norton, 2003); Ignacio Ramonet, "Dueling Globalizations: Let Them Eat Big Macs," *Foreign Policy* (Fall 1999): 116–121, 125–127; Thierry Linard de Gueterchin, S. J., "A Christmas Present for the Ford Workers in the ABC of Sao Paulo," Centro Cultural de Brasilia: Global Economies and Culture Project, in conjunction with the Woodstock Theological Center, Georgetown University, Washington, DC, April 6, 1999; Dani Rodrik, *Has Globalization Gone Too Far?* (Washington, DC: Institute for International Economics, 1997).

18. Amy Chua, *World on Fire: How Exporting Free Market Democracy Breeds Ethnic Hatred and Global Instability* (New York: Anchor, 2004); James Mittelman, *The Globalization Syndrome: Transformation and Resistance* (Princeton, NJ: Princeton University Press, 2000); Mark Juergensmeyer, "The Worldwide Rise of Religious Nationalism," *Journal of International Affairs* 50 (1); Benjamin R. Barber, *Jihad vs. McWorld: How Globalism and Tribalism Are Reshaping the World* (New York: Ballantine, 1995); Samuel Huntington, "Clash of Civilizations," *Foreign Affairs* 72(3), 22–28.

19. National Intelligence Council, *Global Trends 2015: A Dialogue About the Future with Nongovernment Experts* (Washington, DC: U.S. Government Printing Office, December 2000), <www.cia.gov/cia/publications/globaltrends2015/>.

20. Benjamin Barber, "Mutual Aid Society on a Grand Scale," *Los Angeles Times,* (Nov. 17, 2002), <www.democracycollaborative.org/publications/books/barber_111702.html>.

21. Robert Keohane, "International Institutions: Two Approaches," *International Studies Quarterly* (1988): 379–396; Steven Weber, "Institutions and Change," in Michael W. Doyle and G. John Ikenberry (Eds.), *New Thinking in International Relations Theory* (Boulder, CO: Westview Press, 1997), 229–265; Stephen Krasner, "Sovereignty: An Institutional Perspective," *Comparative Political Studies* (April 1988): 66–94; Graham Allison and Philip Zelikow, *The Essence of Decision: Explaining the Cuban Missile Crisis,* 2nd ed. (Reading, MA: Longman, 1999); I. M. Destler, *Presidents, Bureaucrats, and Foreign Policy* (Princeton, NJ: Princeton University Press, 1972); Francis Rourke, *Bureaucracy and Foreign Policy* (Baltimore: Johns Hopkins University Press, 1974); Morton Halperin, *Bureaucratic Politics and Foreign Policy* (Washington, DC: Brookings Institution, 1974); Terry Moe, "The Politics of Bureaucratic Structure," in John E. Chubb and Paul E. Peterson (Eds.), *Can the Government Govern?* (Washington, DC: Brookings Institution, 1989); Deborah Larson, *The Origins of Containment: A Psychological Explanation* (Princeton, NJ: Princeton University Press, 1985).

22. Keohane, "International Institutions: Two Approaches," 386–387.

23. Weber, "Institutions and Change," 235; Michael Barnett and Martha Finnemore, *Rules for the World: International Organizations in Global Politics.* (Ithaca, NY: Cornell University Press, 2004); Martha Finnemore, *National Interests in International Society* (Ithaca, NY: Cornell University Press, 1996).

24. Finnemore, *National Interests in International Society.*

25. Krasner, "Sovereignty: An Institutional Perspective," 83.

26. Ibid., 66.

27. Ibid., 79.

28. Ibid., 80.

29. Allison and Zelikow, *The Essence of Decision*; I. M. Destler, *Presidents, Bureaucrats, and Foreign Policy* (Princeton, NJ: Princeton University Press, 1972); Rourke, *Bureaucracy and Foreign Policy;* Halperin, *Bureaucratic Politics and Foreign Policy;* Terry Moe, "The Politics of Bureaucratic Structure," in Chubb and Peterson, *Can the Government Govern?*

30. This is the most critiqued part of bureaucratic theory: the idea that "where you stand (on an issue) depends on where you sit (in which organization)." A cottage industry has developed to critique this aspect of bureaucratic theory. As convincing as these studies are that issue positions are not determined by organizational membership alone, it is important to note that Allison never said this was the only determinant of an actor's position; it is one factor among many. Also, many of these studies mistakenly conclude that bureaucratic and organizational dynamics were not involved when no conflict is seen among bureaucratic actors. If agencies often pursue strategic alliances, and especially if actors seek to reduce uncertainty and to be sure in advance of a meeting that they will not be blindsided, then a lack of conflict along agency lines at key meetings might not be evidence that bureaucratic politics theory has been disproved, but the phenomenon might actually be explicable according to the theory. Thus, the problem for Allison's theory is not that it has been proved wrong by numerous critical studies, but that it is too poorly specified to be proved wrong or right. Both evidence of conflict and evidence of its absence among agencies can be interpreted in light of the theory.

31. Charles Heckscher, "Defining the Post-Bureaucratic Type," in Charles Heckscher and Anne Donnellon (Eds.), *The Post-Bureaucratic Organization: New Perspectives on Organizational Change* (Thousand Oaks, CA: Sage, 1994), 27.

32. Moe, "The Politics of Bureaucratic Structure," in Chubb and Peterson, *Can the Government Govern?* 285.

33. Ibid., 329.

34. Larson, *The Origins of Containment,* 341.

35. Ibid., 349.

36. Cusimano Love, *Public–Private Partnerships and Global Problems*.

37. Heckscher and Donnellon, *The Post Bureaucratic Organization*. Also, a growing literature is developing in sociology on diffuse networks; see Mary Durfee and Paul Lopes (Eds.), "Networks of Novelty: The Diffusion of Ideas and Things," *The Annals of the American Academy of Political and Social Sciences* (Philadelphia: AAPSS, November 1999).

38. Al Gore, *Common Sense Government: Works Better and Costs Less* (New York: Random House, 1995); Al Gore, "Report on the National Performance Review," White House press releases on July 14, Sept. 14, Oct. 13, and Dec. 5, 1994, and Jan. 26, 1995; also see White House Documents, Office of the Press Secretary, "Gore Announces Initial Restructuring of Foreign Affairs Agencies," Jan. 27, 1995; Donald F. Kettl, *Reinventing Government? Appraising the National Performance Review* (Washington, DC: Brookings Institution, 1994); Donald F. Kettl and John J. DiIulio, Jr., *Cutting Government* (Washington, DC: Brookings Institution, 1995); Ronald C. Moe, "The 'Reinventing Government' Exercise: Misinterpreting the Problem, Misjudging the Consequences," *Public Administration Review* (March–April 1994): 111–122; Gerald E. Caiden, "Administrative Reform American Style," *Public Administration Review* (March–April 1994): 123–128.

39. James P. Pinkerton, *What Comes Next: The End of Big Government and the New Paradigm Ahead* (New York: Hyperion, 1995).

40. Heckscher, "Defining the Post-Bureaucratic Type," 25.

41. Ibid., 27.

42. Daniel Patrick Moynihan, "Our Stupid but Permanent CIA: What Are We Going to Do about Reforming the Agency? Nothing," *Washington Post* (July 24, 1994): C3.

43. Richard Gates, as quoted in David M. Kennedy, *Sunshine and Shadow: The CIA and the Soviet Economy* (Cambridge, MA: Harvard University, 1991), 18.

44. Only in 2005 did air passenger volume in the U.S. return to pre-September 11 numbers. Only in January 2006 did the New York Stock Exchange return to pre-September 11 levels.

CHAPTER FOURTEEN

Sovereignty: Who Cares?

The Future, and Why Sovereignty Is Not Enough

Maryann Cusimano Love

"We must craft a policy that manages and balances our increasing interdependence with our increased vulnerability . . . expand thinking and policies to encompass a broader understanding of security beyond the security of states."[1]

—Mary Robinson, Executive Director, Realizing Rights: The Ethical Globalization Initiative; UN High Commissioner for Human Rights, 1997–2002; President of Ireland, 1992–1997

"Where once nations depended on sovereignty alone to secure their destinies, today they depend on one another. In a world where the poverty of some imperils the wealth of others, where none are safer than the least safe, multilateralism is not a stratagem of idealists but a realistic necessity. The lesson of 9/11 was not that rogue states could be unilaterally preempted and vanquished by a sovereign United States, but that sovereignty was a chimera—that HIV and global warming and international trade and nuclear proliferation and transnational crime and predatory capital had already stolen from America the substance of its cherished sovereignty well before the terrorists displayed their murderous contempt for it on that fateful morning."[2]

—Benjamin Barber

"Partnerships among all stakeholders in society are increasingly a "must" in a world filled with complex global challenges."[3]

—President William J. Clinton, United Nations Special Envoy for Tsunami Recovery and President of the United States of America (1993–2001), July 2005

Sovereignty—who cares? Why write a book about it, much less three books on the topic? For the more than 2 billion people, nearly one third of the world's population, living in failed or failing states, sovereignty matters.[4] They would like to see more sovereignty, in the form of law and order, good governance, basic capacity, effectiveness and fairness of the public sector—what academics call internal sovereignty, positive sovereignty, or domestic sovereignty. Nigerians traveling to the West are awed by the simple things: the fact that people obey traffic rules, that cars move in predictable patterns, that there are regular, routine, and transparent procedures for obtaining a driver's license in the Department of Motor Vehicles, and that money or connections will not excuse you from these procedures. They know a world in which blind men can obtain driver's licenses for the right fee, in which cars and trucks jump median strips and head the wrong way down highways in a high stakes game of "chicken" if it will get drivers around traffic tie-ups.

For the families of the 13.3 million people killed in major armed conflicts over the past ten years,[5] almost all of which are internal, civil wars, sovereignty matters. Many are fighting for control over the sovereign state; others are fighting for self-rule, to break away and form their own sovereign state. Some are fighting for democratic sovereignty, to have the institutions of the state accountable to the people. For people of the former Eastern bloc and Soviet Union, of South Africa, Brazil, Argentina, Palestine, and East Timor, democratic sovereignty matters.

For the 2.4 billion people (37 percent of the world's population) living in repressive states, and the 1.2 billion people (19 percent of the world's population) living in only partly free countries, sovereignty matters. It matters when the police throw your loved one in prison for criticizing the government, or for some unnamed or fabricated offense.[6] The 170 million killed at the hands of their own government leaders over the past century[7] knew the evils of sovereignty intimately. All these people daily experience predatory sovereignty, personal sovereignty (law is whatever the leader says it is, without democratic process or constraints), and criminal sovereignty (the co-optation of the state by criminal elements). What academics call negative sovereignty or the right of noninterference in states' internal affairs is what Kofi Annan decries when he says that "The sovereignty of States must no longer be used as a shield for gross violations of human rights."[8]

For the millions of immigrants killed, imprisoned, or deported due to failure to obtain proper legal entry permission, and for the 13.2 million refugees in the world today,[9] pushed out of one country's borders but unable to begin life anew in another country, sovereignty matters, as the sovereign effectively denies access to jobs, food, shelter, health care, education, travel—opportunities that glimmer out of reach across the border.

Yet for those of us lucky enough to live in functioning, developed, democratic states, with positive sovereignty and democratic sovereignty, sovereignty is not enough. It is better than living in failed states, predatory states, and non-democratic states, to be sure, but sovereignty isn't all it is cracked up to be. For the nearly 3,000 families who lost loved ones on September 11, the unquestioned sovereignty of the United States could not protect or save them from marauders in the sky armed with box cutters. For the 40 million people around the world infected with HIV or AIDS, sovereignty cannot save them from traveling, devastating pathogens.

As people everywhere move beyond sovereignty, they do so for different reasons. For people in failed and failing states, and for people in predatory and criminal states, they look beyond sovereignty to networks of IGOs, NGOs, and even MNCs to help save them from their crumbling or abusive sovereign structures. For people in developed, democratic states, we look beyond sovereignty because even generally fair and functioning states cannot save us from pressing global problems that go beyond borders.

Sovereignty is not extinct; it persists, but in new forms and functions. We reinvent it in practice each day in our struggles to manage global issues.

GLOBALIZATION'S UNINTENDED CONSEQUENCES

Much of this book has been about globalization's unintended consequences. States, IGOs, and MNCs worked to build international markets and to create the political, economic, and technological infrastructure that made the global marketplace possible. States courted foreign direct investment and technological advancement. Through a variety of economic and political liberalization policies, states deliberately worked to increase the size of the private sector while curtailing public-sector expenditures so the private sector would not be "crowded out." They pursued these policies to increase economic development and prosperity, believing that wealthy states are strong states.

Western states sought to promote open societies, believing that democratic states are more stable trade partners and are less likely to go to war with other democracies. States did not intend, however, to create the infrastructure for global problems to thrive. State governments did not realize that the new actors and dynamics created by globalization would also drain autonomy, choice, and freedom of action away from states. Sovereignty is based on territory, yet the new economy and new actors' prosperity does not derive from territory, making them less beholden to states. How can these new dynamics and actors be managed within a system of sovereign states? How can states maintain law and order, justice and peace against licit and illicit private-sector actors who are increasingly powerful?

POLICY PRESCRIPTIONS

Policy prescriptions for managing globalization and the global problems created by open societies, economies, and technologies fall into three main categories: state-centric (public-sector) approaches, nonstate-centric (private-sector) responses, and mixed (public–private) responses.

The State-Centric Approach

The state-centric approach to global problems suggests that states strengthen their capacity to fight global problems, enhancing law and order institutions, control over borders, markets, multilateral cooperation among states, and inter-agency cooperation within states to increase states' efficacy of response.[10] In essence, this approach argues that the same forces that facilitate global problems and undermine sovereignty (open technologies, economies, and societies) can be harnessed or managed to fight global problems. States need to better use the same new technologies and market forces that are being used against them in global problems. If we could just make states smarter and get them to work together better, then states would be able to meet these challenges more effectively. If states were equipped with better technologies, with enhanced state capacity, then cooperating and sharing information and implementation would be possible and more effective across and within governments. After all, terrorists and drug traffickers are using the most advanced emerging technologies and are developing strategic relations with other criminal cartels. Why can't states do the same in their efforts to stop these illicit activities? State-centric responses can be unilateral, focusing on building the capacity of states internally. They can also be multilateral, focusing either on increasing IGO capacity or on federal, functional cooperation among government agencies (as when police or judges share information and cooperate across borders).

Anne-Marie Slaughter argues that government agencies and officials at all levels are working together across borders in unprecedented government networks to manage global problems. These harmonization, enforcement, and information networks help address capacity and jurisdiction gaps. And to the degree that government actors are democratically elected, these government-to-government networks are more legitimate, democratic, and accountable than partnerships with unelected actors such as MNCs, and NGOs. Horizontal networks coordinate action and information across governments, while vertical networks allow international coercion through state-to-IGO delegation. The result is a "New World Order" of "disaggregated sovereignty." Sovereign units respond to global problems, but they do so through new government networks.[11]

State-centric responses are seen most often in the efforts to fight the global problems of terrorism, drug smuggling, cyberthreats, transnational crime, and WMD proliferation. This is not surprising: These issues touch most closely to the security sectors where state identity and activities are strongest and where states have always been active. Interdiction, improved intelligence and law enforcement capabilities, interagency and IGO efforts to improve information sharing, cooperation, and enforcement are all examples of state-centric responses to global problems. The Proliferation Security Initiative is an example of a state-centric approach to improve countries' abilities to interdict WMD weapons and materials. Even progressive and creative programs that are fully in the cooperative security rubric—such as the Cooperative Threat Reduction programs to stem proliferation from the former Soviet Union (FSU)—fit into this category. Attempts to increase nuclear material protection, control, and accountability (MPC&A) by increasing security at FSU nuclear labs and facilities by installing security cameras, detection devices, modern accounting and storage procedures, and so on are oriented at strengthening the capacity of states.

The Nonstate-Centric Approach

The nonstate-centric policy approach emphasizes the importance of the private sector in responding to global problems. It also emphasizes the limitations of trying to work through the state for help in curtailing activities that largely fall in the social and economic sectors where the reach of liberal, capitalist states is the shortest. If state capacity is (or should be) weakening, then why ask the state to solve global problems? Why not go directly to the private sector, where the resources exist to attack the problem?

This approach emphasizes developing new responses and infrastructure that utilize nonstate actors such as NGOs and MNCs. Corporate codes of conduct to improve international environmental and labor standards, shareholder and consumer activism to change MNC policies, efforts to get pharmaceutical companies to voluntarily reduce prices and increase access to essential medicines for poor countries and people, market solutions to overcoming poverty problems through FDI, increased trade, and microbusiness (for example, Nakornthon Bank) are nonstate-centric policy prescriptions. Direct action campaigns by NGOs to change corporate or consumer behavior (for example, convincing the tuna industry to adopt dolphin-safe fishing techniques) effect change regardless of governmental participation. Efforts to fight global problems of refugee flows, disease, and environmental degradation tend to focus more readily on nonstate-centric approaches.

NGO activities have traditionally been strongest in these areas. The efforts of the Gates Foundation to immunize children in Africa, and the efforts of ProMED (the Program to Monitor Emerging Diseases), a global electronic mail network that facilitates reporting on and discussion of disease outbreaks around the world, are also nonstate-centric responses.

Mixed or Public–Private Approaches

Finally, there is a third way. If public- and private-sector responses alone cannot effectively manage global issues, then why not combine the two? Public–private partnerships can reap the benefits of each separate approach while minimizing some of the problems of one approach alone. By combining the benefits of state legitimacy and enforceability with the flexibility and resources of the private sector, more traction can be brought to bear on difficult global issues.

The state still has important levers that can be used to fight global problems. David Victor of the Council on Foreign Relations invokes a *Star Wars* analogy. The dark side of enthusiasm about using private-sector responses is that you still need the force of the state. A state can provide threats or force, serve as negotiator or facilitator of private-sector interactions, and backstop private-sector initiatives with a safety net baseline of law that provides more universally implementable and enforceable norms. States provide not only the sticks but also the carrots of incentives, and they can focus direction. The state has the added advantage of being familiar and available. But neither the state nor the private sector can do it alone. The choices are not between multilateralism and unilateralism, integration and fragmentation, federal government and local government, and public sector and private sector. To manage global problems, we must use all of the networks at our disposal. Choice of the institutional instrument will be based on who has the established network assets in a sector. She who has the network becomes the partner with the foreign policy organizations.

For example, Stephen Flynn argues that greater cooperation between the government and private-sector shipping firms through information sharing, transparency, and increased security measures at the point of origin would greatly reduce trafficking in refugees, persons, drugs, and weapons, as well as terrorism. The private sector wins with faster, more assured shipping, less money lost to stolen shipments, less time lost to backups at the border, and fewer invasive border inspections. The government wins allies in trying to manage global problems and gains information with which to better target government border control resources.[12] Debt-for-nature swaps, the

World Commission on Dams, the United Nations Global Compact—all of these are public–private partnerships.

Thorsten Benner and Jan Martin Witte note, "Governance has gone global—and so have questions of legitimacy and accountability. The old 'club model' of international politics as a closed shop involving just governments is defunct. International organisations, non–governmental organisations (NGOs), transnational companies—all play vital roles alongside national officials in global policymaking. Why bother with partnerships? A more appropriate question should be: What other useful mechanisms are available?"[13]

Benner and Witte argue that problems of transparency, accountability, and legitimacy can be addressed by building checks and balances into the partnerships, not with a single mechanism but through "pluralistic systems of accountability." These can include leveraging reputational accountability, peer accountability, financial accountability, process accountability, transparency about sources and uses of funding, and performance accountability.[14]

If states alone cannot adequately respond to global problems, then why is it important that they be part of the multipronged approach? The most important advantage states have is that they exist. They do not have to be built from scratch. They are familiar, with addresses and known processes that are understood and available for interaction, allowing the opportunity for transparency and accountability. States may not have the ability to command or compel resolution of a global problem, but they are uniquely positioned to coordinate, communicate, facilitate, and cajole action from a variety of other actors who look to the state to fill that conduit function. States are a focal point for citizen imagination and demands. Whether or not states can solve global problems alone, the question is still raised by the public and the media, "What is the state doing about it?"

In addition, governments are often perceived to have the political legitimacy to act on behalf of the populace in foreign affairs. Although foreign policy bureaucracies in democracies are generally not staffed by elected officials, they are created and funded by elected officials, and they can be held responsible to elected officials. Thus, state institutions must have some degree of political support to exist at all; on the other hand, it is not clear whom MNCs and NGOs represent, to whom they are accountable or how they can be held accountable, or how much political legitimacy and support they command. Why not use the institutional advantages states have of being available as a forum?

Underlying these differences over how to best respond to global problems are different assumptions about the future of the sovereign state. Is the sovereign state retreating, its power becoming more diffuse in a globalized economy? Susan Strange argues that power is moving from states to markets as states either abdicate more functions to nonstate actors or vacate certain functions altogether.[15] There is some evidence from the preceding chapters in favor of this view. Nonstate actors are increasingly taking on functions that were traditionally performed by states, even in the security sector. The example of debt-for-nature swaps supports Rosecrance's idea of the declining importance of territory relative to the rising importance of market forces.[16] If states are losing power to nonstate actors and market dynamics, then responses to global problems should be aimed at nonstate actors and market forces.

Others argue that the sovereign state is still the fundamental unit in the international system. Sovereignty took centuries to develop and will not disappear in a few decades, and there are no well-developed alternative organizing units ready to replace sovereign states.[17] The preceding chapters offer some evidence to support this view. Terrorism highlights that the state is still important enough to be worth fighting for. If this is the case and state actors still reign supreme, then efforts to fight global problems should still be aimed at states and strengthening state institutions or perhaps at developing more cooperative ventures among states.

There is a third way. If sovereignty is denigrated but not dead, then fighting global problems may require a combined approach in which a wide spectrum of policy responses are undertaken and coordinated, aimed at both state and nonstate sectors. If we are in a period of transition or turbulence[18] —in which a changed economic system has created new actors and dissipated the power of states in crucial economic and social sectors, but in which state actors are still important in the law enforcement and security sectors—then a combined approach is necessary. Just as new interstate highways are often built alongside existing two-lane highways, new networks using new actors must be built while the old state actors are still functioning.

For all of the advantages of pursuing public–private partnerships, there are also obstacles. Many were discussed in the last chapter, but there are also the problems of working with many different actors and integrating a wide variety of responses. More actors require greater coordination, communication, cooperation, prioritization, transparency, and accountability, which increases the level of difficulty. Pursuing a combined approach also necessitates vigilance for threshold effects and unintended consequences. For example, policy responses may need a certain level of funding for a protracted period of time before a program may yield results. But if policy responses are split over a variety of state and nonstate venues, then resources may be diluted or a plan of attack may be pursued for too short a period, never reaching the threshold necessary for effective action. Unintended consequences apply to every approach. Because action must be coordinated among a wider variety of players, it may be more difficult to anticipate the full ramifications of a wider array of actions in public–private partnerships. For example, funneling attention and funding to nonstate actors and sectors could further undermine state sectors and actors. As new highways are built, sometimes the old roadways fall into disuse.

Continued monitoring and attention to coordination, prioritization, and accountability are necessary. Yet none of these critiques is unique to public–private approaches, though they may be more intense with them. State-centric and nonstate-centric prescriptions also share these obstacles. For example, government bureaucrats are not elected, and government bureaucracies are not necessarily transparent, accountable, democratic, or legitimate. Combating terrorism, organized crime, or drug trafficking in one sector or region may merely drive it into another area. All approaches require building political support, coordination, communication, prioritization, transparency, and accountability—and all may encounter resistance to change by existing organizations, threshold effects, and unintended consequences.

DOES SOVEREIGNTY STILL REIGN?

If state-centric responses are still necessary along with other approaches in dealing with global problems, then does this mean that Krasner and Spruyt are right? Is there no competitor to the sovereign state out there right now, so sovereignty still reigns by default? Not exactly, because sovereignty is changing in significant ways. Vertical and horizontal linkages may still anchor sovereignty in place, but they are breaking down. The anchor is becoming dislodged.

It is instructive to remember Hendrik Spruyt's story of how fundamental change came about the last time and ushered in the sovereign state: the economy changed. New elites were created who benefited from the new economic system and needed a new form of political organization to better accommodate them and their economic practices. Ideas changed, new organizational forms emerged and competed, and, after centuries of flux, the sovereign state eventually won out.[19]

There are many parallels today. The economy has changed. The new economic system is increasingly based on information, technology, and services, which are less dependent on the control of territory. The means of production, capital, and labor are mobile, not fixed. Players who make use of modern information, communication, transportation, and financial technologies reap the benefits of increasingly open borders and economies.

Political systems that make room for the new economic system reap profits in foreign direct investment, and so regime types as distinct as the Chinese communist system, the Mexican emerging democracy, and the Iranian theocracy are all simultaneously undertaking reforms to make themselves more attractive to investors' capital and technology flows.

New elites are emerging who profit from the new economic system. Typified by George Soros, Bill Gates, and Ted Turner, these "new imperialists"[20] increasingly follow no flag. They are passionate about expanding technologies and markets, and they are frustrated by what they see as anachronistic state barriers to investment and trade flows. The international business classes attend the same schools, fly the same airlines, vacation at the same resorts, eat at the same restaurants, and watch the same movies and television shows. Independent of national identities, these elites mobilize to try to make states facilitate market dynamics. Some call it the "Davos culture" after the Swiss luxury resort where the annual World Economic Summit met.[21] Sociologist Peter Berger calls it the "yuppie internationale," a culture typified by the scene in a Buddhist temple in Hong Kong of "a middle-aged man wearing a dark business suit over stocking feet. He was burning incense and at the same time talking on his cellular phone." Berger believes these cultural ties have made peace talks in South Africa and Northern Ireland go more smoothly: "It may be that commonalities in taste make it easier to find common ground politically."[22] Can it be that leaders who all shop at the Gap and Benetton and eat at McDonald's find political antagonisms quaint and unnecessary? In what he dubs the "Golden Arches Theory of Conflict Prevention," Thomas Friedman argues that no two countries with McDonald's restaurants have ever gone to war with one another.[23] Even though clearly there are many economically underprivileged people around the world who do not partake in this lifestyle, the values of this new elite percolate into the rest of society as people mimic the behavior of the elites and strive to better their economic situations to one day rise into the wealthier classes.

Ideas are changing (including ideas of authority, identity, and organization), facilitated by the new information technologies and changes in the economy. Never before in human history have we been able to spread ideas so quickly and widely. Modern communication technologies allow an ever-wider swath of the planet to be tuned in to the same advertisements, the same television shows, and, thereby, to some of the same ideas about consumerism and personal freedoms. Identity is becoming less tied to territory. If identity and authority do not stem from geography, then what is our new church, our new religion? In the European Middle Ages, identity came from Christendom, the Church, while authority stemmed from spiritual connections. In the modern era, identity was tied up with the nation state; authority corresponded with geography. Now authority and identity are increasingly contested. Strange believes we now have Pinocchio's problem: The strings of state control, authority, and identity have been cut, but no new strings have been fastened.[24] States no longer are the supreme recipient of individual loyalties, especially because they no longer fulfill basic services and functions and other actors have stepped into the gap. Firms, professions, families, religions, and social movements have all significantly challenged the state's territorial and security-based claim to individual loyalty. We are left to choose among competing sources of allegiance, authority, and identity, with no strings to bind us like puppets to one source of authority, and with more freedom to let our conscience be our guide.

Certainly the new economy would like identity to be formed around consumer products—you are what you wear, what you consume. Advertisers spend billions to imprint brand loyalty at an early age, and all the advertising of Planet Reebok, I'd-like-to-buy-the-world-a-Coke, and Microsoft's One World Internet Explorer icon share a common theme: that identity stems not from national borders but from consumer products. Identity is therefore just as mobile as the economy. You are not born with it. You can buy it. Alternatively, some see identity as increasingly flowing from professions and firms: You are what you do, and your commitment is to your profession rather than to a specific state. As Rosecrance describes it, "Today and for the foreseeable future, the only international civilization worthy of the name is the governing economic culture of the world market."[25] Benjamin Barber refers to this popular, consumer market culture as "McWorld."[26] As market values permeate various cultures, certain ideas emerge as prized: the value of change, mobility, flexibility, adaptability, speed, and information. As capitalism becomes our creed, with technology as our guide, distinct national and religious cultures are becoming permeated with common market values.

There are alternatives to market values, however. Religious organizations and NGOs promulgate alternative ethics to materialism, a globalization in which we are not merely consumers or a governance problem but human beings, each with irreducible sacred dignity. This vision of globalization prescribes putting people before profits, ethical values before market values. These organizations use the tools of globalization to promote their views of humanizing globalization. For example, the Internet is a popular tool for organizing and proselytizing by many faith groups, including traditional Islam.[27]

Ideas of organization are also changing and are based on models from the marketplace and technology: computers, the Internet, and the market are diffuse, decentralized, loosely connected networks with a few central organizing parameters but strong ties to the activities of individual entrepreneurs. Foreign policy organizations are, in some instances, going beyond bureaucracy, creating flexible, innovative, coordinating networks.

Creative public–private partnerships are the wave of the future in solving global problems. Rather than trying to become draconian, big brother states (which would conflict with the goals of open societies, open economies, and open technologies), it makes sense for governments to look toward civil society for help in managing global problems. But states must be aware of the costs of contracting out. In privatizing, not only do governments lose some control over policy, but also private entities may present obstacles to the government's agenda as profit or other motives conflict with important public policy goals.[28] Although *privatization* and "moving beyond bureaucracy" are popular buzzwords and phrases in today's budget-conscious political climate, changes in state architecture have consequences for how we think about political authority, identity, and organization.

Ideas drawn from experience of the new economic system are helping to shape new ideas of political organization. A resurgence of IGOs simultaneous with increased attention to local governance may not seem at all strange to a civilization used to surfing the Internet and using a system that is simultaneously globally connected and only as good as the local link.

Rosenau believes that as individuals become more analytically skillful, the nature of authority shifts. People no longer uncritically accept traditional criteria of state authority based on historical, legal, or customary claims of legitimacy. Instead, authority and legitimacy are increasingly based on how well government authorities perform.[29] Love and Hellmuth's description of the numbers of refugees and migrants voting with their feet seems to support this claim. Thus, while scholars disagree about the sources of identity and authority in the emerging era, they agree that these ideas are changing.

Finally, new forms of political organization are beginning to emerge, as evidenced by the European Union and the increasing roles and profile of IGOs. Thus, even if, as Spruyt maintains, the sovereign state is still supreme, three out of four of his indicators of fundamental change are already here: Changes in economy, elites, and ideas are in evidence, and even though no new form of political organization has unseated the sovereign state, new forms are beginning to emerge around the sovereign state that are chipping away at functions previously performed by it and changing its role.

GOING GLOBAL VERSUS GOING LOCAL: THE STATE CONTRACTS OUT

Are new forms of political organization emerging to accompany these changes? Many commentators have noted the irony that globalizing forces are spreading and deepening at the same time that virulent forms of nationalism are evident in internal wars.[30] There are several reasons why this is not surprising. First of all, scholars on nationalism note that ties to ethnic or national groups increase under threat.[31] Therefore, it makes sense that at precisely the time when globalizing forces threaten local identities, there is resurgent attention to local ways of life.

Threat is only one piece of the puzzle, however. Transitions to liberal economic and political forms are destabilizing. Virulent nationalisms can be resuscitated as a means of finding a scapegoat for tough times. The fact that there once was a violent form of nationalism does not mean, however, that future conflicts will break out along national or ethnic lines. Many of the most highly developed states today once endured bloody civil wars—the United Kingdom, the United States, and France.

Previous conflict by itself is neither an indicator nor an explanation for later conflict. For example, most journalists and pundits described the cause of conflict in the Balkans as "ancient ethnic hatreds."[32] But this no more explains the conflict than does noting that the sun rose before the fighting took place, and because A came before B, A therefore caused B. Poland and Czechoslovakia also experienced "ancient ethnic hostilities," yet violent nationalism did not plunge these societies into internal war as occurred in the former Yugoslavia. Economics was a pivotal trigger in bringing violent nationalism to Yugoslavia, while Poland and Czechoslovakia had gentler transitions from communism. As the economic situation deteriorated in Yugoslavia, politicians sought to protect their own national groups. Leaders exploited nationalist tensions to explain away economic woes and distance themselves from their communist pasts, often using the media as their megaphones of hate.[33] Michael Brown notes that bad leaders, bad neighbors, bad internal problems, and bad neighborhoods can also fire nationalism into internal conflict.[34] There is no straight causal line between violent nationalism in the past and violent nationalism in the future. However, states undergoing difficult transitions can be more vulnerable to such violent forms.

Going global and going local are connected in another way as well. A study of twelve states over the past twenty years showed a correlation between indicators of open societies, open economies, and open technologies and government decentralization. States that increased in openness over the time period also increased in government decentralization (the amount of money and decision-making power that went to the local government level as opposed to the central government). States that stayed closed in the same time period did not experience government decentralization. Correlation is not causation, and so the forces of open economy, open technology, and open society and government decentralization might be caused by some third factor (the IMF, for example, as international investors pressure states both to decentralize governments and to privatize markets). But initial evidence does show that there are "simultaneous trends in globalization and decentralization."[35] Decentralization and open society, open market, and open technology forces go together.

By this view it is not an accident that the highly centralized states of the communist Soviet Union and Eastern Europe, the apartheid state of South Africa, the military regimes in Argentina, and the social-welfare states of the United Kingdom and the United States are undergoing decentralization simultaneously. Big government is generally being downsized all over the planet,[36] and power is increasingly moving to local governments in federated systems and to nonstate actors. Sometimes the central state government retains authority over certain functions but no longer performs the functions itself, as when Australia contracts refugee camps out to private companies or Britain debates hiring mercenary soldiers:

> Global changes occurring today are creating new, complex, and decentralized systems of networks that are radically different from the old centralized systems of governance which controlled the process of international activities and decision making.[37]

How can it be that local government is making a comeback all over the globe at the same time that IGOs are becoming more important? The state is contracting out functions to several actors simultaneously: IGOs, NGOs, MNCs, and local governments. The strong central governments of the twentieth century—the fascist states, the communist states, and the Rooseveltian social security state—are receding. In the twenty-first century, the sovereign state remains. But this is not the state that we drove into the last century. This is not your father's Oldsmobile.

THE SPEED OF CHANGE

If the sovereign state is changing and new forms of political organization are emerging, then will change take centuries this time around? When sovereignty emerged, competing political forms coexisted for centuries before feudalism receded and the sovereign state emerged as the standard. Skeptics believe that it will take a similarly long time before current changes in economic or social structures mount a fundamental challenge to the sovereign state system, in part because those who benefit from the existing state system will fight to keep it. But the end of feudalism and the rise of sovereignty took place in an era when the modes of transportation and communication were horseback and slow-moving ships. Might change occur more quickly now in an era of jet planes, the Internet, faxes, e-mail, personal computers, and cell phones?

The rate of change is different from what it used to be. As Susan Strange notes,

> What is new and unusual is that all (or nearly all) states should undergo substantial change of roughly the same kind within the same short period of twenty or thirty years. The last time that anything like this happened was in Europe when states based on a feudal system of agricultural production geared to local subsistence gave way to states based on a capitalist system of industrial production for the market. The process of change was spread over two or three centuries at the very least and in parts of eastern and southern Europe is only now taking shape. In the latter part of the twentieth century, the shift has not been confined to Europe and has taken place with bewildering rapidity.[38]

Ideas are spread instantaneously in an era of satellite television, as fast as an Internet connection. The "one world" advertising themes of Nike, IBM, and UPS may contain a grain of truth in highlighting the ramifications of a wired planet to which many of us are plugged in.

The idea of punctuated equilibrium draws the analogy that institutional change may occur rapidly over a limited period of time in unexpected ways. Rather than the Darwinian idea of change as slow, steady, continuous, and gradual, punctuated equilibrium stresses that change is "usually accomplished rapidly when a stable structure is stressed beyond its buffering capacity to resist and absorb.... These evolutionary shifts can be quirky and unpredictable as the potentials for complexity are vast."[39]

Is the fast rate of change that open economy, society, and technology forces have unleashed comparable to the rate of change of sovereign states to keep up with new environmental circumstances? This is particularly important as more states become democratic, because democratic state institutions are often slow to act, with opportunities for gridlock and delay built into the state structure. Democracy was never organized to be effective or efficient. Shared powers and separate institutions with checks and balances among them is a hedge against tyranny, not a recipe for efficiency. By putting different parts of government at each other's throats, it was hoped that government might stay off the people's backs and that deliberation and perspective might result from democratic procedures. Tyranny has many faults, but it can act quickly. The government does what the ruler says, whether it is right, just, legal, or in the public interest. The Nazi government, for example, was chillingly systematic and efficient in its use of industrial technology to conduct the Holocaust. Government becomes much more slow and bothersome when those in charge have to consult others about what to do, and when they have to factor in civil rights, civil liberties, and accountability to the law. In an era of e-mail, cell phones, and laptop computers, where the economy and technology place great value on speed and efficiency, we forget that democratic institutions were not built for speed. As Alexis de Toqueville noted, the miracle of the system is that it works at all.

If the rate of external change vastly exceeds the institution's ability to respond, then will sovereign institutions be stressed beyond their ability to evolve and adapt? Buffeted by external blows, sovereignty continues to limp along, pocked by capacity, jurisdiction, and other institutional gaps. But as the speed of technological change outpaces the sovereign state's ability to hobble and hotwire responses, the limp may become more pronounced and perhaps (though no time soon) eventually fell the sovereign state.

CONCLUSION: THE SHIP OF STATE

At what point do we have a new ship of state? Scholars agree that change is occurring. The sovereign state is not obsolete and will continue to play a role along with other actors on the international scene. But there is disagreement over sovereignty's future. We are in a period of transition. We do not know yet whether the state can be retrofitted to weather the storms of changes in economy, elites, and ideas, or whether these changes will someday bring about new forms of political organization.

The situation is analogous to a famous puzzle in the study of philosophy: the ship of Theseus. There are three different ways the ship of Theseus problem is discussed. The first stems from its origins in Greek mythology. Theseus was the son of Aegeus, the king of Athens. Theseus sailed away to fight a heroic battle, but after slaying the Minotaur he forgot to change the sails to indicate the victory to his father. Sailing in the same old sails unwittingly brought about tragedy, as his father did not realize the battle had been won because the changed situation was not immediately apparent by viewing his son's ship. In a fit of despair, Theseus's father committed suicide, throwing himself from a cliff into the sea.[40] The analogy here is to the discussion in Chapter 13 about institutions. Many of our foreign policy institutions were built to fight strong states, not weak states and global problems. We have not changed our institutional sails consistent with the new situation, and we flirt with disaster by traveling with our old sails.

The more pressing analogy, however, concerns the other two ways in which the problem of the ship of Theseus is discussed, questioning the nature of change and identity. If the planks of a ship are removed one by one over intervals of time, and each time an old plank is removed it is replaced by a new plank, then is it a new vessel? At what point did it reach critical mass to call it something new?[41]

This is the question we now face in considering the sovereign state. In Chapter 1, we considered ten functions of states that Susan Strange believed are either no longer being performed or are at least being shared with other, nonstate actors. Scholar William Zartman posts his own list. In discussing failed or weak states that are collapsing, he lists five basic roles states perform: as the decision-making center of government; as a symbol of identity; as controller of territory and guarantor of security; as an authoritative and legitimate political institution; and as a system of socioeconomic organization, the target of citizen demands for providing supplies or services.[42] Although Zartman offers this list as a litmus test for when weak states are failing because basic state functions are no longer being performed, many of these functions correspond with Strange's and other authors' observations of roles that all states (weak and strong) formerly undertook but no longer fulfill.

The chapters of this book show that states are no longer the sole decision-making centers. MNCs, IGOs, and NGOs increasingly make decisions about matters that were traditionally handled by states. Economic decisions increasingly take place in corporate boardrooms, on the floors of international stock exchanges, and in the conference rooms of the IMF, and states increasingly react to, rather than generate, these key decisions. States are being challenged as symbols of identity and as authoritative, legitimate political institutions, as citizens increasingly place their loyalties elsewhere. Even strong states no longer can unilaterally control territory or borders or secure territory from external threats.

Alternative institutions—from MNCs to NGOs and IGOs—are increasingly the targets of citizen demands for services that citizens do not believe the state can supply. If the sovereign state is no longer performing the basic functions associated with sovereign states, then at what point does sovereignty cease? If the primary innovation of the sovereign state was its connection of authority to territory, then what does it mean for sovereignty if the state's connection to territory is being severed and states derive less authority or power from territory?[43] Rosenau argues that authority is no longer automatically conferred to the traditional sources on the basis of customary legitimacy claims, be they legal or geographic, but that people are instead judging legitimacy and authority on the basis of performance. If sovereignty is no longer about territory, then what is it about? If territory is at the heart of sovereignty and territory is removed, then is what's left still sovereignty? How many planks must be pulled for us to recognize it as something different?

The difference between the case of sovereignty and the changes that occurred to the ship of Theseus are these: The ship's planks were replaced exactly in the same manner and to fulfill the same functions. The planks were not altered to turn the ship into a rocket. In the case of sovereignty, however, materials are changing to slowly give the vessel a facelift. Such changes might be correlated to the changes in regime and administrative type from the authoritarian regimes and regimes with the strong central government functions typical of the twentieth century to the decentralized, capitalist, and democratic regimes of the twenty-first century.

However, the changes this volume discusses are not just changes in sovereignty's face or outward appearance; they are changes in its nature. Unlike the ship of Theseus, the ship of state is changing the very functions it performs and how it performs them. If sovereignty is as sovereignty does, and what sovereignty does is changing, is sovereignty itself changing?

The final analogy with the ship concerns the nature of change. Some philosophers argue for foundationalism—that sound principles need to be laid out first before new concepts can be built on them. But Otto Neurath argues that we seldom have the luxury of changing our ideas in a pristine vacuum and starting from scratch. Instead he argues that "we are like sailors who must rebuild their ship on the open sea, never able to dismantle it in dry dock and to reconstruct it there out of the best materials."[44]

Certainly this is analogous to the descriptions of change offered by political psychologists, as forged in experience. Humans learn by doing, and as we experiment with states contracting out and public–private partnerships, we learn new ways of thinking about human organizations. These experiences are changing how we exercise and think about sovereignty. The ship's wheel is being replaced while the ship is still in operation. New planks are added and old functions are jettisoned while we are under way. Nonstate actors are cropping up and assuming functions that states used to perform. New policies toward global problems are evolving, utilizing nonstate sectors at the same time that state responses are being fine-tuned. We are not dry-docked and awaiting the emergence of a new ship of political organization, but we must go forward while we are in the midst of major construction.

The problem with our ability to track changes in the sovereign state is that we are used to the system; we are not good even at contemplating what the alternatives to sovereignty might look like. We are truly conceptual prisoners. Ideas matter, and outdated ideas can kill. Changes can occur in unintended ways, and they can occur rapidly when threshold effects are reached. Even though Krasner concludes that the sovereign state "will not be dislodged easily, regardless of changed circumstances in the material environment" and that sovereignty is so entrenched that "[i]t is now difficult to even conceive of alternatives," he acknowledges that surprises are possible.[45]

The *Titanic* was a supposedly unsinkable ship that hit an iceberg in the dark and sank within hours, killing more than 1,500 passengers and crew members. Similarly, the sovereign state is hitting many unforeseen obstacles in the dark side of globalization. Gaps in our institutions are already painfully apparent. Because the seas of change are turbulent, we have a moral obligation to think about the unthinkable, build better institutions, and consider alternatives if the impossible were to occur and the ship of sovereignty turned out not to be unsinkable after all. Urgently needed are new thoughts on how we might better organize humans, as well as more specific ideas about the organizational shapes into which sovereignty might morph or that might rival or replace sovereignty at some time in the unknown future. These ideas are developing out of our experiences of economic and technological change as our ideas about organization are informed by the new organizational structures we use in the marketplace and on the Internet.

Sovereignty is not going away, but it is evolving, decentralizing, and contracting out. States increasingly coordinate policy among a wider variety of public and private actors. Richard Neustadt describes a U.S. political system in which the president is more powerful than other political actors but rarely has the ability to command or compel. Instead, the president must persuade others to pursue his preferred outcomes.[46]

The state is entering a similar position. It may be more powerful than NGOs, IGOs, and MNCs, depending on the case and the situation, but it rarely has the power to command or compel outcomes on global problems. Instead, states have to assume new roles as coordinators, facilitators, initiators, and salesmen in order to persuade action on global problems. This places burdens on state institutions, requiring organizational changes and adding more functions for states to undertake though not necessarily control. Neustadt notes that an increase in duties does not equate to an increase in power or in the capacity to fulfill new duties, and that adding more duties without means is equivalent to being a glorified clerk, not a powerful entity. For the immediate future, sovereignty will be first among competing forms, but there will be a "return to history" in the sense of a return to cross-cutting, nonhierarchical, ad hoc, and relative forms of order and organization.

Yet integrating action among a wider variety of players also opens new opportunities for policy and offers greater possibilities for effectively managing global issues than old-style unilateral responses. NGOs and MNCs frequently "forum shop"—that is, move an issue across borders to a more hospitable institutional venue for a chance at better resolution. We are no longer stuck with sovereignty only; we can often choose from and move among a variety of institutions. We are engaged in an exciting period of organizational pluralism and experimentation. International political problems have gone beyond sovereignty. We must also go beyond sovereignty in theory and in practice, changing our ideas and our institutions to better respond to the life-and-death challenges of globalization's gaps.

ENDNOTES

1. Mary Robinson, "The Ethical Globalization Initiative: Realizing Rights," <www .realizingrights.org/>; <www.eginitiative.org/>.
2. Benjamin Barber, "Declare Our Interdependence!" September 13, 2003, <www .thinkingpeace.com/pages/Articles/Archive1/arts040.html>.
3. President Clinton, as quoted in the endorsements for Jan Martin Witte and Wolfgang Reinicke, UN Global Compact Office, "Business UN usual," 2005, <http://globalpublicpolicy.net/businessUNusual/>.
4. Foreign Policy and the Fund for Peace, "The Failed State Index," *Foreign Policy* (July/August 2005), <www.foreignpolicy.com/story/cms.php?story_id=3098>.
5. <http://unstats.un.org/unsd/mi/pdf/MDG%20Book.pdf>
6. Freedom House, *Freedom in the World 2005,* 2, <www.freedomhouse.org/research/freeworld/2005/essay2005.pdf>.
7. Greg Noone, "Genocide and Crimes Against Humanity," presentation 2004.
8. Kofi Annan, Nobel Prize Acceptance Speech, December 10, 2001.
9. UNHCR, *2004 Global Refugee Trends,* June 17, 2005, 2.
10. Francis Fukuyama, *State-Building: Governance and World Order in the 21st Century* (Ithaca, NY: Cornell University Press, 2004).
11. Anne-Marie Slaughter, *A New World Order* (Princeton, NJ: Princeton University Press, 2004).
12. Stephen Flynn, "America the Vulnerable," *Foreign Affairs* (Jan.–Feb. 2002).
13. Thorsten Benner and Jan Martin Witte, "Everybody's Business: Accountability, Partnerships, and the Future of Global Governance," in Susan Stern and Elisabeth Seligmann (Eds.), *The Partnership Principle: New Forms of Governance in the 21st Century* (London, Archetype Publishers, 2004).
14. Ibid.
15. Susan Strange, *The Retreat of the State: The Diffusion of Power in the World Economy* (Cambridge, UK: Cambridge University Press, 1996), 189.

16. Richard Rosecrance, "The Rise of the Virtual State," *Foreign Affairs* (July–Aug. 1996): 59–60.

17. Stephen D. Krasner, *Problematic Sovereignty: Contested Rules and Political Possibilities* (New York: Columbia University Press, 2001); Stephen D. Krasner, *Sovereignty: Organized Hypocrisy* (Princeton, NJ: Princeton University Press, 1999); Stephen D. Krasner, "Sovereignty: An Institutional Perspective," *Comparative Political Studies* 21 (April 1988): 74; Kenneth Waltz, "Globalization and Governance," *PS: Political Science & Politics* (Dec. 1999): 693–700; William H. McNeill, "Territorial States Buried Too Soon," *Mershon International Studies Review* 41 (1997): 269.

18. James N. Rosenau, *Turbulence in World Politics* (Princeton, NJ: Princeton University Press, 1990).

19. Hendrik Spruyt, *The Sovereign State and Its Competitors* (Princeton, NJ: Princeton University Press, 1994), 62, 75.

20. Mark Leibovich, *The New Imperialists* (New York: Prentice Hall, 2002).

21. Samuel Huntington, *The Clash of Civilizations and the Remaking of World Order* (New York: Simon & Schuster, 1996).

22. Peter L. Berger, "Four Faces of Global Culture," *The National Interest* (Fall 1997): 24.

23. Thomas L. Friedman, *The Lexus and the Olive Tree: Understanding Globalization* (New York: Farrar, Straus & Giroux, 1999), 195–196.

24. Strange, *The Retreat of the State,* 199.

25. Richard Rosecrance, *The Rise of the Virtual State: Wealth and Power in the Coming Century* (New York: Basic Books, 2000), 59–60.

26. Benjamin R. Barber, *Jihad vs. McWorld* (New York: Ballantine Books, 1996).

27. Jon W. Anderson and Dale F. Eickelman (Eds.), *New Media in the Muslim World: The Emerging Public Sphere* (Bloomington: Indiana University Press, 1999).

28. Peter Passell, "U.S. Goals at Odds in a Plan to Sell Off Nuclear Operation," *The New York Times* (July 25, 1995): A1.

29. Maryann Cusimano, "James Rosenau and Monica Lewinsky," *PS: Political Science and Politics* (Dec. 1999). Interestingly, Rosenau's thesis explains why President Clinton's approval ratings did not diminish and even improved during his impeachment hearings. The media and conservative thinkers have been at a loss to explain why the U.S. public was not more exercised about President Clinton's extramarital affair, its moral implications, and its effects on the dignity of the presidential office. But if the public judges legitimacy and authority by performance criteria, not by appeals to tradition or moral authority, then breaches of tradition and morality would not affect the public's perception of Clinton's legitimacy or authority. If performance criteria are all that matters, then Clinton's poll ratings make sense given the low unemployment rate and strong performance of the U.S. economy during his administration, especially while European and Asian economic growth rates were simultaneously flat or declining. According to Rosenau, it would seem that political leaders can "get away with" quite a bit as long as it does not interfere with their record of concrete achievements.

30. Amy Chua, *World On Fire: How Exporting Free Market Democracy Breeds Ethnic Hatred and Global Instability* (New York: Anchor, 2004).

31. Ted Robert Gurr, "Minorities, Nationalists, and Ethnopolitical Conflict," in Chester Crocker, Fen Osler Hampson, and Pamela Aall (Eds.), *Managing Global Chaos* (Washington, DC: U.S. Institute of Peace, 1996), 53–78; David Little, "Religious Militancy," in Crocker et al., *Managing Global Chaos,* 79–92; Ernest Gellner, "Nations and Nationalism," in Richard Betts (Ed.), *Conflict after the Cold War: Arguments on the Causes of War and Peace* (New York: Macmillan, 1994), 280–292; Louis Kriesberg, "Regional Conflicts in the Post–Cold War Era: Causes, Dynamics, and Modes of Resolution,"

in Michael Klare and Daniel Thomas (Eds.), *World Security: Challenges for a New Century* (New York: St. Martin's Press, 1994), 155–174; Donald L. Horowitz, "Ethnic and Nationalist Conflict," in Klare and Thomas, *World Security,* 175–187.

32. Robert D. Kaplan, *The Coming Anarchy: Shattering the Dreams of the Post Cold War World* (New York: Vintage Books, 2001); Robert D. Kaplan, *Balkan Ghosts: A Journey through History* (New York: Vintage Books, 1994).

33. Susan Woodward, *Balkan Tragedy* (Washington, DC: Brookings Institution, 1995).

34. Michael Brown, *The International Dimensions of Internal Conflict* (Cambridge: MIT Press, 1996), 579.

35. Jong S. Jun and Deil S. Wright, *Globalization and Decentralization: Institutional Contexts, Policy Issues, and Intergovernmental Relations in Japan and the United States* (Washington, DC: Georgetown University Press, 1996), 1.

36. President Clinton declared the era of big government dead, referring to the end of welfare as we knew it and reforms that downsized the federal government to the smallest it had been since the Kennedy administration. Similar downsizing efforts have been underway internationally as privatization and "e-government" spread. Structural adjustment policies trim government spending in developing countries.

37. Jun and Wright, *Globalization and Decentralization,* 3–4.

38. Strange, *The Retreat of the State,* 87.

39. Krasner, "Sovereignty: An Institutional Perspective," 79.

40. Robert E. Bell, *Dictionary of Classical Mythology: Symbols, Attributes and Associations* (Santa Barbara, CA: ABC-Clio, 1982), 207.

41. Rodrick M. Chisholm, *Person and Object: A Metaphysical Study* (LaSalle, IL: Open Court, 1976), 89–92.

42. I. William Zartman, *Collapsed States* (Boulder, CO: Lynne Rienner, 1995), 5.

43. Rosecrance, *The Rise of the Virtual State.*

44. Otto Neurath quoted in A. J. Ayer (Ed.), *Logical Positivism* (Glencoe, IL: The Free Press, 1959). This is sometimes referred to as "Neurath's ship."

45. Krasner, "Sovereignty: An Institutional Perspective," 80.

46. Richard E. Neustadt, *Presidential Power and the Modern Presidents: The Politics of Leadership from Roosevelt to Reagan* (New York: The Free Press, 1990).